THE DEFEAT AND ATTRITION OF THE *12. SS-PANZERDIVISION HITLERJUGEND*

THE DEFEAT AND ATTRITION OF THE
12. SS-PANZERDIVISION HITLERJUGEND

Volume I: The Normandy Bridgehead Battles 7–11 June 1944

ARTHUR W. GULLACHSEN

CASEMATE

Pennsylvania & Yorkshire

Published in the United States of America and Great Britain in 2024 by
CASEMATE PUBLISHERS
1950 Lawrence Road, Havertown, PA 19083
and
47 Church Street, Barnsley, S70 2AS, UK

Copyright 2024 © Arthur W. Gullachsen

Hardback Edition: ISBN 978-1-63624-347-4
Digital Edition: ISBN 978-1-63624-348-1

A CIP record for this book is available from the British Library

Printed and bound in the United Kingdom by CPI Group (UK) Ltd, Croydon, CR0 4YY

Typeset in India by Lapiz Digital Services, Chennai.

For a complete list of Casemate titles, please contact:

CASEMATE PUBLISHERS (US)
Telephone (610) 853-9131
Fax (610) 853-9146
Email: casemate@casematepublishers.com
www.casematepublishers.com

CASEMATE PUBLISHERS (UK)
Telephone (0)1226 734350
Email: casemate@casemateuk.com
www.casemateuk.com

Contents

Acknowledgements

The team critical to the production of this work, most of whom were present for the writing process with my last two books for my publisher, Casemate Publishers, again provided invaluable support in helping me get to the finish line. Without them, the whole production process falls apart, and even though my name is on the cover of this book, it is very much a group effort at times. This work on the *Waffen-SS*, the military arm of the Nazi Party of wartime Germany, is in no way, shape or form an attempt to glorify its military record or whitewash its horrific record of war crimes. The trust that the publisher has placed in me to produce an objective historical analysis of the events of June 1944 that will stand the test of time is very much appreciated.

In thanking specific individuals, I would first and foremost like to thank my wife, Michele Connor, for her unwavering support during the period the manuscript for this book was written. This support allowed me the time to accurately translate wartime German primary sources, review maps and take important notes from secondary sources to produce the most detailed picture possible of the German military effort on the eastern flank of the Normandy bridgehead in the period 7–11 June 1944. She is my biggest champion, and I am thankful for her every day.

Mrs Ruth Sheppard, the publisher at the heart of Casemate Group, is my key enabler in that without her presence, this book would not have been written. Her flexibility and patience with my many idiosyncrasies is very much appreciated, and her team of excellent staff help me make sure all the pieces of the puzzle fall into place.

Again, my friend and co-worker Dr Asa McKercher provided key assistance with his indexing skills and taking the time to look over the manuscript with a fine-tooth comb for any grammatical errors and other oversights. A non-Panzer enthusiast, his oversight is critical in making this book understandable to the average reader or book buyer with an interest in Second World War military history.

My regular battle map graphic artist, Mr Mike Bechthold of Waterloo, Ontario, has been enlisted once again to enhance my scanned scribbles in the way of rough map sketches into the polished creations you see today. These maps are detailed to a degree that has not been presented before regarding the fighting 7–11 June 1944 north and north-west of the city of Caen, and his contribution to this book in this area was critical.

I am also very much indebted to British military historian and specialist on the Second World War history of the 46 Royal Marine Commando, Mr Keith Taylor of Hamburg, Germany. Keith was kind enough to share with me a vast treasure trove of *Hitlerjugend* primary documents used to construct parts of his two-volume self-published set on the campaign of the 46 Royal Marine Commando (46 RMC) in North-West Europe, *The Waist-High Cornfield*, and *Broken Bridge, Rivers to Cross.*[1] This act of kindness allowed me to redirect funding to the purchase of photographs and the production of maps by removing the need to purchase reproductions of archival material. While this book will provide a detailed account of the fighting in and around the village of Rots, his book *The Waist-High Cornfield* is and will continue to be the definitive account of the battle and the role of the Royal Marines in the fighting. His research was also especially important, as it helped me understand the fighting as experienced by the Fort Garry Horse (10th Canadian Armoured Regiment), now a Canadian Army Reserve regiment in Winnipeg, Manitoba, Canada. I joined this regiment as a university student while at the University of Manitoba studying to receive a bachelor of arts degree in history and am interested in its wartime operations. It played a prominent role in the fighting in Rots and Le Hamel on 11 June, and its war diary for the month of June 1944 was unfortunately lost during the Second World War.

Finally, the RMC Office of the Vice President of Research at the Royal Military College of Canada, my employer, was one of my most important 'enablers' in that they provided the funding to acquire research materials for me to produce the manuscript. Without these research funding awards, I would not have been able to obtain the primary documents from the Czech military archives as well as important secondary sources, such as Keith Taylor's book, which were key to conducting the research needed and not found in libraries.

Arthur W. Gullachsen
Kingston, Ontario, March 2024

Battle map unit abbreviations

British Army units and formations

3rd Br Inf Div	British 3rd Infantry Division
50th Br Inf Div	British 50th Infantry Division
8 BAB	British 8th Armoured Brigade
69 BIB	British 69th Infantry Brigade
185 BIB	British 185th Infantry Brigade
1 D	1st Battalion, The Dorsetshire Regiment
2 RUR D Coy	2nd Battalion, Royal Ulster Rifles, D Company
6 GH	6th Battalion, The Green Howards
7 GH	7th Battalion, The Green Howards
KOSB	1st Battalion, The King's Own Scottish Borderers
ERY A Sqn	East Riding Yeomanry A Squadron, RAC
SRY	Sherwood Rangers Yeomanry, RAC
24 L	24th Lancers, RAC
4/7 DG	4th/7th Royal Dragoon Guards, RAC
61 Recce	61st Reconnaissance Regiment, RAC
62 A/T elmts	62nd Anti-Tank Regiment, Royal Artillery
46 RMC*	46 (Royal Marine) Commando
Y/B/A Tps	Y, B and A Troops of 46 Royal Marine Commando
S Tp	S Troop of 46 Royal Marine Commando
2 RMASR	2nd Royal Marine Armoured Support Regiment

*Though still part of the Royal Marines and thus the Royal Navy, the 46 (Royal Marine) Commando was part of the 4th Special Service Brigade of the British Army in the late war period, the Royal Marines infantry battalions joining the British Army Commandos Special Service Force structure in 1942.

Canadian Army units and formations

3rd Cdn Inf Div	3rd Canadian Infantry Division
7 CIB	7th Canadian Infantry Brigade

7 CIB HQ	7th Canadian Infantry Brigade Headquarters
8 CIB	8th Canadian Infantry Brigade
9 CIB	9th Canadian Infantry Brigade
2 CAB	2nd Canadian Armoured Brigade
SDGH	The Stormont, Dundas and Glengarry Highlanders
NNSH	The North Nova Scotia Highlanders
NNSH sp	The North Nova Scotia Highlanders Support Company
RRR	1st Battalion, The Regina Rifle Regiment
RRR HQ	1st Battalion, The Regina Rifle Regiment, Headquarters
RWR	Royal Winnipeg Rifles
RWR HQ	Royal Winnipeg Rifles Headquarters
RWR Sp	Royal Winnipeg Rifles Support Company
RWR CP	Royal Winnipeg Rifles carrier platoon
1 CSR	1st Battalion, The Canadian Scottish Regiment
QOR	The Queen's Own Rifles of Canada
R de Ch	Le Régiment de la Chaudière
Sp	Support Company
CH	The Cameron Highlanders of Ottawa
SFR	The Sherbrooke Fusiliers Regiment, the 27th Armoured Regiment, CAC
FGH	Fort Garry Horse
HQ Tp	Headquarters Troop, SFR
1 H	1st Hussars, the 6th Armoured Regiment, CAC
1 H elmts	1st Hussars Elements
3 A/T	3rd Anti-Tank Regiment, Royal Canadian Artillery
12 RCA	12th Field Regiment, Royal Canadian Artillery
13 RCA	13th Field Regiment, Royal Canadian Artillery

German Army (*Heer*) units and formations

716. Inf.Div. elmts	*716. Infanterie-Division* elements
21. Pz.Div.	*21. Panzerdivision*
Pz.Lehr	*Panzer-Lehr-Division*
Pz.Rgt. 22	*Panzerregiment 22*
Pz.Gren.L.Rgt. 902	*Panzergrenadier-Lehr-Regiment 902*
KG Rauch elmts	*Kampfgruppe* Rauch elements
Pz.Gren.Rgt. 192	*Panzergrenadier-Regiment 192*
II/902	*II. Batallion(Gepanzert)/Panzergrenadier-Lehr-Regiment 902*

Hitlerjugend (*Waffen-SS*) units and formations

12. SS-Pz.Div.	*12. SS-Panzerdivision Hitlerjugend*
SS-Pz.Gren.Rgt. 25	*SS-Panzergrenadier-Regiment 25*
SS-Pz.Gren.Rgt. 26	*SS-Panzergrenadier-Regiment 26*
SS-Pz.Rgt. 12	*SS-Panzer-Regiment 12*
I/25	*I. Batallion/SS-Panzergrenadier-Regiment 25*
1/25	*1. Kompanie/SS-Panzergrenadier-Regiment 25*
2/25	*2. Kompanie/SS-Panzergrenadier-Regiment 25*
3/25	*3. Kompanie/SS-Panzergrenadier-Regiment 25*
II/25	*II. Batallion/SS-Panzergrenadier-Regiment 25*
5/25	*5. Kompanie/SS-Panzergrenadier-Regiment 25*
6/25	*6. Kompanie/SS-Panzergrenadier-Regiment 25*
7/25	*7. Kompanie/SS-Panzergrenadier-Regiment 25*
III/25	*III. Batallion/SS-Panzergrenadier-Regiment 25*
9/25	*9. Kompanie/SS-Panzergrenadier-Regiment 25*
10/25	*10. Kompanie/SS-Panzergrenadier-Regiment 25*
11/25	*11. Kompanie/SS-Panzergrenadier-Regiment 25*
13/25	*13. Kp.(Geschütz)/SS-Pz.Gren.Rgt. 25*
15/25	*15. Kp.(Aufklärung)/SS-Pz.Gren.Rgt. 25*
I/26	*I. Batallion/SS-Panzergrenadier-Regiment 26*
1/26	*1. Kompanie/SS-Panzergrenadier-Regiment 26*
2/26	*2. Kompanie/SS-Panzergrenadier-Regiment 26*
3/26	*3. Kompanie/SS-Panzergrenadier-Regiment 26*
4/26	*4. Kp.(Schwere)/SS-Pz.Gren.Rgt. 26*
II/26	*II. Batallion/SS-Panzergrenadier-Regiment 26*
5/26	*5. Kompanie/SS-Panzergrenadier-Regiment 26*
6/26	*6. Kompanie/SS-Panzergrenadier-Regiment 26*
7/26	*7. Kompanie/SS-Panzergrenadier-Regiment 26*
8/26	*8. Kp.(Schwere)/SS-Pz.Gren.Rgt. 26*
III/26	*III. Batallion(Gepanzert)/SS-Pz.Gren.Rgt. 26*
9/26	*9. Kp.(Gepanzert)/SS-Pz.Gren.Rgt. 26*
10/26	*10. Kp.(Gepanzert)/SS-Pz.Gren.Rgt. 26*
11/26	*11. Kp.(Gepanzert)/SS-Pz.Gren.Rgt. 26*
SPW Elements	*SPW 251 halftrack elements of III. Btl.*
13/26	*13. Kp.(Geschütz)/SS-Pz.Gren.Rgt. 26*
II/SS-Pz.Art.Rgt. 12	*II. Abteilung/SS-Panzerartillerie-Regiment 12*
III/SS-Pz.Art.Rgt. 12	*III. Abteilung/SS-Panzerartillerie-Regiment 12*
2/AR 12	*2. Bttr.(Gepanzert)/SS-Pz.Art.Rgt. 12*
7/AR 12	*7. Batterie/SS-Panzerartillerie-Regiment 12*
8/AR 12	*8. Batterie/SS-Panzerartillerie-Regiment 12*

9/AR 12	*9. Batterie/SS-Panzerartillerie-Regiment 12*
II/SS-Pz.Rgt.12	*II. Abteilung/SS-Panzer-Regiment 12*
I/12	*I. Abteilung/SS-Panzer-Regiment 12*
1/12	*1. Kompanie/SS-Panzer-Regiment 12*
2/12	*2. Kompanie/SS-Panzer-Regiment 12*
3/12	*3. Kompanie/SS-Panzer-Regiment 12*
4/12	*4. Kompanie/SS-Panzer-Regiment 12*
5/12	*5. Kompanie/SS-Panzer-Regiment 12*
6/12	*6. Kompanie/SS-Panzer-Regiment 12*
7/12	*7. Kompanie/SS-Panzer-Regiment 12*
8/12	*8. Kompanie/SS-Panzer-Regiment 12*
9/12	*9. Kompanie/SS-Panzer-Regiment 12*
SS-Pz.AA.12	*SS-Panzer-Aufklärung-Abteilung 12*
2./SS-Pz.AA.12	*2. Kp.(Pz.Späh)/SS-Pz.Aüfkl.Abt. 12*
3./S-Pz.AA.12	*3. Kp.(Aüfkl.)/SS-Pz.Aüfkl.Abt. 12*
SS-Pz.Pio.Btl. 12	*SS-Panzerpionierbatallion 12*
1/Pio.	*1. Kp./SS-Pz.Pio.Btl. 12*
2/Pio.	*2. Kp./SS-Pz.Pio.Btl. 12*
3/Pio.	*3. Kp./SS-Pz.Pio.Btl. 12*
4/Pio.	*4. Kp.(Schwere)/SS-Pz.Pio.Btl. 12*
Beglt	*SS-Divisionsbegleitkompanie 12*
4/Flak 12	*4. Batterie/SS-Flak Abteilung 12*

Introduction

1944 was a year of catastrophes for the German *Wehrmacht*, the title for the wartime German armed forces (literally 'defence power'), encompassing all three regular services of the army, navy and air force during the Second World War. If there was any doubt for the average German that the war was lost for his or her nation, the events of this year confirmed it. One of the most significant defeats for German arms on the Western Front during June 1944 was the failure to destroy the successful Allied landing and lodgement on the European continent, Operation *Overlord*. The focus of this book is on the frontline events 7–11 June 1944 in the eastern sector of the Normandy bridgehead, focusing specifically on the German military response to the amphibious landings there. During this period, the *12. SS-Panzerdivision Hitlerjugend*, known henceforth as the *Hitlerjugend*, a formation of the *Waffen-SS*, the military arm of the German *Nationalsozialistische Deutsche Arbeiterpartei*, more commonly known in the West as the Nazi Party, attempted to capture and hold the battlefield initiative and in conjunction with other German *Panzerdivisionen* (armoured divisions) to throw what would become the British Second Army into the sea.

The title of this work, *The Defeat and Attrition of the 12. SS-Panzerdivision Hitlerjugend*, ties into the two main historical questions this work will address. First, why exactly did the powerful German armoured forces, among them some of the best-equipped new *Panzerdivisionen* of both *Das Heer*, the German regular army, and the *Waffen-SS*, fail to drive the Anglo-Canadian forces on the eastern flank of the Normandy bridgehead back into the sea? Secondly, in their attempts to do so, severe losses were suffered by these formations during the many determined attacks launched in the period 7–11 June 1944. What was the exact nature of these losses?

To address these two historical questions, this book, Volume I of a planned multi-volume series, will analyse the combat record of the *12. SS-Panzerdivision Hitlerjugend*. This formation of the *Waffen-SS* lacked for very little in the way of personnel and resources by the standards present within the German armoured forces, the *Panzerwaffe*, in the year 1944. It was a very well-equipped division, and its core of officers and non-commissioned officers (NCOs) was composed of *Waffen-SS* combat veterans from the Eastern Front. The remainder of its ranks were filled with mostly 18-year-old, extremely fit, politically indoctrinated and highly trained former members of the Hitler Youth organisation, the *Hitlerjugend*, the compulsory youth paramilitary organisation that had existed in Germany since July 1926. To many interested in the history of the German armed forces during the late war period, it may seem incomprehensible that this armoured division, one of the most powerful within the German land forces, which were arguably at the peak of their expansion and military power in the year 1944, led by veteran leadership, failed to achieve the main goal it was tasked with; destroying the eastern sector of the Allied Normandy bridgehead.

The main thesis presented is that despite this division's best efforts, they were defeated by a firm Allied defence, anchored by the twin giants of overwhelming field and anti-tank artillery combat power and total tactical air superiority. These offensive and defensive strengths drove back the uncoordinated and often ad hoc offensive operations of the *Hitlerjugend*, eventually robbing the Germans of the initiative in a grinding series of attritional battles that saw no decisive outcome north and west of the Norman city of Caen in the period 7–11 June. As a result of these bloody battles, tremendous losses in personnel and equipment were suffered by the Germans that, in the face of no reinforcements and unrelenting defensive responsibilities, forced the division's leadership to assume a defensive, rather than offensive, stance. Very little had been accomplished in the period 7–11 June, other than denying the city of Caen to Anglo-Canadian forces and establishing a firm defensive front that contained the bridgehead. Using the *Hitlerjugend* as a case study, this work uses primary archival and secondary sources to support this argument.

Expanding upon the main argument presented, several sub-factors also helped to deprive the *Hitlerjugend* of victory against Anglo-Canadian forces in the critical first days of combat in the Normandy bridgehead. First, quality command and control at the corps, divisional and regimental level, made worse by poor communication, was lacking at times within the German forces on the eastern sector of the bridgehead. Simply put, poor leadership, communication and staff work at all levels contributed to less than satisfactory operational outcomes in cases when victory was more than possible. In the first week of fighting, a profoundly anxious urgency, overconfidence and lack of experience persisted to impair combat performance. The *Hitlerjugend* were fighting a totally new enemy whose technological capabilities were unknown to the veteran Eastern Front *Waffen-SS* unit and formation commanders, who did not expect the Anglo-Canadian forces to be so strong and resilient. The ability of the *Waffen-SS* to coordinate and command combined arms battlegroups and to utilise all available assets at key points was weak at critical times, leading to tactical defeats and irreplaceable losses in the short term for the combat units.

Decisive leadership at the *Armeegruppe*, *Armee* and *Armeekorps* levels was also lacking. Following the successful 6 June 1944 Allied amphibious assault, the Operation *Neptune* segment of the larger Operation *Overlord* invasion, questions as to which *Armeekorps*-level formation commanded the *Hitlerjugend*, where it was to be deployed, and when it was released from *Oberkommando Des Wehrmacht* (*OKW*) reserve were, for a very critical period of time, unanswered. To achieve the best military outcome in the critical short-term period after Allied combat units were ashore, the division had to be decisively employed at once, as soon as the majority of its fighting components could be assembled near the beaches. This did not happen.

These initial missteps, chronicled in Chapter 6 of this work, were made infinitely worse by the absence of key commanders from the area of operations, most critically *Generalfeldmarschall* (*G.F.M.*) Erwin Rommel, *Oberbefehlshaber* of *Heeresgruppe B* (*Commander-in-Chief of Army Group B*), who was visiting his wife and son in Germany. Also missing was *7. Armee Oberbefehlshaber General* Dollman, who was off organising a training exercise, and *I. SS-Pz.Korps Kommandeur Ogruf.* Sepp Dietrich, who was in Belgium. Luckily, within the *7. Armee* area of operations the *LXXXIV. Armeekorps Oberbefehlshaber, General der Artillerie* (*Gen.d.Artl.*) Erich Marcks was present, and his energy on 6 June was responsible for what German response did occur.

There was also the lack of a rehearsed, clear, previously war-gamed plan of action of what exactly to do if an invasion in a certain sector of northern France took place. With a firm plan in place, the German response may have been more effective given the inevitable collapse of the German *Atlantikwall* bunker-based static defences on the coast. As it was, a chaotic lack of coordination occurred on D-Day, as the Germans were unclear of where the main Allied blow might fall and thus hesitant to commit their forces to what might turn out to be the wrong decisive point. An especially harmful factor was the location of the *Hitlerjugend* on D-Day; this formation was too far away from the invasion beaches when the actual landing occurred to intervene decisively on the first day, 6 June 1944.

Nothing less than a re-run of the excellent German defensive effort with minimal forces against the Anglo-Canadian Dieppe amphibious operation of 19 August 1942 was what was needed to repel the invasion of June 1944. Given the large increase in Allied assault forces and the resources to support this later landing, German *Panzerdivisionen* had to be close to the beaches to fight as combined arms teams with the weak German static defenders of Hitler's vaunted *Atlantikwall* defences. They were simply too weak to do it alone without *Panzer Kampfgruppen* (armoured battlegroup) support. This did not happen, and the one *Panzerdivision* close enough to launch an attack, the *21. Panzerdivision*, had its forces frittered away piecemeal in multiple efforts, failing in them all. The vital hours in which to 'Dieppe' the Anglo-Canadian invaders of the eastern section of the D-Day beaches slipped away, and by evening the Allied forces were ashore in strength, with only the hapless *21. Panzerdivision* having contacted Anglo-Canadian forces in a series of inconclusive meeting engagements.

As stated earlier, poor German leadership in the chaotic first days of combat saw a lack of proper planning and coordination to allow correct combined arms tactics to be exercised, with horrendous results. The successful integration of *SS-Panzergrenadiere* (armoured infantry), *SS-Panzer-Artillerie* (armoured artillery), *SS-Panzer-Pioniere* (armoured combat engineers) and *SS-Panzer* (armoured) units to maximise the impact of any operations was frequently lacking, with key elements missing from both defensive and offensive operations at times. It is astonishing that this occurred, as the *Hitlerjugend* had had a very long training and expansion period by 1943/44 standards and had conducted multiple unit and formation live fire training exercises by late spring 1944. With only the armoured units or armoured infantry units attacking by themselves during the early bridgehead battles, Anglo-Canadian forces exploited the lack of combined arms coordination on the German side, turning back attack after attack with the liberal use of field and anti-tank artillery. Being spread too thin, *Hitlerjugend* officers simply could not mass an overwhelming amount of combat power to defeat Allied forces.

Secondly, the Germans suffered a lack of plentiful resources in the way of replacement personnel, vehicles and equipment. This inability to reconstitute itself while deployed to the front was especially damaging for the division as it arguably curtailed the *Kommandeure* (commanders) from being especially aggressive given there were no new resources coming to replace those lost in combat. In order to prevail in the decisive battles in the period immediately after the invasion, massive forces in the way of troops, vehicles and ordnance needed to be concentrated at a critical point to break through the Allied lines of defences. The 1944 Normandy campaign was one of attrition, and for its commanders to prevail, large resources had to be available for immediate use. The *Hitlerjugend* officers realised very rapidly that if a severe disaster was to occur in which very heavy losses were suffered, the results could be catastrophic.

Thirdly, the total lack of air support from the *Luftwaffe* and the total impotence of the German *Kriegsmarine* naval forces against the Allied amphibious operations and subsequent logistical effort contributed significantly to making the *Hitlerjugend*'s military objectives unattainable. The air support Anglo-Canadian forces enjoyed over the bridgehead in the first days of its existence absolutely prevented German routine administrative travel, resupply efforts and the redeployment of units above the company level in broad daylight.

Fourthly, an inability to deploy combat power quickly at key points was present due to the overtasking of the division and forcing it to cover too much of the German front in the eastern side of the bridgehead. The elimination of the *Atlantikwall* defenders and the lack of a regular *Heer Infanterie-Division* (German army infantry division) to simply hold the line, freeing up the *Hitlerjugend* to mass for an attack at a critical weak point in the Allied front as per practised *Panzerwaffe* (armoured forces) doctrine, forced this armoured formation into a role it was never intended to take on for long periods of time. Planned to be an elite armoured strike force, instead it was forced to dig bunkers and take on the role of front-line cannon fodder.

Finally, the defensive strength of the Royal Canadian Artillery (RCA) and Royal Artillery (RA) field artillery, anti-aircraft and anti-tank forces, fighting hard to support the front-line infantry and armoured forces and driving off the occasional *Luftwaffe* attack, proved decisive in halting and inhibiting German operations. Harassing and concentrated field artillery fire, occurring around the clock day and night, curtailed the movements of the *SS-Panzergrenadiere* at the *Kompanie* level and above, often leaving the Panzer units alone to try to make headway against Allied attacks or defensive positions. While Anglo-Canadian combat arms operations by infantry and armoured units sometimes floundered, the supremacy of the RA and RCA never wavered, continually pounding German combat units and formations, not to mention their rear area headquarters and logistical units.

The structure of this book will follow events chronologically and provide supporting chapters covering events before the invasion to properly set the stage for the reader. After an introductory chapter and two chapters that introduce the German and Anglo-Canadian forces involved, briefly chronicling their formation, structures and training, the following chapters cover the D-Day assault and the response of the German static and armoured forces, followed by detailed analysis of the fighting of the *Hitlerjugend* in the following sectors: the area north-west of Caen, Putot-en-Bessin, Bretteville-l'Orgueilleuse, Norrey-en-Bessin; the static front north of Caen, Hill (or Point) 102; Le Mesnil-Patry; and finally Rots and Le Hamel. These chapters will be followed by a conclusion in which the main ideas presented will be reinforced.

As the first volume of a planned multi-volume work, this book will chronicle what the author defines as the 'first battle of Caen', this being the fighting around and for the city and the area north and west of it by the *Hitlerjugend* in the period 7–11 June 1944. The German divisional historian of the *Hitlerjugend* and its former *Chef des Stabes* (chief of staff), the late *Waffen-SS* veteran Hubert Meyer, defines this battle as 7–10 June 1944, and this definition is based on the period of attacks by the *Hitlerjugend* on Canadian and British forces, 10 June seeing the division switch its tactical focus over to the defensive after losing the battlefield initiative. The author has chosen to include these first defensive battles, the fighting at Cristot, Le Mesnil-Patry, Le Hamel and Rots on 11 June, as part of this 'first battle of Caen'. While the *Hitlerjugend* had transitioned to the defensive by the close of 10 June, this fighting was not its first purely defensive fight, the forces of *II. Btl./SS-Pz.Gren. Rgt. 26* having been driven out of the village of Putot-en-Bessin on the evening of 8 June 1944 by reserve forces of the 7th Canadian Infantry Brigade.

12 June 1944 saw a definite halt to the fighting of the *Hitlerjugend*, apart from some minor infantry clashes and artillery bombardments to the west in the sector of the neighbouring *Panzer-Lehr-Division* (*Panzer-Lehr*). As a result, the author has chosen the day previous as the end of the period of historical study for this book. Virtually no major Anglo-Canadian offensive operations or major defensive efforts

by the *SS-Panzergrenadiere* of the *Hitlerjugend* occurred on this date. The very next day, 13 June, major combat broke out on the left flank of the division, as the British 50th Infantry Division and 7th Armoured Division of the British 30th Corps launched their major attack with the aim of capturing Villers-Bocage in a sweeping envelopment operation. Hence, 12 June 1944 will be the starting point for the next volume of this series, entitled *The Defeat and Attrition of the 12. SS-Panzerdivision Hitlerjugend, Volume II: Operations* Epsom, Windsor *and* Charnwood, *11 June–12 July 1944.*

Key supporting data will be presented in a series of detailed appendices that will contain German personnel, equipment and armoured losses during the battles and losses inflicted on the Allies. As was the case with previous works by the author, every opportunity to utilise the correct wartime unit and formation titles, ranks and military terms utilised in wartime primary documents will be used. Due to the needs of brevity, the official German administrative rank title will be written out only once, and abbreviations will be used from that point forward (*Stubaf.* instead of the full *SS-Sturmbannführer*).

What this means within the book is that the anglicizing of the German military for historiographical purposes for an English-speaking audience will not take place. Instead of '*Waffen-SS* Major General Fritz Witt', *Brigadenführer* (*Brig.Fhr.*) Fritz Witt will be used, with the abbreviated version used after the first mention of the historical figure or personality. Instead of anglicised British Army regimental style '12th SS Panzers', the correct *12. SS-Panzerdivision Hitlerjugend* or *Hitlerjugend* abbreviated form will be employed. This correct historical approach will also be applied to formations in the 1944 British and Canadian armies by accurately utilising the correct administrative title they used during wartime in written headquarters documents. Instead of the British 'I Corps', the correct '1st Corps' will be employed, the second version being the correct title used in wartime, within both operational orders and the most mundane administrative documents. The author will however insert 'British' as needed to separate British Army formations from Canadian Army formations. The use of roman numerals for British corps is an unfortunate post-war invention of anglophone historians attempting to mimic US Army corps numerical designations to provide uniformity in their manuscripts. The attempts of anglophone historians to apply the British regimental system to the *Waffen-SS* and *Heer* formations and their units (12th SS Panzers) can only be explained as a practice that grew out of British Army Camberley Staff College battlefield tours in the 1950s and 1960s.

Time is also a topic that will be corrected in this book. Many publications have stated that the time used by the British Second Army in Normandy during the June 1944 period was one hour behind that used on German military clocks. This is untrue.

Without going into extensive detail that might be boring to the reader, the British nation used Greenwich Mean Time, also known in documents as Universal Time Coordinated (UTC) pre-war. The time used in German-controlled occupied France was Time Zone 'A' (Alpha Time Zone) and this translated into the equivalent of British Greenwich Mean Time (GMT) plus one hour (GMT +1 hour). During peacetime in Britain, one hour was added usually to this time in the summer months; the result being 'British Summer Time' (BST = GMT +1).

However, this status quo changed in Great Britian in 1939 after the declaration of war with the introduction of Defence Summer Regulations, which added one hour to the clock year-round to save energy in wartime. The result, in summer, was called 'British Double Summer Time' (BDST = GMT +2). As an aside, this change also occurred in winter, the added hour being still in place (GMT +1). British Double Summer Time only ended on 17 September 1944; the Normandy campaign having concluded at this point.

Over on the German side of the English Channel, the same time changes occurred in occupied France and the Low Countries. During the summer months, the Germans applied special summer time (+1 hour) to their Time Zone 'A' (including northern France), so the clocks were adjusted to plus two hours (GMT +2 equivalent).

What is the end result for the historian when comparing British and German wartime accounts, primary documents and other war diaries? Absolutely nothing. The times were the same.[1] Given this assessment, the supposed time difference is but another Normandy historiography 'myth' that has had to be deconstructed, which unfortunately affects the quality of numerous works on the Normandy campaign. Why were events recorded at different times in war diaries of the opposing armies involved? Events were communicated by exhausted men in the field to equally tired unit operations and intelligence officers who were conducting other tasks simultaneously. Recording events at exact times was often not a priority.

As this is but one book of many on the subject, one being produced roughly every five years or so on the *Hitlerjugend*, the *Waffen-SS* and the German forces in the Normandy campaign, an effort was made to make this book historically significant. It had to be made new and interesting to the average Normandy enthusiast, historian, or specialist in the Canadian Army or German forces of the late war period. To accomplish this, the research process for this book used hard to obtain copies of German *Waffen-SS* primary sources available through the Czech military archives in Prague or held by other historians as the main primary source research materials. Hungarian and French military historians have utilised these war diaries to varying degrees in other works on the *Hitlerjugend*. These rare and difficult to obtain primary sources were used to a much greater degree to both chronicle events and analyse the operations of the *Hitlerjugend* against the British and Canadian armies to an extent not regularly present in anglophone works on the subject. The failure to utilise these war diaries and other German documents is a significant research shortcoming within previous *Hitlerjugend* works. These documents will be used to illustrate in detail for the reader why the operations of the *Hitlerjugend* against British and Canadian forces largely failed or were only temporarily successful.

This work will not include an extensive historiography section and will not discuss in detail each work that has been produced on the *Hitlerjugend* in the 78 years (at time of publishing) since the surrender of the Third Reich, apart from what is arguably most comprehensive work on the subject to this point, *The History of the 12. SS Panzerdivision Hitlerjugend* by its former *Ia Generalstabsoffizier* (divisional chief of staff) and eventual *Obersturmbannführer* (*Ostubaf.*) Hubert Meyer, not to be confused with the more infamous *Brigadenführer* (*Brig.Fhr.*) Kurt Meyer, the former divisional commander. Published in a German multi-volume edition in 1982, these works were compiled and translated into English in 1990.[2] Over the course of decades, Meyer reconstructed the division's history from Allied and surviving German primary documents, veteran interviews, and his own memory of operations. It is a spectacularly detailed work, and it can conservatively be stated that no German or Allied division history published in English is as good. It is, however, not without its faults.

Criticism of Meyer's divisional history consists of two main issues. The first is the complete omission of a very difficult topic for German Second World War veterans to discuss in writing, this being the war crimes of the division. The infamous Canadian Army prisoner executions, some of which will be discussed in this volume, are entirely omitted as if they never happened. This is explained by Meyer's work being very much a combined effort from a multitude of divisional veterans and regimental commanders as well as its having been completed as a unit history written for the benefit of the surviving *Hitlerjugend* veteran community in Germany rather than an objective historical work. There was never a possibility that Meyer or the *Hitlerjugend* veteran community would wish or allow themselves as former unit and formation *Kommandeure* to be defined as war criminals, which is exactly what some of the surviving officers and senior non-commissioned members in the post war era were, these men being guilty of war crimes as defined under the Geneva Convention.

Secondly, and very importantly, Meyer's work lacks a critical appraisal of German tactical operations, such as the pattern of quickly planned operations without proper resources to support them and rapid defensive counterattacks on Allied offensive operations in Normandy, which often led to horrendous losses. In the period covered within this book, the *Waffen-SS* at times did not have the combat power or tactical élan to mount effective attacks, and many of these were repeatedly demolished in the face of huge amounts of Allied artillery and anti-tank fire. This pattern of operations caused irreplaceable losses and destroyed the morale of the units involved. But since Hubert Meyer himself was part instigator and planner of many of these counterattacks while working in the division *Gefechtsstand* (headquarters), his lack of criticism is understandable. This calls into question the effectiveness of *Heer* and *Waffen-SS* late-war armoured doctrine, and whether Meyer was smart enough to comprehend that the Allies understood the German tactical approach to armoured operations, specifically planning to defeat them with massed artillery and air power, using the hapless and anticipated German counterattacks as tactical opportunities.

Following the conclusion of the Second World War, accounts of the fighting began to be produced by various historians in the West. An explanation for the Allies' perceived slow progress in the breakout of the Normandy bridgehead was sought, and it was at this point that the paradigm of German tactical superiority was born. Quite simply that of superior performance of one's units and men with less materiel and fewer assets, taking on and slowing down the Allied juggernaut. While the Germans did fight with skill at times, it is a bridge too far to say that they possessed a superior tactical élan and stood out on the battlefield as superior in every way in their infantry and armoured operations, some of which were catastrophic failures.

Not surprisingly, Meyer supports the view that the Germans fought desperately and with some skill to conduct their defence, but the overwhelming superiority of Anglo-Canadian forces simply bludgeoned them back. Again and again the message of Allied material superiority is given to the reader in Meyer's history as the reason for the German defeat, though other factors were certainly at play, most prominently strategic and tactical blunders.

Also, one of the biggest holes in Hubert Meyer's divisional history is any kind of assessment of the leadership of the first divisional *Kommandeur* of the *Hitlerjugend*, *Brigadenführer* Fritz Witt, who as *Division-Kommandeur* directed operations from his *Gefechtsstand* in Venoix in the period studied within this book. His deployment to Normandy as divisional *Kommandeur* was incredibly short, with Witt being killed by Royal Navy naval gunfire on 14 June 1944. It is as if he is a somewhat invisible figure in the historiography of the division, with his actions, decisions, and communications largely struck from the record by Meyer, who concentrates almost solely on the front-line action and the actions of the Allies when discussing the period 7–11 June, which is arguably the critical period when the Normandy Bridgehead survived German counterattacks and was enlarged.

This gap in the historiography of the division extends to Anglophone works on the *Hitlerjugend*, as Canadian and British works on the division say very little, if anything, about Witt and his divisional headquarters, the focus in the existing books on the *Hitlerjugend* being almost strictly discussing *Standartenführer* Kurt Meyer and the *Obersturmbannführer* Wilhelm Monke and Max Wünsche, the lead personalities in charge of regimental-sized formations whose personal accounts or war crimes fill many books analysing the fighting in the time frame 7–11 June 1944.

While Hubert Meyer wrote a very detailed divisional history on *Hitlerjugend*, he seems to have also omitted his role as *Ia* or divisional chief of staff in leading the division in the fighting and influencing the decisions of Witt and other key *Gefechtsstand* staff officer personalities behind the front lines. Was Witt effective as a battlefield commander, and what effect did he have on operations? This work will attempt to fill this gap and draw some basic conclusions on Witt, his headquarters and their role as an influence on the battles and provide a basic summary of the decisions taken by these entities.

While some may consider the *Hitlerjugend*, other *Heer* and *SS* formations and the German defensive campaign in Normandy to be an exhausted historical topic, this book will illustrate that those interested in the subject still have a considerable amount to learn from the events that took place in the summer of 1944. Though the subject of the *Waffen-SS* is a terribly important part of the military history of the 20th century, it is arguable that German scholars have barely scratched the surface with regards to its study, and some of the best books on the subject may have yet to be written.

Within Canada, as this manuscript was being typed, a 98-year-old Ukrainian *Waffen-SS* veteran was mistakenly invited by the Speaker of the House of Commons through the office of a member of Parliament from the ruling Liberal Party, and given a standing ovation as a 'Ukrainian veteran who fought for Ukrainian independence against the Russians' during a state visit from the current Ukrainian President.[3] This disrespectful event showed a lack of historical comprehension of and education on the Second World War, and reflects the importance of new and ongoing efforts to study its events. What is worse, it must have been a terrible blow to the families of many Canadian servicemen who fell or were executed as prisoners of war by the *Waffen-SS* in Normandy during the summer of 1944. While some may state that the Western Front and the more 'Germanic' *Waffen-SS* divisions such as the *Hitlerjugend* were an entirely different kettle of fish than Eastern Front foreign legions such as the *14. Waffen-Grenadier-Division der SS (Galizische Nr. 1)*, there were abundant numbers of Ukrainian, Russian and other foreign fighters within the *Hitlerjugend*, one of the more famous being the driver and bodyguard of the then-*SS-Standartenführer* Kurt Meyer, the Cossack Michel (surname unknown), who was a constant companion of the regimental and eventual divisional *Hitlerjugend Kommandeur* in the summer of 1944 in France.[4] The *Waffen-SS* was truly a force of many nations, all of the fighters united in their loyalty and belief in the twisted, racist and murderous global perspective of Adolf Hitler, *Der Führer* of the Greater German *Reich, Grossdeutschland*. As I do mention to others when discussing this matter in academic and public settings, all members of the *Waffen-SS* wore the uniform with the swastika and eagle on the left arm, and all had sworn the oath of allegiance. This book will take its place in the historical discourse over the late war period and play its part in making sure the past is never forgotten.

CHAPTER I

The plans for defending northern France in spring 1944

Before discussing the status of the *12. SS-Panzerdivision Hitlerjugend* pre-invasion, a brief overview of the German plan for defending northern France, its inherent flaws, and the impact of Allied deception measures, is needed. This overview is needed to illustrate where the *Hitlerjugend* fit into the grand defensive plan for northern France and what conflicting views German commanders held concerning how best to defeat an Allied amphibious invasion.

The task of coordinating the planning for the German military response to such a landing was the responsibility of the *des Oberbefehlshabers* (*O.B.* – commanders-in-chief) of *das Heer*, the two most prominent of these being *Generalfeldmarschall* (*G.F.M.*) Gerd von Rundstedt, *O.B. West* and *Kommandeur* of *Heeresgruppe D* (Army Group 'D' later on 1944 changing its title to the simpler *O.B. West*), which controlled all of occupied France, and his subordinate, the *O.B.* of *Heeresgruppe B* (*H.Gr.B.*), *G.F.M.* Erwin Rommel, the commander of a significant number of *Heer* formations in northern France. A third figure was present in the picture, subordinate to von Rundstedt but not yet part of Rommel's command by 1 June 1944. This general officer was *General der Panzertruppe* (*Gen.d.Pz.Tr.*) Leo, Geyr von Schweppenburg, the *Oberbefehlshaber* of *Panzergruppe West* (*Pz.Gr.West.*), which had under its command the powerful *I. SS-Panzerkorps*, the *Hitlerjugend* being one of the *Panzerdivisionen* within it.

Since March 1944, Rommel's *H.Gr.B. Hauptquartier* (higher headquarters) was located in La Roche-Guyon on the Seine River, about 50km north-west of the capital. The area of responsibility for *H.Gr.B.*, one of the two *Heeresgruppen* in France (*Heeresgruppe G* being responsible for southern France), was from the coast of the Netherlands in the north-east to the port of Cherbourg in the west. In northern France, *H.Gr.B.* had two armies under its command that were deployed to defend against an invasion. These were the *15. Armee* under *Generaloberst* Salmuth, headquartered in Tourcoing, and the *7. Armee* under *Generaloberst* Dollman, whose

Hauptquartier was at Le Mans. Rundstedt's *H. Gr. D. Hauptquartier* was located in St Germain, just outside Paris. *Pz. Gr. West*'s command staff under von Schweppenburg was also near Paris, and thus while von Rundstedt's and von Schweppenburg's staffs enjoyed a luxurious life near the city, they were physically and somewhat mentally separated from the possible future landing zones and areas of operations. They did not regularly meet the *Armee Befehlshaber* or Rommel, who in contrast constantly travelled north to the coast to meet *Division*, *Armeekorps* and *Armee*-level headquarters staff officers and their *Kommandeure*.

In June 1944 the German *OKW Hauptquartier* was located in Zossen, roughly fifty kilometres south of Berlin, but for all intents and purposes had its key element located in Hitler's *Wolfsschanze* (Wolf's Lair) headquarters complex near Rastenburg, East Prussia. Hitler rarely left the *Wolfsschanze* in 1944, though he did sometimes travel to Berchtesgaden, his mountain retreat and other locations for short periods.[1]

While Rommel was nominally under the command of *Oberbefehlshaber West*, *G.F.M.* von Rundstedt was directly under the command of *OKW*, which was effectively Hitler, with *Generalfeldmarschall* Wilhelm Keitel, as *OKW Chef des Stabes* and *Generaloberst* Alfred Jodl, the *Chef des Wehrmachtführungsstabes* (Chief of Operations Staff) assisting him. All *Kriegsmarine* and *Luftwaffe* forces in France answered to *OKW*, as well as *Organisation Todt*, which was responsible for military construction projects in occupied France.

Though von Rundstedt was *O.B West*, Hitler regularly went over his head in planning and controlling even the most minor military details, as was his manner throughout the war. Though von Rundstedt was his superior, Rommel still enjoyed a high level of status and independence due to his victories in North Africa that allowed him to gain audiences with the *Führer*. This celebrity status allowed him some independence, and most certainly allowed the *Panzerdivisionen* (armoured divisions) deployment controversy, which this chapter will discuss shortly, to exist. Rommel had arrived in Paris to meet von Rundstedt in December 1943 to inspect the *Atlantikwall* defences and advise on how to counter the invasion itself, initially acting as an advisor but eventually moving his command, *H. Gr. B.*, into northern France.[2]

The German problem of how to deal with an invasion the like of which had previously occurred in Italy and Sicily has been well documented within the Normandy campaign's historiography. Perhaps the best summation of the issues confronting the Germans is contained in the seventh volume of the official German history of the Second World War, *Germany and the Second World War*, published by Oxford University Press and co-written by a team of established German scholars.[3] The main crux of the disagreement at the highest levels of the German high command was where to deploy the powerful German *Panzerdivisionen*, who had control of them, and decisions on determining how they were initially employed when D-Day finally came. An effective defensive plan for northern France was hampered by many factors, but the biggest by far was the failure to place a majority of Germany's most powerful and mobile land forces in France, these being the armoured reserves, under the command of one headquarters. This headquarters then would have the ability to deploy them to locations close to the beaches in order to employ them as rapidly as possible and to maximum effect. This much more logical approach to controlling, deploying and employing the *Panzerdivisionen* in actual combat operations was not adopted by *OKW* due to Hitler's desire for strict control and the lack of an *OKW* strategic reserve.

The need for this reserve had been forced upon Hitler when it was made abundantly clear to him, after a period of looting occupied France for new formations for the Eastern Front, that the forces of the *Westheer* (German army of the west) were being rapidly denuded and its ability to defend France and act as an *OKW* strategic reserve were being removed. This 'looting' in March 1944 had seen the *19. Luftwaffen-Felddivision* (*Luftwaffe* Field Division) as well as *Sturmgeschütz-Abteilungen* (assault gun battalion) *326, 346* and *348* deployed to the Eastern Front, followed by the complete *II. SS-Panzerkorps* with its two brand-new, nearly fully equipped *Panzerdivisionen*. These departures had badly reduced the fighting power of *O.B. West*, and Jodl and others within the *Wolfsschanze* had brought the issue forcefully to the *Führer*'s attention. The final straw was the deployment of the very last *OKW* reserve, the *1. Gebirgs-Division*, to the Carpathian Mountains.

As a result of these events, Hitler ordered that many under-strength formations in France be rapidly brought up to strength, but the damage had been done in the short term. German industry at this point simply lacked the capability to instantly re-equip the still forming divisions still located in France. While it is out of the scope of this book to detail the buildup that followed, by June 1944 a large number of re-equipping and combat-ready armoured divisions had been somewhat brought up to strength in France.[4] It was very fortuitous for the Germans that the Normandy landings did not occur until June, as the combat power of the *Westheer* in France had been badly eroded earlier in spring.

The *Panzerdivisionen* of *Pz.Gr.West*, though intended to support the two defending armies in northern France, by June 1944 were almost a third independent *Armee*, and would in fact become one in all but name in July 1944. Schweppenburg wanted control of all the armoured divisions, and to deploy them away from the beaches to be concentrated in defeating the Allies inland, in battles of encirclement. This was, in fact, in line with existing German doctrine. Supporting von Schweppenburg, *Inspector der Panzertruppen Gen.O.* Heinz Guderian and *G.F.M.* von Rundstedt argued that the danger of naval gunfire could not be ignored and noted the catastrophic effect that this firepower had had on German armoured forces in Italy and Sicily.

Rommel was adamant that this strategy was now incorrect, and that if the Allies were not attacked immediately by strong armoured forces in their assault phase they would not be dislodged afterward.[5] Rommel believed that it was all or nothing on the first day of the invasion and wanted a linear deployment of Panzer forces to immediately swarm any landing. This would make them vulnerable to naval and air attack, but this was a price Rommel felt it was necessary to pay. In the spring of 1944 he declared:

> You have no idea how difficult it is to convince these people [his colleagues]. At one time they looked on mobile warfare as something to steer clear of at all costs, but now that our freedom of manoeuvre in the west has gone, they are all crazy after it. Whereas, in fact, it is obvious that once the enemy gets his foot in, he will put every anti-tank gun and tank he can into the bridgehead, and let us beat our heads against it, as he did at Medenine. To break through such a front, you must attack slowly and methodically, under cover of massed artillery, but we, of course, thanks to the Allied air forces, will have nothing there in time. The day of the dashing cut-and-thrust tank attack of the early war years is past and gone – and that goes for the east too, a fact which may, perhaps, by this time, have gradually sunk in.[6]

Wargames in March 1944 were conducted by *Gen.d.Pz.Tr.* von Schweppenburg with *Gen.O.* Guderian and *G.F.M.* von Rundstedt in attendance. These wargames were designed to win over these influential men to von Schweppenburg's viewpoint and further his pursuit of complete control of all the available armoured forces in a massive reserve. The result of these games was that Guderian and Rundstedt were convinced that von Schweppenburg was correct, deepening the divide in overall strategy.

How did *OKW* deal with these competing personalities and their arguments? Rather than commit to a workable, realistic strategic and tactical plan for dealing with a major Allied landing in northern France, the German supreme commander in the person of *Der Führer*, Adolf Hitler, seemingly endorsed multiple approaches, all the while not committing seriously to one major plan. Largely detached from reality in his East Prussian *Wolfsschanze* headquarters which contained key personnel from the *Oberkommando der Wehrmacht* headquarters in the months before the invasion, he attempted to hedge his bets by allocating partial resources to the powerful personalities of von Rundstedt, Rommel and von Schweppenburg and their often-contrasting approaches to the defence of northern France.

Rommel felt his hands were tied by the presence of the von Schweppenburg group and felt interference from von Rundstedt in his defence plan, Rundstedt being in the von Schweppenburg camp. Rommel, though the *Oberbefehlshaber* of *H.Gr.B.*, could not control the best assets that might help him succeed, the most powerful of these being the *Panzer-Lehr* and *Hitlerjugend*. These divisions could not be released until authorised by *OKW*, despite being nominally under the control of von Rundstedt.

The deployment of armour was thus a muddled mess, and it was not under the unified command of one man in the theatre itself.[7] This was a recipe for disaster. This confused command structure was at least partly responsible for the failures that followed and profoundly affected the military potential of the *Hitlerjugend* in the first days of the invasion. As of 1 June 1944, the *2., 21.* and *116. Panzerdivisionen* were allocated to Rommel's *H.Gr.B. H.Gr.D.* under von Rundstedt had control of the rest of the *Panzerdivisionen* and its parent training and command organisation, *Panzergruppe West*, but with the catch that they could only be released by order of the *OKW*.[8] Then, and only then, could they be transferred to the command of *Pz.Gr. West* under von Schweppenburg, which would then transfer them to the command of an *Armee* or *Armeekorps* that would employ them on the battlefield. Thus, most armoured formations in France and Belgium, these including the *1. SS-Panzerdivision Leibstandarte Adolf Hitler*, the *Hitlerjugend*, the *Panzer-Lehr Panzerdivision* and *17. SS-Panzergrenadierdivision Götz von Berlichingen*, were in a kind of limbo. With regard to the remaining operational or re-equipping *Panzerdivisionen* located in the south of France, many of these were not ready for immediate combat.

Further throwing the Germans into disarray was the overwhelming perception by the *Westheer* high command that the invasion was to occur in the Pas-de-Calais, the shortest route from Great Britain to the continent. This idea was fuelled by Allied misinformation and deception measures. This ruse, to be discussed later in in this work, would turn out to be very effective. On top of this was the Allied breakthrough in decrypting the German Enigma machine's coded messages at the Bletchley Park estate in Milton Keynes, England. The intelligence that resulted from these broken encrypted transmissions, Ultra, gave the Allies a tremendous insight into German overall strategy. Delivered from June 1941 on, Ultra provided an enormous intelligence windfall that was crucial for a total intelligence picture of German deployments, plans and intentions. Each *Panzerdivision*, as an example, had at least one Enigma machine.

So where did this leave the *Hitlerjugend*, the subject of this book? In June 1944 it was nominally part of *Pz.Gr.West* under von Schweppenburg for training and supply matters, but under the operational control of *O.B West/H.Gr.D.*, which had command of the *I. SS-Panzerkorps*, its parent *Panzerkorps*. Complicating matters even more, the actual employment of the division or moving it had to be approved by *OKW*, as it was also an *OKW* reserve formation. Thus, theoretically, it could be swiftly released if necessary, but this approval had to come from Hitler.[9]

The *I. SS-Panzerkorps* – commanded by *SS-Obergruppenführer und General der Waffen-SS (Ogruf.)* Josef Dietrich, and ably assisted by his *Chef des Stabes*, *Brigadeführer* Fritz Kraemer, a former *Heer* staff officer – was headquartered in Septeuil, just west of Paris.[10] The location of this *Korps Hauptquartier*, while central to other German headquarters near Paris, had the potential to be problematic if it had to move north quickly.

Since the *Hitlerjugend* was in Dreux, France, and its surrounding area, it was at least one day's march, fuel allowing, from the coast in any direction. They would have to endure a lengthy road march, virtually guaranteeing that they would not engage in combat operations on the first day of an invasion. The way the division was deployed, it was in a location to confront the Allies using the Schweppenburg plan, drawing them into France and then destroying them, out of range of the naval guns and to a certain extent short-range fighter bombers. To ask it to conform, suddenly, to the Rommel plan for responding to an invasion quickly would be impossible at short notice.[11]

The one German leader effectively tasked to immediately repel an invasion with all forces at his disposal was the aforementioned *G.F.M.* Rommel, the *Oberbefehlshaber* of *H.Gr.B.* He had been its commander since its third wartime deployment in northern Italy during the fall of 1943, disarming the Italian armies located there after the nation's armistice with the Allies and facilitating the German military occupation of the northern and central parts of the country. Still a powerful public figure for the Nazi's propaganda machine and the architect of several triumphs in North Africa before the disastrous events of spring 1943 and the fall of Axis-held Tunisia, Rommel was retained to oversee *H.Gr.B.* in its fourth wartime deployment as of winter 1944, to defend northern France against the coming Allied invasion.

Rommel was a realist and being a student of the events in Sicily and the boot of Italy during late 1943, he knew that if the Allies were given a chance to establish a beachhead, they would never be removed. He also understood the scale of technology and materiel employed in supporting Allied operations and had seen first-hand the impact of Allied tactical fighter bombers on German armoured operations in North Africa. These events had convinced Rommel that, if an invasion was to take place, it would have to be 'Dieppped' within a very short period of time by all German forces in the area. These forces would have to re-enact the outcome of the disastrous 19 August 1942 Anglo-Canadian raid on the French coastal casino town of the same name, which saw Allied forces defeated in detail. Rommel knew that the armoured and mobile formations he had at his disposal would have to work with, not fight for resources against, the static defenders of the *Atlantikwall*.

What help was there for the German land forces in the spring of 1944 in the way of naval and air forces? A pitiful amount was allocated in the way of real combat power, and the war in the air and on the high seas had turned against Germany in a dramatic fashion by June 1944. Support for the land forces of the *Heer* in France was negligible compared to Allied strengths in the air and on sea in spring 1944: the strengths of both the *Kriegsmarine* (German navy) and the *Luftwaffe* (German air force) were at a low ebb by spring 1944, the Battle of the Atlantic having already been decisively lost by the Germans in May 1943, and the spring of 1944 having seen the United States Army Air Forces (USAAF) run rampant throughout the airspace over Germany. This decisive US onslaught in the air had forced the *Luftwaffe* to commit the majority of its still sizeable, but dwindling, resources there.

The combat power of the *Luftwaffe* in France had been steadily depleted by June 1944. *Führer Befehl 51* (Leader order number 51), issued by Hitler on 3 November 1943, directed that more squadrons be sent to France and the Low Countries, but this was not enough to stem the Allied fighter bombers, medium bombers and airborne reconnaissance aircraft that increased their schedule of operations over northern France. This increase was part of the ongoing Anglo-American 'Transportation Plan' air offensive to destroy the French transportation infrastructure. The German *Luftflotte 3* (Air Fleet 3), partially based in northern France, did contain nearly five hundred aircraft, but by June 1944 many of these were non-operational. While some were based near Normandy, many were in Belgium and other parts of central France. The only workable strategy the *Luftwaffe* generals and their headquarters staff could come up with in the months leading to Operation *Overlord*, the Allied invasion of the continent, was to plan to 'surge' the number of *Geschwader* (wings) and *Gruppen* (large squadrons) in any potential Allied landing zone by ruthlessly stripping them from other fronts. It was planned that forces from southern France, Germany, Italy, Denmark and Greece would quickly react and fly into the theatre of operations to turn the tide. The reality of numerical inferiority against the Allies was making its presence felt, and these operational plans came from desperation in an impossible situation.[12]

The main weaknesses of the *Luftwaffe* in occupied France were the aforementioned lack of available aircraft and the correspondingly small number of *Luftwaffe Flak Batterien* (batteries) in northern France. The infrastructure in the way of fighter and night fighter radar installations (Douvres-la-Délivrande, France as an example), established logistics networks, airfields, repair facilities, concrete emplacements for the anti-aircraft *Flak Batterien*, and command and control headquarters, was still present in northern France and had been increased steadily since 1940. Despite a large defensive infrastructure, the *Luftwaffe* had been steadily losing control of the airspace over the *Reich* due to the deployment of the P-51 Mustang fighter in the long-range role for the USAAF. Using this new long-range fighter, the USAAF had worked steadily in a bludgeoning manner to destroy the *Luftwaffe Tagjäger* (day fighter) force and the German aviation industry since February 1944's Operation *Point-Blank*. This operation marked the beginning of the USAAF effort to find and destroy all *Luftwaffe* fighter forces and their factories within Germany. As a result of this Allied effort and the inevitable and obvious turning of the tide against the *Luftwaffe* in the skies over Germany, the vast majority of *Luftwaffe Geschwader* had been slowly but surely relocated to the *Reich*. Supporting this effort on the ground was the *Luftwaffe* controlled *Flak* forces and the radar and command and control centres to control and organise the defence, all under the command of *Luftflotte Reich*.

Give the paucity of available fighter, bomber and reconnaissance units left over or behind in France, which numbered 481 and of which only roughly 100 were fighters, the conditions were exactly right for an increase in Allied medium bomber and fighter-bomber operations.[13] Utilising southern and central England, which could rightly be described as a massive airfield by June 1944, these aircraft easily reached targets in France. The Allied fighter bombers, flying a constant series of daytime raids every time the weather allowed it, quickly established air superiority over some portions of northern France by early June, and the situation would only worsen for the Germans after D-Day.

The *Kriegsmarine* in France and the Low Countries was in a hopeless state of inferiority, and this state of affairs was ripe to be exploited by the upcoming massive Allied amphibious operation within the larger parent Operation *Overlord*, this being Operation *Neptune*, planned to launch from the English Channel ports. In northern France there were two major German naval groupings, one responsible for the western coastline from Cherbourg to the mouth of the Orne, the other from the Orne to the mouth of the Somme in the east. Naval strength in the way of warships within the western grouping, *Seekommandant Normandie* under *Kriegsmarine Konteradmiral* Walter Hanneke, was very weak. The entire German *Marinegruppenkommando West* (Naval Group West) surface fleet in France was composed of a grand total of 3 destroyers, 5 torpedo boats, 34 E-boats and 163 minesweepers.[14] The German U-boat command had 37 U-boats based in France, and these were virtually trapped within the French bases due to overwhelming Allied air and sea power. Allied naval power in the way of the nearly seven thousand vessels primarily of the United States Navy (USN), Royal Navy (RN) and Royal Canadian Navy (RCN) forces were slowly concentrated prior to June within the English Channel ports, these protected by an Allied air power umbrella. As a result of this massive supremacy, even the smallest German convoys along the coast were major undertakings, and even minor attacks launched against Allied shipping were just as difficult.[15]

The final German forces designated to combat Allied forces immediately on the day of an amphibious landing were the ground forces within the coast static defences. The *Atlantikwall* defences were a major commitment of scarce resources, time and effort, and meant, whether Hitler or other German commanders liked it or not, that the first actual front line during an invasion would be the coastal beaches themselves. The massive deployment of resources, much of it under the command of the paramilitary Nazi construction force *Organisation Todt*, created a large number of bunkers, obstacles and minefields, and the Germans intended, if possible, to make a large effort to prevent any successful landings from the very moment Allied forces disembarked.

G.F.M. Rommel, as *O.B. H.Gr.B.*, wanted to employ the armoured divisions as close as possible to the beaches to fight *with* the *Atlantikwall* defenders rather than have them arrive there long after they had been overwhelmed. He was convinced that this was the only chance he, as *Heeresgruppe Oberbefehlshaber*, had to prevail. Rundstedt and Schweppenburg, on the other hand, had argued against the employment of the *Panzerdivisionen* near the beaches, effectively splitting up *Panzerkorps* to simply assign their battlegroups to different possible beach sections identified as most likely for invasion. *Panzerkorps*, with all their divisions, had to be employed as per German doctrine (at least in their eyes) to exercise maximum force at the critical point during a battle of manoeuvre. In their opinion this was not necessarily immediately after Allied forces had landed.[16] The argument was also made that the coastline of northern France was so vast that the existing armoured divisions could not cover it all, and thus, they should be concentrated inland. Seemingly endless wargames fought in Paris by members of the German high command validated this view.[17]

Rundstedt and Schweppenburg would also hold up examples from the fighting in Italy and Sicily to boost their arguments, citing the effect of Allied battleships and cruiser's naval gunfire. These warships were, however, by 1944 an irrelevant concern, given the potential impact of massed tactical airpower over the battlefield, southern England being one massive aircraft carrier for launching strikes and achieving air supremacy over the beaches. Rommel understood this, and the impact of naval and air forces was something entirely missing from the operational experience of both von Schweppenburg, an Eastern Front veteran, and Rundstedt, who was born in 1875, and at the age of 69 was arguably too old to comprehend, never mind adapt operationally, to the massive threat that Allied airpower posed. Powerful displays of naval and airborne firepower were something simply not experienced on the Eastern Front to the scale that would be present in Normandy.

Further expanding on the differences described in the command styles of von Rundstedt, von Schweppenburg and Rommel, while Schweppenburg and Rundstedt were tied to their headquarters, the study of maps, and delegating duties to their staff officers, such as Rundstedt's capable *Chef des Stabes, General der Infanterie* Günther Blumentritt, Rommel did the exact opposite. Rommel was very 'hands on', and visited as many areas as he could during a workday, constantly making inspections of units and defences. This is not to say he did not carry out the appropriate headquarters role of an *Oberbefehlshaber*, but that he was engaged in determining for himself the true reality of a situation rather than receiving a briefing from a staff officer based in a luxurious château in Paris.[18]

As such, the deployment of the *Hitlerjugend* as another *Panzerdivision* deep within the interior of northern France, orchestrated by Rundstedt and others, reflected a calculated refusal to support the German troops that would be fighting first on the beaches, this despite the deployment of sizeable amounts of artillery and the construction of extensive defensive works there. The placement of powerful armoured formations away from the beaches was an attempt to appease Schweppenburg and other supposed armoured 'experts' who thought, incorrectly, that a massive Punic War Cannae-style battle of encirclement would occur within northern France. Some more extreme proponents of the 'interior battle of encirclement' wanted to even stop the *Panzerdivisionen* from intervening for five to six days.[19] Rommel and other German Mediterranean campaign veterans understood that once the Allies had landed and entrenched themselves, there was no defeating them without a massive Kursk-like 1943 Operation *Zitadelle*-style offensive, and this fact was simply beyond the mental capabilities of their opponents. Rundstedt and Schweppenburg's approaches were simply wrong, and terribly so. With regard to German fortunes, it was unfortunate that Hitler and his *OKW* staff officers, the only ones that could enable Rommel, could not bring themselves to understand history would repeat itself.[20]

The correct and realistic approach, despite the past experience of the impact of naval gunfire in Sicily and Italy, was to have the *Panzerdivisionen* close to the beaches, dispersed to avoid the worst of any naval bombardment. In this way the Germans could 'mate' the *Panzerdivisionen* temporarily to *Atlantikwall* forces located in northern France before an armoured division's rotation back to the Eastern Front. By doing so, these armoured forces, the cream of the *Heer* and *Waffen-SS*, would be ready and able to drive any Allied landing back into the sea rapidly. This goal would have to be accomplished within a set period of time, less than a day ideally, or the Allies would simply reinforce their gains and establish an iron-clad defence, backed by naval gunfire and tactical and strategic airpower, which would make their defeat a near impossibility.

The allocation of resources to the *Atlantikwall* system of obstacles, mines and concrete bunkers added strength to the operational viewpoint of Rommel that the seashore itself was the main battle area, and that this front line against any invasion needed to be manned in force. Though Rommel had promised Hitler that by 1 May 1944 the *Atlantikwall* would be in reasonably defensive shape, this goal had only been partially completed by 1 June. But enough in the way of construction strides had been made since the fall of 1943 to make it capable of putting up a significant defensive fight, this after German generals in France had first realised their defensive measures were entirely inadequate.[21]

The total coastline of northern France, from the Belgian border to the port of Cherbourg area, was nearly 445 kilometres. The *Atlantikwall* simply could not be strong everywhere, or present in any real depth in a similar manner to German First World War trench lines in Belgium and France during 1917–18. There simply were not enough construction resources, personnel or time remaining from January 1944 onward for a German *Wehrmacht* that was already fighting a ground campaign in two theatres and fighting a strategic naval and air campaign on multiple fronts. As the invasion loomed, Rommel worked intensively to complete fortifications and obstacles that were in the construction phase and not begin planned ones. Without his dynamic leadership as *O.B. H.Gr.B.*, what German resistance did occur on D-Day against invading US and Anglo-Canadian forces would not have been as intense as it was.

When the actual invasion event did transpire, the aims and plans of Rommel, Schweppenburg, Rundstedt and *OKW* in the form of Hitler himself would all collide and result in tremendous friction and a scattered, inefficient response. Top secret Allied Ultra intelligence, the product of the decryption of German military Enigma machine communications, had provided the Allies with insight into German disagreements at the highest level of their command, which the Western powers spurred along by establishing phantom armies in northern and south-western England. The threat of multiple potential landing sites gave weight to Schweppenburg and Rundstedt's viewpoints that a strong central reserve of *Panzerdivisionen*, located in central France, needed to be flexibly responsive to counter potential threats in multiple locations.

By May 1944, it is arguable that it was apparent to *OKW* and *H.Gr.D./O.B. West*, though it is up for debate if anything was clear to them in this disastrous year, that a massive build-up of Allied forces was underway in southern England.[22] Due in no small part to the determined effort towards deception by the Allied high command and intelligence services, the Germans concluded that a likely invasion would most probably occur in the Pas-de-Calais region opposite Dover with a force of approximately twenty divisions initially, and this event was expected to occur in mid-July 1944.[23]

The Allies' main deception plan, *Bodyguard*, was divided into two sub-operations, 'Fortitude North', and 'Fortitude South'. Due to these efforts, the Germans were made to believe through 'Fortitude South' that a fake army group in southern England, the First United States Army Group, was ready to assault the Pas-de-Calais. Through 'Fortitude North', the Germans were led to believe that an army in Scotland, the Fourth British Army, also existed and could be used in potentially multiple landing sites.[24] The presence of the First US Army Group, purportedly commanded by none other than the well-known US Lieutenant General George. S. Patton, was intended to menace the Pas-de-Calais and alarm the Germans to the real possibility of an invasion there. It was then hoped that the Germans would deploy most of their first-class formations there and the usual poor quality static defensive units and formations would be placed near the real locations for the actual invasion. A sophisticated campaign of deception, ranging from subverted former German agents captured in England to inflatable dummy Sherman tanks and mockup aircraft, was utilised to reinforce this illusion.[25]

It was not all smooth sailing for the Allies in the months leading up to Operation *Overlord*. The reconnaissance overflights of aircraft belonging to *Luftflotte 3*, based in the north of France, had revealed the inexorable build-up of all manner of ships and landing craft in the port of Southampton and others. As a result, German intelligence officers had produced an accurate report that argued that an invasion would likely occur in the area Cherbourg–Le Havre. This analysis had been made after a series of *Luftwaffe* overflights, though the number of these flights that had reached their objectives had been limited due to the overpowering nature of the Allied air defences in southern England.

Allied intelligence desperately watched for any mass German movement away from the Pas-de-Calais of the best German infantry formations that were suited to repel Allied invasion forces within hours of them landing. Amazingly lucky by any standard of the imagination, no major German troop movements occurred, though the Normandy sector was reinforced as May and June 1944 approached. Allied headquarters staffs and members of the intelligence services had watched with bated breath from southern England as the time crawled by.[26] But the overall effort of Operation *Bodyguard* was effective, and the threat of the fictitious First US Army Group would continue to pay important dividends well past 6 June 1944.

While it was impossible to somehow destroy or attrit all German land forces in France prior to the Allied landing, it was possible to influence their locational deployment away from the real landing beaches. What could be achieved by the Allies was achieved, and thus Operation *Overlord*'s chances of success were increased severalfold by this brilliant deception campaign. Also beneficial for the Allies, neither the *Hitlerjugend* nor *Panzer-Lehr* moved even slightly closer to Normandy, their deployment locations remaining the same as a result of the Panzer controversy. In the end, Rommel, Schweppenburg, Rundstedt and even Hitler and his entourage high in the *Berchtesgaden* complex in early June 1944 were convinced the Allied amphibious landing would come in Pas-de-Calais, and ensured the best German static defences were there, ready to fight an assault that would never come.

CHAPTER 2

The *Panzerwaffe* in France and the *Kampfgruppe* battle

Before the *Hitlerjugend* as a *Panzerdivision* is discussed in the next chapter, it is important to address the question of what sort of forces it was intended to fight alongside as part of a *Panzerkorps* in France. What *Panzerwaffe* (German army tank arm) standards did these formations in France meet, or not meet, with regard to strength, capabilities, and structure at the beginning of June 1944? In the first part of this chapter, the author will briefly examine a *Heer Panzerdivision*, one that would fight shoulder to shoulder with the *Hitlerjugend* for the period studied within this book. By doing this, the work can illustrate some of the challenges faced by the *Westheer* on the eve of its decisive defensive campaign, and illustrate how *Heer Panzerdivisionen* were weaker in some ways than those of the *Waffen-SS*.

A second important question to be addressed is, once battle was joined with an invading Allied invasion force, how were the vaunted armoured divisions of Germany expected to fight in France? The author will present a short summary of German tactical armoured doctrine centred on the *Kampfgruppe* (battlegroup) in order to provide the reader with insight as to how the defenders of occupied France planned to use these divisions to crush the enemy.

Addressing the first question, while there were favoured, well-known formations that were extremely well equipped, trained and organised along somewhat standard lines such as the lavishly equipped *Panzer-Lehr*, others epitomised the chaotic nature of the German war industry and its inability to standardise equipment and vehicles within armoured divisions. The reality in 1944 was that many German *Panzerdivisionen* seemingly could not conform to ordered organisational structure standards, which was made impossible by the then constant state of expansion due to Hitler's orders, the lack of new vehicles and equipment, and the ongoing effort to rebuild old worn-out divisions, which took resources. While it was all well and good for the *Generalinspekteur der Panzertruppen*, *Generaloberst* Guderian, to issue new organisational structures periodically for the *Panzerdivisionen*, more often than not it was partially impossible for the divisional headquarters staffs to fully carry out these reforms due to a lack of personnel, vehicles and equipment or time away from combat operations.

Deployed closest to the invasion beaches south of what would become the eastern sector of the Normandy Bridgehead was the *21. Panzerdivision*, based south and south-east of Caen. This division had been ordered reformed on 6 May 1943 after the surrender of its former iteration in Tunisia as part of the mass German and Italian North African capitulation. Commanded by *Generalmajor* (*Gen.Maj.*) Eduard Feuchtinger, it had been allowed to evolve without resources and mutate over the course of the previous year with official *OKH* support due to its unique status as a *Panzerdivision* largely equipped with captured French tanks and vehicles.

On 1 June 1944 its structure partially resembled that of a *Panzerdivision*, but it was unique within the *Panzerwaffe*. This use of *Beutepanzer* armour (captured 'loot' tanks) was part of the German effort to use every possible resource, regardless of this impact on standardisation, in the year 1944 to fend off a looming massive military defeat on all fronts.

Gen.Maj. Feuchtinger cannot be described in any way as a qualified expert in mobile operations or defensive warfare using armoured forces, having last served in combat as an *Artillerie-Regiment Kommandeur* on the Eastern Front during the initial operations in the USSR in 1941. Pre-war, this First World War veteran had cultivated close ties to the Nazi Party as the organiser of *Heer* participation in several political rallies and later as part of the organising committee for the Summer and Winter Olympic Games in 1936. In truth, Feuchtinger owed his appointment in occupied France more to loyalty to Hitler and the Nazi Party than merit or a wartime record of successful operational command. He enjoyed a luxurious life in occupied Paris while overseeing the organisation of his new division, but had little interest in forming a feasible plan to actually use it to drive the Allies into the sea using its combat power in a concentrated manner.

As an *Oberst* in 1943, in an effort to utilise his gifted subordinate *Major* Alfred Becker and others, Feuchtinger had been charged with raising *Schelle-Brigade West*, a formation which was intended to employ captured French vehicles as a mobile strike force against an Allied landing. He was a gifted organiser, and despite his reputation as a playboy and free spirit, he did achieve results in an environment starved of resources. Later he was charged with the creation of the *Neu* (new) *21. Pz.Div.*, and by June 1944 it was completely rebuilt and ready, in the eyes of some of the German high command, to be the first to combat an invasion.

The key formation within any *Panzerdivision* was its *Panzerregiment*, and *Pz.Rgt. 22* was weak. Most glaringly, *Pz.Rgt. 22* did not possess the standard *Pantherabteilung* (Panther tank battalion), which was intended to equip the first battalion of every *Panzerregiment* in 1944 and be its cutting edge. A 1944 *Panzerregiment* was supposed to have one Panther and one Panzer IV *Abteilung*. *Pz.Rgt. 22* only had enough

Panzer IV medium tanks (104 such tanks) to form one strong Panzer IV *Abteilung*. The rest of the second *Abteilung* was composed of captured obsolete French tanks with a smattering of Panzer IVs.

Another powerful source of strength for the division was its *Sturmgeschütz-Abteilung 200* assault gun battalion, led by the previously mentioned *Maj.* Becker. Composed of four *Batterien* with 40 assault guns, this unit was intended to be both the offensive and defensive power of the division in its mobile operations and was powerfully equipped with numerous self-propelled guns based on French tank chassis.

The division's four, fully manned *Panzergrenadiere-Bataillone* within its two *Panzergrenadierregimenter* were very strong by *Heer* standards, these being well equipped with all manner of heavy weapons, two of them being completely mounted on captured French Unic P 107 half-tracks. That said, these regiments did not have the three *Bataillone* the SS-*Panzergrenadierregimenter* had.

Its powerful, fully equipped *Panzer-Artillerie-Regiment 155* artillery regiment was largely composed of a mix of captured Russian and better German towed artillery pieces. Other units such as *Panzerjäger-Abteilung 200* (anti-tank battalion) and *Panzer-Pionier-Bataillon 220* (combat engineer battalion) were also completely either mechanised or motorised and fully equipped. The *21. Pz.Div.* had a rather long training cycle by 1944 standards and was inspected by *G.F.M.* Rommel in the spring of 1944. While the division did not lack armoured fighting vehicles, its ability to maintain the captured French vehicles and other weaponry would be limited in high-intensity combat operations in which these items broke down or were damaged.

While the division did have some talented and veteran commanders, such as *Oberstleutnant* Hans von Luck, *Kommandeur* of *Pz.Gren.Rgt. 125*, others, such as *Pz.Rgt. 22 Kommandeur Oberst* Hermann von Oppeln-Bronikowski, were average, the latter being responsible for the failed *22. Panzerdivision Pz.Rgt. 204* counterattacks during the November 1942 Soviet Operation *Uranus*, which saw the Red Army encircle the German *6. Armee* at Stalingrad. While a sprinkling of veterans were present in the *21. Pz.Div.*, some with experience on the Eastern Front and North Africa, the soldiery was mainly composed of new conscripts that had various levels of training.

The *21. Pz.Div.* was the closest German armoured division to the beaches, being located within the Caen area, and if dynamically led, it had the potential to deliver a tactical defeat on a portion of a future Allied amphibious landing. Good command and control would be key to the division's success when it was finally employed in its first combat operations. What it needed was a seasoned veteran commander with dynamic drive who could concentrate its forces for use towards a single point to cause maximum damage on the enemy in the shortest amount of time. The *21. Pz.Div.* was unfortunately missing this type of *Kommandeur* in Feuchtinger, and as a result, nothing in the way of dynamic success would be achieved when the real invasion came on 6 June.

Regarding the armoured formations of the *Westheer*, how were they intended to fight as part of the German tactical doctrine in the year 1944? What was the German tactical doctrine? More importantly, how was it hoped these divisions would perform when contact with the enemy in France was made?

The strengths and weaknesses of the *Heer* were very glaring by 1944 and were obvious to its enemies. Earlier in the war, the British Army had concluded that if a method of fighting could be developed to disrupt the German army's mobile operations and drag them into a battle of attrition, then *Das Heer* could be defeated. The difference between the tempo and style of military operations the Germans wanted and their realistic ability to conduct said style of fighting in spring 1944 played an enormous part in deciding the outcome of the Normandy campaign. The choice by the author to study the *Hitlerjugend* provides an excellent case study to illustrate what the German land warfare doctrine was in the late-war period, and exactly what type of combat formation they thought could achieve their desired objectives with. The unsuccessful offensive operations of the *Hitlerjugend*, to be discussed within this work, would highlight the clash of Allied and German doctrines.

The German army was designed for and had attempted, throughout the war up to this point, to fight a battle of aggressive manoeuvre where it had the capability to do so. This *Blitzkrieg* or 'lightning war' style of fighting grew out of a mixture of the German *Truppenführung* (Handling of Combined-Arms Formations) manual of tactical warfare doctrine and the influence of proponents of armoured warfare such as *Generaloberst* Heinz Guderian and *G.F.M.* Erwin Rommel.[1] The latter two and others were influenced greatly by the inter-war writings of German military theorists on mobile warfare. The experience of the victories in the West, Poland, and the USSR had established the Panzer as the dominant land weapon system in the eyes of the *Heer* high command and the upper echelons of the *Waffen-SS*. Though some ideas were picked up from British military theorists, British influence has been massively overstated.[2] This fluid battle concept stressed the Panzer and motorised infantry units as the key elements. Joining the pre-First World War strategic thinking of Field Marshal Alfred von Schlieffen with 1930s approaches to motorised mobile warfare resulted in an armoured, mobile approach to war that saw success in outflanking, surrounding and ultimately destroying their opponents through massed attacks at their weakest point as the primary objective. A self-contained divisional *Kampfgruppe* (battlegroup), using its own organic combined arms to maximum advantage with maximum mobility, was to crush the enemy rapidly. The focus was not on gaining ground, but destruction of the enemy forces.

The German *Heer* could not fight how it wanted to without all combined arms being in motion and functioning well at high tempo. An artillery-based tactical doctrine, such as the kind evidenced during the First World War in France, was very undesirable to the field marshals in charge of the Third Reich's forces in 1944. Fighting the battle with artillery as their centrepiece would mean being tied to the fire-plan of high command and not outrunning or manoeuvring beyond the range of the guns. This was anathema to the *Panzer Kommandeure* of the early war period, most of whom were participants in the early *Blitzkrieg* campaigns or students of the *Gen. O.* Guderian school of armoured tactics.[3] Armoured manoeuvres and the 'cult of the offensive' had vastly reduced the need for artillery in an operational plan, other than for temporary shock value, as was evidenced in the Battle of France in 1940.[4]

In the autumn of 1943, the Germans were still winning tactical battles on the Russian front with armoured formations conducting roughly the same tactics as in 1941, albeit with better Panzers.[5] Briefly explained, this manner of fighting saw one combined arms *Kampfgruppe*, or a combination of them, acting on different or common objectives in a manner loosely controlled by corps and divisional-level headquarters. Non-armoured *Kampfgruppen* would usually participate in non-offensive flanking moves or simply follow up to occupy ground and repel counterattacks after the armoured *Kampfgruppen* had seized objectives. The difference between these operations and those staged by British or Canadian formations was that most weapons involved and decisions on how to fight the battle were in the hands of the *Kampfgruppe Kommandeur*. While under the thumb of the divisional commander and charged with achieving operational objectives, depending on the situation these could be flexible and in some cases even optional if the situation changed. As military historian Dennis Showalter states: 'Successful operations were exemplified by the successful execution of *Auftragstaktik*, the necessity of subordinate commanders to act independently within a general framework, responding to specific conditions and exploiting specific opportunities without reference to higher headquarters', adjusting their tactics and doctrine as the situation demanded.[6]

The *Kampfgruppe Kommandeur* had to have his finger on the pulse of the situation and take advantage of opportunities as they arose. The divisional *Kommandeur* could take a strong hand in the control of the *Kampfgruppen* or just let them operate towards achieving their objectives in a hands-off manner, the divisional *Gefechtsstand* monitoring their progress via wireless situation reports.[7] All firepower within the armoured and totally mechanised *Kampfgruppen* had to move with it. Towed *Artillerie Batterien* could support operations, but the *Kampfgruppen*, with their own organic tracked firepower, were not tied to them. The same was true regarding air support. These two methods of support could provide effective destructive firepower, but on the vast open steppes of the USSR and the plains of France and Poland, the battle during the early years of the war had often moved so fast and so far in short periods of time that these assets were left behind or not used. Virtually the only factors that hamstrung armoured mobile operations were strong enemy opposition that could not be bypassed, a lack of fuel or other key supplies or munitions, or poor road conditions.

Packed into the *Kampfgruppe* was everything that was needed to do the job. The up-front fighting edge to the formation consisted of *Panzer* or *Sturmgeschütz* units, with as many vehicles as could be mustered. *Panzergrenadiere* and *Panzerpioniere* mounted on SPW 251 half-tracks or on the backs of the armoured vehicles were a key part of the spearhead, always ready to support the armoured advance and dismount and assault at a moment's notice. Light self-propelled artillery would follow the lead columns at a distance with their howitzers mounted on converted tank chassis. Such artillery was seen as a brief shock weapon more than anything else, to soften up the objective for the armoured group (*Gepanzertgruppe* or *Panzergruppe*), and they had only limited ammunition supplies. Following this were towed and self-propelled anti-aircraft *Flak* elements to fight off enemy aircraft, and these assets could often be employed in the ground role. Following at a distance further back were numerous ammunition carriers and supply and maintenance vehicles, maintaining a link with divisional rear areas.[8] All divisional support elements held at the divisional level that did not fit into a *Kampfgruppe* and could not be moved quickly were reasonably distant from the fighting in rear laager areas. These consisted of the divisional *Gefechtsstand*, armoured vehicle repair units, larger divisional logistic units, units controlling fuel and ammunition dumps, medical clearing stations and the like.[9]

Providing more detail on how the divisional artillery, so central to Allied doctrine and the 'Queen' of its battlefield by 1944, fit into the picture of the German *Kampfgruppe*-style offensive battle, one adjective comes to mind: *reduced*. The artillery was tasked with softening up the enemy's defensive positions in the zone of the designated area for initial break-through of the *Kampfgruppen*: nothing more. Any strongpoints of infantry or tanks were to be reduced by this *Artillerie* in a violent, brief, shocking fashion. But the artillery was always a temporary support asset, and never viewed as vital to the objective of destroying the enemy. Due to a lack of ammunition in the late war period, the *Panzer-Artillerie* could engage the enemy with counterbattery fire for a very short period, only attempting to temporarily silence any enemy field artillery from bombarding the *Kampfgruppe* assembly area prior to an operation. They would, however, play a bigger role in defensive operations of the *Kampfgruppen*, something of an almost daily role in the last year of the war, seeking to smash enemy assault formations in their assembly areas and using the *Flak* units of the division to annihilate ground targets if no enemy aircraft were present to engage with.

The *Kampfgruppe* commander would have the support of the divisional *Artillerieführer*, or *Ar.Fu.*, with the regular field and rocket *Nebelwerfer* artillery *Batterien* at his command for the initial part of an offensive operation. The ability of German divisions to rapidly coordinate artillery forces for a massive bombardment of a specific battlefield sector was very limited. While there was a higher *Artilleriekommandeur*, or *Ar.Ko.*, at the German *Korps* and *Armee* level, any *Heer* equivalent to the British Army Group Royal Artillery grouping was decidedly inferior, and terribly hamstrung by a lack of ammunition, motorisation and wireless capability in the face of the Allied radio signal triangulation threat that led to counterbattery fire. Massed fire from German *Korps*-level *Nebelwefer*, *schwere-Artillerie* and *Flak Brigaden* could only be utilised in the late war period for specific missions or during military emergencies.[10]

An important conclusion can be drawn from the above paragraphs on artillery in general in the German army; it was not the dominant weapons system. That distinction belongs to the Panzer. If the German *Heer* and *Waffen-SS* were confronted by Allied armies who had an artillery-based operational planning process, such as the British and Canadian armies, and if the *Panzergruppe* could not prevail in a shocking, violent fashion immediately, there would be challenges to say the least.[11] Specifically, if a *Kampfgruppe* was forced to fight a well-equipped enemy dug in for defence, it would be highly likely that the sufficient weight of artillery fire needed to annihilate the defensive positions would not be available. The German *Artillerie* arm could not match the Allies in extended artillery duels, nor could it destroy their concentrations in massive, army-level fire attacks. Moreover, because the massed use of field artillery was not part of German doctrine, they never developed the manufacturing capability back in Germany to actually employ such a tactical approach. Vital also to artillery-based tactical thinking was an effective supply system to bring the shells themselves into the theatre. This existed in the way of the French railway system in northern France in May 1944, but Allied air forces rendered it non-serviceable in places as a result of their spring 1944 'Transportation Plan' air offensive.[12]

With regard to defensive operations – and hundreds of these had taken place in Africa, the Mediterranean and the Eastern Front following the German loss of the overall initiative in late 1942 – the armoured *Kampfgruppe* was viewed as vital to quickly sealing off any penetration of the German *Hauptkampflinie* (main line of resistance) and restoring the previous positions, destroying the enemy in the process. A quick response was seen as essential to restore the situation before the enemy could fortify its newly won real estate, giving them the ability to inflict massive casualties on a German counter-attacking force.[13] In the fighting on the Eastern Front and North Africa, attacking Allied enemy armoured and infantry forces, having hopefully first been worn down by defending German defensive positions consisting of infantry and anti-tank guns, would then be attacked from the flank or rear by armoured 'fire-brigades', sent in from locations near the break-through sector to restore the line and inflict casualties on the Allied forces. The immediate German defensive counterattack, if not done quickly, was a risky option against a prepared opponent. If it failed against a defence organized around massive anti-tank and field artillery firepower, losses would be doubled, and the casualties suffered by the initial defending force would be compounded by those in the counterattacking force. For these reasons, German defensive doctrine was based on the shock of a quick counterattack supported by brief – but usually powerful – preparatory barrages from indirect fire.

The key factor on which any armoured *Kampfgruppe*'s success hinged was the most important one in the practice of *Blitzkrieg* armoured warfare: attack the enemy not where he is strong, but where he is weak. To batter your unit or formation or allow its advance to be bogged down against the enemy's strongest bulwark was perceived by the Germans as inviting defeat, and in the later war years this would result in large equipment and personnel losses that German formations could not afford to replace. Importantly, a German *Kampfgruppe* in 1944 simply did not have access to a sophisticated fire-support network in place to call down overwhelming firepower on a fortified enemy position or line if it encountered one in its advance. Decisive action and exploitation had to be sought at the enemy's weakest point, not the strongest.[14]

To conclude this summary of German armoured tactics in the late war period, according to well-established German doctrine, the defeat and destruction of the enemy was to be brought on by the most powerful units within a *Kampfgruppe*, operating with speed and daring. The battle would either be won or lost by their ability to succeed in destroying the enemy rapidly. It was always intended for the *Luftwaffe* to provide support, but it was not seen as the most important factor. Likewise, the mobile artillery firepower within the *Kampfgruppe* was seen as sufficient to get the job done in the shortest amount of time, helping to crush the enemy quickly. By keeping an offensive tempo high and the enemy off balance, the Germans believed they could prevail in offensive and defensive operations in the late war period. The Germans' Achilles heel lay in the imperative placed on themselves to repeat the successes of the early war *Blitzkrieg* victories. If the German approach to operations of mobile manoeuvre was thwarted in any way, be it by a strong enemy defence or the inability to supply an armoured spearhead, the doctrine would unravel, and the Nazi war machine would be dragged into a battle of attrition it could not win.

CHAPTER 3

The *12. SS-Panzerdivision Hitlerjugend* in June 1944

Returning to the *Hitlerjugend*, this division was selected by the author as a case study in part because of it being the epitome of what the Third Reich believed to be an ideal military formation, one with which they sincerely believed they would win the war, or at least postpone defeat. The *Panzerdivisionen* were viewed as the elite of the *Heer* and *Waffen-SS* formations, and responsible for virtually all the battlefield successes achieved from 1939–43. The mobile battle with hard-hitting armoured formations was, by 1944, the only acceptable doctrine for a land force somewhat lacking in numbers of personnel, armour, artillery and other resources comparable to its enemies, and by spring of that year it was also lacking tactical air support. If the *Westheer* had any hopes for success in the anticipated invasion battles, they were pinned on the *Panzerabteilung* and *Panzergrenadiere Bataillone* of the *Hitlerjugend*.

The *12. SS-Panzerdivision Hitlerjugend* was established in June 1943 by administrative order No. *784/43 gK*. The initial assembly area which its new recruits and veteran cadre would be concentrated in was in Beverloo training area north of Brussels, this establishment formerly being a Belgian Army training ground that was appropriated by the German *Heer* following the surrender of Belgium and its occupation in 1940.[1]

Taking most of its new recruits that year from the *Hitlerjugend* (Hitler Youth) organisation, hence its name, it was hoped the division would symbolize the commitment of Germany's youth to the war effort, the survival of the *Reich*, and National Socialism. The majority of its new *SS-Panzergrenadiere* were teenagers born in the year 1926, and as all new members of the *Waffen-SS*, swore an oath of allegiance to *Der Führer*, Adolf Hitler.

From the start, the intention was to create an elite *Waffen-SS* armoured division. It was to be identical in structure and strength to the *1. SS-Panzerdivision Leibstandarte Adolf Hitler*, and together these divisions would form an *SS-Panzerkorps* of two armoured divisions. The veteran cadre needed to accomplish the goal of raising and training a brand-new armoured division of over twenty thousand men would require the infusion of senior- and junior-level *Waffen-SS* commissioned and non-commissioned officers, nearly all of whom would come from the *Leibstandarte*; only a small percentage would come from the *Heer*, other *Waffen-SS* formations and training schools. This 'splitting' process, which was carried out with many 'named' formations in the German land forces in the years 1943–45, the most notable examples being the *Grossdeutschland Panzergrenadier-Division* and the *Herman Göring Fallschirm-Panzerdivision*, usually had a horrendous effect on the division that supplied the necessary cadre, as it was often forced to give up half its officers and junior leaders. In the case of some divisions, entire *Bataillone* and *Abteilungen* would disappear in one fell swoop. The effect of 'splitting' the *Leibstandarte* arguably degraded its military effectiveness just prior to the failed Kursk Offensive, Operation *Zitadelle*, and its disastrous 1943–44 deployment to Ukraine in which it fought to annihilation over a period of months, suffering severe losses with little to show for it except a continuous retreat.[2]

The reasons behind the formation of the *Hitlerjugend*, its training and equipment have been well documented, the best example being the Meyer divisional history mentioned in the introduction regarding the historiography of the division. And, it is the combat record of the division, not its establishment, that is the subject of this work. It is however worthwhile to briefly discuss the division's key personalities, its composition, and the Eastern Front combat experience its core cadre possessed and which influenced how they approached future operations. The *Waffen-SS* also had some unique approaches to military training versus that of the Allies and the *Heer*, and this will be briefly mentioned.

By early June 1944 the *Hitlerjugend*'s training period was virtually complete. It was, by Germany's standards in 1944, a very highly trained, well-equipped division – intended to be the perfect example of the type of formation used to execute the *Heer* doctrine of quick, mobile campaigns of encirclement and deep penetration.[3] By 1944 the war had turned conclusively in the Allies favour, and this now meant it was almost certainly to be used for defensive counterattacks and defeating Allied offensive operations, and this was understood, though not publicly stated, by the German high command.

The core of the division, coming mainly from the *Leibstandarte* with a sprinkling of *Heer* personnel, were soldiers of great experience and quality. Their calibre, proven in combat over two winters on the Eastern Front in some of the most difficult tactical situations imaginable, could not be higher. The designated commanding officer of the division on its formation in 1943 was the former commander of the *SS-Pz.Gren.Rgt. 1* of the *Leibstandarte*, then-*Oberführer* Fritz Witt. A member of the *Leibstandarte* since the 1930s, Witt had fought in Poland, Greece, France and Ukraine.[4] Highly decorated and militarily capable, he was admired by his subordinates and fellow *Waffen-SS* officers. The second most admired soldier of the *Leibstandarte* was the then-*Sturmbannführer* Kurt Meyer, the former *Kommandeur* of the *SS-Pz.Aüfkl.Abt. 1*, the reconnaissance battalion of the *Leibstandarte*. He had also fought in all the *Leibstandarte* campaigns and was now designated to be leader of *SS-Pz.Gren.Rgt. 25*, which contained more strength than a 1944 British Army infantry brigade and was one of the two *SS-Panzergrenadierregimenter* within the division. A pure soldier and natural leader, he was fearless in battle and aggressive to the point of being reckless. Mated with these features was a record of having the innate natural ability to judge a combat situation and make the correct decision. By spring 1943 his star was rising within the *Waffen-SS*, and he was the senior of the two *SS-Panzergrenadierregiment Kommandeure*.

Then-*Stubaf.* Max Wünsche was slated to become the designated *Kommandeur* of the new *Hitlerjugend Panzerregiment, SS-Pz.Rgt. 12*. He had recently led a tank battalion of the *Leibstandarte* in the spring 1943 Kharkov battles with great distinction. He was also a veteran of the Russian campaign from the beginning and was perceived as one of the most talented young armour commanders in the Third Reich.

The brutal combat of the battles in France, Greece and Russia had hardened these men. Each had shown personal courage and was revered by the new recruits in Belgium and France as near super-soldiers. Each was a natural leader, who could, and would themselves attempt to do anything that was asked of their men.[5]

Unfortunately, while these key leaders were battle-hardened veterans, it must be noted that the early *Blitzkrieg* campaigns and the war in Russia was something entirely different from the desert campaign in Africa, the fighting in Italy and the coming battles in France. Tactics and warfare, especially with respect to Allied air power and field artillery, not to mention the treatment of civilians and POWs, were entirely different in the West. Many non-commissioned officers and officers had been brutalised by their experience in the East, and they had come to treat their enemies with contempt – seeing them as less than human, as vermin to be exterminated, and many blindly accepted the propaganda that all Slavs were 'Untermensch', racially sub-human. Their approach to human life had become negligent at best, and brutally criminal at worst. Many, such the new *SS-Pz.Gren. Rgt. 26 Kommandeur Ostubaf.* Wilhelm Mohnke, believed all battlefield enemies and anyone in the way of his operations deserved nothing more than a bullet. The direction for the *Waffen-SS* to see themselves as members of the master race led them to see captured or wounded enemy soldiers, even in the West, with anything but compassion. They did not think these wounded enemy soldiers needed the treatment required by the Geneva Convention or fair treatment. The enemy was to be destroyed, and whether he fought or surrendered did not make much difference. Far from exclusively a *SS* or *Waffen-SS* practice, regular *Heer* units on the Eastern Front also routinely shot civilians, communists, partisans, surrendered prisoners and anyone else even moderately interfering with their operations. This criminal ruthlessness would be brought to France by the former *Leibstandarte* elements and filtered into the young *Hitlerjugend* soldiers.[6]

This factor was made worse by the severe shortage of non-commissioned officers (NCOs), the *SS* equivalents of squad leaders. These were especially needed since the entire non-officer or non-commissioned officer (NCO) manpower of the division in the summer of 1943 was 17- and 18-year-old *Hitlerjugend* members who needed discipline to become effective combat soldiers. The lack of these more mature junior leaders in the way of sufficient numbers of *Unterscharführer* and *Scharführer* would result in a lack of discipline and rampant risk-taking behaviour on the battlefield. This behaviour was also due to their being indoctrinated in the past to take the initiative in all situations they encountered within their stages of training within the *Hitlerjugend* youth organisation. These 18-year-olds, mated with the transferred veteran *Waffen-SS* and *Heer* personnel, filled a basic framework, but it was numerically short of the war establishment model for a *Waffen-SS Panzerdivision* with regard to officers and non-commissioned junior leaders. This deficiency was partially remedied by selecting outstanding potential officer and NCO candidates and running crash-training courses, a process that was only partially complete by spring 1944.[7]

Earlier in September 1943, the *Hitlerjugend* sub-division structure had been established. The main body of the division was based in the aforementioned Beverloo, Belgium, and it is surrounding localities, while the *SS-Panzerregiment* was based in Mailly-Le-Camp, near Rheims, France. The order of battle was that of a typical *Waffen-SS* type 1943 *Panzerdivision* with a few minor variations.[8] Despite problems in rapid military equipment acquisition for the new division, training went ahead as scheduled, albeit with a very different basic training program compared to that of the Western Allied armies. It is important to mention this factor, because this training that occurred in the fall/winter of 1943/44 set the *Hitlerjugend* apart from its enemies and allowed them to function effectively in the field and overcome numerical inferiority and other obstacles in combat on occasion.

Divisional *Kommandeur Obf.* Witt decided on three main priorities to develop the youths into *SS-Panzergrenadiere*. These were, in order of priority: physical hardening through sport, character training in a classroom setting and through team exercises, and finally weapons training in a realistic outdoor environment. Contrary to western Allied armies, parade ground drill was virtually abandoned, except for route marches or special occasions. 'Square Bashing' was frowned upon and seen as a useless skill considering the military situation Germany found itself in. Heavy pack route marches were also looked down upon as damaging to health and morale. Progressive marksmanship training in a realistic outdoor or urban environment was stressed as a basic combat skill. Live-fire exercises began soon after, especially for the *SS-Panzergrenadiere*. Instruction in the application of camouflage, field-craft and ambush tactics soon followed. The teaching of bunker construction with interlocking defensive fire schemes was also introduced. Junior officers and non-commissioned junior leaders were active participants in field training exercises with the young *SS-Panzergrenadiere*. It was seen as important for the younger soldiers to observe the leaders as part of their team and respect them for the example they set, and not as part of a different social strata, as was the case in the late war British Army.[9]

Classroom lectures on the values of the National Socialist political system and party went on unabated, and the thoroughly indoctrinated youth as of June 1944 absolutely did believe in the thousand-year *Reich* of Adolf Hitler and the need to defend it and Europe against the dangers of Judeo-Bolshevism, presented to them as a real and serious threat to Germany. It was important for the leadership of the division, the Nazi Party and the *Waffen-SS* that these men who would carry out the fighting knew what they were fighting for, as twisted and perverted as the ideology was. It was clearly perceived that the military fate of Germany would rest upon the shoulders of these young men. To have them properly motivated for combat was key in the eyes of the divisional commander. Under the direction of *Obf.* Witt, every effort was made to instil in the young *SS-Panzergrenadiere* the ideals of sacrifice and teamwork for the success and survival of the *Reich*.[10]

This psychological indoctrination, paired with the advanced and realistic training methods, formed a cadre of highly motivated soldiers possessing combat skills that made them potentially very effective in the field. They had an increased bond with their leaders, and this bond led to a higher degree of devotion to their unit and team. Often the *Hitlerjugend SS-Panzergrenadiere* during the coming Normandy campaign would have the unreasonable asked of them. That they were able to deal with these demands reflects their commitment. The argument is made by Anglophone military historians that this over-commitment brought on self-sacrificing behaviour and undue casualties were incurred due to this 'fanaticism'. There are problems with this assessment, as British or Canadian soldiers who fought hard in impossible situations and did not surrender at the drop of a hat are portrayed by these same historians as 'heroic' within their unit histories. Putting this assessment aside, the ultra-aggressive style of offensive warfare was perfect for the short-term environment, but in a long-term attritional campaign or series of battles, this style of fighting could quickly diminish *SS-Panzergrenadiere* unit strength in a rapid manner.[11]

Each of these individuals was moulded into a team player within his unit or sub-formation within the division.[12] When all these units acted in unison the *Waffen-SS Panzerdivision* became a terrifyingly effective force utilising the doctrine of the mobile battle.

Laying out the structure of the division and its main manoeuvre formations, the most powerfully destructive formation within the *Hitlerjugend* was its *Panzer*, or armoured, regiment, *SS-Panzerregiment 12*, which fielded two *Abteilungen* (battalions). Critical for future battlefield successes in Normandy was the leadership of the *SS-Panzerregiment* commander, by June 1944 the aforementioned *Obersturmbannführer* Max Wünsche. He and many of the *SS-Panzerregiment 12 Zug* (platoon) and *Kompanie* (company) *Kommandeure* were combat veterans, which gave the German crews an edge over the incoming green Allied crews they would face. The new crews were trained to a very high standard in realistic simulations of combat. Combined with this experience were the tanks, which were advanced examples of German weapons technology. The Panther *Ausführung* A and G variants were superior in nearly everything but serviceability to the Allied tanks, while the Panzer IV Ausf H model was roughly comparable to the Allied Sherman but had a much better high-velocity tank cannon. For anti-aircraft defence, the *Flak Zug* of *II Abt./SS-Pz.Rgt. 12* contained four Panzer IV *Wirblewind* turretless Panzers with a quad mount 2cm cannon installed on them.

Also stressed was training in tank repair and recovery, something that was viewed as important in view of the abysmal delivery rates of new tanks from German industry within the *Reich*. The sum of its leaders, vehicles, and training made *SS-Panzerregiment 12* potentially the most powerful and effective formation within the *Hitlerjugend*, something that it was to arguably demonstrate once actual combat began. The fast-flowing mobile battles Germany had fought to conquer a large part of Europe were based upon this weapons system. Victory in divisional defensive or offensive operations to a large extent would depend upon this regiment.[13]

The motorised and mechanised infantry of the divisions was contained in two regiments. These were *SS-Panzergrenadierregiment 25* and *26*, and each contained three *Bataillone*, all of them fully motorised or mechanised. One of these *Bataillone*, *III. Btl.(Gepanzert)/SS-Pz.Gren.Rgt. 26*, was fully equipped with *Schützenpanzerwagen 251 (SPW 251)* armoured half-tracks. The *SS-Panzergrenadiere* were very well outfitted, and the complete opposite equipment wise to the bicycle-equipped *Grenadier-Bataillone* that rode into battle in some 1944 model German *Infanterie-Divisionen*.

Each truck-mounted motorised *Bataillone* of *SS-Panzergrenadiere* had literally dozens of the highly advanced MG-42 belt-fed machine guns.[14] Also present were liberal amounts of the *Panzerschreck* (tank terror) single-shot anti-tank bazookas and the more advanced disposable *Panzerfaust* (tank fist) infantry anti-tank weapons. The outer part of their uniform consisted of a camouflage smock or in some cases they were issued the full camouflage uniform, which was highly advanced for 1944, giving the *SS-Panzergrenadiere* an edge in concealing themselves or ambushing their opponents. Each *Bataillone* had four *Kompanien*, and the fourth was the *Schwere* (heavy) *Kompanie*, which contained several *Züge* with different types of heavy weapons. This weaponry consisted of three MG-42 machine guns with tripod mounts, six 8cm *Granatewerfer* 34 mortars, three towed *Pak 40* 7.5cm anti-tank guns and four short-barrelled 7.5cm *leichtes Infanteriegeschütz*.[15] One *SS-Panzergrenadierregimenter* together could boast a total of thirty-two 12 and 8cm mortars, twelve 7.5cm *Infanterigeschütz* infantry howitzers, and six 15cm *Schwere*

Infanterigeschütz howitzers. This was not insignificant indirect firepower, and could be used in conjunction with the *SS-Panzerartillerieregiment* of the *Hitlerjugend*, to be discussed shortly. The scale of weaponry and vehicles for the SPW 251 mounted *III. Btl.(Gepanzert)/SS-Pz.Gren.Rgt. 26* was much higher, and much of it was mounted on half-tracks themselves.[16] And, on top of the three *SS-Panzergrenadiere Bataillone* per regiment were the four separate regimental *Kompanien*, these being the *13. (schwere Infanterie-Geschütz), 14. (Flak), 15. (Aufklärung)* and *16. (Pioniere) Kompanien.*[17] Leading directly up to the invasion, the state of infantry training and equipment was quite good considering the varying standards present in other new divisions of the *Waffen-SS* and *Heer* being built in 1944, and spectacular with regard to vehicles and equipment in comparison to a similar division that had spent two to three months in combat on the Eastern Front. The standard present was more than equal to that of an Anglo-Canadian infantry brigade, especially in weapons.

The separate *SS-Panzerpionierbataillon 12* (Combat Engineer) and *SS-Panzer-aufklärungabteilung 12* (Reconnaissance), were separate from the *Regimenter* within the division but were also powerful combat units. Somewhat different from the company-strength field engineer units of the Commonwealth armies, *SS-Pz.Pio.Btl. 12* was unique in that it could carry out an infantry role as well as its primary combat engineer tasks. It could excel in urban warfare and was outfitted for the task with explosives, flamethrowers and mortars. It could also bridge rivers, level buildings, cut down sections of forest and build field fortifications. The reconnaissance unit of the *Hitlerjugend, SS-Panzeraufklärungabteilung 12*, was the eyes of the division. This *Abteilung* was well equipped with every sort of half-track and wheeled armoured car designed for armed reconnaissance, and also possessed a variety of motorcycles and sophisticated communication equipment. It was also issued some anti-tank guns and mortars, but on a lighter scale. Paired with this were the previously noted *Aufklärung Kompanien* in *SS-Pz.Gren.Rgt. 25* and *26* and a *Zug* within *SS-Pz.Rgt. 12*.

The field artillery regiment of the *Hitlerjugend, SS-Panzerartillerieregiment 12*, was very powerful. On paper, it was outfitted with a vast array of powerful towed and self-propelled artillery pieces that equipped the *Batterien* in all three *Abteilung*. Combined with everything in the divisional arsenal at or over 8cm, the *Hitlerjugend* could in total boast a staggering 224 pieces of artillery. This was much more than that assigned to an Allied infantry division. Provided it had enough ammunition, the division could deliver devasting indirect fire power to win a mobile battle that was hoped to be won in a quick, decisive manner. It should be noted however that despite this powerful artillery, German doctrine did not demand sustained indirect fire support for extended First World War-style bombardments characteristic of British Army doctrine. Therefore, there was no plan to provide the guns with ammunition on a lavish, bottomless scale – with perhaps the exception of 8cm mortar rounds.

While the division was forming in France, rapid equipment acquisition was a severe problem for *SS-Pz.Art.Rgt. 12* as well as the posting in of veteran artillery instructors with technical expertise. Rather than having a standard towed or self-propelled gun equipping each *Abteilung*, the regiment was issued with a bewildering array of equipment reflecting no attempt at standardisation. Its three *Abteilung* present in June 1944 possessed twelve 10.5cm Wespe self-propelled howitzers, six Hummel 15cm self-propelled howitzers, eighteen 10.5cm towed field artillery pieces, twelve 15cm towed field artillery pieces and four 10.5cm towed cannons. A fourth *Abteilung*, on paper consisting of twenty-four 15cm and six 28cm Nebelwerfer rocket launchers, was intended to be the powerful crown jewel of the divisional artillery, but unfortunately this unit had not been equipped as of June 1944.[18]

Not attached to the artillery regiment, though containing some of the deadliest large-calibre guns, was the anti-aircraft *SS-Flak Abteilung 12*. It contained twelve 8.8cm dual-purpose anti-aircraft and anti-tank guns, and nine 3.7cm flak guns in four *Batterien*.

Divisional artillery was supplemented by brigade groupings of guns at the *Armeekorps* or *Panzerkorps* level, to be assigned as needed. Experience in Russia and North Africa had begun to turn war production in the Third Reich towards an increased artillery output, and this was beginning to be reflected in orders of battle at the *Korps* level. The ever-growing power of Allied artillery in the east and west was beginning to be noticed. The defensive firepower of massed artillery was needed then more than ever in the ongoing defensive struggles of 1944 onwards, even though the ammunition to supply these *Batterien* was often absent.[19]

During the winter and spring of 1944, the division trained intensively in several large-scale exercises in Belgium, and was visited by senior German commanders, including *G.F.M.* von Rundstedt, *Gen.d.Pz.Tr.* von Schweppenburg and their entourages. As fuel and ammunition were made available in fits and starts, other smaller combined arms exercises were carried out, often with the staff of the parent *I. SS-Panzerkorps* in attendance as units carried out manoeuvre and live fire training demonstrations during these visits.

The expected trucks, armoured personnel carriers, tanks, prime movers, artillery pieces and anti-tank guns did not arrive all at once, but in dribs and drabs that illustrated the German war economy's production challenges in equipping the new formations Hitler had demanded be created. For the tank regiment, *SS-Pz.Rgt. 12*, training went on intensively as much as possible, this often being curtailed by the lack of fuel and having to share tanks, many of which had not yet been delivered to the two *Abteilungen* and the regimental *Stab Kompanie*. Instead of the war establishment *SS-Panzerregiment* tank strength of 81 Panthers, 4 Panzer IIIs and 101 Panzer IVs it was supposed to have, on 1 June 1944 it possessed 98 Panzer IVs, 48 Panthers and 2 Panzer IIIs. While this was not perfect, it was a sizeable number of armoured vehicles for a German *Panzerdivision* in 1944. Exercises with the *SS-Panzergrenadiere* were conducted to build tank–infantry co-operation, something essential to future success on the battlefield.

Continuing to exercise in the vicinity of Beverloo and its surroundings, a second large *Hitlerjugend* combined arms exercise went on 16 March 1944, in front of *G.F.M.* von Rundstedt. The results were again positive and were intended to show that the division was ready for large scale mobile *Panzer* operations. Shortly afterward the division took its place as an active unit within the *I. SS-Pz.Korps* order of battle, along with the now-returned *Leibstandarte*, which had returned to Belgium to rebuild. The now promoted *Obf.* Witt declared the former youths of *Hitlerjugend* to be young military men who knew their craft and could defeat the enemy.

The end of March and the dispatch of the *II. SS-Pz.Korps*, comprising of the *9.* and *10. SS-Panzerdivisionen*, respectively, to Eastern Galicia, saw the redeployment of the *Hitlerjugend* to the sector formerly held by the *10. SS-Panzerdivision* in France. Centred around the city of Dreux in the Evreux, Bernay–Vimoutiers–Gacé–Montagne–Dreux semi-circle east of the Orne, the *Hitlerjugend* was placed in an anti-invasion role to initially counter any airborne landings and immediately afterwards liquidate any amphibious landings. Initially *H.Gr.D/O.B. West* had wanted to deploy the division to Lisieux, closer to the coast, but *Gen.d.Pz.Tr.* von Schweppenburg had the deployment order changed in accordance with his philosophy that the *Panzerdivisionen* should be placed in the interior of France.[20] On 1 April 1944, 90 trains took the division to its new home.[21] The move took place over two days and went smoothly except for an ambush by French partisans near Ascq, France. As the train carrying *SS-Pz.Aüfkl.Abt. 12* was moving in the marshalling yard, an explosion shook the track, derailing two flatcars and prompting an exchange of gunfire.[22] In the ensuring roundup of suspects, 86 Frenchmen were shot dead on the orders of *Ostuf.* Walter Hauck, in a war crime now recognised as the Ascq Massacre.

Once moved into its new former *10. SS-Panzerdivision Frundsberg* billets, the *Hitlerjugend* now took its place in the defence scheme for occupied France and the Low Countries. For training and administrative purposes, it was to function under the umbrella of *Panzergruppe West*, which was subordinate to *H.Gr.D/O.B. West* as an *OKW* reserve. If an invasion came, it was to be subordinated to the operational control of *I. SS-Panzerkorps*. Three deployment plans were drawn up for possible combat theatre employment. Routes (A–C), orders of march, and battlegroups were made up for the major components of the division.[23]

By 1 June 1944, the mass of the division was designated combat ready and capable of offensive operations. The strength of the division in France on 1 June stood at 18,102 men, and a total of 98 *Panzer* IVs and 66 Panthers had arrived for *SS-Pz. Rgt. 12.*[24] The *SS-Panzerartillerie* and *SS-Panzergrenadiere* units contained their exact war establishments of self-propelled, heavy and light field artillery pieces. Of the total number of men in the division, 14,360 were within the combat arms units.

Some deficiencies were present, however. Most glaring was the human resource situation. The shortage in officers and NCOs was 144 and 2,192, respectively. The

48% shortfall in non-commissioned officers was particularly damaging despite the best efforts of the divisional staff to run as many leadership courses as possible.[25]

Vehicle and equipment shortages were also still a problem on the eve of the invasion. *SS- Panzerjäger-Abteilung 12* was still in Belgium waiting for its tank destroyers, and the *Nebelwerfer*-equipped *IV. Abt./SS-Panzerartillerieregiment 12* was completely without transportation. Also, a *Batterien* of *SS-Flak.Abt. 12* was still without vehicles, this after waiting for nearly a year. The missing *Nebelwerfer* and *SS-Panzerjäger* units amounted to a total authorised strength of 1,191 men, who would only reach the division with their units in mid-June and July 1944, along with the final 13 Panther tanks for *I. Abt./SS-Pz.Rgt. 12.*[26]

The loss of the *SS-Panzerjäger Abteilung* from the order of battle cost the division three *Batterien* of the potent Jagdpanzer IV L/48s, which had a high-velocity 7.5cm tank gun mounted on a Panzer IV chassis. Within *SS-Pz.Rgt. 12*, Bergepanther recovery tanks and command Befehlspanzer tanks were lacking, as well as heavy stocks of fuel to effectively march or fight the regiment in battle.[27] The resource and financial cost of modern war, especially where Panther tanks were concerned, was appallingly high. It is arguable that the German war economy simply could not support the military doctrine the *Heer* had in place, that of masses of tanks and half-tracks, while on the other hand, the industrial and financial colossus of the Western Allies could superbly support theirs.

In land warfare equipment, the German army certainly favoured quality over quantity. They often had the best and most sophisticated weapons systems available, but their weakness lay in their inability to replace them if lost in battle and the lack of munitions to feed them. The battered and bombed war economy of the *Reich* was simply not up to it, as was brutally evidenced in the long, drawn-out process of simply equipping the division.[28]

Despite some shortcomings, the division was very powerful, and one of the best equipped German *Panzerdivisionen* in the Normandy theatre when D-Day arrived.[29] It was sufficiently well trained and equipped for a short, violent *Panzer* thrust. It was perfect for the Rommel approach to attacking an Allied beachhead. Extended combat operations, however, presented a potential problem.

If the division was confronted by a peer enemy that was well equipped and reasonably well led, it was very likely that the *Hitlerjugend* could expect heavy equipment and personnel casualties if it was forced to fight an extended pitched battle. To take part in any sort of artillery-based attritional defensive or static battle, the division would need access to huge stocks, which were not present in France as a standing reserve of munitions.

Also, simply moving the division in long marches was a problem. Fuel was not plentiful and there was also the growing awareness that Allied tactical air forces were very powerful and their aircraft were present in large numbers. It was obvious *SS-Flak. Abt. 12* could not drive them all off, raising the potential of destruction from the air.

To prevail in combat long term against an enemy mighty in numbers and materiel, the division would need all its anti-tank and artillery components, which it did not have. It also needed access to replacement tanks, men, anti-tank guns and all sorts of other resources that would be expended or lost in combat to maintain the fighting strength of the division.[30] But for the short-term 'Rommel' battle, being deployed close to the beachhead and driving violently into it very quickly, the division was in an excellent state. Potentially, it had two very powerful battlegroups based off each *SS-Panzergrenadierregiment*, and in comparison to other German formations in the area, could dole out and accept a considerable amount of damage in the short term.

Putting the *Hitlerjugend* into a long-term slugging match-style campaign of attrition was not what it was designed for, nor what it could long withstand. The German replacement system, terribly inefficient at quickly getting tanks and equipment to units on a monthly basis, was even worse in terms of human replacements. Divisions in combat on the Eastern Front and in Italy were allowed to get worn down to the core. This core would then be re-equipped in a quiet sector of an occupied country or the *Reich* itself with everything it needed in the way of men and materiel. Then the process would repeat itself. The lightning *Panzer* campaigns of 1939–40 had not seen this attritional bleeding occur, since they were over rather quickly. But the struggle for manpower confronting the *Wehrmacht* in 1944 was getting worse and funnelling large numbers of trained men into a division like the *Hitlerjugend* at weekly or monthly intervals, like the Allies, to keep it sustained in a long-term campaign of attrition, was literally impossible.[31]

So how did G.F.M. Rommel hope to use the *Hitlerjugend* if he managed to get control of it as *Oberbefehlshaber* of *H.Gr.B.*? In an ideal 'Rommel' situation for the *Hitlerjugend*, the infantry of the *Atlantikwall* would be only partially overwhelmed, or even better repel a portion of the invaders or contain them to the beaches themselves, like at Dieppe in 1942.[32] Into this battle zone the *Hitlerjugend Kampfgruppen* would pile in, one after another, simply driving the Allies into the sea in a concentric counterattack. At the same time other mobile *Kampfgruppen* would confront airborne operations and surround and destroy them. This ideal scenario depended, crucially and as mentioned in Chapter 1, on the German battlegroups being deployed close to the English Channel. Long marches could be severely hampered or totally interdicted by air power.

Prioritising taking time to understand the strengths of the Allies, not attacking them in force immediately with armoured units, could lead to the possibility of never removing them once they had entrenched themselves in their lodgement, and this was very much Rommel's fear.

The *Hitlerjugend*, tragically stuck in the von Schweppenburg-style deployment on 6 June far from the beaches and airborne landing zones, was hoped to be one of the designated armoured divisions that would defeat the Allies in a battle of encirclement. It, along with some of the other most powerful *Panzerdivisionen* in

France, was not deployed in the preferred Rommel deployment close to the beaches, but far away from them. This immediately decided the outcome of the Normandy campaign and fated the *Hitlerjugend*, along with many other German divisions, to a long, slow demise, attempting to fight a battle of attrition that was not suited to their tactics and doctrine.

CHAPTER 4

The British Second Army in England, June 1944

In May 1944 the entire area of southern England (up to a point close to the city of Sheffield) was taken up by the assembly areas for the army corps of the US First and Third Armies, the British Second Army, and the First Canadian Army. These field armies were very powerful, and each would comprise of at least two army corps when they saw action in France and the Low Countries in 1944, with each corps consisting of at least two divisions.[1] Some of these combat divisions were new and untried in combat, while others, with their experienced personnel had been redeployed from the Mediterranean theatre. These veteran divisions had been given a period of recuperation where they were rested and totally re-equipped in England in preparation for their roles in Operation *Overlord*, the invasion of occupied France.

In addition to these regular armoured and infantry divisions were formations such as the British 79th Armoured Division, made up of bridge-laying, mine-clearing and other specialist armoured vehicles to facilitate the assault on German defences, and the British and US airborne divisions. The airborne divisions were to be employed in airborne assault roles to secure the eastern and western flanks next to the amphibious landing sectors, as well as important bridges.

The divisions of the British 30th Corps, led by Lieutenant General Gerard Bucknall, and those of the British 1st Corps, commanded by Lieutenant General John Crocker, were slated to assault the eastern, Anglo-Canadian Normandy beaches on D-Day. Both of these corps were assigned to the British Second Army, this being the first Commonwealth Army chosen by General Montgomery to deploy to the continent. After carrying out their role of successfully landing and overcoming the beach defences, the divisions within these corps were expected to defend their lodgements past Gold, Juno and Sword Beaches against the expected German counterattacks with armour. These forces would be the ones to combat the *Hitlerjugend*, and this chapter's main effort is describing the operational plans, doctrine and composition of these Commonwealth forces.

The two Allied divisions that engaged in combat operations with the *Hitlerjugend* in the British 1st Corps sector were the British 3rd Infantry Division and the 3rd Canadian Infantry Division. Significant combat on the left flank of the *Hitlerjugend* discussed within this book was with the British 50th Infantry Division, this being part of the British 30th Corps. Powerful attached forces, these being corps level artillery formations, independent armoured brigades, non-divisional supporting arms such as British and Canadian field engineer companies and specialist infantry units such as those from the British Royal Marines supported all three of these divisions.

From west to east, brigades from the three infantry divisions were to land between 0700 and 0800 on 6 June, supported in their actual landings by amphibious armour from three independent armoured brigades, combat engineer units and specialist armoured engineer vehicles. Landing at low tide, the landing craft would have their best chance to avoid defensive obstacles such as the Belgian Gates, re-purposed anti-tank obstacles relocated by the Germans from Belgium that looked like iron cages and log pyramid-type obstacles with German anti-tank *Teller* mines emplaced on them.

The brigades of the British 50th Infantry Division were to land on the western Gold Beach, overwhelming the defences and at the same time securing the site of the future 'Mulberry B' artificial harbour to be built at Arromanches-les-Bains. These brigades and their sub-units were to also advance south-west to capture the important transportation hub of Bayeux, secure the Caen–Bayeux highway and also link up with US forces to the west. Following the capture of these areas, the units were to assume a defensive posture facing south and west to withstand expected German counterattacks. The role of the 3rd Canadian Infantry Division, once past the German defences on Juno Beach in the centre, was to charge south with its infantry brigades to cut the Caen–Bayeux railway and road communications, dig in and with British forces withstand the anticipated German armoured counterattacks.[2] The British 3rd Infantry Division, with supporting units, was also to charge forward after it had overwhelmed the Sword Beach defences to the east, seize Caen proper on D-Day, and to link up with parachute units that had landed in the 'Airborne Bridgehead' on its left flank beyond the Orne River until further follow-on forces could be landed.

It was important that the assaulting units push past the beaches as soon as combat was completed, as follow-on forces and the first logistic efforts of the invasion would need all the space they could to land and move forward themselves.

While there is not space to describe in detail all of the Anglo-Canadian divisions and independent brigades that would fight the *Hitlerjugend* in the period 7–11 June 1944, this chapter will briefly examine the 3rd Canadian Infantry Division and to an extent the 2nd Canadian Armoured Brigade as examples to properly illustrate for the reader the training, equipment, organisation and battlefield doctrine of the Anglo-Canadian Commonwealth invasion forces. While every division and brigade had its own character, organisational spirit and idiosyncrasies, these two formations can be utilised as examples because of the strict uniformity and standards enforced within the Commonwealth armies with regard to weapons, vehicles, organisations and strengths of units. This overview is also necessary to aid the reader in understanding the strengths that allowed the Anglo-Canadian forces to withstand the German armoured counterattacks in the timeframe 7–11 June.

Within this overview will be a short treatise on how these units would utilise, or would have trouble utilising, combined arms tactics to overcome the enemy during their attacks and defensive operations. The author has already written a book that touches on this subject, *An Army of Never-Ending Strength: Reinforcing the Canadians in Northwest Europe, 1944–45*, though its main focus is describing in detail the organisation of the First Canadian Army and its formations and units 1944–45 and how exactly it was reconstituted in the field after suffering combat losses.[3]

The 3rd Canadian Infantry Division and 2nd Canadian Armoured Brigade were the first Canadian formations to see combat in Normandy from 6 June onward; respectively, they had spent the better part of three and one years in southern England, training for combat operations that seemingly would never come. These were some of the formations left behind in Great Britain, not chosen to deploy to Sicily and Italy. By the spring of 1943, they were what remained of the First Canadian Army that had originally comprised of two complete army corps in England.

The other forces left in England were the First Canadian Army Headquarters, the 2nd Canadian Corps Headquarters, independent corps and army-level units and formations such the 2nd Canadian Army Group Royal Artillery, and the complete logistical, training and administrative tails that were attached to them. The combat arms formations that made up the 2nd Canadian Corps, the 1st Canadian Corps having departed to the Mediterranean, comprised of the 3rd Canadian Infantry Division, the 2nd Canadian Infantry Division, the independent 2nd Canadian Armoured Brigade intended to support them both and the 4th Canadian Armoured Division.[4]

The 3rd Infantry Division and the 2nd Canadian Armoured Brigade would not prove to have the ability to attack an enemy of equal strength using combined arms tactics and destroy these forces in the field in the days following the Juno Beach battle on 6 June. Attacking and destroying an enemy that was well equipped and occupying strong defensive positions would take overwhelming and massive force, and at the very least involve a pitched armoured engagement and the devastating use of lengthy artillery bombardments and barrages. On top of this, heavy air attacks would have to be utilised to add to the destruction unleashed on the enemy before and during the battle itself. All of this required a supreme level of skill at combined arms warfare, and sadly this level of coordination was not practised in the months leading up to D-Day.

What was practised was the actual D-Day amphibious assault, and the overwhelming of the concrete fortifications of the *Atlantikwall* defences. The majority of the Canadian formations within the British 1st Corps, taken as an example, had not seen combat before. While some Canadian senior non-commissioned officers and senior officers such as Brigadier Wyman of the Canadian 2nd Armoured Brigade had extensive operational experience in the Mediterranean, others, such as Brigadier Foster of the 7th Canadian Infantry Brigade, had little.

Allied tactical doctrine in the British and Canadian armies, the opponents of the *Hitlerjugend* in Normandy, has come to be called 'Bite and Hold' by military historians. This was an artillery-based doctrine that had evolved out of the First World War, and by 1943 it had morphed to incorporate some of the concepts of an armoured battle, but with infantry still leading the way. Unlike the German operations, on a tactical level it was highly centralised and followed a set-piece plan. Like the German system of mobile manoeuvre warfare, this system of fighting had advantages and disadvantages.[5] However, it had evolved from the period of fighting in North Africa from 1942 onward to deal specifically with German offensive armoured operations, especially hasty counterattacks.

The entire offensive and defensive doctrines of the Commonwealth forces were based around the concentrated fire of field artillery. To minimise casualties like those incurred in the First World War, a huge emphasis was to be placed on the firepower of the Royal Artillery (RA) and Royal Canadian Artillery (RCA) Field and Medium regiments. The utter failure of Commonwealth forces to exercise armour-alone battle tactics in the face of powerful German Pak anti-tank positions had been burned into the minds of senior commanders, especially British ones. A new approach was adopted from November 1942 onwards; it was put into operational practice by British General Sir Bernard Montgomery.[6] In the attack, infantry would lead in close conjunction with powerful tank support, leaning into an intense artillery barrage that consumed a huge number of shells.

As a result of successes won in North Africa and later Sicily and Italy, the vast majority of brigade-level attacks in the late war period in north-west Europe were led by the infantry, supported massively by field artillery fire, and attacking fighter bombers if the weather was good. A field artillery concentration of varying length of time and intensity would be fired against an objective, and then an infantry assault, supported by the battalion Support Company and often a squadron of tanks, would attempt to capture it. If this assault by the infantry line companies was successful, the entire assault force and the supporting armour would immediately dig in on their objective against the expected German counterattack. This was an immediate second opportunity for the Allied forces to inflict heavy casualties on the Germans. If all worked out well, the limited battalion objective, taken at reasonable cost, would suddenly transform itself into a defensive breakwater in which the enemy would destroy himself by counterattacking against immensely powerful coordinated artillery and anti-tank fire, unleashed at the correct moment.[7]

The quality of the Canadian infantry platoons within the infantry line companies in England was very good. They had every reason to be, as many of the first infantry battalions of the 3rd Canadian Infantry Division to arrive in Great Britain had been training since 1941. These men were all volunteers, and each Canadian soldier had an acceptable level of fitness and overall health. They were well fed, allowed to rest, given time off, treated fairly and not brutalised. Morale was on average good to acceptable and would rise considerably when it became clear that the invasion of France would occur and they would be part of it. The infantry companies were cohesive units within the regimental families that were the Canadian one-battalion infantry regiments. There was a large reinforcement structure in place, and what was thought to be an acceptable number of infantry reinforcements were present in southern England to keep all battalions up to strength.[8]

The Canadian infantry battalions were immensely strong combat units. The head of the entire unit was the tactical headquarters of the battalion and contained the battalion commander, several key staff officers and a number of radio-equipped vehicles which could travel around the battlefield as needed. Behind this was the administrative battalion headquarters company, which contained the typists, stretcher bearers, supply echelon personnel and their truck and jeep motor pool. This company also contained, in the summer of 1944, the Scout-Sniper Platoon, which was not numbered, often understrength and at times was detached and placed under the control of the Support Company. The signals and administrative platoons, numbered 1 and 2, were deployed mainly within the battalion headquarters company to facilitate the battalion's communications with its companies and the higher infantry brigade headquarters and carry out administrative tasks.

Containing the heavy weapons of the battalion, the Support Company also possessed the bulk of the battalion's Universal and T-14 tracked carriers and radio equipment. It was an organisation designed to do exactly what its name implied, to support the battalion's line companies in whatever role or operation they were engaged in. The Support Company consisted of the Carrier, Mortar, Pioneer and Anti-Tank Platoons; these platoons being numbered 3 through 6. In June of 1944 a Canadian infantry battalion comprised of four line infantry companies: A, B, C and D, each of roughly one hundred and twenty men. Each company had three platoons, and these were numbered 7 through 18 within the four line companies.[9] Each platoon had three sections commanded by a corporal, and each section comprised of a rifle and Bren gun sub-section. In command of all this was the platoon headquarters, commanded usually by a lieutenant or newly promoted captain.

There was a major effort in southern England in the years 1940–44 to keep Commonwealth battalions that had not been deployed to the Mediterranean at a high level of combat readiness. From 1942 onward the 'Battle Drill' training mania had overtaken Canadian infantry brigades, and these tactics were practised at the section, platoon and company level. In combat scenarios, whatever unit was involved in combat with the enemy would immediately split into two teams: the rifle 'assault' team and the 'fire' team that contained the Bren squad automatic weapons. At the section level, the assault rifle team was led by the section commander, and the fire support team was led by the section second-in-command, or 2 I/C. Once contact was made in the way of either hostile fire or sighting enemy movement, the first job was to locate the enemy position. Second, the fire team, with all weapons including their squad Bren gun and 2-inch infantry mortar, would immediately attempt to suppress it. The assault team would use fire and movement to maneuverer close to the enemy positions. Once the range was closed, they would use all arms, including grenades, to close with the enemy and destroy them as a fighting force so that they were not capable of further resistance.[10] For an infantry battalion-level attack, a massive number of these 'Battle Drill' assaults would be taking place simultaneously, executed by the soldiers of the infantry companies.

The weapons carried by the infantrymen of the platoon were the best the Commonwealth war economies could supply in the late war period and were believed to be good enough to carry out the battlefield tasks asked of them. The problem with these infantry weapons was that they were of a First World War level of technology, and advanced self-loading rifles such as the American M1 Garand and an equivalent of the belt-fed German MG-34 or MG-42 section level machine gun was not present within Canadian infantry platoons. Thus, while machine-gun and rifle ammunition were not wasted by overconsumption through rapid fire, the sheer weight of fire often needed to win a firefight or defend a position was not there in comparison to the weight of fire a German *Panzergrenadier* or US infantry platoon could wield at a critical moment. Fire won firefights, and the First World War Lee-Enfield rifle was not cutting-edge technology.

Next, all four echelons of the attacking infantry battalion – covering, the assault force carrying out the Battle Drill attack, support and reserve – often with supporting armour or engineers if required, would then move onto the newly won objective. The composition of these groupings depended on the battalion or regimental commander and could be accompanied by regular tanks or specialist Armoured Vehicles, Royal Engineers (AVREs) to deal with anti-tank ditches, fortifications, mine fields or a counterattack.[11] Once ground was taken, the assault group consolidated, with heavy weapons moving in to take positions to crush the expected German response. This was known as a 'tactical bound'. A heavy consolidation, if the attack movement or operation was ending, was termed a 'fortress position', or 'pivot'.

Once this consolidation and fortification was completed, and the infantry battalion position was bristling with heavy weapons and anti-tank guns, it would be ready to repel all comers. If the attacking infantry battalion had tanks attached, some might emplace themselves in ambush positions as previously stated. Then once darkness fell they would join the rest of their squadron or regiment in a rear laager area for the night to refuel, re-arm and be on standby in the counterattack role.

If an objective was taken, the initial force would not push on if the opportunity to exploit was there unless explicitly told to do so. Exploitation, if agreed upon beforehand, was undertaken by another unit that would pass through the lines of a friendly unit that had just captured an enemy objective. As a rule, no movement was to be made beyond the range of the supporting RCA or RA field artillery batteries. Only once the enemy was clearly broken, and on the run, would a war of movement begin.[12]

The leading disadvantage of this doctrine was that it was slow and deliberate. It was more steamroller than rapier thrust, with the speed of the dismounted infantry setting the pace. Ground which had been taken was fortified immediately, rather than swiftly moving as far as you could forward in rapid, *blitzkrieg*-style thrusts. Snap decisions to grasp opportunities to encircle, flank, march on or cut off enemy formations were often not taken up after a defeat of the enemy.[13] The fluidity that took place on the Eastern Front was not present in the Anglo-Canadian operational approach. The concept of *Blitzkrieg* or rapid envelopment and destruction of an enemy force was alien. A German defender could anticipate the moves a long way off and if he had proper resources, counter them quite effectively.[14]

Advantages of the Allied system lay in what it was based on: firepower. The level of field and medium artillery wielded by Allied forces in the west after 1943 was tremendously powerful. Mated with this were the Allied tactical air forces that operated in air superiority from this period onwards. Provided the support firepower was strong enough, the speed of movement did not matter, and they could achieve what they wanted to achieve, albeit in a slow, grinding fashion. The logistical ability and mechanisation of the Allies also gave them the ability to use the firepower-based system to its utmost by keeping it in good supply, though, naturally, the odd occurrence of an artillery ammunition shortage did occur.

With rapid fortification of gains done properly, virtually any counterattack could be beaten off effectively. The level of cooperation between the assault group commanders and the air and artillery assets was vital, however, and if communication was poor success could not be guaranteed. Using this system to its maximum, an enemy that presented himself in the open could be severely mauled without even seeing his enemy on the ground.[15] An individual Royal Canadian Artillery (RCA) forward observation officer (FOO) attached to a Commonwealth unit could quickly bring down the fire of every field or medium artillery piece within range in a matter of minutes; a tremendous feat of coordination and sheer power, totalling up to one thousand guns. German troops in Normandy suffered greatly from this defensive and offensive power on a daily basis, as the gun crews would only stop firing to sleep.

In contrast to the overwhelming strengths of the Canadian Army was the capability of the Canadian Armoured Corps. It is very important to discuss the issues confronting the CAC, as the events of 7–11 June would see not one but two difficult defeats for Canadian armoured regiments that would arguably influence their tactics for the remainder of the Normandy campaign and beyond. While well led, supplied and maintained, challenges to Canadian armoured regiments in the way of lack of combat experience, weak tank armour and tank armament hindered their performance on the battlefield. Canadian military historian Sean Summerfield argues that some 2nd Canadian Armoured Brigade units preparations for combat in France suffered due to decisions made pre-invasion at the brigade, regiment and squadron levels.[16] Summerfield makes the case that these failures would go on to contribute to high casualties and tactical defeats in the bridgehead battles following the success of the amphibious phase of Operation *Overlord.*

The matter of equipping the armoured regiments was a significant challenge leading up to *Overlord.* The Sherbrooke Fusilier Regiment (SFR – the 27th Canadian Armoured Regiment), taken by Summerfield as a case study, had arrived in southern England in late 1942 but had not been issued a sizeable number of tanks to train with until May 1943. On 10 May 1944, less than a month before the invasion, many of the tanks used by the regiment in some of its final British exercises, such as Operation *Fabius III*, were the older and obsolete Ram and Crusader type. These types would not be operated by the regiment in Normandy, their place taken by the more modern US-built lend-lease Sherman III and the Sherman 17-pounder variant, the Firefly.[17]

On 16 May 1944, 12 Sherman Fireflies were delivered to the SFR, but they were found to possess a myriad of teething problems related to the new 17-pounder main armament, and many of these problems would continue to be present right into the period 7–11 June 1944. While the delivery of the new Sherman amphibious Duplex Drive (DD) and Sherman Firefly tanks was anything but a reduction of the combat power of the SFR, the crews had to be familiar with the equipment in order to effectively utilise it, and all aspects of the vehicles had to function on the battlefield. There were many challenges in this department.

Field training at the troop and squadron level in England was also a problem, as troops had to 'break in' the new tanks, and with the training focus being on the amphibious assault, it was not possible to conduct field exercises utilising the new equipment to be fought with in France due to the immediate nature of the invasion and time constraints. The effectiveness of tanks crews in battle would absolutely depend on their familiarity with their equipment. Lightning-fast reactions were needed when utilising weapons systems to destroy the enemy and successfully carry out their mission. The fact that the Canadian Army in southern England and Canada as a Commonwealth nation was entirely dependent on the British Army for issuance of major weapons systems, such as tanks, in some cases hindered the combat capabilities of its military. Whatever was spared by the British Army was the only option Canada had in the complete absence of a pre-war arms industry or military industrial complex.

Personnel issues with the Canadian armoured regiments were also a problem, As the reality of the invasion and imminent combat began to become apparent, a flurry of transfers took place in the SFR, with 130 men being transferred in or out of the regiment, and this does not count the number of men moved between troops and squadrons. This destroyed unit cohesion in the squadrons, as the crew members that had exercised together in southern England in the previous months were interchanged with new, unfamiliar faces.[18] The jostling and reshuffling of the squadrons and their troops within them caused havoc for the regiment, and while the true impact of this on the battlefield in the period 7–11 June is difficult to quantify, it cannot have added to the SFR's combat effectiveness.

The ability of the armoured squadrons to effectively cooperate with infantry battalions at short notice was also an area in which the Canadian Army had room to improve. Known as joint operations or 'joint ops' within the British Army, combined arms performance in the Commonwealth armies was good in some respects and poor in others. The regimental system, embedded in Commonwealth armies since their creation, continued to inhibit the inter-arms and interservice cooperation and coordination that war in the 20th century required. Infantry regiments, as an example, were concerned with what was happening to them first and foremost, not the field engineer company or armoured squadron that was attached to them. All-arms and combined-arms warfare was often a foreign subject to many units, rather than the status quo, and emphasis on the assault phase of Operation *Neptune* and the amphibious landings of Operation *Overlord* inhibited combined arms exercises and training. The ability of infantry companies and tank squadrons to conduct offensive operations was lacking, as neither side had any idea of how the other arms were to properly support, interact and communicate with them on the battlefield in order to achieve their operational goals. This was not the case with the Royal Artillery and Royal Canadian Artillery, as both organisations aggressively sought to best integrate their liaison and forward observation officer (FOO) teams into both armoured and infantry units successfully. Both had an outgoing approach to working with armour and infantry units, as the RA and RCA commanders understood this was critical in order for their artillery barrages, concentrations and counter-battery fire to be effective.[19]

Despite the challenges listed above that would arise in operations past the D-Day beaches, the first job at hand confronting all the D-Day assault units of the British and Canadian armies – attacking and overcoming the *Atlantikwall* defences to avoid another Dieppe Raid disaster – was something they were totally prepared for. This would be a mission that they would execute nearly perfectly in an awesome display of combat power against concrete fortifications manned by a determined enemy.

CHAPTER 5

The Anglo-Canadian D-Day assault, 6 June 1944

As the focus of the book is a case study of the *12. SS-Pz.Div. Hitlerjugend*, only a general overview will be provided of the events of 6 June on the Gold, Juno, and Sword invasion beaches, three of the five invasion beaches that were assaulted as part of the larger Operation *Overlord* that day in the Allied invasion of Europe. These three beaches were where the first forces of the British 1st and 30th Corps landed, these being the initial two corps that would constitute the British Second Army in the Normandy bridgehead.

This overview is necessary to explain why and how the Anglo-Canadian positions and the overall frontline were located where they were by the morning of 7 June 1944, when the first powerful forces of the *Hitlerjugend* assembled near the battlefield north-west of Caen. This overview is primarily drawn from secondary sources, as the research efforts towards obtaining primary documents logically focused on those surviving documents that concern or are from the *Hitlerjugend* during June 1944 and that survived the war.

This chapter will summarise the landings on the Sword, Juno and Gold Beaches as well as the Anglo-Canadian airborne landing zones east of the river Orne in order to briefly summarise the speed and military prowess displayed in the amphibious and airborne landings all along the eastern portion of what would become the Normandy bridgehead. There is not space within the book to detail the landings in all three sectors, but the author has chosen to place focus on the somewhat forgotten amphibious assault of the 3rd Canadian Infantry Division on Juno Beach to detail exactly how the *Atlantikwall* was overcome. This beach and its battle has been largely ignored by British and American authors in their historiography of the 6 June Normandy landings, despite Canadian tanks pushing further inland than US or British forces that day. It was the front line of the Canadians that the *Hitlerjugend* would batter away against primarily in the period 7–11 June, and thus this focus is justified. Complementing this, shorter summaries of the Gold and Sword beach landings will be presented.

The actual invasion of France, which began on the night of 5/6 June with the airborne assaults to provide flank protection for the main amphibious landings that morning, was a triumph of concentration of forces, excellent training and planning, ably supported by a large amount of firepower and innovative technology designed to overcome the concrete linear nature of the *Atlantikwall* defences.

These defences had been recently strengthened in order to counter what the Germans believed was the unlikely, but still possible, event of a landing there, the Pas-de-Calais being identified as the more likely landing zone because it had the shortest route possible through the English Channel from Dover.

Regarding the improvement in German defensive strength in the area from the Cotentin Peninsula to along the Normandy coast, the majority of this work had occurred in the period immediately leading up to June 1944 and had been instigated by the direction of *OKW* and *Der Führer*, Adolf Hitler, who had been influenced to improve the strength of forces to the west of the Pas-de-Calais by the results of *Luftwaffe* photo reconnaissance overflights. These reports, when analysed by the German *Kriegsmarine Marinegruppenkommando West* high command in France, had led to analysis forwarded to *OKW* that suggested that while a landing in the Pas-de-Calais was possible, the amount of landing craft in southern English ports to the west of Dover and along the entire stretch of Channel coastline indicated only one thing, an operation in the immediate future that involved landing somewhere to the west. By April 1944, Hitler had received enough information from his daily briefings to command the *Chef des Wehrmachtführungsstabes im Oberkommando der Wehrmacht* (Chief of the *OKW* Operations Staff), *Generaloberst* (*Gen.O.*) Afred Jodl, to immediately order *O.B. West G.F.M.* von Rundstedt to deploy available forces to the Cotentin peninsula and to Normandy. The object of these moves was to ensure a higher level of resistance immediately behind the *Atlantikwall* before armoured reserves could be brought in to decisively deal with the Allies.[1]

The first day of the conflict in Normandy was a vital time for *das Heer*, the German army. At this point an Allied initial lodgement on the French coast would be at its most vulnerable, and to succeed in destroying it the *Heer* needed to penetrate its perimeter in a rapid manner, as their doctrine of highly aggressive mobile warfare demanded. As aforementioned, *G.F.M.* Rommel recognised the danger of letting the Allies entrench themselves in the beachhead in strength; he believed if German forces could not succeed in rapidly crushing a landing, the *Wehrmacht* would ultimately be defeated in France.[2]

6 June 1944, D-Day, saw the mass landing of Allied amphibious and airborne forces on a broad front along the Normandy coast. The force summoned to carry out the amphibious part of the larger Operation *Overlord* – Operation *Neptune* – would employ over 285 warships, 4,100 landing craft and 1,600 support vessels that would make up two naval task forces, both possessing an overwhelming amount of naval power.[3] Crushing resistance all along the *Atlantikwall* in bitter fighting, by midday powerful Allied forces were ashore and making advances inland.

The successful assault on Juno Beach, this being the landing zone between Gold and Sword Beaches, is held up by Canadian military historians as one of the most successful operations within the nation's military history. In carrying out this assault, the 3rd Canadian Infantry Division and attached forces gained a solid foothold in occupied France, which had been under the heel of German occupation since 1940. Highly rehearsed, the successful Canadian landings erased the stigma of the crushing defeat of the Dieppe Raid in August 1942, the Canadian Army's previous attempt to penetrate the German *Atlantikwall* defences.[4] The result of this landing would also establish a front line of Canadian defences near the Norman city of Caen, largely solidified by 8 June, that would successfully repel the repeated *Hitlerjugend* assaults that are studied within this book.

The sector that was to be attacked was roughly three miles across and consisted of flat, hard-packed sand at low tide for roughly 300 meters in places, which disappeared at high tide, followed by a sea wall that was up to 2.4 meters high. Behind the line of villages in the Canadian zone were paved road networks of high-quality, pre-war standard French construction. Beyond the beaches were a vast array of topographical features, these being farm fields, wooded areas and large tilled fields of relatively open, flat terrain broken by the occasional stream or river. Some farming areas to the south were perfectly flat, which would prove to be very advantageous for the future construction of airfields.[5] However, unfortunately for the Allies, none of the Utah, Omaha, Sword, Juno or Gold Beach Sectors contained a major town or city with intact, large or deep water port facilities.

The specific role of the 3rd Canadian Infantry Division was to participate in the initial amphibious assault with two infantry brigades and the aforementioned attached forces, consolidate its hold on the initial beachhead area for further follow-on forces, then advance forward to enlarge the beachhead, within the limits of what landed forces could adequately defend. Once the coastal towns had been secured and the beach defences cleared, the division would then land its last remaining infantry brigade, the third regiment of the 2nd Canadian Armoured Brigade as well as further engineer, artillery and specialist troops. Elements of four self-propelled (SP) RCA field artillery regiments would also land, and their batteries would deploy into the area near the beaches. Using combat engineer assets to clear the beaches of obstacles, it was planned that routes would be opened to allow the passage of armour and vehicles rapidly off the beaches to support the infantry. If all went well, the paved, high-quality road network would be utilised to move quickly to push inland, rapidly expanding the size of the bridgehead during the first day of its existence.[6]

The 7th Canadian Infantry Brigade, under Brigadier Foster, was to assault the western section of beaches, at the centre of which were the seaside town of Courseulles-sur-Mer and the mouth of the Seulles. The 8th Canadian Infantry Brigade, under Brigadier Blackader, would attack the eastern beaches of Juno, these around and in front of the seaside towns of Bernières-sur-Mer and St Aubin-sur-Mer.

Both brigade groups would have sizeable amounts of amphibious armour and AVREs, as well as combat engineers and other specialist troops to support them on the objective. One full squadron of amphibious 'swimming' Duplex Drive (DD) Sherman III tanks would be employed to support each landing infantry battalion. These tanks were waterproofed and equipped with propellers mounted on the rear hull near the tracks and a large raised 'apron' that stopped the sea from swamping the tanks. Two squadrons from each regiment would support the two infantry brigades in their landings.[7] The ARVEs were supplied by the 5th Assault Regiment, Royal Engineers, and a number of 95mm howitzer-gunned Centaur tanks were also to be landed from the 2nd Royal Marine Armoured Support Regiment. It was planned that these tanks would support another Royal Marine unit, 48 Royal Marine Commando (48 RMC), assigned to assault objectives on the 8th Canadian Infantry Brigade sector's left flank.[8]

The 7th Canadian Infantry Brigade would land two of its infantry regiments, the Royal Winnipeg Rifles of Canada (RWR) and the 1st Battalion, the Regina Rifle Regiment (RRR), with one company of its third regiment, the 1st Battalion, the Canadian Scottish Regiment (1st Can Scots) in support of the RWR west of Courseulles. This objective area was the Mike sector, the beaches being Mike Green and Mike Red, and one beach of the Nan sector, Nan Green. In support would be two squadrons of 1st Hussars (6th Canadian Armoured Regiment) tanks, one for each battalion sector, slated to 'swim' in five minutes before the infantry arrived in their landing craft.[9]

The 8th Canadian Infantry Brigade planned to land two of its regiments, the Queen's Own Rifles of Canada (QORC) and the North Shore (New Brunswick) Regiment (NS), against the remaining sectors of Nan beach, these being Nan White and Nan Red. In support and slated to hit the beaches before the infantry were combat engineers and the Sherman DD tanks from two squadrons of the Fort Garry Horse (10th Canadian Armoured Regiment).[10] The reserve regiment of the 8th Canadian Infantry Brigade was the Francophone Le Régiment de la Chaudière, and it was ready to land as a second wave.

If all went well, the reserve battalions for each brigade would land a short time after the first two, as well as the self-propelled artillery of the four RCA field regiments, and parts of the 3rd Anti-Tank Regiment, RCA, and the 4th Light Anti-Aircraft Regiment, RCA. These last two regiments would establish strong anti-tank and anti-aircraft defences of the areas captured. Slated to land last after both brigade areas had been secured was a third wave of the division consisting of the reserve 9th Canadian Infantry Brigade and the reserve armoured regiment of the 2nd Canadian Armoured Brigade, the Sherbrooke Fusiliers Regiment (27th Canadian Armoured Regiment), along with more specialist beach control parties and other troops.[11]

Pushing past the three main built-up areas of Courseulles-sur-Mer, Bernières-sur-Mer and St Aubin sur-Mer, the Canadian forces had three specific phase lines to pass in their planned advance south. The first phase line was 'Yew', and it was just past the three built-up localities on Juno Beach. Second was phase line 'Elm', on the line Creully–Pierrepont and Le Fresne-Camilly and Solomby-sur-Thaon. The third and most ambitious phase line was 'Oak', with its axis on the line Putot-en-Bessin–Carpiquet–Caen, the northern suburbs of this city being the final objective for D-Day. To reach this line, the infantry regiments would have to utilise all manner of available motor transport and armoured vehicles to travel the distance. The utmost in aggression and speed would be needed. A fourth planned phase for the forces involved would be to reorganise themselves on 'Oak' in anticipation of German counterattacks.[12] This final phase line was roughly seventeen kilometres inland, an ambitious distance for a unit that had just landed.[13]

Part of the static German *716. Infanterie-Division* (*716. Inf.Div.*) manned the defences in the Juno Beach objective area. Its *Grenadier-Regiment 736* (*Gren.Rgt. 736*), very much a second-rate formation, had bunkers within all three localities of Courseulles-sur-Mer, Bernières-sur-Mer and St Aubin-sur-Mer. The sub-unit of *Gren.Rgt. 736* on the front lines was the *II. Btl./Gren.Rgt. 736*. Its *7. Kompanie* was in the 'Mike' Sector, the *6. Kompanie* in Courseulles itself, the *5. Kompanie* in Bernières-sur-Mer and the *9. Kompanie* in the "Nan" sector near St Aubin. Their defences consisted of concrete emplacements with anti-tank guns of the 5, 7.5 and 8.8cm types, supported by MG-42 machine-gun positions and a network of fighting positions and trenches near the seawall, in houses and open fields. In the area of Juno Beach there were in total eleven 8cm mortars, one 8.8cm gun, one 7.5cm gun and six 5cm guns. There were also command bunkers and some sections of communication trenches that were underground. Each fighting position could be supported by mortar fire, and the positions were designed to support each other through direct fire, be it from anti-tank guns or machine guns. The size of the bunkers varied, but they were placed roughly one every five hundred meters. The bunker firing ports were designed to not open out to sea and thus be vulnerable to direct fire from a warship or landing craft. The firing ports opened in a lateral fashion, giving the gunners the ability to sweep a section of the beach with enfilade fire, hitting all targets lined up on the beach or held up by obstacles.

In the way of obstacles, a belt of *Teller* anti-tank and *S-3* and *Schu-Mine* antipersonnel mines was laid which was three hundred to eight hundred yards wide. Obstacles in the water consisted of wooden posts, Belgian Gate iron anti-tank barriers taken from the Belgian frontier and tetrahedra made up of logs to catch the undersides of landing craft.[14] All of these obstacles were mined. The overall defence ribbon was strong but it had no depth, as this could not be accomplished by the Germans over the whole length of the *Atlantikwall*. In reserve 1.6 kilometres to the rear were four more *Grenadier Kompanien* of the *Gren.Rgt. 736*, and a *Kompanie* of captured French tanks. On the western flank of the front-line defences were two battalions of former Polish and Russian prisoners of war, now serving in the German army with German officers. On paper the defences looked formidable, and at the very least they were enough to repel a sizeable infantry assault force like that of the August 1942 Dieppe Raid.[15]

Air support on D-Day itself consisted of a large RAF Bomber Command raid on several German coastal gun emplacements located behind the beaches judged to be capable of bombarding the amphibious assault forces. These emplacements were hit by heavy and medium bomber raids on the night of 5/6 June. The targets included coastal and inland *Batterien* and nearby ammunition, barracks and command bunker complexes. The majority of these had been heavily fortified in the years of the German occupation and had been built with reinforced concrete. These emplacements were located at Houlgate, Fontenay, La Pernelle, Logues, Maisy, Merville, Mont Fleury, Pointe du Hoc, Ouisterham and St Martin-de-Varaville.

All these targets were obscured by heavy cloud, and the bombing had to be completed using the OBOE blind bombing system technology equipping RAF bombers in 1944. In all 1,012 aircraft took part, and only three were lost.[16] Many of these aircraft were Royal Canadian Air Force (RCAF) Halifaxes and Lancasters, and their crews were very accustomed to night-time bombing. The results of the bombing were as good as could reasonably be expected, considering it was conducted during obscured conditions. The aerial bombing runs went on from 1130 hours on 5 June until 0515 hours the next morning.[17]

Several of these artillery emplacements were later attacked either by paratroopers or Royal Marine Commandos, and if the initial bombing did not disrupt their operations, the later infantry assaults did put the guns out of action. One of the heaviest bombed emplacements was at Pointe du Hoc, the area being made a moonscape. Ironically, this was for naught as the guns had been moved to another location.

The RCN and RN bombardment force in support of the Juno Beach landings was Force 'E', part of the larger overall Naval Force 'J'. Having total naval superiority and having cleared most of the German sea mines from the area of their operation, these forces could manoeuvre at will as close to the shore as possible to obtain the best firing positions. As there was also total air superiority, the naval force did not have to worry about *Luftwaffe* anti-shipping attacks. The naval bombardment to directly support the Juno Beach landings was very powerful and caused considerable damage to the three defended localities that contained the German defensive positions. This naval gunfire unfortunately caused heavy French civilian casualties but successfully suppressed and in some cases stunned and demoralised the German defenders. It did not however destroy the enemy or totally crush their ability to resist.

Destroyers of the Royal Canadian Navy (RCN), Royal Navy (RN) and other Allied navies in the Anglo-Canadian landing zones, placed in direct support of the assault wave preparing to surge onto the beach, targeted the bunker lines on or near the seawall and beach areas, firing at them directly from short ranges. The destroyer forces bombarding the *Atlantikwall* bunkers with this direct 'Drenching Fire' consisted of 11 destroyers that would manoeuvre close to the beaches: HMS *Kempenfelt*, HMS *Faulknor*, HMS *Venus*, HMS *Fury*, HMS *Vigilant*, HMS *Bleasdale*, the Canadian HMCS *Algonquin*, the Norwegian HNoMS *Glaisdale*, the Canadian HMCS *Sioux*, the HMS *Stevenstone* and Free French *La Combattante*. This bombardment began at 0610 hours and was very accurate in a way that the aerial bombardment could not be, in that the fire was adjusted on targets in plain view.[18] Firing indirectly on targets further inland, the RN cruisers HMS *Diadem* and *Belfast* attacked the Beny-sur-Mer and Vers Battery south of the invasion beaches and some targets south of Juno Beach.

Despite their best efforts, only about 14 percent of the German *Atlantikwall* positions on Juno Beach were damaged or destroyed. In comparison, at least 90 percent of the civilian buildings on the shoreline were damaged or destroyed.[19] The strength of the German pillboxes and bunkers, which were constructed from very thick concrete and reinforced with rebar, stood up to the pounding. The main effect was to stun, concuss or incapacitate the German defenders sheltering in the bunkers. The bombardment continued until the first landing craft and DD tanks were near the beaches at 0745 hours. This gave the captains of the destroyers significant time to expend many shells and do their utmost to destroy German positions. Some of the inland German *Artillerie Batterien* were also attacked again for good measure using naval bombardment from the cruisers and fire from larger battleships further offshore.

The formation of the assault craft as they approached Juno Beach on the morning of 6 June had been well thought out by the British and Canadian forces prior to the invasion. There were a multitude of different types of smaller craft involved in *Neptune* and each one had a specific purpose. As an example, looking at the array of craft that would assault the 'Left Brigade' target beaches of Nan Red and Nan White as they were steaming forward at top speed at H-30 on the morning of 6 June 1944, they were arranged as follows: First to reach the beach but not actually land were the Landing Craft Support (Medium) (LCS (M)), which had forward observation teams from the Royal Canadian Artillery (RCA). These spotters would do their best to direct fire from the RCA M7 Priest 105mm self-propelled artillery firing on the move as their craft sailed forward, deployed to the rear of the successive waves of landing craft. Planning to have their armoured vehicles 'swim' to the beach, next up behind the LCS (M) were the Landing Craft (Tank) (LCT) landing craft, which carried a variety of armoured vehicles, from the British RE AVRE bridge layers to Sherman DD swimming tanks to additional M7 Priest 105mm self-propelled guns. Within the ranks of the LCT landing craft were also the LCT (CB) or 'concrete buster' landing craft, carrying Royal Engineer AVREs armed with the 105mm assault mortars.

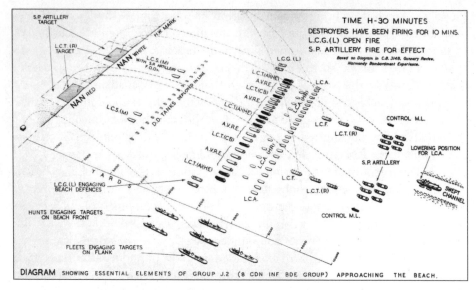

Formation of the 8th Canadian Infantry Brigade assault craft and supporting warships, Operation *Neptune*, 6 June 1944. (DND Military History and Heritage, Canadian Participation in the Operations in North-West Europe, 1944. Part 1: The assault and subsequent operations of 3 Canadian Inf Div and 2 Canadian Armd Bde 16–30 Jun 44. Appendix A to E Maps. 30 June 1952)

The next wave consisted of 10 Landing Craft Assault (Hedgerow) (LCA (HR)) with Hedgerow rocket banks mounted on them. These were 24 British Spigot mortars that could be launched to clear an identified beach obstacle. Behind these were the smaller Landing Craft Assault craft (LCA), each carrying 35 assault infantry. These LCA infantry craft were the most manoeuvrable, but also the smallest and flimsiest of the landing craft, and most vulnerable to direct and indirect fire, obstacles or sea mines.[20]

Next were Landing Craft Tanks (Flak) (LCT(F)), armed with an array of 20mm Oerlikon and 2-pounder Oerlikon 'Pom-Pom' anti-aircraft guns. Behind these were Landing Craft Tank (Rocket) (LCT (R)) vessels, with the hulls specially built to house and fire large quantities of indirect-fire rocket artillery. Fully loaded and ready to fire, each LCT (R) vessel had 1,000 British 60-pound RP-3 rockets ready for launching and 5,000 rockets stowed below decks. There were four of these vessels for Juno. Behind this grouping were more LCT Armoured High Explosives (HE) carrying the RCA M7 105mm self-propelled guns. Alongside these were RN and RCN Control Motor Launches, controlling the vast array of landing craft moving forward at top speed. Past these were the accompanying RN and RCN minesweepers, which had just cleared a path to the beach for the assault force and its destroyers.

All the landing craft armed to engage the beach defences in some manner would be scheduled to fire at specific times as they approached the target beaches, the matrix for this fire support effort being titled the 'Joint Fire Support Plan'. [21]

The effects of the bombardments, both aerial and naval, including the self-propelled 105mm M7 Priest fire, did not completely destroy or incapacitate the defenders at Bernières that were be attacked by the waves of landing craft described above. Though possibly deafened and concussed, the German soldiers were now very alert and could still man their weapons and engage the Canadian assault craft as soon as they landed. While some casemates had been demolished and some heavy weapons incapacitated, the majority were still serviceable, and it became a matter of whether the German commanders could summon their troops out of the bomb shelters and lower levels of bunkers to man their positions when the first Canadian assault landing craft neared the coast just before 0800 hours.

The actual amphibious assault on the beaches was designed to overwhelm the Germans by the sheer amount of personnel, resources and firepower from armour deployed against the defences. The most western portion of the assault beaches were Mike Red and Mike Green, these being the objectives of the RWR, and one company of the 1st Can Scots. The LCA of the RCE beach assault party, the first two RWR companies and 1st Canadian Scottish Company landed first at 0735 hours, beating the B Squadron DD Sherman tanks of the 1st Hussars to the beach. Following a period of heavy fire in which many RWR soldiers were machine gunned while they were chest-deep in water as they disembarked among the half-submerged beach obstacles, the LCTs with the AVREs and DD tanks came ashore and assisted in engaging the beach defences, some already cleared by the RWR. The 1st Can Scots Company encountered little resistance, the pillbox it was responsible for destroying having been silenced by naval gunfire.

The German soldiers were active in their defence measures on the seawall and in fighting positions in Courseulles itself, its small harbour and the Mike Red beach area as more and more landing craft came ashore. Determined RCE and RWR assault tactics, combined with the Sherman DD tank fire, silenced the German positions one by one within the town itself. The Canadian infantry immediately began to push into the village and the side streets, the thin crust of defences having been penetrated at this point. The other two companies of the RWR subsequently landed, and overall combat for this town ended by mid-morning. Later that afternoon the battalion pushed forward to the village of Cruelly and was consolidated by 1700 hours. [22]

The other beach in front of Courseulles and part of the 7th Canadian Infantry Brigade's area of responsibility was the Nan Green beach on the eastern side of Courseulles, the area adjacent to the RWR objective. Here two companies of the RRR assaulted the beaches, supported by A Squadron of the 1st Hussars, with AVRE tanks and RCE assault parties in support. Here too the Sherman DD tanks managed to land at a similar time as the infantry, and immediately began to engage an anti-tank gun in a concrete casemate. The infantry cleared several trenches and strongpoints, but the Germans in this sector were determined, and managed to remerge in some cases and try to reinfiltrate. However, the infantry with tank support managed to defeat the defenders and the RRR pushed forward south into Fontaine-Henry, a village south of the beaches on report line 'Elm', that evening.

The third reserve battalion of the 7th Canadian Infantry Brigade, the 1st Can Scots minus one company, landed by mid-morning and pushed forward as the right flank of the brigade, taking up positions in Cainet and Le Fense-Camilly by the end of the day. At 0900 hours that morning the 12th and 13th Field Regiments, RCA, landed and began to offload their M7 105mm Priest self-propelled artillery and other vehicles, setting up battery positions near the beaches. Pushing forward, the 7th Canadian Infantry Brigade headquarters established itself in Colombiers-sur-Seulles that evening.

The most western beach of the 8th Canadian Infantry Brigade area, Nan White, encompassed the seawall in front of the village of Bernières-sur-Mer and was the exclusive objective of the Queen's Own Rifles of Canada (QORC) infantry regiment. Supporting the QORC was B Squadron of the Fort Garry Horse, as well as RCE combat engineer assault parties and AVRE vehicles. Due to high seas and the risk of being swamped, the DD tanks landed very close to the beaches, arriving just a short time after the infantry assault LCA craft had touched down. The German soldiers were active in their defence measures, with intense MG-42 machine-gun fire and mines causing heavy casualties among the assaulting troops, the armoured support for the Canadians in this area unfortunately recorded as being ineffective. Despite having to run a long distance among mined obstacles to the seawall and landing right in front of a resistance nest, surviving QORC soldiers managed to successfully assault strongpoints and fighting positions one by one, and by mid-morning they were subdued. Once the pillboxes had been cleared of resisting Germans, the infantry immediately began to push into the village and the side streets. Major combat in this sector also ended by noon and Bernières was declared clear.[23]

Also within the 8th Canadian Infantry Brigade sector was the village of St Aubin-sur-Mer, and this village, protected by a seawall, had some sections of it defended by German soldiers determined to fight. The infantry regiment charged with assaulting the beach with two of its infantry companies was the North Shore (New Brunswick) Regiment (NS). One company's LCA assault craft landed successfully, but the infantry immediately began to take casualties from machine-gun fire from pillboxes. The tanks and AVRE tanks were landed successfully, just after the infantry, but some vehicles were immediately knocked out by German 5cm anti-tank Pak fire. Intense Sherman DD tank and AVRE fire did adequately support the infantry, and the tanks were able to subject the bunkers to heavy fire, silencing them. The NS reported the area of western St Aubin clear by midday, but notably, other strongpoints in the village resisted until 2010 hours.[24]

On the left flank, the other NS company made very good progress into the village with minimal difficulty, and the two follow-on companies landed later pushed into the south part of St Aubin and cleared the village of Tailleville to the south.[25] The Royal Marines of 48 Royal Marine Commando (48 RMC), supported by the 2nd Royal Marine Armoured Support Regiment's 95mm Centaur tanks within this sector of Nan Red, pushed into parts of the neighbouring town east of St Aubin, Langrune-sur-Mer, where it was halted by German resistance. This fighting made a link-up with the neighbouring British 3rd Infantry Division impossible for the moment.

The success on Juno, though well supported by air and naval assets, was mainly due to the tactics of Canadian Army units specifically trained for the amphibious assault role, overcoming well-defended concrete emplacements of the German *Atlantikwall* defences. Canadian forces carried out their mission due to the successful exercise of combined arms warfare on the objective, defeating strong German defences whose troops were alert and ready to fight. Fighting determinedly as the British would do on Gold and Sword Beaches, the use of all arms, these being armour, armoured engineer vehicles, artillery, combat engineers and assault infantry, conquered one defensive strongpoint after another and the coastal towns of Saint Aubin-sur-Mer, Bernières-sur-Mer and Courseulles-sur-Mer were liberated.

Apart from later combat on the right flank and near the outskirts of Douvres, the overall front of the 3rd Canadian Infantry Division was largely free of heavy fighting by midday, and parts of the two landed infantry brigades of the division, once regrouped, could begin to move inland in order to attempt to claw their way forward to their intermediate objective lines for the day. Taking the North Shore (New Brunswick) Regiment (NS) as an example to illustrate the overly ambitious nature of the day's operations, its part in the second phase was to attempt to capture Tailleville, the wooded area near the village, and finally subdue the *Luftwaffe Nachtjäger* radar station at Douvres, held by *Luftwaffe* troops emplaced within a large subterranean bunker complex with underground phone lines. After clearing the radar station, it was intended that the battalion would take its place in what was planned to be the 8th Canadian Infantry Brigade 'fortress' south of Anguerny, 11 kilometres north-west of Caen. Achieving all of these tasks would have been almost insurmountable unless all the Germans in the immediate area of operations of the NS chose to surrender. To ask the men of the regiment to continue to attack after hours of gruelling combat was a very tall order, as the platoons were exhausted and had taken significant losses. After a period of inconclusive combat in the afternoon and gaining the first view of the radar station's formidable defences in the way of bunkers and barbed wire, the NS dug in for the night.

At 1050 hours, after seeing that major combat in the three seaside towns was being successfully concluded, Major General Keller, the commander of the 3rd Canadian Infantry Division, ordered the third brigade of the division, the 9th Canadian Infantry

Brigade led by Brigadier Cunningham, to land on Nan White.[26] Just before this the remaining landing craft carrying self-propelled 105mm M7 Priests had landed in the 8th Canadian Infantry Brigade sector, and shortly afterward the last remaining armoured regiment of the 2nd Canadian Armoured Brigade also came ashore.

The beaches were now clogged with damaged and half-sunk assault craft and the vehicular traffic of those leaving the beach area or just landing. The German obstacles still present continued to cause problems. Despite the chaos, RCN and RN beach parties and RCE personnel successfully created vehicle crossings on the seawall where required, and the slow crawl of traffic out of the three seaside towns began, despite more and more vehicles and personnel piling up behind those moving out.

At this stage a great effort was made to move the units and their equipment inland, and despite continuing pockets of German resistance, Canadian forces attempted to reach their various phase lines. German resistance, never being completely subdued during 6 June, flared up in several locations as the infantry and armour surged down the roads south leading inland.

As an example, in the afternoon the vanguard of the 9th Canadian Infantry Brigade began an effort to push through the 8th Canadian Infantry Brigade units towards Beny-sur-Mer. This force, the North Nova Scotia Highlanders (NNSH) infantry regiment, with the armoured Sherbrooke Fusiliers Regiment (SFR), in support, pushed forward at 1605 hours. Having landed in the second wave, both units were nearly up to establishment strength and had experienced little combat. Three NNSH companies married up with the three Sherbrooke Fusiliers Regiment armoured squadrons, leaving the fourth infantry company to march on foot as the tanks ahead pushed forward in three columns. Not moving forward at the same pace, the two remaining infantry regiments of the brigade did not accompany this force.

Having landed in the second wave, the Sherbrooke Fusiliers were very near their establishment strength in tanks, with 49 Sherman IIIs mounting short 75mm guns, and 12 Firefly variants, four of which had been allocated to each squadron. The 11 Stuart light tanks of the recce troop, armed with weak 37mm guns, gave the regiment a total of 72 tracked armoured fighting vehicles.[27]

Breaking free of the coastal traffic jam, the three columns arrived in their assembly area of 'Elder', the code name for the assembly area of the 9th Canadian Infantry Brigade vanguard, at 1645 hours. Arriving with the rear decks filled with Canadian infantry, these tanks and other vehicles were prime targets for a *Luftwaffe* that was luckily totally absent from the skies; this unimpeded movement showing how weak their presence was over the beachhead on this day.

From the 'Elder' position the three columns pushed on, B Squadron reaching La Mare via Basely. A Squadron with its infantry advanced to Colomby-sur-Thaon, and C Squadron with its company of NNSH soldiers pushed in between the previously mentioned two forces.[28] D Company of the NNSH marched along behind the three companies mounted on the tanks, and was followed by the battalion headquarters and the NNSH Support Company.

German resistance was never totally eliminated, and the Canadian infantry was shot at continually in each successive village and from German positions some distance away, this fire forcing the NNSH infantry to dismount and march behind the tanks as they advanced. As an example of this scattered resistance, a German mortar position, manned by soldiers from the *716. Inf.Div.*, was taken out with grenades and tank fire from an A Squadron tank as it pushed through the fields.[29] The tanks of A Squadron then continued to advance, making contact with the other two squadrons near Ainsy in their push forward. The SFR recce troop, in front of the three advancing squadrons, encountered a position with two German 8.8cm guns near Basly, also from the *716. Inf.Div.*, which were quickly destroyed. These German troops and others like them located behind the beaches usually fought for a period of time, then usually surrendered rapidly when they realised the number of tanks and infantry they were up against.

When it reached early evening and dusk began to fall, British Second Army Commander General Sir Miles Dempsey, overall commander of the eastern portion of the newly won invasion bridgehead, decided that the ability of the Anglo-Canadian forces which were ashore to establish a strong defence would be impaired if they continued to push forward. All three divisions under his command were signalled to stop their advance via the British 1st Corps headquarters. Canadian units were thus ordered to cease the advance at roughly 1820 hours and to dig in and establish defensive positions in depth, in anticipation of the expected German counterattacks with armoured forces.[30]

The southern-most ground captured by Canadian forces that evening had been seized by the NNSH battlegroup from the 9th Canadian Infantry Brigade. The tanks of the three SFR squadrons assembled in Villons-les-Buissons, and assumed an all-around defence centred on the area around the village and the surrounding fields. D Company of the NNSH, following behind the three squadrons of tanks with the other companies, arrived later that night with the NNSH Support Company and battalion headquarters. German infantry in the way of scattered pockets of resistance were located near Villons-les-Buissons, and these groups were dealt with by NNSH infantry patrols. The position of the vanguard's infantry was oriented south and was centred around the Ainsy-Villon-les-Buissons crossroads. The SFR tanks stayed with the infantry for a period while they dug in and consolidated, with an almost peacetime southern England training exercise environment present, this being encouraged by the lack of German artillery fire and non-presence of the *Luftwaffe*. The final positions of the 3rd Canadian Infantry Division as of midnight on 6/7 June were a significant distance inland but were only halfway in some places to the phase line 'Oak', this running roughly along the east–west Caen–Bayeaux railroad line and highway.

Firm contact in the form of a solid line of positions to the right flank of the British 3rd Infantry Division had not been established, and significant German defences, mainly in the form of the Douvres radar station, had not been cleared. There was a significant gap between the Sword and Juno Beaches, and this was due to the resistance of the eastern-most strongpoint at St Aubin, and other strongpoints at Langere-Sur-Mer and Petit Enfer. The defenders of the German concrete casemates were led by NCOs and officers determined to fight, and the aforementioned landing of the 48 Royal Marine Commando (48 RMC) at 0843 hours on the eastern sector of Juno Beach had seen the marines take heavy casualties from machine-gun and mortar fire.

At Le Fresne-Camilly the 7th Canadian Infantry Brigade had established a brigade fortress, with the Royal Winnipeg Rifles forming the western left-flank oriented south, the 1st Battalion, the Canadian Scottish Regiment in the middle, closest to the village of Le Fresne-Camilly, and the 1st Battalion, the Regina Rifle Regiment just to the north-east of the village. Behind the infantry regiments were the tanks of the 1st Hussars, supported by parts of the Cameron Highlanders of the Ottawa Machine Gun Battalion and the 3rd Canadian Anti-Tank Regiment, RCA.

The aforementioned four field artillery regiments of the RCA – these being arguably the most powerful combat arms units within the 3rd Canadian Infantry Division, as the events of the next few days would illustrate – had taken up battery positions north of the infantry brigade fortresses, and were ready to carry out any sort of fire mission that night. The gun crews with their M7 105mm Priest self-propelled guns were still near full strength despite the loss of some vehicles during the landings, and were in firing range of any enemy units that might attack the Canadian infantry in the night.

However, if the Canadian infantry brigades were to advance the next day, as was planned, the Commander, Royal Artillery (CRA) of the division, Brigadier Todd, would have to ruthlessly drive the field regiments forward to take up new firing positions in order to support the brigades in their advances if enemy forces were encountered. As will be discussed in Chapter 7, this would only be partially achieved.

By the end of the day Canadian forces were consolidated past phase line 'Elm', but though tremendous progress had been made, they had not reached phase line 'Oak'. However, the forces on 'Elm' were able to consolidate and were ready to offer a stiff defence if any serious German counterattack against Canadian forces on 6 June materialised. It did not.

The role of the German *Panzerdivisionen* under the control of *G.F.M.* Rommel had been to quickly, where possible, move from their deployment areas in a unified fashion and liquidate the invaders before any serious lodgements could be established. This had not occurred, but key Canadian objectives on phase line 'Oak' had not been captured, and some would not fall until July 1944.

Stopping early did allow Canadian forces to have time to plan to push forward the next day. Extremely heavy fighting would occur on 7 June, and the 'early stop' to operations ordered by British Second Army commander General Dempsey arguably allowed for Canadian defensive positions to be arranged in depth, helping to effectively absorb German offensive operations north of Caen the following day, 7 June.

Canadian military operations on 6 June had been remarkably successful, and there were very few serious setbacks apart from some Canadian soldiers, mainly paratroopers, being captured during the night of 5/6 June and later in the day. Though the fighting was fierce, in general it was over on most beaches within the Juno sector in under two hours. Though the final objective for D-Day, reaching the line 'Oak', had not been achieved, the forces inland that had pushed forward from the beaches were now in place 9.65 kilometres inland.[31]

Due to the summer weather and the time of sunset in Normandy, a further push could have been possible for Canadian forces. Given the lack of progress for some Anglo-Canadian units, had the 9th Canadian Infantry Brigade vanguard pushed forward further, it would have been dangerously exposed and without flank protection. The neighbouring battlegroups, infantry and armoured battalions simply did not or could not advance at the same pace following the combat at the beachhead. The decision to halt at Villons-les-Buissons was the correct one.

Looking at the British landing zone to the west of Juno Beach, the Gold Beach assault was carried out primarily by two infantry brigades of the very experienced British 50th Infantry Division under Major General Douglas Graham, supported by units of the British 8th Armoured Brigade and various other Royal Engineer (RE) and specialist units, such as the 47 Royal Marine Commando (47 RMC). This division and the supporting 8th Armoured Brigade would be the first formations of Lieutenant General Gerald Bucknall's British 30th Corps to land, the forces to the east on the Juno and Sword Beaches being under the command of the British 1st Corps. Following the two assault brigades landing, two further brigades were to land and press forward inland. One of them, the British 56th Infantry Brigade, had been temporarily attached to give the division increased combat power for the assault and subsequent consolidations. Gold Beach was divided into two landing zones for the assaulting British units: 'Jig' in the west and 'King' to the east, the first being approximately 3,200 meters wide (2 miles) and the second 2,400 meters wide (1.5 miles).

Defending the Gold Beach Sector were other parts of the *716. Inf.Div.* under *Generalmajor* (*Gen.Maj.*) Wilhelm Richter, these forces being the two remaining *Bataillone* of *Grenadier-Regiment 726*, which had strongpoints around Le Hamel and the *441. Ost-Bataillone*, which actually occupied the beach defences. The eastern edge of Gold Beach was defended by *Grenadier-Regiment 736*, which would form the main force which was to oppose the Canadian landings at Juno Beach to the east. Providing *Artillerie* support in this area was *Artillerieregiment 1716*, which had both towed and emplaced guns east and west of the village of Crépon. The very western tip of the Gold sector was defended by *Grenadier Regiment 916* of the *352. Infanterie-Division*, its *Grenadier-Regiment 915* forming the basis for the reserve *Kampfgruppe* Meyer, which was motorised and based south-east of the city of Bayeux. Providing more field artillery support for this area was *Artillerieregiment 352*, which contained four *Abteilung*, consisting of 12 *Batterien* equipped with 10.5cm and 15cm howitzers, totalling 48 field artillery pieces.[32]

Supported by a force of Allied cruisers and destroyers that comprised Bombarding Force K, the units of the British 69th and 231st Brigades stormed the beaches, with the 231st Infantry Brigade assaulting the western Jig sector and the 69th Infantry Brigade assaulting the eastern King sector. In some areas the British infantry overcame resistance very quickly, but in others it faced a sustained battle that went on for hours. The preliminary naval bombardment had begun at 0530 hours, this being followed by the landing craft beginning their landings in the two sectors at 0725 hours. Bad weather in the way of high winds gave the landing craft a difficult time, and the Sherman DD tanks and RE AVRE tanks supporting both the Jig and King infantry assaults were landed as close as possible to avoid them being swamped. Fire was received from the Longues-sur-Mer German coastal battery, but British Royal Navy cruiser fire managed to disable three of its four guns, reducing its effectiveness.

Landing on the western Jig sector of Gold Beach, the 231st Brigade, after crushing resistance, pushed west to capture Arromanches and sought to contact US forces

Generalmajor Wilhelm Richter, *Kommandeur* of the *716. Infanterie-Division* on the *Atlantikwall* on 6 June 1944, photographed here as an *Oberst* circa 1943. (Bundesarchiv via Wikimedia Commons)

assaulting Omaha Beach. The British 69th Infantry Brigade, landing on the eastern King sector, moved east to link up with Canadian forces that had landed on Juno Beach, making contact later that day. The German strongpoints at La Rivière and Le Hamel possessed 8.8cm and 7.5cm guns respectively in concrete casemates, and these gun crews fought hard, firing at the British infantry and supporting DD and AVRE tanks until tank fire managed to silence both of them. Fortified houses in La Rivière, Le Hamel and Asnelles-sur-Mer resisted stubbornly until overcome, and there was no massed surrender of German forces, each fortification fighting on for some time.

Landing to the west, the 47 Royal Marine Commando (47 RMC) lost several landing craft to mined obstacles, taking heavy casualties in the process, and were held up by German resistance on the way to capture their objective, the small port of Port-en-Bessin. More German resistance ensured they did not reach it that day, the Royal Marines only Capturing Hill 72 and the small village of La Rosière that night.

The second wave of landings later that morning, consisting of the British 56th and 151st Infantry Brigade forces, landed without major difficulties apart from the landing of the first brigade, which had planned to land on Jig but was re-routed to King because of resistance at Le Hamel. These forces quickly moved out from the beachhead and advanced in the direction of Bayeux, the high ground near the paved Route Nationale 13 (RN 13) highway, as well as the Caen–Bayeux railroad to the south and the area between the Aure and Seulles rivers. In the later afternoon British forces met the German mobile reserve *Kampfgruppe* Meyer of the *352. Infanterie-Division* east of Bayeux at Villers-le Sec, which they destroyed, killing its commander. It had previously been thrown into disarray by a heavy Allied air attack, and the subsequent British infantry and tank fire scattered its infantry sub-units.

As was the case with the Juno Beach assault, the British forces on Gold Beach did not achieve all their designated objectives, but they had destroyed nearly all the *Atlantikwall* forces they encountered. Most defences had been overcome by 1000 hours, and yet some holdouts kept fighting until the afternoon, this difference illustrating the varying degrees of resistance and weapons available to the Germans which influenced whether they kept fighting or gave up.

A link up with US forces to the east at Omaha Beach had not been affected, and while this had occurred with Canadian forces to the west, German resistance had held up the advance straight along the coast. With regard to the objective 'lines', these were only partially attained by the British 50th Infantry Division forces because of a multitude of reasons, traffic jams and ongoing German resistance being the most prominent. The advance of British forces was very respectable, though, and the victory over *Kampfgruppe* Meyer of the *352. Inf.Div.* had been the crowning success. At the end of the day, the British 50th Infantry Division held the line Arromanches-les-Bains–Vex-aux Aures–St Sulpice–Esquay-sur-Seulles–Brecy–Creully, where contact was made with Canadian forces. British casualties in the Gold Beach Sector were an estimated 1,000 to 1,100 men, and a significant number of armoured vehicles were disabled or destroyed.

The assault on Sword Beach by the British 3rd (Assault) Infantry Division and attached forces, commanded by Major General Rennie, was very much resisted by the German defenders on the beaches, and unlike some of the combat on Gold and Juno Beaches, it went on uninterruptedly right into the evening. This beach was also unique in that it was the only one to have a German *Panzerdivision*, this being the *21. Pz.Div.*, actually assault its invasion forces on 6 June.

Beginning with naval bombardment from 0300 hours, this was followed by the landing craft setting out for the beaches from 0725 hours onward. Overcoming heavy resistance in the Queen Beach landing zones in front of Hermanville-sur-Mer, the British 8th and 9th Infantry Brigade forces, supported by the 1st Special Service Brigade commandos to the east, successfully crushed German resistance over a number of hours. Overcoming the heavy anti-tank gun fire which destroyed several tanks, the British managed to clear enough of the seawall and construct several exits from the beach area from which follow-on forces flowed in the late morning and afternoon. To the east, defences at Ouisterham were cleared after heavy fighting, and subsequently in the afternoon the Special Service Brigade forces commandos made contact with the British 6th Airborne Division's forces east of the Orne canal.

By afternoon, the front of the British beachhead was solidifying, with the British 8th Infantry Brigade defending Hermanville-sur-Mer, the British 9th Infantry Brigade digging in near Périers-sur-le-Dan and the 41 Royal Marine Commando (41 RMC) holding part of Lion-sur-Mer on the coast. Units of the 1st Special Service Brigade had crossed the Orne Canal and the imposing Lébisey Wood ridgeline north of Caen was now within reach of the British 185th Infantry Brigade, which, having landed, was now assembling to advance south.

It is important to go into some detail concerning the British attempt to drive south towards Caen in the afternoon in order to explain why Caen did not fall to the British Army on D-Day. By 1100 hours the three infantry battalions of the aforementioned intermediate brigade to land, the British 185th Infantry Brigade, were ashore and marching to assigned assembly areas just south of the beaches. The brigade headquarters at this time was located at Hermanville. Arranged west to east were the 1st Battalion, Royal Norfolk Regiment (1 RNR), the 2nd Battalion, King's Shropshire Light Infantry (2 KSLI) and the 2nd Battalion, Royal Warwickshire Regiment (2 RWR). The 2 KSLI were deployed on the main road south to Caen and near midday were waiting for the tanks of the British 27th Armoured Brigade to move up to support them. It was planned that these tanks would take three companies of the battalion on their rear engine decks and move in column via the paved road right into Caen. The remaining two infantry battalions, without armoured support, were to advance on the left and right flanks. Due to terrible traffic congestion on the beaches, the Sherman tanks of the Staffordshire Yeomanry armoured regiment were delayed.

Brigadier Smith of the British 185th Infantry Brigade decided at roughly noon that enough of a delay had occurred, and he had to attempt to advance, with or without supporting armour. If the armour did arrive, it would just have to catch up with the infantry. He would advance with the dismounted infantry companies over the ridge near the Périers-sur-le-Dan high feature and then push forward to the Biéville–Beuville twin villages, through the Lébisey village and wooded area. Directly south of this last location were the outskirts of Caen, the objective for the British 3rd Infantry Division on D-Day.[33]

As the infantry companies set out to advance on foot, one and a half squadrons of the Staffordshire Yeomanry armour arrived in the assembly area of the 2 KSLI shortly after midday. There was a wet, marshy area on one side of the crossroads south of Hermanville-sur-Mer leading south, and on the other side was a minefield. on arrival, the tanks and other vehicles piled up nose to tail and were thus caught in a second massive traffic jam.[34] It was unclear to the battalion commander if he should continue to wait or simply begin to march south in a dismounted advance.

At Sword Beach a terrible situation developed with regard to the RN's ability to land more vehicles via landing craft and landing ships, as the low tide of early morning had turned into high tide and shrunk the amount of beach available to disembark armoured vehicles on. The landing ship tanks (LSTs) had to manoeuvre as close as possible to the beach exits, which had been created by Royal Engineers bridging or creating gaps in the seawall, and thus the unloading of vehicles was severely impaired by delays. That more vehicles had not been unloaded earlier had been due to the heavy combat that ensued from daybreak until mid-morning. Making matters worse, the loss of several Sherman DD tanks due to combat and floundering in rough seas reduced the number of serviceable tanks for combat south of the beaches by midday.

Deciding the matter shortly after midday, the commanding officer of the KSLI was ordered by the British 185th Infantry Brigade to advance, regardless of the reduced number of Shermans. The KSLI, with its flanks secured by the other two battalions, would advance straight down the present-day D60 paved Hermanville–Caen road. No major German forces were detected by the British at this time other than stragglers belonging to the *716. Inf.Div.*

At this moment a critical unit necessary to support the British advance broke free of the traffic jam north near Hermanville-sur-Mer and got into open farmers' fields where its guns were deployed to support a further advance south. This was the 7th Field Regiment, RA, and it had made it off the beaches with nearly its entire vehicle establishment.

Despite this success and the decision to advance, many factors continued to hold the British up. German mortar and artillery fire was a problem for units attempting to reach and support the British 185th Infantry Brigade vanguard, as German gunners firing from further east near the mouth of the Orne had successfully adjusted the range of their artillery pieces using the visible wind socks the RN beach personnel had planted in the beach sands. These were promptly removed once German artillery fire intensified. Hastily moored barrage balloons, set up to deter *Luftwaffe* air attacks, were also used by the *Heer Artillerie* to calculate ranges for field artillery pieces and shore batteries still firing in the afternoon, and though they were removed quickly, the artillery rounds disrupted the efficient movement of traffic struggling to break free of the coast.[35] Also, the loss of key personnel in the initial fighting had also done its part to impair the British advance south, as the commander of the 5th Assault Regiment, RE, and the 5th Beach Group, RN, had both been killed by mid-morning.[36] While these key leaders had been replaced by their second in commands, the temporary impact of their loss did impair the effort to organise the traffic chaos near the beachhead.

With a reduced number of troop-carrying Sherman tanks of C Squadron Staffordshire Yeomanry in the lead, followed closely by dismounted KSLI infantry, the vanguard of the British 185th Infantry Brigade pressed forward. Far behind, more British forces in the way of B Squadron Staffordshire Yeomanry, RA tank destroyers and FOO parties for the 7th and 33rd Field Regiments, RA, pushed forward to join them. This was fortuitous, as A Squadron of the same armoured regiment had been detached temporarily to help reduce German strongpoints holding out to the rear.[37]

Advancing south towards the ridge near the village of Périers-sur-le-Dan, the C Squadron Staffordshire Yeomanry tanks with it KSLI infantry mounted on their engine decks initially encountered very little resistance. Cresting the ridge and moving down the forward slope towards Beuville, the column was fired upon by a German *Artillerie Batterie* from the *716. Inf.Div. Artillerieregiment 1716.* Its *Batterie* positions were ringed with barbed wire, protected by machine guns and the captured Russian 12.2cm howitzer crews fired intensely at the leading elements of the British once they were sighted. An 8.8cm gun from *Panzerjäger-Abteilung 200* of the *21. Pz.Div.* was also in action, and several British tanks were knocked out.[38]

By 1425 hours a 2 KSLI infantry company had encircled the *Batterie* position and RA field artillery fire was called in, but the Germans continued to fight and man their guns when not being shelled or machine gunned. Eventually a limited number of the German gunners managed to break out of the encirclement in late afternoon and fled south into a nearby wooded area. As this fight was going on, the main body of the armoured column reached the Biéville–Beuville twin villages at 1600 hours. Near the villages mortar and rifle fire was encountered as the column cleared the area and pushed on towards the high ground near Lébisey Wood and the nearby village of the same name. As the main body advanced towards the rise, B Squadron of the Staffordshire Yeomanry was detached to try to retain the Periers-sur-le-Dan high ground, should a German armoured counterattack appear.

As the Staffordshire Yeomanry recce troop Stuart light tanks pushed into the wooded area near the high ground, word came that a large number of German tanks had been spotted to the south and were approaching at a fast rate of speed straight up the paved road from Caen. Luckily, A Squadron of the Staffordshire Yeomanry returned at this point to take up defensive positions with the main body, this being C Squadron of the Staffordshire Yeomanry, the anti-tank guns of the 2 KSLI Support Company and a M-10 tank destroyer troop of 41 Battery, Royal Artillery.[39]

While one of the *21. Pz.Div. Kampfgruppen* built around *Pz.Gren.Rgt. 125* was fighting east of the Orne against British paratroopers, the remainder of the division had finally been deployed forward, after much delay and indecision, to protect the northern approaches to Caen and the city itself. *Pz.Gren.Rgt. 192* under *Oberstleutnant* Rauch had its *Panzergrenadier Kompanien* scattered north of the city, and these were beginning to make contact with the brigades of the British 3rd Infantry Division by midday, exchanging fire at long range.

Gen.d.Artl. Marcks, the *Oberbefehlshaber* of the German *LXXXIV. Armeekorps*, had only one uncommitted *Kampfgruppe* based upon *Pz.Rgt. 22* of the division available as his last reserve to stop Caen from falling. The reserve, the aforementioned reported column of *Panzer* IVs and other vehicles, was reported by the British at 0945 hours to be south of Caen, marching north. As the Panzer IV *Panzergruppe* with elements of *I.* and *II. Abt.* and the regimental staff moved forward cross country to avoid air attack, the British engaged some parts of *Pz.Gren.Rgt. 192* near Périers, and it was these elements that also fought the British in the twin villages of Biéville–Beuville. As this was happening, the Panzer IV *Kompanien* had to find ways around Caen, it and all its bridges being under heavy fighter bomber air attack at this time.

Meeting with *Gen.d.Artl.* Marcks near Caen, *Oberst* Oppeln-Bronikowski of *Pz.Rgt. 22* and *Gen.Maj.* Feuchtinger, *Kommandeur* of the *21. Pz.Div.*, were ordered by Marcks to attack and break through with the Panzer IV *Panzergruppe* to the beachhead at all costs. Breaking up the *Panzergruppe* into two groupings, *II. Abt./ Pz.Rgt. 22* was tasked to clear the twin villages of Biéville–Beuville while *I. Abt./ Pz.Rgt. 22*, which was set to arrive later, was directed to seize the Périers-sur-le-Dan ridge area. After this orders group, during which Marcks had verbally dressed down Feuchtinger for incompetence regarding the delayed nature of the attack, the Panzer IV tank columns set off. It was not possible for the author to determine exactly how many tanks set off in the two groupings, but a conservative estimate would be sixty.

Encountering heavy British anti-tank and tank fire north of Lébisey Wood, some *II. Abt./Pz.Rgt. 22* Panzer IVs, without close *Panzergrenadiere* support, began to take hits and burn. Moving west, more tanks were hit around Biéville. *I. Abt./Pz.Rgt. 22*, arriving later, moved to the west to attack the Périers-sur-le-Dan high feature, now occupied by British tanks, anti-tank guns and a number of self-propelled M-10 tank destroyers. Engaging both German groupings, the British defensive fire was intense and accurate at long range. Despite some attempts to move west in order to outflank the British, the Germans continued to suffer losses, also taking fire from B Squadron of the Staffordshire Yeomanry and from other British anti-tank guns that had been moved into position. In the fighting that lasted roughly an hour, 13 Panzer IVs were lost. The British forces after this encounter remained in their defensive positions, awaiting further attacks. After this defensive victory, the British advance south towards Caen was halted. Seeing burning Panzer IV wrecks, the following *Pz.Gren.Rgt. 192* infantry elements supporting the attack had pulled back with the remaining tanks.

Meanwhile, on the British right flank of Sword Beach, the 41 RMC which had been attacking Lion-sur-Mer had suffered heavy losses from machine-gun and mortar fire. This resistance would continue, and responsibility for subduing this village would later be assigned to the British 8th Infantry Brigade.[40] Holding this German salient on the coast were determined defenders from the *716. Inf.Div.* who refused to give up. At the same time as the combat occurred near Lébisey Wood, Biéville–Beuville and Périers-sur-le-Dan, a German *Panzergrenadier* thrust by *Pz.Gren.Rgt. 192*, supported by a few detached Panzer IVs, reached the coastline near Lion-sur-Mer. It then pulled back, as its flanks were totally exposed and it had observed a massive armada of gliders flying overhead to the positions of the British 6th Airborne Division east of the Orne. Feuchtinger, concerned it would be cut off, ordered that the *Panzergrenadiere* turn back towards Caen, leaving a *Kompanie* of *Panzergrenadiere* to help defend the *Luftwaffe* Douvres radar station with its soon to be surrounded garrison.[41]

Concluding this summary of the British landing in the Sword Beach Sector, the forces involved had performed admirably, linking up with airborne forces to the east over the Orne canal, advancing a significant distance towards Caen, fighting off poorly organised or simply late German *21. Pz.Div. Kampfgruppen* attacks and inflicting heavy casualties on all enemy forces they encountered.

There was no question of the British division simply landing and 'driving on to Caen', as it was busy from the initial landings until midnight with uninterrupted combat, not only with parts of the *716. Inf.Div.*, but with the vanguards of *Gen. Maj.* Edgar Feuchtinger's *21. Pz.Div.*, whose tanks and armoured personnel carriers had at times swarmed around its perimeter.

East of the Orne, the British 6th Airborne Division's attack had been as successful as it realistically could have been, and key bridges on the Orne canal, such as the now famous 'Pegasus Bridge', had been taken. German attention had been dragged away from the assault beaches, and by noon the paratroopers, having landed just after midnight, were well established in what would become their 'Airborne Bridgehead', and were waiting to be reinforced. Canadian participation within the British 6th Airborne Division airborne operations, though out of the scope of this book, consisted of the 1st Canadian Parachute Battalion, and they were successful in their part of the airborne landings near Varaville, fighting a battle against the German defenders near a manor house and successfully accomplishing their objectives for the most part. On 6 June they established their part of a strong eastern flank blocking German reinforcements and potential counterattacks along the coast against the landing beaches.[42]

To conclude, the day had been one of outstanding military success. That said, Anglo-Canadian attempts past noon on 6 June to advance on Caen had not been fanatical, and the farthest the British 3rd Infantry Division's forces had advanced that day was to Biéville. While the British Second Army headquarters and its Operational Order No. 1 on 21 April 1944 had detailed the importance of capturing Caen, formation-level operation orders distributed by the British 1st Corps had weakened this directive in the eyes of the brigade and divisional commanders, especially those in the British 3rd Infantry Division. As a result, far less impetus and importance was placed on the capture of some or all of the city by last light. Reviewing points C and D of the *Neptune* Operation Order reprinted in the Canadian official history of the campaign in north-west Europe, Point C outlines 'possible conditions that may forestall or delay the capture of the city', one of these being strong enemy resistance or threat of immediate counterattack. As these 'conditions' were present, this was enough for the British brigade commanders to not drive forward with reckless abandon. In addition to real and threatened possible German countermoves, especially from the regrouped *21. Pz.Div.*, the British high command very much believed it was imperative that their forces had to be ready to defend against these possible attacks in order for their bridgehead to survive. Thus, they constrained their forces from an all-out push south that evening.[43]

CHAPTER 6

The march of the *12. SS-Panzerdivision*, 6–8 June 1944

Within France, the *Wehrmacht*'s most powerful land forces, among them the *Hitlerjugend*, were deployed very poorly to rapidly react to an invasion on the coastline of northern France, that is, to fight the Allies on the beaches. The impact of the poor planning of *Gen.d.Pz.Tr.* von Schweppenburg and *G.F.M.* von Rundstedt had hampered the military capability of *G.F.M.* Rommel's *H.Gr.B.* to a tremendous degree, placing the majority of the *Panzerdivisionen* too far from the realistic front line of the beaches to react within the critical window of time during which the Allied units in the landing stage of amphibious operations were vulnerable. Many *Panzerdivisionen* were also not under Rommel's control, and though this would change later in the Normandy campaign, what mattered was the present. German doctrine demanded maximum effort at the *Schwerpunkt* (focus point) of any Panzer attack. If the *Panzerdivisionen* were scattered throughout France's interior or were not accessible due to them being *OKW* reserves, they could not be assembled quickly near the coast in a concentrated manner.

The aforementioned deployment of the *Hitlerjugend* had the division widely spread out in the Bernay–Gacé–Elbeuf–Louiviers–Dreux area, destroying its military capability to reach the beaches quickly. Instead, it would spend the entirety of 6 June either preparing to move or involved in an extended route march to the invasion sector, harried – though not as badly as some German formations – from the air by Allied fighter-bombers during daylight hours.

The D-Day response of the *Hitlerjugend* to the invasion was as effective as possible given the leadership and direction it was provided with from higher levels of command. Due to the incredibly poor German intelligence capabilities, the division was totally in the dark in the days leading up to the invasion as to the massive Allied operation in its final stages of preparation.

At roughly midnight on 5 June, the first reports began to filter into the *Hitlerjugend* divisional headquarters west of Acon from the sector of the *711. Inf.Div.* east of the

Orne in the coastal area of responsibility of the German *15. Armee.* These reports consisted of accounts of dummy parachutists being dropped over the area near Houlgate. It was assessed that these actions were not a major military operation but rather an attempt to see how the German forces within France and the *Atlantikwall* might react, as well as to see whether they could be diverted away from a true amphibious landing site. The German military response at the headquarters level was made difficult for the headquarters staffs involved, as the airborne landings had occurred very close to the *Armee* boundary between the *7. Armee* and the *15. Armee,* the Orne River. Both sets of headquarters were now reporting to the *Hauptquartier* of *H.Gr.B.*, clogging its signals sections with messages and overwhelming the overnight staff and duty officers.

At 0130 hours *H.Gr.B. Chef des Stabes, Gen.Maj.* Speidel, received reports of paratroopers from *7. Armee Chef des Stabes Gen.Maj.* Pemsel that paratroopers were in contact with German forces. Speidel was not entirely convinced at this stage that this was anything more than a raid or diversion. This would turn out to be a critical impediment to the successful response of German forces in the area. *7. Armee* units on the coastline also reported a large number of warships in the Channel, ironically detected by artillery sound ranging equipment, not radar, these installations having been destroyed or incapacitated by weeks of non-stop air attack.[1]

While mass confusion occurred within the German *OKW* and *H.Gr.D./O.B. West Hauptquartiere* on the night of 5/6 June as to what was really occurring and where, rapid individual reports began to filter into the *Hitlerjugend Gefechtsstand* near Tillières-sur-Avre, France, shortly after midnight concerning the airborne drops with dummy paratroopers in the sectors of the *Atlantikwall* units to the north-west.[2] Communication with said units and the neighbouring *21. Pz.Div.* did not result in a clear intelligence picture being delivered, and the situation remained unclear.[3] Due to poor *Luftwaffe* and *Kriegsmarine* intelligence gathering abilities, *OKW* had no idea even on 5 June that thousands of ships were steaming out of their ports on the southern English coast into the Channel, and that the decisive event, one of the greatest of the Second World War, was underway.[4]

Brig.Fhr. Witt first received these reports with his staff at his manor house headquarters, and initially there was no great cause for alarm. The divisional staff went to bed, but Witt remained awake, and at 0130 hours the first combat reports of paratrooper landings near and to the east of the Orne were reported, and the divisional commander woke up the *Ia, Stubaf.* Hubert Meyer, in order to discuss with him whether to put the division on high alert.

Still in darkness, the château of Tillières-sur-Avre exploded into a flurry of activity as the divisional *Gefechtsstand* of the *Hitlerjugend* came to life upon receiving updated news of the invasion. These were more detailed reports on the drops of actual US, British and Canadian paratroopers on both flanks of what would become the Normandy invasion beaches. After a flurry of radio and field telephone traffic, the division received the message it was subordinated to the *I. SS-Panzerkorps*, but after this, any clear orders or first communication from this *Korps Hauptquartier* never arrived. Amazingly, the *Hitlerjugend*'s parent *Panzerkorps*, commanded by *Ogruf.* Dietrich, would not be alerted until 1000 hours, meaning this headquarters lost critical planning and coordination time. The situation was made worse by Dietrich's absence, as at the time he was in Brussels, Belgium.[5]

Brigadenführer Witt, on his own initiative, had by this stage put the formations and units of the division on high alert. The staff of the divisional headquarters had immediately swung into action, alerting all the units and formations within the *Hitlerjugend* which were spread throughout the surrounding area, as well as those involved in exercises put on by the two *SS-Panzergrenadierregimenter*. Slowly but surely over the next few hours all parts of the division came to life in their various locations.

The mass of the *Hitlerjugend*, if it was to travel west from Bernay straight to Caen and then straight north to the coastal town of Bernières-sur-Mer, was at its closest point 102 kilometres away from the invasion beaches. As time passed and the division frantically readied itself in the darkness for a road march in the shortest time possible, more reports and orders arrived at 0230 hours, first from *H.Gr.B.*, relaying a request from *15. Armee Hauptquartier* for reconnaissance forces from the *Hitlerjugend* be sent north to the sector of the *711. Inf.Div.*, located to its immediate north. This static division, neighbour of the *716. Inf.Div.* west of the Orne, was now involved in combat with British 6th Airborne Division forces. The aforementioned *Hitlerjugend* reconnaissance forces were requested to gain information on which enemy forces had landed, and to make contact with the *711. Inf.Div.* Reports from the *Gefechtsstand* on this static division at Chateau Le Quesnay, north of Glanville and nine kilometres north of Pont-l'Évêque, indicated heavy combat with British airborne units and that the sounds of battle could be heard nearby.[6]

By 0240 hours, the *Hitlerjugend* received orders to increase its march readiness from *H.Gr.B.*; similar commands at this time were being issued to several German *Divisionen* located within the interior of northern France.[7] While this was all well and good, and the higher headquarters had to give increased readiness orders prior to directing a fighting formation to advance into a combat zone, precious time was slipping away. The Germans were still somewhat blind to the main threat in the way of an armada already in the English Channel and bearing down on the second rate *Atlantikwall* defences. This would only change at 0325 hours, when the *Kriegsmarine* Naval Group West alerted *H.Gr.D./O.B. West* that hundreds of landing craft and other vessels were literally filling up the Channel off the Calvados coast. Shortly afterward, at 0410 hours *H.Gr.B.* put both the *7.* and *15. Armeen* and all their respective *Atlantikwall* units on high alert.[8]

Acting aggressively and understanding speed was of the essence, at 0445 von Rundstedt made the formal request to *OKW* to have access to the armoured divisions.

This was followed by the telephone lobbying of *7. Armee Chef des Stabes Gen.Maj.* Pemsel to *H.Gr.B.* to secure the release of the *21. Pz.Div.* to *LXXXIV. Armeekorps* for immediate action against the attacking British airborne forces.

It is important at this time to observe, incredibly, that when the real invasion occurred, the Panzer debate on whether to engage the invading Allied enemy on the beaches or hold off and engage them in a battle of envelopment within northern France, which had gone on for months, was completely forgotten in the frenzied efforts of the German high command in France and Germany to react in a speedy manner.

By late afternoon on 6 June, elements of several German *Divisionen* were alerted, en route or preparing to engage Allied units on the beaches or as close as they could get to them. The impact of the poor deployment decisions that had been made which placed German forces inland was immediately felt by German unit and formation commanders, who, while they were not completely ignorant of Allied fighter bombers, were about to feel the full impact of their bombing and strafing. The fighters would be present as soon as there was enough light to fly on 6 June and would immediately begin to attack any and all German reconnaissance units that had driven forward on the roads during the early morning on their way north to the Caen–Bayeux sector.

By 0500 hours, the *15. Armee*, in whose area of responsibility a small part of the airborne landings occurred, requested the release of the *Hitlerjugend* from *OKW* reserve in order to deploy it immediately to the area north-east and north-west of Lisieux in order to support the *711. Inf.Div.* in its battle with airborne forces. By this time, it is important to note that no actual landing forces had reached the beaches in the eastern part of the landing zone, these being Gold, Juno and Sword. The situation was very unclear to the Germans, and while this would change quickly in the hours to come, for the moment they were literally blind to events right off the coast, the Allied ships being largely hidden in the darkness.

As time slipped by, the *Oberbefehlshaber West*, G.F.M. von Rundstedt, took matters into his own hands and on his own initiative and responsibility released the *Hitlerjugend* to *H.Gr.B.*

At 0550 hours the first deployment order came from *H.Gr.B.* to *Pz.Gr.West*, to which the division had been subordinated prior to the invasion, for the *Hitlerjugend* to deploy to a new assembly area, Bernay–Lisieux–Vimoutiers, as soon as possible to be ready to support the units of the *15. Armee* in action east of the Orne.[9] On arrival its leadership was to establish contact with the *Gefechtsstände* of the nearby *84. Inf.Div.* and *711. Inf.Div.*, in order to coordinate future operations. Additional *Flak* units were to be deployed to support the movement of the division and provide some protection from roving Allied fighter-bombers.[10] At approximately 0700 hours, the order to move was transmitted to *Brig.Fhr.* Witt and his headquarters staff.[11]

Shortly after these events, at 0645 hours, *H. Gr. B. Chef des Stabes Gen. Maj.* Speidel finally released the *21. Pz. Div.*, a not insignificant force containing 104 Panzer IV tanks, 40 self-propelled guns on French tracked chassis and a number of obsolete French tanks.[12] An important observation at this time is that as these critical hours slipped by, the *21. Pz. Div.*, the *Panzerdivision* closest to the coast, was having its ability to attack en masse (with the aim of achieving one main objective or clearing one area) slowly reduced. Each report of paratroopers was forcing it to consider responding to everything, and it was failing to concentrate forces or keep them in reserve to do so. Its headquarters, missing its *Kommandeur Gen. Maj.* Feuchtinger along with his *Ia Generalstabsoffizier*, the former having to be dragged from a Paris night club in the early hours of the morning, was being distracted by a multitude of reports from dozens of sectors, all seemingly awash with paratroopers.

The problem with moving the *Hitlerjugend* north-west into an area north of Lisieux was that its new concentration zone compressed the division into a smaller area than had been planned, and there were only two viable routes with an equally reduced number of bridges instead of the four routes that were chosen for the previously arranged *Aufmarch B* plan. Moving the *Hitlerjugend* would involve thousands of vehicles, and two routes instead of four would slow its movement considerably. To the *Hitlerjugend Gefechtsstand* staff, this movement order seemed totally arbitrary, and it appeared the higher headquarters had ignored the previous planning effort which the division had made to organise routes to the coast. The order also ignored the current deployment of the division, as some of its units had deployed north of the east–west line Lisieux–Bernay. These parts of the division would have to travel south-west and then north-west to get to the new assembly area, wasting time. Ridiculously, some parts of the division would temporarily march away from the airborne landing zones and then be redirected north due to the road network.

These decisions made in the middle of the night under pressure and in haste seemingly did not consider the size of the *Hitlerjugend*, it being a near-fully equipped *Panzerdivision* with thousands of wheeled and tracked vehicles. Moving the formation was no easy task, and it was difficult for it to correct its course of march quickly once it was underway. As mentioned previously, the immediate response of the *Hitlerjugend* divisional and regimental *Gefechtsstand* staff when the news of the deployment order reached them one was one of dismay, as an entirely new planning effort to move the division in a coordinated manner would now have to be enacted again, and this would take time.

As the *Hitlerjugend* assembled its vehicle columns, the reports from west of the Orne became more serious. The first amphibious landings had taken place and the *Atlantikwall* bunkers were under attack. At 0925 hours the German *LXXXIV. Armeekorps* reported that Canadian and British tanks were overrunning the coastal artillery positions and their bunkers behind the invasion beaches. At this point *Gen. d. Artl.* Marcks, *LXXXIV. Armeekorps Oberbefehlshaber*, ordered the *21. Pz. Div.*

to redeploy those of its forces which could be moved west of the Orne to do so and confront the British.

At 1000 hours, the first units of the *Hitlerjugend* in France finally began to move, departing via a series of routes to take it to new concentration area. As it moved, communications intensified between various German senior *Kommandeure* at the *Armee*, *Armeegruppe* and *OKW* levels. Very luckily for the division, in the area of Lisieux there was low cloud, strong winds and intermittent rain showers, helping reduce the fighter bomber presence in the area.[13] Bizarrely, as the division began to move, *Gen.Maj.* Jodl of *OKW* countermanded the order releasing the *Hitlerjugend*, returning it to its previous status as a *OKW* reserve, but allowed its current movement to continue. Luckily for the Allies and tragically for the later military fortunes of the *Panzer-Lehr*, this formation was also ordered to remain for the moment in its assembly area south-west of Paris. It was hoped by *OKW* at this stage that the *7. Armee* could 'Dieppe' the Allied forces that had landed with its own resources. This was wishful thinking to say the least, and reflected a lack of appreciation of the situation from the *OKW* staff officers with the *Führer* in Berchtesgaden. That said, there was also the perception by Hitler and others back in Germany that this was not the 'real' invasion, but a diversionary operation.[14]

At 1415 hours, Rundstedt, made painfully aware of the situation west of the Orne, north of Caen, again petitioned *OKW* to release the *Hitlerjugend* for action north of Caen. At 1430 hours, much to the relief of the *7. Armee*, the *Hitlerjugend*, which had not yet reached its new assembly area north of Lisieux, as well as the *Panzer-Lehr*, were finally released to *H.Gr.B.* and later *7. Armee* direct command. Nearly 14 hours since the beginning of the airborne assault on Normandy, the *Hitlerjugend* would finally be deployed to Caen to combat the Allied ground forces advancing ever closer to the ancient Norman city.

Accordingly, the *7. Armee* issued orders to both divisions through the correct chain of command, this again being through the *Hauptquartier* of *Panzergruppe West* instead of directly to the divisional *Kommandeure*. Inexplicably, these new orders only reached the *Hitlerjugend* at 1700 (!) hours, and vital time was lost. The key excerpt from the *7. Armee* telephone log message to *Pz.Gr.West* is translated as follows:

> The *12. SS-Panzerdivision* is to move forward immediately north of the axis Alecon–Carrouges–Flers into the area around Evrecy. The division subordinated initially to *LXXXIV. Armeekorps*.
> Assignment: Operating on the left flank of the *21. Pz.Div.*, it is to throw the enemy west of the Orne into the sea and destroy him.
> To *Panzer-Lehr Panzerdivision*: As ordered by *H.Gr.B.*, the division to advance immediately south of the said axis and reach initially the area Flers–Vire.[15]

The *Hitlerjugend*, now entirely in motion, had to re-route itself, and coordinate its columns to re-orient themselves onto the routes identified for *Aufmarch C*, the deployment plan previously rehearsed to send them to into the Orne sector. As night approached, the columns of the *Hitlerjugend*, many using a wide variety of routes rather than just one or two due to their shift in direction of movement, began to snake closer to Caen. Some immediately used the excellent, paved Route Nationale 13, which led straight to Caen on a near east–west axis from Lisieux.[16]

While the *Hitlerjugend* was temporarily subordinated to the *LXXXIV. Armeekorps* of *Gen.d.Artl.* Marcks, this would just be for a short time, as the *I. SS. Pz.Korps*, temporarily led by *Chef des Stabes Brig.Fhr.* Kraemer until *Ogruf.* Dietrich could return from Belgium and meet up with his now travelling *Hauptquartier*, was placed under the command of the *7. Armee* at 1500 hours. This was done by *G.F.M.* von Rundstedt with the express purpose of coordinating the action of *Panzerdivisionen* in action or on the way to the area west of the Orne, these being the *21. Pz.Div.*, *Panzer-Lehr* and *Hitlerjugend*.

In order to reach Normandy, the *I. SS-Panzerkorps Hauptquartier* departed immediately with its more mobile elements via the route Nantes–Foreux–Trun to Falaise, suffering heavy air attack during the remaining daylight of 6 June as it got closer to the front.[17] Kraemer mentions in his post-war account that he met *Brig.Fhr.* Witt south of Caen and discussed its deployment. Both men had time to acclimatise themselves to the situation in order to assist them in planning and writing orders, but, conversely, they also lost precious time in reaching the battle zone. This was at roughly the same time as the *Hitlerjugend* was re-routed, which was likely between 1400 and 1600 hours on 6 June. At 1610 hours *SS-Pz.Gren.Rgt. 25* reported in its *Kriegstagebuch* entry for 6 June that it was now on *Aufmarch* (route) 'C' – this being a prearranged route to the Caen sector and which was near St Pierre-sur-Ifs.[18] Very challenging for all staff officers and *Kommandeure* at this time was the complete radio silence order given by *H.Gr.D./O.B. West* regarding any and all radio traffic, and the overwhelming fighter bomber presence on all main roads, stopping columns again and again as the drivers and occupants of vehicles dove into ditches as the fighters screamed overhead in their strafing runs. On the evening of 6 June *I. SS-Pz.Korps Oberbefehlshaber Ogruf.* Dietrich would finally reach Normandy, meeting his *Chef des Stabes Brig.Fhr.* Kraemer at 2000 hours in St Pierre-sur-Dives and managing to visit the *21. Pz.Div. Gefechtsstand*.[19] An appalling scene met Dietrich as he reached this headquarters, the division *Kommandeur* being missing and only the *Ia* staff officer present. The *21. Pz.Div.* forces were spread all over the front on both sides of the Orne River and had been completely rebuffed by the British in their late afternoon aborted counterattack (described in the previous chapter). Thus, the possibility of another concentrated thrust against the Allies by this division alone was, at this time, impossible. It was the only German formation holding the front line in many areas, as the *Atlantikwall* forces by now had largely been destroyed. What was left of the *716. Inf.Div.* were scattered fragments and rear area troops. The *711. Inf.Div.* east of the Orne, part of the *15. Armee*, had anxiously demanded, and received, elements of *Pz.Rgt. 22* to help it take on British paratroopers.[20] On top of this situation, it was clear by the fall of darkness on 6 June that the *Hitlerjugend*, marching towards

Caen and bedevilled by fighter-bombers the closer it got to it, would not be ready for combat operations before 7–8 June. Considering this situation and the current known and unknow locations of the main bodies of the *Hitlerjugend, 21. Pz.Div.*, and *Panzer-Lehr*, Dietrich reportedly made the decision then and there that no coordinated action would be possible until 8 June at the earliest.[21]

As previously briefly discussed, the first unit of the division to deploy to the combat zone was composed of the reconnaissance patrols of *SS-Panzeraufklärungabteilung 12*, the armoured reconnaissance battalion of the division. Led by *Stubaf.* Gerd Bremer, the *Abteilung* was fully mechanised and contained a wide variety of vehicles. At 0230 hours it was alerted to prepare a series of recce patrols towards the combat zone, primarily into the area of the *711. Inf.Div.* on the eastern flank of the invasion zone. The *1. Kompanie* of the *Abteilung* was broken up into patrols of several vehicles, each led by an officer or senior non-commissioned officer (NCO) and well equipped with fuel, ammunition and stores to allow for an extended period of operations over several days. These patrols were to cover a vast area, from the mouth of the Seine to the city of Bayeux. The patrols were directed to ascertain what enemy forces were present and where, what they had achieved by this time, and what their intentions were, if possible.[22]

One of the patrols of *1. (Panzerspäh) Kompanie* of *SS-Pz.Aüfkl.Abt. 12* under *Kompanie-Chef Ostuf.* Hansmann pushed north to its assigned sector of Caen, though the congested roads and streets of villages were now clogged with assembling *Heer* forces, much of them from the *21. Pz.Div.* On reaching the city in the foggy early morning of 6 June, the soldiers of *SS-Pz.Aüfkl.Abt. 12* had trouble finding the Caen military *Kommandeur* to gain information, and their progress through bombed out streets was further hindered by a mass of *Heer* vehicles and dismounted troops gathering beside the roads in the half light. As they passed, they witnessed *Heer Feldgendarmerie* struggling to impose some kind of order on the traffic movement going in and out of the city in all directions.

Pushing further north-west of Caen toward Bayeaux and the invasion beaches, Hansmann and his patrol of eight-wheeled Sd.Kfz.234 armoured cars bypassed Bayeux, then under attack from fighter-bombers, and advanced north to approach the Bay of Arromanches and the village of Arromanches-les-Bains. Ironically, this would be the future home to the mammoth Allied Mulberry Harbour logistics offloading area, one of two later established during the Normandy campaign to support the Allied forces. On arrival, the Germans set out to inch their way towards the British soldiers now observed in the sand dunes with armoured support in the way of Sherman DD tanks. On reaching a high point near the Bay of Arromanches to observe the whole spectacle, the armoured car crews saw the great swath of ships offshore, seemingly hundreds of them, with flashes of gunfire emerging from cruisers, destroyers and battleships.[23] The time would have been roughly 0800 hours, the British by this point having overwhelmed parts of the beach defences. There was still significant fighting going on, but the reconnaissance forces of the *Hitlerjugend*, true to their role, did not get involved in combat but continued their observation of the battlefield and sending reports. In the course of making radio transmissions, they were taken under naval gunfire and forced to withdraw. As they withdrew, they did observe the effects of naval bombardment, seeing houses set on fire in Tracy, St Sluice-Sur and Arromanches as they pulled back from this first *Hitlerjugend* contact with the enemy.

Hansmann's translated radio report reads:

> Hundreds of enemy ships sighted, protected by large balloons. British infantry and heavy equipment coming ashore virtually unopposed. A dozen heavy tanks counted. Coastal defences either out of action or overrun. Enemy infantry in battalion strength moving south towards Bayeux. The city itself, and the roads leading into it, under naval bombardment.[24]

Far to the east, at various vital crossings over the Seine, the *Batterien* of *SS-Flak.Abt. 12*, the motorised anti-aircraft battalion of the division, had received orders that it was to prepare to move again. In order to help defend these Seine crossings from the ongoing 'Transportation Plan' of the Allied air offensive on northern France in the weeks leading up to the invasion, the *Flak Abteilungen* of both the *Panzer-Lehr* and the *Hitlerjugend* had been deployed to several locations along this river to the east of the main bodies of their *Divisionen*. Once the movements of both *Divisionen* were confirmed on 6 June, both their respective *Gefechtsstand* ordered their *Batterien* to defend new, vital bridge crossings on their anticipated march routes. In due course, on 6 June *SS-Flak Abteilung 12*, whose *Gefechtsstand* was initially located at Louviers, had to move its *Batterien* to the Lisieux area to attempt to beat the divisional units there, then quickly re-deploy as the order came to send the *Hitlerjugend* to Caen.

Word reached *SS-Flak Abteilung 12*, whose record is largely ignored in histories of the *Hitlerjugend*, in its *Gefechtsstand* in Louviers, to increase its readiness level to march at 0600 hours. By 0800 hours it was ordered to march via the route Gaillon–Louviers–Le Neuborg–Lisieux, with the order of march being *1. Batterie, 3. Batterie, Stab, 2. Batterie*, and lastly, *4. Batterie*. These groupings set off at 0930 hours with some parts of *2.* and *4. Batterien* left to defend the Les Andelys crossing of the Seine. By 1800 hours *1.* and *3. Batterien* were emplaced in the area of Lisieux.[25]

Once the new order came to send the *Hitlerjugend* to Caen, the *Flak Batterien* were told to pack up and leave almost as soon as they arrived. They were directed, at 1840 hours, to move towards the west in the tracks of *SS-Pz.Aüfkl.Abt. 12*, in order to protect the Orne crossings at Amayé–Les Moutiers. One by one, the *Batterien* of the *Abteilung* got going again, *3. Batterie* receiving the order to move west at 1900 hours.

All this movement was disrupted by a major air attack on the town of Lisieux on the evening of 6 June by 80 B-24 Liberator four-engine bombers, as recorded in the war diary of *SS-Flak Abt. 12*. Significant damage was done to roads, and the last entry of the war diary for the day indicates that all throughout the evening of 6 June the march columns of the *Hitlerjugend* were under heavy air attack on the route of advance the closer they got to Caen.

Reviewing the *SS-Flak Abteilung 12* actions, all their travel time could have been used to fight fighter bombers that flew at treetop level along the main roads. The anti-aircraft fire the *Hitlerjugend Flak* expended to defend itself on 6 June was thus not intense, and the *Kriegstagebuch* of *SS-Flak.Abt. 12* recorded only thirty-six 8.8cm rounds being fired, and only seven hundred 2cm. This shows that the *Abteilung* was more focused on movement than engaging the enemy 'Jabos' (Jagdbomber).[26]

For *SS-Panzergrenadier-Regiment 25*, the process of readying its *SS-Panzergrenadier Bataillone* for march was more straightforward at the lower-level headquarters as less of a planning process was needed for movement, the requirement to move at very short notice having already been anticipated. Taking *I. Btl./SS-Pz.Gren.Rgt. 25* as an example, the following sequence of events took place:

- The code word 'Blucher' was received (meaning: invasion – be ready to march within 90 minutes) at 0555 hours.
- The *Bataillon* was ready to march by 0600 hours, as its preparatory activities had been going on in a frenzied manner since 0330 hours.
- Later in the morning, orders were received via field phone for Deployment Plan 'Z' to the new assembly area, using route (*Aufmarch*) 'B'. These orders were only received at 1000 hours, reflecting the time the higher divisional headquarters staff consumed to plot new, altered routes for the division.[27]

The actual movement plan for the units and formations of the *Hitlerjugend* was complicated, and march serials had to be devised for the order of the route march to both prevent anarchy from erupting on the roads and to allow units to retain cohesion. The road march of the *Hitlerjugend SS-Panzergrenadierregiment* closest to the invasion beaches, that of the *SS-Pz.Gren.Rgt. 25*, which marched to Caen from near Vimoutiers, was rather uneventful. It did not suffer from enemy action in comparison to the ordeals of the other large groupings from the *Hitlerjugend*.

Looking at events on the regimental level, on 6 June the *SS-Pz.Gren.Rgt. 25 Gefechtsstand* and its attached *II. Abt./SS-Pz.Rgt. 12* Panzer IV *Kompanien* were alerted at roughly 0330 hours. By 0415 hours the Panzer IV *Abteilung* was ready to march and had its *Kompanien* attached to each one of the *SS-Panzergrenadiere Bataillone*. Further direction for the move came at 0530 hours regarding the exact order of march.[28] The *7., 8.* and *9. Kompanien* had approximately 10 Panzer IVs each, while *5.* and *6. Kompanien* had 14 Panzer IVs. No *Kompanie* was at full tank establishment strength due to the decision to establish an unauthorised *9. Kompanie*.[29]

As stated, the march of *II. Abt./SS-Pz.Rgt. 12* within the columns of *SS-Pz.Rgt. 25* was uneventful and the lengthy columns, despite some problems with spacing due to driver inexperience, would miraculously not be attacked by fighter bombers in the move from Vimoutiers on the afternoon of 6 June. The weather did have some rainy periods, but for the most part there was clear flying weather. The fighter bombers of the RAF 2nd Tactical Air Force and USAAF 9th Air Force were occupied with flying over the actual invasion beaches and making their sweeps on main roads and the villages near the coast. It being early on in the Normandy campaign, the Allies were not established in airfields in France yet, and all the RAF, RCAF and USAAF sorties that left from southern England had to fly across the English Channel and back.

Finally moving at 1230 hrs, much later than some *Hitlerjugend* units that had begun moving at 1000 hours, the lead *Bataillon* in the column was *I. Btl./SS-Pz. Gren.Rgt. 25*, with the attached the *7.* and *8. Kp /SS-Pz.Rgt. 12* as well as the *II. Abt./ SS-Pz.Rgt. 12 Gefechtsstand* staff. Attached also to each *SS-Panzergrenadier Bataillon* were parts of *III. Abt./SS-Pz.Art.Rgt. 12*, but it is unclear which *Batterien* were with which *Bataillone*. It was reported that it marched in the order *Fühungstaffel, Stabesbatterie, 9. Batterie, 8. Batterie, 10. Batterie*, and finally *7. Batterie*.[30]

Spaced out at 100-metre intervals, this large column set out on the route initially laid out to take it north of Lisieux. It would then pivot at Livarot, driving to St Pierre-sur-Dives and then to Caen as per the new orders that arrived between 1600 and 1700 hours. Following it in sequence of march was *II. Btl./SS-Pz.Gren.Rgt. 25* with the attached *9. Kp./SS-Pz.Rgt. 12* and then the *III. Btl./SS-Pz.Gren.Rgt. 25* with the attached *5.* and *6. Kp./SS-Pz.Rgt. 12*. To monitor the movement of the Panzer IVs and establish radio contact with the divisional *Gefechtsstand*, *II. Abt./ SS-Pz.Rgt. 12* set up its *Abteilung Gefechtsstand* between St Pierre-sur-Ifs and the Lisieux–Saint-Pierre-sur-Dives road.[31] Total losses on 6 June for the *SS-Pz.Gren.Rgt. 25* columns were two killed, three wounded and six vehicles lost, all to air attack.[32] These losses may have been separate from the *III. Abt./SS-Pz.Art.Rgt. 12* columns, these reporting personnel losses of one killed, nine wounded and one missing, and vehicle losses totalling six.[33]

Further examining the units of *SS-Panzer Regiment 12* and their travels 6–8 June, not all went smoothly. When alerted, *SS-Pz.Rgt. 12* had been involved in exercises, and its two *Abteilungen* were conducting training and separated from their supply and maintenance sub-units when news of the invasion came via field phone to the regimental headquarters, located in Chateau d'Acquingny. *Ostubaf.* Wünsche was woken, and he immediately alerted the regimental staff, the officers of the *Stabskompanie* and the *Gefechtsstände* of the *I.* and *II. Abt./SS-Pz.Rgt. 12*. Using whistles, the men were roused from their sleep by their NCOs in the early morning of 6 June and swung into action.

Shortly after this the *Erkundungszug* (scout platoon) of the regimental *Gefechtsstand* was directed to scout a route for the *SS-Panzerregiment* headquarters and its *Stabskompanie* as well as the *I. Abteilung* Panther tanks. The distance of the planned route was initially judged to be roughly 130 kilometres, and would have to be traversed, it would turn out, during both daylight and nocturnal hours. The route would be marked with the tactical symbols of *SS-Pz.Rgt. 12*, some of these signs being marked with 'Wünsche' or the various sub-unit commanders in order to deprive French insurgents of the knowledge of which units were involved. This motorcycle sidecar-equipped unit was initially to take the route Mézidon–Manerbe towards the invasion beaches, this being the route for *SS-Pz.Rgt. 12* minus the parts exercising with *SS-Pz.Gren.Rgt. 25*. A senior non-commissioned officer and *Zugführer, Oscha.* Wontorra, would scout even further, to Valseme, 14 kilometres north-west of Lisieux.[34]

While they had been exercising with *SS-Pz.Gren.Rgt. 26*, the Panther *Kompanien*, the main combat power of the division, were not attached to this regiment as part of a designated *Kampfgruppe*. Their exercises had been going on since 4 June in the St Andre-sur-L'Eure area, and the individual *Kompanien* of the *Pantherabteilung* were billeted to villages around Le Neuborg. The *Abteilung* staff company was billeted in the town itself, on the eastern edge of the *Hitlerjugend* concentration area. Word of the invasion and the instruction to go on the alert reached all four Panther *Kompanien* between 0300 and 0800 hours. *Ostubaf.* Wünsche had planned out multiple routes for the movement of *SS-Pz.Rgt. 12* prior to the invasion. *Stubaf.* Jürgensen, the *Pantherabteilung Kommandeur*, was under orders to take his designed route, and began to make his *Abteilung* ready for the route march. Significant factors would slow him down. He would have to assemble and move the various maintenance and supply units, some attached to each Panther *Kompanien*, to where the Panthers were, and make sure the tanks were properly outfitted with fuel, munitions and all other consumables to allow the *Pantherabteilung* to go into combat when they reached the front. The supply and logistics units still had part of their vehicles, personnel and all the resources needed to supply the Panthers remaining within their cantonments, which were several kilometres away when news of the invasion came.

Though preparations for an extended route march went like clockwork, as this scenario had been rehearsed previously by the leadership of *SS-Pz.Rgt. 12*, it still took precious time. When the *Pantherabteilung* was finally ready to march, its earliest movement began in early evening. Due to the location of not only the mass of the division but its most powerful fighting element, the *Pantherabteilung*, the entire day passed before it could begin moving. As its elements desperately outfitted the Panthers with fuel and ammunition and made last minute repairs, the Allies were landing thousands of troops, tanks and artillery pieces and all the resources needed for them to fight. Despite this, morale was high. The crews of the Panther tanks were in good spirits and wished for operations to begin immediately. The *Kompanie-Chef* of the *4. Kompanie, Hstuf.* Pfeiffer, gave each *Züge* a speech in which he stated that they were not to be reckless, and that he could not accomplish anything with dead or wounded soldiers.

The order of march when the first columns set out finally at 1300 hours as part of the larger *SS-Pz.Gren.Rgt. 26* series of vehicle columns was *1. Kompanie*, followed by *4. Kompanie*. Setting out with 100-meter intervals between the tanks and the trucks and SPW 251 halftracks of *SS-Pz.Gren.Rgt. 26*, the Panthers found all routes heavily congested, as *Heer* and *Waffen-SS* units in the area became intermixed as they sought to move forward.[35] *Stubaf.* Jürgensen delayed the movement of the *Pantherabteilung* until each *Kompanie* could be partially assembled with the majority of its wheeled and tracked vehicles. The march route for the first two *Kompanien*, *1.* and *4.*, began south of Le Neuborg, and took the route St Andre–Damville–Breteuil–Le Ferte–Fresnil towards Gacé. Following these two lead *Kompanien*, the *3.* and finally the *2. Kompanie* headed out on the roads.

The area near the town of Lisieux was the scene of several heavy strafing and bombing runs by Allied fighter bombers. Though no Panthers were lost, the smooth traffic control practices with regard to vehicle spacing and organisation fell victim to the panic that ensued due to air attack. The darkness was lit up by wreckage still burning, these being the remains of Germans trucks and even some SPW 251 half-tracks knocked out by Allied fighter-bomber activity on all major approach routes to Normandy.

By evening, the *Kompanien* were found in the following locations: *1. Kompanie* had reached Berthouville, *2. Kompanie* was in Barsen, *3. Kompanie* was in Le Thiel–Nolent, and *4. Kompanie* had reached St Claire. The *Abteilung Stabskompanie* (staff company) had reached Boissy. Movement continuing near midnight on the night of 6/7 June saw the *Abteilung* continue west via the route Thiberville–Orbec–Monnai–Gacé.

In the mass movement, Panther *Züge* immediately became separated from their *Kompanie* vehicles and other *Züge* as other units began to intermix with the mass influx north. Free from the fighter-bombers, as the German units struggled forward in the darkness, fatigue and traffic congestion led to accidents, as the vehicles had all been driving with dimmed blackout lights.

From there the march continued all day on 7 June 1944 via Trun–Falaise–Thury Harcourthen to Amaye in the Maizet district as part of the larger *SS-Pz.Gren.Rgt. 26* movement.[36] At this point, while the *SS-Panzergrenadiere* kept moving, the *Pantherabteilung* movement was halted due to lack of fuel. The Panther tanks were dispersed under large trees and waited for fuel throughout the night of 7/8 June 1944. It is noted that at this time, a single Panther tank that had become separated from its *Kompanie* now rejoined it.[37] Frequent maintenance halts and Allied air activity had resulted in major traffic jams, causing delays.[38] Panther crews also drove at less than maximum speed during road moves to preserve engines and transmissions. Night driving would have been conducted in blackout conditions, also reducing speed to a minimum.

The march of the *Pantherabteilung* was much lengthier and more complicated than that of *II. Abteilung* with its Panzer IV tanks. In recent works by Anglophone authors, the mobility of the Panther has been highlighted as a significant weakness. Instances are recounted that suggest rail transport absolutely had to be used to get the Panthers close to the front to save on the wear and tear on highly fragile Panzers, a constant theme present in books on German armour.[39] Firmly addressing this topic regarding the Panther, the cutting edge of the *Hitlerjugend SS-Panzerregiment*, nothing could be further from the truth. The tank's improved reliability in the summer of 1944 allowed its crews to conduct long road moves. This was made evident by *Pantherabteilung* in Normandy conducting regular road marches during June–July 1944.[40]

On being ordered to the invasion front, the fastest way the leadership of the *I. Abt./SS-Pz.Rgt. 12* could get its Panthers there in the shortest possible time was by driving them. The 66 tanks of this unit covered a distance of roughly 140 kilometres to reach Caen, travelling from 6–8 June 1944 under frequent air attack. For a tank unit in the Second World War, this was a sizeable distance. In 1944, due to the level of technology present, a number of tanks per unit would be expected to fall out during a lengthy road march, despite maintenance and other halts, and regardless of an army's nationality.[41]

Combat losses during the march were relatively light for the *Pantherabteilung*. Taken as an example, in terms of the personnel losses to *I. Abt./SS-Pz.Rgt. 1* caused by enemy air attacks during the entire route march to the area south of Caen, one was soldier killed on 7 June 1944. Total vehicle losses consisted of four trucks and a Flakpanzer 38(t) of the anti-aircraft *Zug*. One supply truck was lost due to an accident and six other trucks were temporarily out of action.[42] Upon reaching the area south of Caen 20 kilometres from the front, the battalion had covered a total of 140 kilometres from its former billets at Le Neuborg. It is important to note that within the *I. Abt./SS-Pz. Rgt. 1 Kriegstagebuch* there is no evidence of a large number of vehicles falling out due to mechanical issues. The largest challenges during the march had been supplying the fuel requirements of the Panthers and avoiding losses due to fighter-bomber attacks which caused chaos on the roads leading to the *Invasionfront*.

Records on the 6–8 June movement of *SS-Pz.Aüfkl.Abt. 12*, *SS-Pz.Pio.Btl. 12*, *SS-Pz.Gren.Rgt. 26* and *SS-Pz.Art.Rgt. 12* into the area west of Caen are sparse, and better accounts exist on their final assembly in the area south of Cheux on the night of 7/8 June. Some data is present for *II. Abt./SS-Pz.Art.Rgt. 12*, which marched with its towed howitzers in the order of *4. Batterie*, *6. Batterie*, *5. Batterie* and finally the *Abteilung* supply and ammunition vehicles. Its journey was not peaceful, however, as its *5.* and *6. Batterien* suffered losses from air attack.[43] It is inferred that their movement was very slow and large intervals were placed between each vehicle in columns due to the threat of and actual air attacks. The columns starting from locations the farthest east under the command of *Ostubaf.* Mohnke had to travel 194 kilometres, much further than the *SS-Pz.Gren.Rgt. 25* forces under *Staf.* Meyer. The Panthers of *I. Abt./SS-Pz.Rgt. 12* did travel with *SS-Pz.Gren.Rgt. 26* for a short period and would have arrived with this regiment on the evening and night of 7/8 June had it not been for the aforementioned delayed fuel deliveries along the way and their voracious fuel consumption rates. This unit was not the only one to suffer from lack of fuel. The self-propelled *Artillerie* of *I. Abt./SS-Pz.Art.Rgt. 12* was reported as being stranded for a period at Feugerolles on 7 June, moving again when fuel arrived for it.[44]

Regarding *SS-Pz.Art.Rgt. 12*, the *II. Abt./SS-Pz.Art.Rgt. 12* of *Stubaf.* Schöps with its 10.5cm howitzers and the *I. Abt./SS-Pz.Art.Rgt. 12* of *Stubaf.* Urbanitz with its Wespe and Hummel self-propelled 10.5cm and 1.5cm *Artillerie* pieces did travel within the *SS-Pz.Gren.Rgt. 26*'s main body, arriving in the period 7–8 June. The *III. Abt.(Schwere)/SS-Pz.Art.Rgt. 12* of *Stubaf.* Bartling had already arrived on the night of 6/7 June with *SS-Pz.Gren.Rgt. 25*, and deployed in the Caen area.[45]

The *SS-Pz.Gren.Rgt. 26* order of march can be discerned from the arrival times of the *Bataillone* on the battlefield west of Caen in the period 7–8 June. First to arrive on the western flank of the *Hitlerjugend* across the Mue river (a tributary of the river Seulles) was the attached *SS-Pz.Aüfkl.Abt. 12*, which immediately began conducting recce screening duties as the main body of *SS-Pz.Gren.Rgt. 26* approached, their hundreds of vehicles festooned with foliage of all types to camouflage them. The order of arrival for the regiment was *I. Bataillon*, followed by *II. Bataillon* and lastly the *III. Btl.(Gepanzert)/SS-Pz.Gren.Rgt. 26*, which was impeded by the slower speeds of its SPW 251 half-tracks. Last in the columns was the attached *SS-Pz.Pio.Btl. 12*, which appears to have arrived on 8 June in the Cheux area. This unit was to suffer more than any other within the *Hitlerjugend* during the approach march, with its entire bridging section being destroyed by air attack near Evreux.[46] These strafing and bombing attacks by the Allied fighter-bombers were for the most part successful every time they took place, but not without cost; the *Flak Zug* of *SS-Pz.Art.Rgt. 12* shot down a Mustang on 7 June.[47]

However, the lack of written detail or first-hand accounts concerning heavy losses in *SS-Pz.Gren.Rgt. 26* implies that as a regiment and in comparison to other German formations on the road to Normandy it suffered only moderately from the 'Jabos'. There may be more to the story, but this is apparently lost to history, the *Kriegstagebuch* of *SS-Pz.Gren.Rgt. 26* entries only beginning at 12–13 June 1944, and being written only in pencil (versus the typed entries in the other surviving *Kriegstagebuch* war diaries of the division).[48] Concerning casualties from air attack, the *Hitlerjugend* had suffered, but it could have been far worse. Lost in the movement to the front were 83 casualties; 20 dead, 60 wounded and 1 missing.[49] In addition to the lost personnel, two significant losses had occurred which would impact the fighting in the period 7–11 June: the *I.* and *II. Abt./SS-Pz.Art.Rgt. 12* had a number of ammunition trucks destroyed in the transit period of 6–7 June, the losses in ammunition being 150 rounds of 10.5cm for the first unit and 800 rounds of 10.5cm for the second. Replacement for the munitions lost, as well as the vehicles destroyed – 38 in total for *SS-Pz.Art.Rgt. 12* – would be desperately needed in the fighting ahead.[50]

CHAPTER 7

The first battle of Caen: The 7 June 1944 attack of *SS-Pz. Gren. Rgt. 25*

The attack of *SS-Pz. Gren. Rgt. 25* with its attached armoured forces and support from the *Hitlerjugend* divisional artillery on the afternoon of 7 June has been discussed within many works on the *Hitlerjugend* and the bridgehead battles of the 3rd Canadian Infantry Division. There are a multitude of different historical appreciations of the event, and while the purpose of this chapter is to describe in detail the day's military operations, it will allow the author to present an encompassing conclusion on the outcome of the fighting. The day's events would be important, and this chapter will also summarise what military goals were attained, what losses were suffered by both sides and outline a series of war crimes that occurred post-combat. While this was but one day of fighting on one specific part of the Normandy bridgehead, this fighting would determine the front-line north of the city of Caen for nearly a month to follow and effectively rob the *Hitlerjugend* of the ability to launch concentrated counterattacks due to it being forced to hold this section of the line.

The events that led to only one half of the *Hitlerjugend* being committed to intense combat with British and Canadian forces on 7 June, instead of the entire division en masse on a limited frontage in close cooperation with other German forces, utilising maximum force, make up one of the greatest military failures of *H. Gr. B.* during its campaign in France in 1944. It was critical to defeat the Anglo-Canadian forces within the beachhead in a conclusive manner that drove them right back into the English Channel quickly, and this did not occur. While some tactical victories were won, the decisive all-or-nothing stroke was not achieved.

The chief protagonist for the day's events was the force which held the initiative for the first part of the day: the NNSH-SFR vanguard force of the 9th Canadian Infantry Brigade, described in detail in Chapter 5. Examining events from midnight within the Anglo-Canadian lines on 7 June, sporadic combat continued into the hours of darkness. During this time small groups of German forces aggressively attempted to establish themselves in the area north of Caen with mixed results, and many Canadian patrols ventured south.

The front lines of the 3rd Canadian Infantry Division's 8th and 9th Canadian Infantry Brigades, supported by the armour of the 2nd Canadian Armoured Brigade, were anything but straight on divisional situation maps on the night of 6/7 June 1944. These lines curved wildly due to German resistance and the Allied halt order issued during the late evening on 6 June that froze the movement of Canadian units in their most advanced positions at the conclusion of D-Day. The 9th Canadian Infantry Brigade forces had dug in for the night facing south and occupied a line spanning Beny-sur-Mer–Basly–Villons-les-Buissons–Anisy, these areas captured in the last push forward in the evening of 6 June. On the rear left flank of the division facing south, the German strongpoint of the *Luftwaffe* Douvres radar station remained uncaptured, and the villages of La Deliverance and Luc-sur-Mer remained in German hands. A large gap of 5.4 kilometres still existed between the Juno Beach lodgement and the British-held Sword Beach, the British 3rd Infantry Division forces only holding parts of the coastal town of Lion-sur-Mer. On the left flank, forces of the British 185th Infantry Brigade had advanced significantly on D-Day and had possession of the two towns of Biéville and Beuville. But German *21. Pz.Div.* forces were now in front of the British, holding Lébisey village, the nearby wooded area and the high ground on which both locations lay.

Sporadic contact with German forces continued through the night. In the early morning, a German reconnaissance force attacked the western perimeter of the Le Régiment de la Chaudière and the North Nova Scotia Highlanders (NNSH) within their brigade 'fortress' positions. Moving aggressively in darkness to detect the forward positions of Allied forces, one small *Zug* grouping of these half-tracks was detected and fired on by Canadian tanks and NNSH infantry, a number of vehicles being destroyed and the *Panzergrenadiere* who had not been killed being captured in the process. However, a larger second group of half-track mounted infantry did inflict heavy losses on A Company of Le Régiment de la Chaudière, this *Kompanie*-level night attack destroying part of the Francophone company and taking 41 prisoners in the raid. It is unclear which unit the Canadians were in contact with due to a gap in the *21. Pz.Div.* historiography of the period, but it was most probably *Hptm.* Hoegl's newly arrived *Pz.Pio.Btl. 220*, which was part of the *Pz.Gren.Rgt. 192 Kampfgruppe* Rauch and charged with holding the line on the left flank of the division.[1]

Once this combat finished, a process which had been ingrained into the Canadian tank crews after several years of exercises undertaken in southern England – that of harbouring for the night – took place. All the tanks from the three SFR squadrons, as well as from the recce troop moved back to La Mare, just north of Anguerny, for the night. Once there they re-armed, refuelled and let the crews sleep in or under the tanks for a few hours, which sheltered them from artillery.

Despite the success of the 9th Canadian Infantry Brigade and its supporting armour up to this point, a serious incident occurred this night that would have lasting repercussions. Travelling back to the 2nd Canadian Armoured Brigade headquarters from the SFR regimental headquarters in two armoured cars, the SFR regimental signals officer and adjutant stumbled into a German ambush near the Colomby-sur-Thaon crossroads. The Canadian occupants of both vehicles fled into the darkness, but unfortunately some were captured or shot in the process. Within the scout car of the signals officer, brigade-level signals codebooks were found, and these were used by the Germans in the following days during combat operations against Anglo-Canadian forces.[2]

As morning broke on 7 June, the Canadian units of the vanguard prepared to press on. It can be said with some certainty that almost every soldier and officer within the NNSH vanguard force in the beachhead was suffering from some form of sleep deprivation, and in some cases the night of 6/7 June was the second night in a row in which they had little to no sleep. 6 June had been very busy with the disembarkation, relentless waiting in traffic, slow movement due to traffic congestion and finally some minor combat with weak German screening forces. An important question to consider is how this affected the planning, command and control of future operations on D +1.

Canadian advances planned for 7 June called for the 9th Canadian Infantry Brigade vanguard to move quickly to secure those D-Day objectives which had not been attained on 6 June, these being along the 'Oak' phase line. On the left flank of the 3rd Canadian Infantry Division facing south, this push would involve the vanguard pushing south past the Route Nationale 13 highway, the Caen–Bayeux rail line and finally onto the Carpiquet airfield west of the suburbs of Caen.

Unknown to the headquarters of the 9th Canadian Infantry Brigade, on 7 June the British 3rd Infantry Division on its left flank had largely abandoned plans for a renewed advance on Caen proper, and only select units of the British 185th and 9th Infantry Brigades had received orders to advance. Its operation would be halted on the aforementioned high feature of Lébisey Wood, north of village of the same name, by stiff resistance from *21. Pz.Div.* forces. Instead of a massive onslaught south, British efforts on 7 June would concentrate on establishing firm links with the Canadian forces on its right flank along the coast, eliminating any remaining *716. Infanterie-Division* pockets of resistance on the *Atlantikwall*, and redeploying forces to reinforce the British 6th Airborne Division in the 'Airborne' bridgehead east of the Orne.[3]

To the rear of the 9th Canadian Infantry Brigade, the 8th Canadian Infantry Brigade was ordered to establish a firm left flank for the 3rd Canadian Infantry Division, in effect a virtually insurmountable barrier should a large German counterattack emerge from Caen during the day. The Regiment de la Chaudière, the North Shore (New Brunswick) Regiment and the Queen's Own Rifles of Canada thus worked to establish strong defensive positions and launched minor operations to clear small, bypassed groups of German troops behind the front line. Chief among the isolated groupings of Germans was the *Luftwaffe* Douvres night fighter radar station, with its underground maze of concrete tunnels and strong fortifications. The German *Luftwaffe* personnel and a *Kompanie* from *Pz.Gren.Rgt. 192* were determined to hold out, and were confident that an attack by strong German forces would soon relieve them.

Moving south from the village of Tailleville, the North Shore Regiment immediately became mired in the wooded area just south of the village, two companies encountering sporadic resistance on their way to the radar station. With its first elements reaching the radar station and its bunker complexes at 1600 hours, the regiment made little progress, and the M7 105mm Priest self-propelled artillery of the 19th Field Regiment, RCA and British Churchill AVRE tanks in support made little impact on the German defenders protected by thick concrete walls. The other two infantry regiments of the 8th Canadian Infantry Brigade, Le Régiment de la Chaudière and the Queen's Own Rifles of Canada, had a relatively easier time of it, sweeping the areas near their final 6 June positions for isolated German stragglers, then establishing a brigade fortress position around Anguerny.[4]

While this was occurring, the remaining two regiments of the 9th Canadian Infantry Brigade, the Stormont, Dundas and Glengarry Highlanders and the Highland Light Infantry of Canada, concentrated on either flank of the NNSH and SFR grouping, ready to be called forward to support the drive south along the road to Carpiquet. In the hours of the early morning, the NNSH and its supporting SFR squadrons finalised plans to press forward in exactly the same manner they had on the afternoon of 6 June. It is impossible for historians to evaluate if the officers of the brigade vanguard believed the going would be as relatively easy as it had been the previous day.

Before this chapter discusses the major battle that takes place on 7 June north of Caen, an important question to be addressed is whether the leadership of the 3rd Canadian Infantry Division knew what was in front of them in the way of enemy formations and their strengths. Did the Canadian brigadiers, the divisional staff and Major General Keller have a solid intelligence picture of the enemy when ordering Brigadier Cunningham of the 9th Canadian Infantry Brigade forward, and what was the level of coordination with the British 3rd Infantry Division, the formation to the west? From the lack of historical evidence to suggest otherwise, it appears Keller had no idea what was in front of him, and little knowledge of overall British 3rd Infantry Division operational plans.

Prisoners had been taken from the *21. Pz.Div.* on the night of 6 June, and while some elements of the 8th and 9th Canadian Infantry Brigades had recorded and passed this information on, the vanguard of the 9th Canadian Infantry Brigade arguably had no idea that elements of a powerful German formation such as the *Hitlerjugend* were immediately south that morning. Examining the situation at daybreak, another important question to consider is did the NNSH and its supporting armour have enough combat power to fight a major armoured battle if they needed to do so?

Looking back with the benefit of hindsight, the possibility that they would simply reach their objectives relatively unmolested and fortify them, effectively turning the newly won objective into a 'fortress' before powerful German armoured reserves arrived on the scene, was near zero.

The artillery support arranged for the advance of the 9th Canadian Infantry Brigade was very inadequate for the task ahead and not deployed correctly. This will be discussed shortly in detail. This was problematic in the extreme, and not having this support ready and on hand was a disaster waiting to happen. Missing also was a reliable, foolproof means to communicate effectively via wireless with the RN warships lying off the coast of Bernières-sur-Mer and the RCA field artillery regiments, there now being four of these in the bridgehead.

Regardless of a lack of artillery support, the NNSH-SFR vanguard moved out at roughly 0745 hours, led by the tanks for the SFR, and advanced south.[5] Another problem for the SFR and the NNSH was that while there were many east–west roads, there was only one main route south through Villons-les-Buissons, Les Buissons, Buron, Authie, Franqueville and finally Carpiquet. If an enemy blocked this one main route south there would be a problem for the armour, possibly forcing the entire vanguard to halt its progress or go cross-country. With its nearby *Luftwaffe* airfield, the vanguard's final objective was now abandoned by its former inhabitants as word spread of the powerful Anglo-Canadian forces pushing inland.

The ground the NNSH and SFR vanguard was to advance over was perfect tank country. It was broken by small, wooded areas and gently rolling fields in places without significant hill features, and was crisscrossed by excellent east–west roads, many of which were paved, others being dry farm tracks. Villages were compact in order to maximise farmland and each one had some form of a combination of gardens, orchards, stone barns and farmhouses. In each was a series of walls that divided one property from another. In the middle of each small cluster of buildings was a paved road intersection, at which there was usually an elementary-level school for the village, a mayor's office and a church. The patchwork of farmland outside the village was worked by the farmers who often had their homes and barns located within or near the clusters of buildings. On the larger farms operated by more well-off families, a fully separate cluster of buildings would exist, usually with a barn or two-story farmhouse. Some of the buildings were hundreds of years old by 1944, yet were extremely sturdy with cellars resilient to artillery fire or airstrikes.

The area of Buron, Authie and Franqueville was not completely free of the enemy, and the equivalent of a weak and poorly equipped *Infanterie-Bataillon* had been scraped together during the night of 6/7 June from the remnants of *Gren.Rgt. 736*. Immediately behind this weak screening force were other small groupings of German forces from the *21. Pz.Div.* These forces had been deployed to this sector temporarily to act as a screen until further German forces, these being from the *Hitlerjugend*, arrived. The *21. Pz.Div.* forces were part of *Kampfgruppe* Rauch, led by *Oberstlt.* Rauch of *Pz.Gren.Rgt. 192.* It consisted of the *2.* and *3. Kp./Pz.Pio. Btl. 220,* reinforced by parts of *II. Abt./Pz.Art.Rgt. 155.* Also present was a small force from *Pz.Jg.Abt. 200,* with a number of towed 8.8cm anti-tank guns.[6] These weak screening forces and their limited defensive capabilities did not bother *Staf.* Kurt Meyer of *SS-Pz.Gren.Rgt. 25,* who is recorded to have arrived at the *716. Inf. Div. Gefechtsstand* bunker near Caen at 0015 hours. It was during discussions with officers of this division and *21. Pz.Div.* that he made his infamous comment 'Bah, little fish, we will throw them into the sea'.[7]

The route march of the *SS-Pz.Gren.Rgt. 25,* the first *SS-Panzergrenadierregiment* set to arrive, had not been completed by daybreak on 7 June, and many units still had many kilometres to drive. The advance units of *SS-Flak Abteilung 12,* as noted in its *Kriegstagebuch* entry for 7 June, reported that it was only on that morning that units of *SS-Pz.Gren.Rgt. 25* took over security in the St Germaine–Carpiquet–Verson area, which its lead elements had just reached. *SS-Flak.Abt. 12,* like the rest of the division, was completely strung out, with the only nearby elements being the *3. Batterie* at Les Moutiers, the *Abteilung Gefechtsstand* located 700 meters south-west of St Laurent and the *1. Batterie* in the Amaye area. Advancing northward that morning, the *Stabsbatterie* of the *Abteilung* reported itself still in transit near Bretteville-l'Orgueilleuse on the Orne. During this time the *3. Batterie* shot down a Typhoon at 0919 hours, and Jabo air activity over all roads near Caen was recorded as very heavy. Also, that morning, *2. Batterie* was deployed north-east of St Laurent at 1130 hours.

As noon approached, the mass of *SS-Pz.Gren.Rgt. 25* and *II. Abt./SS-Pz.Rgt. 12* had arrived in the western Caen–Bayeux highway area. Its deployment was coordinated from the Abbaye Notre-Dame d'Ardenne's monastery south of Cussy, where the *SS-Pz.Gren.Rgt. 25 Gefechtsstand* had been established at 0830 hours. *Staf.* Meyer was soon met by *Brig.Fhr.* Witt at 0915 hours. This meeting was followed by a briefing at 0930 by the divisional *Ic Generalstabsoffizier, Ostuf.* Doldi, who briefed Meyer in detail on the enemy units opposing him, and their locations.[8]

The location of supporting *Artillerie* and other units will be discussed in more detail later in this chapter. *SS-Flak.Abt. 12,* in order to support all *Hitlerjugend* units in the vicinity of Caen, was subordinated to support *SS-Pz.Gren.Rgt. 25,* but strangely this was not ordered until 1630 hours.[9] The *Gefechtsstand* of the division was established in Venoix, just south-west of Caen, and the divisional *Ia Stubaf.* Meyer and his staff began to oversee operations from this location as *Brig.Fhr.* Witt toured various unit locations and met with *Kommandeure.*[10]

As the mass of *SS-Pz.Gren.Rgt. 25* assembled near the front, *Brig.Fhr.* Witt ordered *Staf.* Meyer to attack on that morning with all he had, time being of the essence. A regimental copy of the divisional attack order, retrieved from *SS-Pz.Art.Rgt. 12*'s war diary appendix, has survived, and is reproduced below. It is very general, and through its lack of specific detail it allowed the *Kommandeur* fulfilling *Brig.Fhr.* Witt's intent to adjust their actual attack plans as dictated by the situation. It is

A b s c h r i f t

12. SS-Panzer-Division
"Hitlerjugend"
Abt. I a   My./S.   Div.Gef.St., den 7.6.1944

B e f e h l für den Angriff am 7.6.1944
===

1. Am 6.6. zwischen Dives- und Ornemündung abgesprungene Fallschirmjäger halten in Linie Petiville - Bavent - Ranville
   der westlich der Orne seegelandete Feind in Stärke von etwa
   zwei Divisionen hat die Linie BENOUVILLE - CREULLY - RYES -
   ASNELLES im Angriff nach Süden überschritten. Augenblicklicher
   Standort der Angriffsspitzen ist nicht bekannt. Eigene Kräfte
   verteidigen sich noch in Benouville, Cresserons, Mathieu,
   Buron, St.Gabriel.

2. Die Division greift den westlich der Ornemündung gelandeten
   Feind, links an die 21.Pz.Div. angelehnt, an, stößt bis zum
   Meer durch und nimmt die Orte St.Aubin und Bernieres. Die
   Panzer-Lehr-Div. wird nach Eintreffen links neben 12.SS-Pz.Div.
   zum Angriff angesetzt werden. Schwerpunkt des Angriffes wird an
   den inneren Flügeln der 21.Pz.Div. und 12.SS-Pz.Div. liegen.

3. Hierzu stellen sich bereit in den befohlenen Versammlungsräumen:
   a) Rechts verstärktes SS-Pz.Gren.Rgt.25 (Verstärkt durch
      III./SS-Pz.Art.Rgt.12; Unterstellung I./SS-Pz.Rgt.12 wird
      aufgehoben). Grenze zur 21.Pz.Div. Straße Caen, Douvres,
      Langrune.
   b) Links SS-Pz.Gren.Rgt.26 mit z.Zt versammelten Teilen.
      (II./SS-Pz.Art.Rgt.12 bleibt unterstellt, Unterstellung
      I./SS-Pz.Rgt.12 wird aufgehoben); III./SS-Pz.Gren.Rgt.26
      ist als Divisions-Reserve im erreichten Raume bereitzu-
      stellen.
   c) Die übrigen Verbände verbleiben b.a.w. in ihren Versamm-
      lungsräumen zur Verfügung der Division oder erreichen sie
      zu diesem Zweck.

4. Aufträge:
   a) Verstärktes SS-Pz.Gren.Rgt.25 stößt in enger Anlehnung an
      die 21.Pz.Div. tief gegliedert bis zur Küste durch und
      nimmt St.Aubin.
   b) II./SS-Pz.Rgt.12 folgt dem Angriff des SS-Pz.Gren.Rgt.25,
      um gegebenenfalls auf Befehl der Division dessen Angriff
      zu unterstützen oder über SS-Pz.Gren.Rgt. 25 hinweg anzu-
      greifen. Es ist beabsichtigt, nach Eintreffen I./SS-Pz.Rgt.12
      und I./SS-Pz.Art.Rgt.12 hinter II./SS-Pz.Rgt.12 nachzuführen.
   d) SS-Pz.Gren.Rgt.26 stößt mit Masse seiner vorhandenen Kräfte
      zwischen Chiromme und Seulles zum Meer durch und nimmt
      Bernieres, mit ausreichenden Kräften schirmt es gegen den
      Seulles-Abschnitt ostwärts der Linie Loucelles - St.Gabriel
      ab, bis Pz.Lehr-Div. im Angriff die gleiche Höhe erreicht.
      Trennungslinie zwischen SS-Pz.Gren.Rgt. 25 und 26:
      Bachlauf von St.Manvier bis Zusammenfluß 2 km westl.
      Comby - Beny (für Rgt.26) Bahnübergang 800 westl.
      St.Aubien.

-2-

-2-

e) ⅏-Pz.Aufkl.Abt.12 klärt auf gegen Linie CREULLY - RYES -
Port-en-Bessien- Trevieres, sie schirmt in Anlehnung
an ⅏-Pz.Gren.Rgt.26 gegen Seulles-Abschnitt ab, bis
Pz.Lehr-Div. im Angriff dieselbe Höhe erreicht hat.

f) Durch sämtliche in der forderen Linie eingesetzten Verbände
ist bis Angriffsbeginn intensive Gefechtsaufklärung vorzutreiben.

g) Feuereröffnung der Artillerie nach Ermessen der Kampf-
gruppenführer.

h) Mit Angriffsbeginn am 7.6. mittags ist zu rechnen. Er
wird rechtzeitig durch die Division befohlen. Die erfolgte
Bereitstellung der einzelnen Verbände ist der Division
zu melden. Es muß damit gerechnet werden, daß vor Eintreffen aller Verbände der Angriff begonnen wird.

5. Nachrichten-Verbindung:

Funk wie bisher.

6. Hauptverbandsplatz wird im Raum um Missy erkundet und
eingerichtet.

7. Meldungen sind unter Benutzung der Bezugspunktkarte
Fall "Cäsar" zu erstatten.

8. Div.-Gefechtsstand bis auf weiteres Waldstück 1ooo m
südlich Les Moutiers, später hinter ⅏-Pz.Gren.Rgt.25.

Vom Erfolg des Angriffes insbesondere unserer Division hängt die
weitere Entwicklung der Lage in hohem Masse ab.

gez. W i t t

⅏-Brigadeführer und
Generalmajor der Waffen-⅏

F.d.R.d.A.:

⅏-Obersturmführer und
Rgts.-Adjutant.

Regimental copy of the *12. SS-Panzerdivision Hitlerjugend* divisional operation order for the attack on 7 June 1944, most probably written by *Ia Stubaf.* H. Meyer, present in the *SS-Pz.Art.Rgt. 12 1944 Kriegstagebuch Analgen.*[1] (Vojenský ústřední archiv) very illuminating in that it recognised the absence of the *Panzer-Lehr, SS-Pz.Gren. Rgt. 26* and that success would depend on close coordination with the *21. Pz.Div.* in order to drive to the coast and reach the attack objective for *SS-Pz.Gren.Rgt. 25* provided by Witt, St Aubin-sur-Mer, within the heart of Juno Beach.[11]

It must be noted that the lengthy road march from the exercise area around Vimoutiers had taken a toll on both the vehicles and personnel of *SS-Pz.Gren.Rgt. 25*. A tremendous amount of fuel had been consumed, and apart from what the divisional supply *Kompanien* attached to Meyer's force had carried with it, there were not large amounts of ammunition and other supplies in the area. The resource needs of a fully engaged SS-*Panzerdivision* with regard to fuel, food and munitions were voracious. The fact that every Allied fighter-bomber flying over the battlefield was aiming to destroy such supply convoys, caches and dumps did not help the situation.

On arrival, the *SS-Panzergrenadiere* disembarked from their trucks, organised themselves, and took up positions in the wooded areas and villages immediately north of Caen. The trucks of *SS-Pz.Gren.Rgt. 25* then had to be placed in wooded hides to conceal them from the roving fighter bombers, and the heavy weapons attached to each *SS-Panzergrenadier Kompanie* were deployed a distance back from the immediate battle area to reduce losses from air attack and Anglo-Canadian artillery. The troops and drivers, exhausted from a long, stress-filled road march under conditions of complete enemy air superiority, now had to fight through exhaustion and carry out the tasks ordered of them by their officers as the three *SS-Panzergrenadier Bataillone* shook themselves out and prepared for battle.

The situation regarding the German Panzer IV tanks was another matter. All five *Kompanien* of *II. Abt./SS-Pz.Rgt. 12* were involved in the battle on 7 June or located very near to it, but the number of serviceable tanks available was roughly 50 from an *Abteilung* strength on 1 June of 101 tanks. The reason for this? Due to the level of automotive technology present in 1944, one could not drive a group of 25-ton tracked vehicles for over 100 kilometres on paved roads without a number falling out, even with regular stops for preventative maintenance and driver rest. Secondly, many had run out of gasoline.

The memoirs of former *8. Kompanie Kommandeur Ostuf.* Hans Seigel, given in February 1969, illuminates the haphazard fashion in which the *Kompanien* of *II. Abt./ SS-Pz.Rgt. 12* were committed to the action. From strength reports, it is apparent the *II. Abteilung* was fully up to strength in the way of tanks on 1 June, and yet on 7 June only five Panzer IVs of Seigel's *Kompanie* were available for combat from a paper *Kompanie* strength of 17. While all five went into action, the combat power of the *Kompanie* was severely limited.

In the year 1944, the Panzer IV tank had roughly the same automotive reliability on road moves conducted on western paved highways as the German Panther and Tiger medium and heavy tanks. Any blanket assumption of historical 'tank reliability' in both Allied and Axis armies is inaccurate. Automotive reliability for heavily armoured tracked vehicles had just not advanced that far in the 25 years since the conclusion of the First World War. This was not exclusively a German problem, and was not the fault of German over-engineering or the inability to design a reliable tank. As would be evidenced during the lightning Allied advance across France of the First Canadian Army at the conclusion of the Normandy campaign in August–September 1944, tanks simply broke down in large numbers.

Due to the air threat, the tanks would often camouflage themselves off the main route and thus motorcycle messengers and other *Kompanie* supply trucks would have trouble finding them during the conditions of radio silence. These conditions and driver fatigue on 6 and 7 June led to an interrupted supply of spare parts, fuel and meals for stranded Panzer IV crews. Delays occurred, and because of this only five Panzer IVs of *Ostuf.* Seigel's *Kompanie* arrived just before noon north of Caen.

Other Panzer IV *Kompanien* that figure prominently in the day's fighting arrived with more tanks, and the *8. Kompanie* seemed to have suffered the most with regard to tanks falling out for one reason or another.[12] It appears Seigel was so delayed in his road march he moved ahead on a motorcycle and thus had time to meet with *Stubaf.* Karl-Heinz Prinz, the *Abteilung Kommandeur*, and the regimental *Kommandeur* of *SS-Pz.Gren.Rgt. 25*, *Staf.* Meyer, at the new Abbaye Notre-Dame d'Ardenne headquarters that Meyer had established that night. Properly briefed on the situation and notified of the rapid approach of several *8. Kompanie* Panzer IVs, Seigel then left to meet them, guiding them to a position behind *I. Btl./SS-Pz.Gren. Rgt. 25*, situated south of Cambes, where he remained on combat alert until the order to attack came later that afternoon.[13]

High in the towers of the Abbaye Notre-Dame d'Ardenne, *Staf.* Meyer observed the advance of the Canadian vanguard in the distance. More specific and realistic objectives had been given to the *SS-Panzergrenadier Bataillone Kommandeure* that replaced the rather vague goal of the divisional order to capture St Aubin-sur-Mer on the coast: the *I. Bataillon's* objective was Anguerny and the *II. Bataillon's* objective was La Gare. The *III. Bataillon's* objective was Basly, and all *Bataillone* were ordered to be prepared to advance from any time after 1300 hours.[14]

As *Staf.* Meyer sat in the tower talking with the *SS-Pz.Rgt. 12 Kommandeur Ostubaf.* Wünsche, present in his Panzer IV command tank near the structure with a field telephone attached was *Stubaf.* Prinz. He was on standby to move forward, his *Kompanien* of *II. Abt./SS-Pz.Rgt. 12* arranged in readiness positions just north of the Caen–St Germain–Bretteville-l'Orgueilleuse road. In the *II. Abt./SS-Pz.Rgt. 12* war diary, only cursory information is given on the exact positions of each of the *Kompanien*. The *8. Kompanie* is described as being on the 'right' (this being to the east) and the *5.* and *6. Kp./II. Abt./SS-Pz.Rgt. 12* are described as being on the 'side' – the author assumes this to be to the west of *8. Kp.* Located to the rear behind these *Kompanien*, the *7.* and *9. Kompanien* are recorded as being initially in reserve.[15] It is unclear from the records which *Kompanien* were not up to strength, but if the *II. Abt./SS-Pz.Rgt. 12* had only 50 tanks ready for action, some of the *Kompanien*, most likely *8. Kp.* and *9. Kp.*, were very weak. The crews at this time were exhausted from their two days of field exercises and their route march. Despite this, they made their tanks battle worthy the best they could and were as ready for action as they could be by noon. The supply *Versorgungkompanie* columns were parked near Eterville on the road to Venoix, and camouflaged to protect against the never-ending Allied aerial activity. The *Werkstatt-Kompanie* with its irreplaceable maintenance, recovery, and repair vehicles was in Meulles, on the Orbec–Vimoutiers road on the first day of action for the *Abteilung*.[16]

The first element of the NNSH and SFR brigade vanguard initially pushing down the D220 paved road south was led by Major Learment, the officer commanding (OC) of C Company of the NNSH. The order of march for the vanguard was the Stuart tanks of the regimental SFR recce troop, followed by the carrier platoon with the C Company of the NNSH mounted on its Universal Carriers, followed by the Cameron Highlanders of Canada 11 Platoon, with at least four Vickers medium machine guns also mounted on Universal Carriers. Following this group was L Troop from the 105th Composite Battery of the 3rd Anti-Tank Regiment, RCA, equipped with M-10 tank destroyers. Following this was the NNSH pioneer platoon, also mounted on Universal Carriers, and behind this was the NNSH anti-tank platoon with its six 6-pounder anti-tank guns.[17] Behind the anti-tank guns was the tactical headquarters grouping of Major Learment. Following a distance back from the Universal Carriers and M-10s were the three squadrons of the SFR, with the NNSH A, B and D Companies riding on the engine decks of the A, B, and C Squadron Sherman tanks.[18] A Squadron was deployed on the right flank and drove in a wedge formation through the nearby fields, and B Squadron did the same on the left side of the paved D220. The SFR C Squadron marched in column immediately behind the vanguard, and behind this was the battalion headquarters of Lieutenant Colonel Petch, the commanding officer (CO) of the NNSH, escorted by the SFR regimental headquarters troop of Lieutenant Colonel Gordon, the CO of the SFR.

This was not an insignificant force, but not the *overpowering* force required and ready to fight an all-out armoured engagement on the perfect tank country northwest of Caen. For even the smallest of offensive operations, modern Western NATO armies require the odds of 3 to 1 when attacking or preparing to fight a meeting engagement. The total tank strength for the SFR on 7 June was close to 60 Sherman tanks, its war establishment being 61. It had not been committed to heavy combat on 6 June, landing in the second wave of landings after the beachhead combat. The rifle line companies of the NNSH were still at least 110 men on average each, and the battalion had not faced intense combat up to this point.

As the Canadian vanguard pressed forward, tragically there were no Canadian RCA field regiments on the eastern sector of the Canadian front deployed forward. While the 14th Field Regiment, RCA was assigned to provide immediate artillery support in the way of Defensive Fire (DF) tasks to the vanguard, it was not ready nor organised to do so. Its wireless communication net with its forward observation officer (FOO) teams assigned to the battlegroup would turn out to be either non-functional or the victim of German jamming. That morning, the 14th Field Regiment, RCA, had only slowly begun moving off the beach from Beny-sur-Mer with their 24 M7 Priest self-propelled 105mm guns. Its commanding officer had planned to move the batteries forward in a staggered manner, so that at least one battery would always be in contact and ready to provide fire support. By 1200 hours, only one battery had reached a somewhat forward position at La Mare, which was receiving mortar fire from the *Luftwaffe* Douvres radar station.[19]

While there were two FOOs provided to the vanguard, both were with the NNSH battalion headquarters and not forward with the line companies. Also assigned to Lieutenant Colonel Petch for the advance on Carpiquet was a forward officer, bombardment, of the Royal Navy (different from a forward observation officer of the RA). He was supposedly equipped and trained to communicate with the warships supporting land operations, and on 7 June this officer was expected to contact the cruisers HMS *Belfast* and *Diadem* if necessary. These were not the only warships within range. There were others moored just off the Juno, Sword, and Gold Beaches, which could technically provide immediate and devastating fire support.[20] Particularly powerful and within range were the battleships HMS *Rodney* and *Warspite*, taken as examples. HMS *Belfast* was equipped with nine 6-inch guns, and HMS *Diadem* mounted eight 5.25-inch guns. The combined fire of both cruisers on a target could theoretically be the equivalent of RA medium regiment. Both were very stable gun platforms with excellent fire control technology for 1944, and could easily destroy several targets simultaneously. Regardless of their availability, it was not expected to use them as a first option, as it was believed the organic artillery assets within the 3rd Canadian Infantry Division would be the primary option.

It is important to note that the 9th Canadian Infantry Brigade vanguard was ordered to seize what was thought to be weakly defended ground. Once seized, the other two battalions of the brigade were to rapidly march forward to take their place in a brigade 'fortress' on the objective line 'Oak'. Simply put, it is very likely the SFR-NNSH vanguard believed it would easily sweep aside any weak opposition and was prepared to fight against the same type of enemy it had faced the previous day. It was not foreseen that the brigade vanguard would fight a meeting engagement with a powerful peer force that would need to be overpowered and defeated in detail, and certainly not half a *Waffen-SS Panzerdivision*. As later events would illustrate, it would not be in the best tactical formation to engage a powerful peer enemy when forced to fight, and its armoured and infantry forces were not properly supported by artillery with the combat power to drive back or at the very least supress the enemy.

Setting off at 0740 hours, the vanguard assumed a wide arrowhead formation with the lead elements taking the paved D220, and the two armoured squadrons on each flank driving cross-country. These could not keep pace with the advance of the vanguard on the paved road and were soon staggered to the rear.

First contact was made by the NNSH carrier platoon and the attached SFR light tanks when the vanguard overcame an enemy position just north of the small village of Les Buissons (south of Villons-les-Buissons) on the west side of the paved road. This first victory came at the cost of a Stuart light tank of the SFR recce troop, which was knocked out by 8.8cm anti-tank fire. Reacting quickly, C Company of Major Learment immediately dismounted and engaged the Germans firing at the Canadian vehicles. It is of note that the NNSH carrier platoon could not have transported the entire 120-man company, and some troops would have been transported on other vehicles. The weak German forces encountered were stragglers from the *716. Inf. Div.* and the first outpost positions of *6. Kp./Pz. Gren. Rgt. 192* and other forces of the *21. Pz. Div.* Slightly west of the D220 paved road, the aforementioned 8.8cm gun was knocked out by the carrier platoon machine guns and mortar fire from the mortar platoon. It is most likely this gun, and its crew were from *2. Kp./Pz. Jg. Abt. 200.*[21] Another SFR Stuart light tank was knocked out at this moment by fire from another 8.8cm gun. Facing many armoured vehicles, the crew was killed by Canadian tank fire from the rest of the SFR recce troop. The whole lead element of the vanguard then attacked Les Buissons, turning right and leaving the D220. Pushing into the town, the Canadians destroyed three half-tracks from *3. Kp./Pz. Pio. Btl. 220* or part of *II. Abt./Pz. Art. Rgt. 155*, one of which had a rocket launcher mounted on it.

Meanwhile, continuing to push forward on the left (eastern side) of the D220, B Squadron Sherman tanks with B Company of the NNSH mounted on them destroyed another French half-track mounting a rocket launcher, a motorcycle with a side car, and an ammunition truck.[22]

West of Les Buissons, A Company soldiers of the NNSH that had dismounted from the SFR A Squadron tanks ran into a small group of *Grenadiere*, also possibly from *6. Kp./Pz. Gren. Rgt. 192* or *3. Kp./Pz. Pio. Btl. 220*. This opposition consisted of a MG-42 machine-gun position and a self-propelled gun located in a small, wooded area. This group was destroyed by infantry and tank fire.

Les Buissons was declared clear at 0900, though this is debatable as when the Stormont, Dundas and Glengarry Highlanders entered the village later at 1000 hours, they were forced to clear it again, as some German elements remained hidden or moved into the village again after the NNSH continued south on the D220, bound for Buron. Moving to the front, yet still behind the remaining SFR recce troop tanks, was a troop of Shermans from C Squadron, which now led the main body of the vanguard down the D220.

The next target for the NNSH-SFR vanguard was the village of Buron. German resistance here became significantly more intense, and more *Panzergrenadiere* were deployed to the east of the town than had been encountered in the way for the resistance on the line Les Buissons–Cambes.

Pushing forward, the vanguard pushed down the paved road over the crest of a small rise, Hill 75, that had two anti-tank ditches dug on either side of the road. The flanking tank squadrons drove around these obstacles to the west and east to surround the village of Buron. As the first Stuart light tanks approached it down the main road, the vanguard radioed brigade headquarters at 11.50 hours that it was past report line 'Ale'. As mentioned previously, in the village and its surrounding area there was an increased enemy presence. The remaining SFR C Squadron tanks, bringing up the rear of the vanguard, reported 8.8cm anti-tank fire on their left flank. Aggressively charging further forward up the D220 and into the fields beside it, the lead Canadian tanks sighted an 8.8cm gun position with two self-propelled guns of the *21. Pz.Div.* located nearby. These were destroyed by Sherman tank fire.

Dismounting before Buron, the NNSH C Company infantry and the carrier platoon destroyed another 8.8cm gun near the village, and after sighting a third *21. Pz.Div.* self-propelled gun, killed the crew with small arms fire and grenades. These events by no means broke resistance, and German *Panzergrenadiere* continued to shoot at the Canadian infantry and tanks with small arms fire.

As the Canadian infantry fought its way through Buron, an air battle was also observed in the skies above. A formation of German Bf 109s encountered a large group of RAF or RCAF Spitfires directedly above Buron. One German fighter shot down a RAF or RCAF Spitfire, whose pilot bellied in his plane close to the Canadian tanks and was rescued by them.

By 1200 hours, Buron was more or less secured by the NNSH and a number of prisoners had been taken. As the small arms fire died down, the vanguard NNSH infantry remounted the vehicles and pressed forward again. On the left flank just east of the village, heavy German artillery fire was encountered by the vanguard for the first time, hitting the SFR B Squadron tanks and their mounted infantry as they drove south through the fields. This artillery concentration appeared to come from the direction of Galmanche and St Contest, forcing the infantry to dismount. This fire was presumably from *21. Pz.Div.* self-propelled artillery whose strongpoint for the moment was located near Galmanche. Major Mahon, the SFR B Squadron OC, ordered his tanks to fire on the Germans, but it was difficult to gauge what sort of effect the direct fire had at this distance. As the infantry attempted to remount the Shermans during a pause in the German artillery fire, it resumed on the stationary tanks, causing the NNSH B Company infantry to scurry to the outskirts of Buron.

The SFR C Squadron tanks exiting Buron also encountered this artillery fire and attempted to carry out a 'squadron shoot', this being a firing line in which all the tanks would fire on a suspected or identified target area. Unfortunately, the lined-up tanks received further heavy artillery fire that disrupted their effort. Manoeuvring again in the fields further to the west, B Squadron attempted to close in on the enemy. As they did so, three Canadian tanks were hit by anti-tank fire, causing the first Sherman losses, which included the tank of the OC of B Squadron, Major Mahon, and that of Captain Bateman, the squadron second in command. When this occurred, the squadron withdrew to a safe distance away to the north.

Regrouping, Captain Bateman organised two composite troops – one under Lieutenant Davies with the remains of No. 2 and 3 Troops, and another under Lieutenant Steeves with what was left of No. 1 and No. 4 Troops, and prepared to push south again.[23] As this was occurring, the NNSH B Company infantry, now dismounted, pushed through Buron.

Next on the path of the vanguard's advance was the village of Authie. A clear line of sight for the tank commanders dead ahead was somewhat obscured by the sloping nature of the ground south of Buron. This 'dead ground' made it impossible for the tanks and universal carriers to see a distance ahead of them. Despite this uncertainty, the advance continued on the D220, the main column on the road more or less now separated from the tank squadrons to its left and right. Encountering little in the way of Germans in the fields past Buron but ever-increasing levels of German artillery fire, the lead armoured column reached the outskirts of Authie, radioing brigade headquarters that it was now on report line 'Danube'.

The village of Authie did have significantly more resistance within it than Buron, containing three *Panzergrenadier* or *Grenadier* MG-42 machine-gun positions that engaged the Canadian vehicles. These were dealt with in the same manner as all former German positions, the lead Canadian Stuart light tanks shooting up the positions with co-axial machine-gun fire and 37mm shellfire. As the tanks continued to fire, the German small arms fire slackened off, but the artillery fire hitting the village and the surrounding area continued.

At this point in the combat the vanguard's movement and the halting of some elements of it due to shellfire had forced it to lose cohesion, in that it was in no way, shape or form ready to deploy all its forces to bear in a concentrated manner if it needed to. Also, the ability of Lieutenant Colonel Petch, stuck at the back of the column and somewhat out of contact and line of sight with his units, to effect proper command and control was more impaired as the squadrons of the SFR were ever more separated.

At 1300 hours the NNSH-SFR vanguard experienced an increased level of shelling and machine-gun fire from seemingly all directions, and communications attempted by the RCA forward observation officer (FOO) team located with Petch at his tactical headquarters vehicle grouping reported that the 14th Field Regiment, RCA, slated to support the advance, was now out of range. Some batteries of this RCA field regiment had been caught in a vast traffic jam south of the invasion beaches and were inching their way forward to their assigned positions near or south of La Mare in order to try to support the forces of the 9th Canadian Infantry Brigade. All this time the lead Canadian tanks along the D220 south of Authie kept moving, ignorant of the lack of artillery support. Next up for the vanguard was the village of

Franqueville, which lay just before the Caen–Bayeaux railway line, south of which was the Carpiquet aerodrome and its hangars.

At approximately 1430 hours, both SFR A and B Squadrons, minus their infantry companies which had now dismounted due to the shelling and mortar fire, had passed Authie, A Squadron pushing forward on the right flank looking south, and B Squadron, which had resumed advancing on the left flank further to the rear, nearest the Germans. As the two Canadian tank wedges of roughly 15 tanks each converged on Franqueville, the German artillery, mortar and other fire became noticeably more intense.[24] Colonel Petch, interviewed post-war concerning the indirect fire, stated that it came from both flanks and from the front, indicating a large amount of artillery pieces had been deployed to conduct this artillery concentration.

This indirect fire was mainly from *III. Abt./SS-Pz.Art.Rgt. 12*, supported by a number of 7.5cm and 15cm *Infanterie-Geschütz* howitzers and 8cm mortars held at the *Bataillone* level within *III. Btl./SS-Pz.Gren.Rgt. 25*. The *III. Abt./SS-Pz.Art.Rgt. 12 Kommandeur, Stubaf.* Bartling, was photographed on this day with *Stubaf.* Prinz of *II. Abt./SS-Pz.Rgt. 12* and *Stubaf.* Urbanitz of *I. Abt./SS-Pz.Art.Rgt. 12*, the latter which's unit had not arrived yet on the battlefield. The photograph, reprinted in the Hubert Meyer history, shows all three reviewing maps for the upcoming attack. The unit *Kriegstagebuch* entry for *III. Abt./SS-Pz.Art.Rgt. 12* on this date reports that good fire support for *III. Btl./SS-Pz.Gren.Rgt. 25* was provided.[25]

While some historians have stated the Canadian drive south on Carpiquet was ambushed near Franqueville, this was impossible, as the NNSH and SFR tanks had been in continuous combat against forces of the *21. Pz.Div.* and *716. Inf.Div.* for some hours already. The vanguard of the 9th Canadian Infantry Brigade was very much 'blooded' by this stage and should have been on high alert for any large and powerful counterattack coming its way.

It was imperative at this stage that both commanding officers of the NNSH and SFR, Lieutenant Colonels Petch and Gordon, and more importantly the brigade staff and Brigadier Cunningham of the 9th Canadian Infantry Brigade, were ready to act decisively if a mass German armoured attack was encountered. They needed to have a plan in place to conduct an aggressive defence, strongly supported by the fire of the entire SFR armoured regiment and large field artillery assets. If a battalion fortress was not possible, the very least that was needed was a plan to deploy all forces available to fight a decisive meeting engagement, and have this plan potentially include other infantry battalions and armoured squadrons. Perhaps it is the ultimate understatement to state that preparation for any or all of these contingencies appears not to have occurred.

What of Allied fighter-bomber activity at this time, which could have supported the vanguard? It was present, but it seemed to have been concentrated on the advance roads filled with trucks and SPW 251s of the *Hitlerjugend* to the south, with *1. Batterie* of *SS-Flak.Abt. 12* recording the shooting down of a Thunderbolt at 1530 hours. *SS-Flak.Abt. 12* was still dispersed at this time, the *4. Batterie I. Zug*, for example, being ordered to remain at Gaillon at 1700 hours.[26]

According to French military historians Georges Bernage and Frederick Jeanne, *Staf.* Meyer gave the order to attack at 1420 hours. His plan was to attack at 1600 hours originally, but after some small combat had occurred near 1400 hours, the element of surprise had already been partially lost, and it was only a matter of time before the Canadians fully discovered the German forces near the Abbaye Notre-Dame d'Ardenne.[27] The *Kriegstagebuch* for *SS-Pz.Gren.Rgt. 25* reports that at 1630 hours the attack was gaining ground rapidly, but no precise timing is given for when the attack actually commenced.[28]

While accounts state the Panzer IV *Kompanien* were ordered into battle first, it appears that the *SS-Panzergrenadiere* of *III. Btl./SS-Pz.Gren.Rgt. 25* of *Ostubaf.* Milius were already moving through the wheat fields towards Authie. It is mentioned within the war diaries of *II. Abt./SS-Pz.Rgt. 12* that the Panzer IV tanks would later pass the *SS-Panzergrenadiere* as they lay prone in the fields on the way to Authie and Buron, and thus it is logical for the author to come to the conclusion they moved first.

According to the *Kriegstagebuch* for *II. Abt./SS-Pz.Rgt. 12*, enemy tanks were first sighted by the *Abteilung* in Franqueville and Authie. The *I. Zug* of the *5. Kompanie* was ordered north just after 1400 hours to conduct reconnaissance on the road from Franqueville. This ended in disaster for the *Zug* led by *Ustuf.* Porch, as he was subjected to surprise tank fire from the lead Shermans of the NNSH-SFR vanguard. Moving forward with Panzer IVs '515', '516', '517', '518' and '519', the two Panzer IVs edging forward first, '516' and '517', were hit and burned out. Another, '518', was heavily damaged in the brief firefight which saw the Canadian forces react first.[29]

At roughly 1440 hours, *Ostubaf.* Wünsche ordered *Stubaf.* Prinz to move his tanks forward into the attack. Observing from the top of the Abbaye Notre-Dame d'Ardenne, Meyer had decided at this point to seize the opportunity to attack, not ambush, the Canadian vanguard, and had to commit maximum forces rapidly to achieve this goal. It is thus at this point that major combat for the *Hitlerjugend*, still only half deployed on the field of battle, began.

At approximately 1445 hours, *Stubaf.* Prinz relayed the order for the Panzer IVs to move forward. Many of the camouflaged Panzer IV tanks already had the enemy in their sights and did not move, simply opening fire in a one-sided fire strike by multiple tanks of the *5.* and *6. Kompanien*. This fire destroyed or badly damaged 10 to 12 Shermans of C and B Squadrons of the SFR. One *6. Kompanie* Panzer IV crew commander, *St.Obj.* Kurt Mulhaus, appears to have done very well in this firefight, and would go on to claim a total of four Shermans destroyed or badly damaged during the fighting on 7 June.[30]

While there was no close contact ambush of Canadian forces as they approached Franqueville, this initial fusillade by the camouflaged Panzer IV tanks and Pak 40 7.5cm anti-tank guns from the area near the Abbaye Notre-Dame d'Ardenne did catch the Canadian tanks crews off guard and inflicted heavy losses in a very short period of time.[31]

Staf. Meyer's attack order was delivered at absolutely the last minute, and it is arguable that while the German tanks firing from hidden positions achieved tactical surprise, if Meyer's order to attack was not given, the Shermans of the A and B Squadron would have pushed into the actual positions of the *Hitlerjugend* near Franqueville. Meyer had waited as long as he could wait, and his attack was more of a reaction to a tactical opportunity than a planned assault. The advance of the NNSH and SFR had forced Meyer's hand, then exposed its flank.

As Meyer watched, green German tracer and tank fire crisscrossed the open fields. First B Squadron SFR contact with the *SS-Pz.Rgt. 12* Panzer IV *Kompanien* occurred near Cussy at roughly 1500 hours. The aforementioned Captain Bateman, now in command of the reduced B Squadron, had continued to push forward on the left flank of the armoured wedge, taking anti-tank fire as he pressed forward. To his alarm, he saw mass movement of German armoured vehicles as they emerged from the area around the Abbaye Notre-Dame d'Ardenne. This was followed very shortly by another round of intense German Pak 40 7.5cm anti-tank and Panzer IV fire that hit more of his tanks, causing some to catch fire. Lieutenant Davies' tank, a Sherman Firefly with a 17-pounder, knocked out three German tanks, but German return fire was intense and several more Shermans were hit. When this occurred, what was left of the squadron, still commanded by Bateman, began to withdraw.

According to Canadian accounts, a tank battle lasting nearly two hours then occurred, with combat occurring in the area Buron–Authie, not to mention the foray of the *5. Kompanie* tanks that were ambushed by SFR tanks and possibly M-10 tank destroyers of the advance guard.

With the *9. Kompanie* in reserve, the *5., 6., 7.* and *8.* Panzer IV *Kompanien* moved out, advancing up to the positions of the *SS-Panzergrenadiere* and then past them. The *SS-Panzergrenadiere* were lying prone in the fields at this time and after a halt to communicate with some of them, the tank *Kompanien* kept on moving forward.

While the Shermans began to slowly withdraw from the kill zones that were the fields of fire for the Panzer IV gunners, the Canadian infantry sought hedgerow-enclosed fields and orchards near the small towns of Authie and Buron as places to consolidate and set up company-level defensive positions for the moment. The NNSH company and platoon commanders at this time did their best, with a lack of clear orders, to set up some kind of defensive positions before the German tanks or the *SS-Panzergrenadiere* were upon them. As further Canadian tanks and Canadian infantry were encountered, the Panzer IV *Züge* carried out their own battles of fire and movement, the *Zug Kommandeur* speaking to the other three to four tanks on the radio in order to keep them moving, orientated in the same direction and alerted to targets to their front.

As the *6. Kp./SS-Pz.Rgt. 12* advanced with the other *Kompanien* of the *II. Abteilung* north in the area between Buron and Authie, they conducted firing halts to support the *SS-Panzergrenadiere*, then engaged in the first long-range firefights with the NNSH infantry companies. Things went very well at first for the *6. Kompanie* Panzer IVs, as several small groups of Canadian infantry surrendered to them and many Canadian tanks were destroyed. The Panzer IV crews did not dismount, but indicated to the surrendering Canadian troops to go forward without weapons to where the *SS-Panzergrenadiere* were.

A largely unknown participant in the 7 June battle who was quite influential in its outcome was *6. Kp./SS-Pz.Rgt. 12 Kompanie-Chef Hstuf.* Ludwig Ruckdeschel, who led his *Kompanie* into battle, participating in combat until his tank was knocked out by SFR Sherman fire in a separate action away from the later demise of the *I. Zug* of *6. Kompanie*, to be discussed shortly. Taking part in the combat that knocked out several SFR Shermans and other vehicles in the fighting, a submission was made by the commander of *SS-Pz.Rgt. 12, Ostubaf.* Wünsche, to have Ruckdeschel awarded the German Cross in Gold, the award for bravery just below the Knight's Cross and above the Iron Cross first class. An excerpt from the written report is as follows:

> Since 7 June 1944 he has been in action with his Panzer *Kompanie* in the battle for Caen, where he has shown unusual bravery in leading his *Kompanie*. North of Caen, he convincingly smashed the first English [Canadian] armoured opponent, destroying 14 English [Canadian] tanks, three troop carriers [Bren Gun Carriers of the NNSH carrier platoon] and several anti-tank guns on this first day of action.[32]

Despite significant initial success, things did not all go smoothly for the German tanks. Alarmingly, the Panzer IV commanders looking behind them did not see any of the *SS-Panzergrenadiere* of *III. Btl./SS-Pz.Gren.Rgt. 25*. Pinned down by Canadian long-range machine-gun fire when the Panzer IVs had churned past them, they had not followed in their wake. Regardless, *6. Kompanie* continued to advance in wedge formation, its axis of advance being north-west between the towns of Authie and Buron with *5. Kompanie* on its left flank, and *7. Kompanie* further to the east. The lead *Zug* of the *Kompanie*, advancing with six Panzer IV tanks, then received very heavy anti-tank fire near Authie, which could have come from M-10 tank destroyers, SFR tanks still in the area, or 6-pounder anti-tank guns of the NNSH firing at very long range.

Leading the point *Zug* of *6. Kompanie* on the attack was *Ostuf.* Albert Gausch, who was the commander that day of a *II. Zug* vehicle, Panzer IV '628'. With him on the attack was the entire *I. Zug*, totalling five other Panzer IVs with the tactical numbers 615–619. Their axis of advance was on the east side of Authie. The aforementioned defensive fire to hit the Panzer IV *Zug* came as a volley, and all six tanks received hits that either destroyed or severely damaged them. Gausch's Panzer IV '628' was hit and immediately immobilised. Panzer IV '615', commanded by *Ustuf.* Kasemiresch,

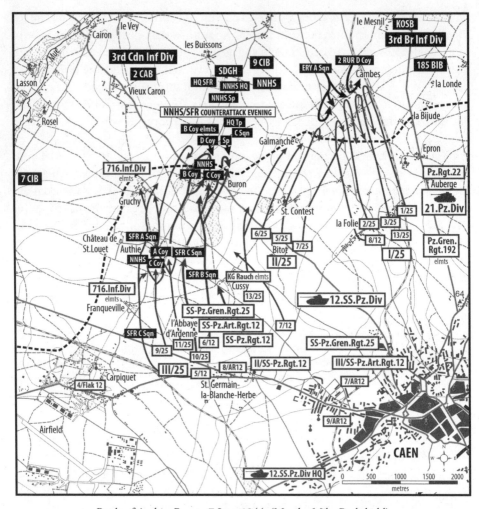

Battle of Authie–Buron, 7 June 1944. (Map by Mike Bechthold)

was also immobilised. Panzer IVs '616' and '617' were very badly damaged, and '618', under *Oscha.* Esser, was hit and burned out, with its commander being badly burned.[33] Panzer IV '619', commanded by *Oscha.* Esser, was also hit and burned out.[34] It is most likely that this firefight was with B Squadron of the SFR.

The experiences of the *6. Kp./SS-Pz.Rgt. 12* Panzer IV tank company indicate to the reader the severe vulnerability of the Panzer IV Ausf H tanks to anti-tank fire of all calibres in the summer of 1944. The armour of the tank was somewhat obsolete in the fall of 1939 and spring of 1940, as losses during the Polish and French campaigns illustrated. By 1943, it had become apparent that despite the best efforts to up-armour and up-gun the tank, it had reached the end of its design potential and was vulnerable to 75mm and 76.2mm Allied anti-tank guns. The addition of *Schutzen* armoured 'skirts' to the turret and running gear improved stand-off spaced armour protection against small calibre weapons and artillery fragments, but counted for little against heavy anti-tank fire from anti-tank or self-propelled guns, which were the premier killers of German armour on both the Eastern and Western Fronts in the summer of 1944.

While its 7.5cm KWK 40 L/43 tank cannon was very good at destroying enemy infantry, anti-tank guns and other tanks, the ability of the Allies to destroy it or damage it with one shot was apparent, the armour in the sides, turret and hull roof being extremely vulnerable. Hits by any kind of anti-tank solid shot from 75mm calibre or above would bore right through the armour of the vehicle and the crew inside, inevitably setting the ammunition or fuel alight and causing the tank to burn out. Only the quickest of the crew to jump out of the tank (or the luckiest) survived with minor injuries, some crewmembers being killed outright or having limbs shot off. The crews of *SS-Pz.Rgt. 12* had also taken advantage of the availability of surplus *Kriegsmarine* U-boat leather trousers and jackets in order to protect them from extreme burns if the tank caught fire.

If the Panzer IV was used aggressively in attacks, heavier losses could occur to the crews in comparison to the level of losses suffered within German Tiger and Panther units. While tanks could be replaced within the *Panzerwaffe*, the experienced and trained crews could not, and the experience lost by forcing the veteran tank crews to fight in the Panzer IV was one of the worst failings of the German war industry. What was needed was for each *Panzerregiment* to be exclusively equipped by the superior Panther tank, but this was impossible for German industry, it being forced to produce a multitude of different designs, each firm clamouring for resources to do so.

A Squadron of the SFR, fighting west of Authie, also began to withdraw under the sustained fire of the rest of the *5. Kompanie* Panzer IVs. It is unknown, in the 7 June fighting, how many A Squadron tanks were lost, or how quickly, and little has been written concerning exactly where they withdrew to following their losses. The author can only surmise they withdrew past Authie and Buron, taking up positions near Les Buissons. Canadian tank crews who had bailed out followed the retreating Shermans on foot, many of them having been badly burned when the tanks caught on fire.

The SFR C Squadron, under Major Walsh, had followed the sounds of battle to the west of Authie to support B Squadron of Major Mahon. It encountered the very same intense 7.5cm tank cannon fire from the Panzer IVs as B Squadron did, and soon it was taking heavy losses as well. The fire was recorded as coming from the direction of Cussy, which meant the possible German unit was *II. Btl./Pz.Gren. Rgt. 192*, firing with its anti-tank guns and possibly some self-propelled guns at the Canadian Shermans in conjunction with the advancing *6. Kp./SS-Pz.Rgt. 12*.[35] As an example of the heavy losses, the SFR C Squadron No. 2 Troop at Authie, while engaged in firing at the Panzer IVs, had three of its tanks – those of Sergeant Reid, Lieutenant Steeves, and Lieutenant Maclean – all knocked out in short order.[36] The surviving C Squadron tanks began to manoeuvre across the battlefield the best they could as the firefight continued. On the southern edge of Authie was an orchard, and in this location many of the SFR C Squadron tanks sought cover and better positions from which to fire on the German tanks. To their frustration and dismay, they encountered several piles of logs, these being trees that had been cut down by the French farmers, and these hampered the movement of the tanks.

As the tank battle raged, the NNSH company commanders and the battalion's commanding officer were not unduly perturbed, and did not, in the assessment of the author, effectively react to consolidate a line of defence where other battalions of the 9th Canadian Infantry Brigade could fight forward to them. Petch and his tactical headquarters were in Les Buissons when the first serious contact with the *Hitlerjugend* Panzer IV *Kompanien* occurred.

It must be acknowledged by the author that Petch did determinedly try to communicate with his companies when the *Waffen-SS* counterattack began, but he had already made serious tactical mistakes that he could not correct because events were spinning out of his control. He had let the NNSH become wildly dispersed since noon on 7 June, and he either could not or did not exert enough command authority to drag his companies back together or order an urgent withdrawal to allow the companies to go firm in a secure location and dig in an all-around defence. It was not as if he did not have the time. The tankers of the SFR squadrons on 7 June had bought him that time, with their blood. The NNSH had been caught in an extended manner attempting to take Carpiquet and achieve their objective, and arguably attempted to do so with little regard for flank security.

In the now cleared Les Buissons, the NNSH tactical headquarters was parked with its vehicles beside those of the SFR regimental headquarters troop. The Stormont, Dundas and Glengarry Highlanders, also of the 9th Canadian Infantry Brigade, had moved or were moving forward at this stage to dig in within this village. Here Petch and Gordon were in regular radio contact with the 9th Canadian Infantry Brigade tactical headquarters and Brigadier Cunningham, and the area was relatively safe and not under heavy shellfire. Petch and Gordon continued to try to organise their units as the German tank counterattack began in earnest. All efforts at communication were hampered by the shelling, mortaring and wireless jamming and false messaging on Canadian channels practised by the *Waffen-SS Nachtrichten* signals troops. The shelling was especially disruptive to the very fragile 1944 radio technology carried on the Universal Carriers and the Sherman tanks.[37]

Reviewing Petch's options, there was no high ground for the NNSH to consolidate on, but as the 7th Canadian Infantry Brigade's 1st Battalion, the Regina Rifle Regiment, would show in the next few days, the stone buildings and walls of the

Norman villages provided excellent defensive positions that could resist tank attack. The ground was flat, and the fields unbroken apart from small orchards and wooded areas near the stone villages from Les Buissons southward. In order to successfully enact a battalion defence in a village, all four-line companies needed to be together, supported by artillery and tanks, and well supplied with ammunition.

At this time, Major Learment, whose progress had halted just north-east of Buron, urged Captain Fraser, also of C Company in Authie to withdraw north with his forces. He then organised the carrier platoon's surviving vehicles to drive south to Authie, to load the C Company men onto them, then pull back. Unfortunately, it appears German fire was too heavy for this column to set out.[38]

Petch had to decide at this moment whether to abandon Authie or try to hold it. Radioing B Company of the NNSH, he ordered its commander to move forward and take a position on the east side of the D220, beside A Company of Major Rhodenizer. The German 8cm mortar fire was so intense this company had to retreat back to the southern area of Buron after its OC was wounded and it could find no good area to dig in, the fields being swept by all types of German fire, direct and indirect. As B Company was struggling, Petch radioed Captain Fraser and his force from C Company to hold his position, and that help was on the way, Petch ordered the carrier platoon to attempt to bring B Company forward again, now under the command of Captain Wilson. But getting them south between the two villages again was a problem due to the artillery, mortar and anti-tank fire, and the planned move south into the area of heavy artillery and mortar fire never took place. B Company remained in its positions.

At roughly 1600 hours, as the tank battle was coming to an end, where exactly were the NNSH line companies as the *SS-Panzergrenadiere* of *SS-Pz.Gren.Rgt. 25* prepared to attack in the wake of the Panzer IV *Kompanien*? Utilising the German anti-tank ditches at Hill 75 south of Les Buissons, the NNSH Support Company had dug itself in with D Company of the NNSH, which had dismounted from the SFR C Squadron tanks during the German shelling and the attempted squadron shoot by this unit. Both units could not in any way influence the coming fight for Authie from this position. Major Learment, the C Company commander who was in charge of the lead element of the vanguard, was dug in just north-east of Buron, with the carrier platoon and one platoon of C Company, and pinned down by heavy German artillery fire. B Company was located on the south-west edge of Buron, and this is where it had withdrawn to following its attempt to push forward to Authie and A Company.

Just east of Authie, two thirds of the NNSH A Company under Major Rhodenizer had dug in with two platoons, this being where they had stopped after heavy artillery and mortar fire began. Rhodenizer had sent forward a platoon to Authie to help reinforce it on his own initiative. A Sherman troop from C Squadron that was still in the area during the tank battle took the platoon to northern Authie, where three tanks of the troop were immediately knocked out. The fourth tank drove quickly to the south of the village and took up a position with the remaining two platoons of C Company under Captain Fraser, who were located in a hedged-in field immediately south of the village. As the two-hour tank battle raged, the NNSH infantry observed events from a distance. As the Canadian and German tanks manoeuvred and fired at each other, the NNSH officers had plenty of time to redeploy and organise their defences. This did occur, but not to good effect.

Hit by fire from multiple Panzer IV *Kompanien* and possibly some *21. Pz.Div.* armoured vehicles in a tank battle they were losing, as mentioned previously the remains of the three SFR tank squadrons all began to pull back after a tank battle of nearly two hours. In effect, this was a second major separation from the NNSH infantry line companies. One of several troop commanders to do so, Lieutenant Davies of the SFR B Squadron pulled back to the area north of Buron, which for the moment was free from the 7.5cm tank fire.[39] It was clear though that if the SFR squadrons had remained south of Buron, they would have been destroyed. By withdrawing to Les Buissons, they could form a new defensive line and regroup. It is unknown who gave the order to withdraw, and if this was done on a squadron or on the regimental radio net. What is clear is that the SFR had fought a major tank battle with its entire regimental strength, one that it had lost.

The reader can of course appreciate that this left the NNSH infantry at the mercy of the Panzer IVs still fit for combat and the *SS-Panzergrenadiere* who were set to follow and set upon the NNSH positions in Buron and Authie, totally unmolested by Allied field artillery or naval gunfire. The SFR tanks, apart from a few stragglers, were now out of the fight for the moment. Where would this leave the NNSH infantry?

South of Authie, Captain Fraser and his C Company soldiers desperately tried to shore up their defences. This was interrupted by heavy shelling that made communication and movement around the area south-east of Authie very difficult.[40] His perimeter consisted of hedges around the orchard that was his defensive position, with part of it bordering the village itself. A Universal Carrier with a crew that had been killed by shellfire was recovered, and its Vickers .303-inch medium machine gun was inserted in a firing position to strengthen the defence. The lone aforementioned Sherman Firefly of C Squadron was also emplaced within the perimeter. Unannounced, the third platoon of A Company under Lieutenant Sutherland arrived at Captain Fraser's position, it having been sent by Major Rhodenizer.

There are no German accounts that describe in detail the attack of the *III. Btl./ SS-Pz.Gren.Rgt. 25* under *Ostubaf.* Milius with supporting forces that cleared the villages of Franqueville, Authie and eventually Buron late in the evening of 7 June. Of important note is that of the four *SS-Panzergrenadiere Kompanien* within the *Bataillon*, two of them were led by serving *Heer* officers temporarily transferred to the *Waffen-SS*, who went into battle wearing regular army uniforms. The *Kommandeur*

Generalfeldmarschall Erwin Rommel, *O.B. Hr.Gr.B.*, inspecting the *Atlantikwall* defences with *Heeresgruppe B Chef des Stabes Generalleutnant* Hans Speidel prior to D-Day. (Critical Past)

Brig.Fhr. Fritz Witt, *Kommandeur* of the *12. SS-Panzerdivision Hitlerjugend*, meeting officers of the division in a photo opportunity prior to D-Day. (Critical Past)

Another photo of Witt from the photo opportunity prior to D-Day. (Critical Past)

Canadian troops landing at Bernières-sur-Mer on D-Day, 6 June 1944. (Critical Past)

Infantry of the North Shore (New Brunswick) Regiment assaulting St Aubin-sur-Mer on D-Day, 6 June 1944. (Critical Past)

Panzer IV tanks of *II. Abt./SS-Pz.Rgt. 12*, on the march to the *invasionfront* on 7 June. (Critical Past)

The *Panzerkommandant* of a Panzer IV tank of *II. Abt./SS-Pz.Rgt. 12*, on the march to the *invasionfront* on 7 June. (Critical Past)

Panzergrenadiere of *Pz.Gren.Rgt. 192* of the *21. Pz.Div.* marching to the front near Caen, June 1944. (Critical Past)

The march route of the Panther tanks of *I. Abt./SS-Pz.Rgt. 12* to the *invasionfront*. The route and distance travelled illustrates the improved mechanical reliability of the tank in the year 1944. (Photo of *I. Abt./SS-Pz.Rgt. 12* route map courtesy of Keith Taylor)

Befehlspanther command Panther '155' of the *I. Abt./SS-Pz.Rgt. 12 Stabskompanie*. It is unknown which *Waffen-SS Panzerkommandant* is in the turret, though it is most certainly not *Stubaf.* Jürgensen. (Alamy Stock Images)

Panzer IV '505', the *Kompanie-Chef* vehicle of the *5. Kompanie*, photographed immediately prior to the 7 June battle. This was the mount of *Ostuf.* Helmut Bando. (Critical Past)

SS-Panzergrenadiere in the fields north of Authie. (Critical Past)

Stubaf. Karl-Heinz Milius, *Kommandeur* of *III. Btl./SS-Pz.Gren.Rgt. 25* conferring with a subordinate. Photographed in the days following the 7 June 1944 fighting in Authie and Buron and the subsequent Canadian prisoner executions. (Critical Past)

An *SS-Panzergrenadier* looks over the Authie battlefield on 7 June, the date marked by the recently knocked out and burning Sherbrooke Fusilier Regiment Sherman tank in the background. (Critical Past)

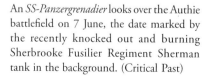

Another *SS-Panzergrenadier* photographed by the German *Die Deutsche Wochenschau* cameraman on the Authie battlefield next to a burned-out Sherbrooke Fusilier Regiment Sherman tank. As the tank is no longer on fire, this may have been filmed in the days after the fighting. (Critical Past)

Panzer IV '536' of *II. Abt./SS-Pz.Rgt. 12* photographed in the days following the 7 June 1944 fighting. (Critical Past)

An *SS-Panzergrenadier* of *SS-Pz.Gren.Rgt. 25* approaching the fighting position of his junior leader, photographed north-west of Caen in the days following the 7 June 1944 fighting. (Critical Past)

A Panzer IV of *II. Abt./SS-Pz.Rgt. 12*, photographed in the fields north-west of Caen in the days following the 7 June 1944 fighting. (Critical Past)

A closeup of the crew of a Panzer IV of *II. Abt./SS-Pz.Rgt. 12*, photographed in the fields north-west of Caen in the days following the 7 June 1944 fighting. (Critical Past)

An 8.8cm Flak of an unknown *SS-Flak Abteilung 12 Batterie* firing at Canadian targets north of Buron in the days following the 7 June 1944 battle. (Critical Past)

of *9. Kompanie*, this being the one that attacked southern Authie, was *Oberleutnant* Fritsch, and the *10. Kompanie Kommandeur* was *Oberleutnant* Dietrich.

During combat, the *Bataillon Kommandeur* would not be with the lead elements fighting the infantry battle, but placed to the rear. This is something important to mention, as many of Canadian military historians have not stated this, placing all the blame for the subsequent prisoner executions and other war crimes on its *Bataillon Kommandeur*, who was of course *Waffen-SS*. While the *Bataillon Kommandeur* was ultimately responsible legally for the actions of his *Bataillon*, it was the individual *Kompaniechefen* who were the battlefield leaders that fought the battles with their *Züge* in the 'thick of it'.[41]

The *Bataillon Kommandeur, Ostubaf.* Karl-Heinz Milius, had not seen action since the French campaign in 1940, when he had commanded no unit larger than a *Zug* as an NCO. Becoming an officer in the years that followed and later commanding a training establishment before being transferred to the *Hitlerjugend* as part of the attempt to offset its serious lack of officers, he lacked recent battle experience. In fact, he had never commanded a large unit in battle, never mind a fully equipped *SS-Panzergrenadier Bataillon* of 1,035 men and a wide array of heavy weapons. Importantly, Milius had served within the *Koncentrationsläger* (*KL*) concentration camp system as a *SS* non-commissioned officer pre-war, an experience that would not exactly enhance his respect for the Geneva Convention and its rules regarding the treatment of civilians on the battlefield and the proper processes for captured prisoners of war.

Yet amazingly, and despite the reported misgivings of *Staf.* Meyer regarding his suitability as an officer and his leadership capabilities, it turned out that on the afternoon of 7 June he would lead the most critical part of the attack for *SS-Pz. Gren.Rgt. 25*, to attack and destroy the vanguard of the 9th Canadian Infantry Brigade and prevent its capture of Carpiquet airfield. If this part of *Staf.* Meyer's counterattack failed, the regiment's other two *Bataillone* would have their left flanks exposed to potential Canadian or British counterattack as they pushed northward against the British from their jumping-off points in Bitot and La Folie. To a certain extent, it all depended on Milius.

The *III. Btl./SS-Pz.Gren.Rgt. 25* had moved into its jumping-off position just south of Franqueville near the RN 13 on the morning of 7 June and had laid in readiness to advance north as part of the larger upcoming regimental operation. Deployed left to right were the *9., 11.* and *10. Kompanie*, with the heavy weapon *Züge* of the *12. (Schwere) Kompanie* deployed within the forward *Kompanie* positions to initially support their dismounted advance. Heavy weapons such as 7.5cm Pak 40 anti-tank guns and 8cm mortars were ready in camouflaged positions, waiting for the Canadian tanks, Universal Carriers and infantry to come into their fields of fire.

It is unclear if the actual plan of attack for the push towards Franqueville, Authie and Buron was devised by Meyer with input from Milius, or if Milius decided which *Kompanie* would attack which objective. With the *Bataillon* start line just north of the RN 13 paved highway, the *10. Kompanie* was ordered to sweep around Authie to the east after pushing around Franqueville in the same manner, advancing towards Buron as its objective. *11. Kompanie* was to do something similar, with its *Züge* pushing east around Franqueville and Authie to converge with the others to launch a three-*Kompanie* attack on Buron. Trailing behind the two leading *Kompanien* would be the *9. Kompanie*, which was ordered to clear Authie proper and a nearby château before potentially moving on to support the other *Kompanien*. Tank support would come from the *5. Kompanie* on the left and the *6. Kompanie* on the right from *SS-Pz.Rgt. 12*, these two near full-strength Panzer IV *Kompanien* supporting the *SS-Panzergrenadiere* by attacking and destroying whatever was in front of them, the *Züge Kommandeur* being charged with running their own aggressive hard-charging battles rather than remaining in a subservient role to the dismounted *SS-Panzergrenadiere*.

Fire support was to be provided by the indirect weapons of the *Bataillon*, and this fire was to be enhanced by heavy *Artillerie* concentrations conducted by the *7., 8.* and *9. Batterien* of the *III. Abt./SS-Pz.Art.Rgt. 12*, its *Batterien* deployed north-west and within Caen. These indirect assets began to intensively pound the Canadian positions in Authie and Buron, pinning the NNSH infantry companies to the ground and hindering their ability to create defensive positions. It was a scene of complete chaos as the moderate to weak resistance the vanguard had encountered up to this point was replaced by a full-on *SS-Panzergrenadiere* attack with supporting armoured and heavy artillery support.

Canadian military historian Howard Margolian states that nine Panzer IV tanks supported the direct attack of the *9. Kompanie Züge* against the two Canadian defensive positions around Authie, the C Company position being in an orchard as previously mentioned, and the position of parts of A Company grouping being the northern border of the village. First contact was made with the southern grouping, the defensive position of Captain Fraser. As soon as the Panzer IV tanks came into view, they were fired on by the .50 calibre Browning machine guns taken from the nearby knocked out SFR Shermans and the lone 17-pounder Sherman. But it was nowhere near a fair fight, as the Panzer IVs lined up to pour fire into the orchard and subsequently into the village itself, pounding the stone buildings with high-explosive fire. The Canadian defensive fire did hold back the *9. Kompanie* initially, but eventually the tank fire proved decisive, as slowly but surely each Canadian fighting position was hit with co-axial MG-34 and 7.5cm tank cannon fire.

As the C Company soldiers were killed, wounded or suppressed in their fighting positions one by one, the *SS-Panzergrenadiere* pushed forward and began to use their MG-42s to pour more fire into the square orchard. Using grenades and fire and movement, they sought to surround the C Company position and eventually push into it from several different directions at once. While the *9. Kompanie* of *Oblt.* Fritsch was delayed at times, its attack was relentless.

As Fritsch destroyed the orchard positions, *11. Kompanie* of *Ostuf.* Stahl, advancing on the right, wheeled left and attacked the NNSH A Company positions of Major Rhodenizer.[42] It is unclear how many *6. Kompanie* Panzer IV tanks were in action here, but the position of A Company was subdued rather quickly, with the NNSH soldiers that did not flee as their ammunition ran out surrendering to the *Waffen-SS*.

After the orchard positions were destroyed, a further attack occurred on the manor house west of Authie, the Château de Louet, and the *9. Kompanie* carried out this attack as well, clearing it. It appears further German Panzer IV tank losses occurred here from either anti-tank guns firing at very long range from the Hill 75 anti-tank ditch position north of Buron, which is unlikely, or SFR Shermans that had withdrawn to a distance firing at the Panzer IV of *5. Kompanie* that were pushing forward to attempt to move into Gruchy. It was reported that a number of burned Panzer IV crewman were encountered by the *SS-Panzergrenadiere*, staggering wounded back towards Franqueville.

A member of *9. Kp./SS-Pz.Gren.Rgt. 25*, *Strm.* Karl Vasold, recalled, as presented in the Hubert Meyer history:

> The order came: Let's go! March! Attack on Authie with Panzer support. We came under a lot of fire and experienced our first losses. Canadian tanks at the edge of the town were knocked out, and the first house to house combat took place, the town was captured. The next attack was on the Château de St Louet, west of Authie. There was concentrated defensive fire from Canadian anti-tank guns. Some of our Panzers were on fire. Critically wounded Panzer comrades were coming to the rear. They had lost hands, suffered severe burns. They were taken back to Authie. There was much coming and going. Only then we received fire from enemy artillery, and the situation became risky. We also took fire from enemy tanks at Buron. They were poor gunners; the explosions were either ahead or behind us. We assembled at the edge of town and discussed the situation.[43]

It appears that Authie and its château were not the limit for the *9. Kompanie* attack, and the *SS-Panzergrenadiere* pushed forward with the other two *Kompanien* to attack Buron. Some elements of this *Kompanie* appear to have taken the village of Gruchy with a number of *5. Kompanie* tanks, an event not included in Canadian military historians' accounts of the battle. There was no combat in this village, as no Canadian troops from the NNSH appear to have been present, all of the remaining elements of B, C, D Companies and the Support Company being in Buron or the anti-tank ditch position to the north of it.

As this combat was occurring, *11.* and *10. Kompanien* of *SS-Pz.Gren.Rgt. 25* pushed north towards Buron, with the remaining tanks of *6. Kp./SS-Pz.Rgt. 12* following at a distance. The tanks of *7. Kp./SS-Pz.Rgt. 12* to the east near Cussy were echeloned right rear and somewhat halted, as the *Bataillon* they were supporting,

II. Btl./SS-Pz.Gren.Rgt. 25, began its push from the village of Bitot, to be discussed shortly. The attack was going very well at this stage, and at 1945 hours the *Kriegstagebuch* of *SS-Pz.Gren.Rgt. 25* reported 14 Shermans destroyed and 8 officers and 117 men taken prisoner. This entry was made with the data at hand, and the totals would turn out to be higher.[44]

As the Germans advanced to the first buildings, a large *Artillerie* fire strike was delivered by *III. Abt./SS-Pz.Art.Rgt. 12* of *Stubaf.* Bartling, hitting Buron in conjunction with mortar fire. In a powerful infantry assault, it appears Buron was taken with a large number of prisoners from the NNSH C and B Companies, giving up after brief combat with the *SS-Panzergrenadiere*. The Panzer IV tanks of *5.* and *6. Kompanien* supported the attack by driving in on the flanks of the defenders at Buron and firing into the town. The Panzer IVs of *5. Kompanie* did this on the left flank as it drove into Gruchy, and *6. Kompanie* did this on the right flank, advancing to a position just east of Buron. The fighting in Buron went on for some time, the remaining NNSH infantry fighting back as best they could against an enemy that outnumbered them at least three to one.

A consistent factor within first-hand accounts of Canadian infantry that surrendered during this battle was a lack of sufficient ammunition for extended infantry combat. The standard load for a Canadian infantryman in June 1944 was ten 5-round clips for his .303 Lee-Enfield rifle, for a total of 50 rounds. This appears to have been the case with all the NNSH companies in combat on 7 June. Either they were not issued or did not carry enough .303 rifle and Bren light machine gun ammunition in magazine box form to defend their positions in a sustained firefight and may not have received extra bandoliers of .303 clips seen on Canadian infantrymen in photographs of the period. Whatever the reason, once out of ammunition the NNSH infantry often surrendered if surrounded.

Could the NNSH Support Company have helped more to defend Buron? The heavy weapons on Hill 75, the site of the anti-tank ditches, appeared to have been in a good position to fire on the Panzer IV *Züge*, but not to fire on the *SS-Panzergrenadiere*, which had marched right up the D220 and the fields to either side of it to assault the town, their approach hidden from Hill 75 by the village.

In the attack of the three *SS-Panzergrenadiere Kompanien* on Buron, Major Learment of C Company was taken prisoner, and only a few members of B and C Companies of the NNSH managed to escape to the next Canadian defence line, the anti-tank ditch positions on Hill 75, where D Company of Major Kennedy was dug in with the anti-tank guns and some Cameron Highlanders of Ottawa Vickers medium machine guns. The 6-pounder anti-tank guns appear to have been in heavy action, firing at the German tanks with the surviving Shermans of the SFR. After the action at Buron, which appears to have occurred up to 1930 hours, *10.* and *11. Kompanie*, with *9. Kompanie* on the left flank, appear to have emerged from Buron and continued to attempt to push north.

Moving through the field of waist-high wheat, the *SS-Panzergrenadiere* came across the positions for D Company, which it appears was dug in on the south forward slope of the Hill 75 in front of the anti-tank ditch. The *SS-Panzergrenadiere* appear to have advanced aggressively, pushing right up the rise, and there was combat within the NNSH positions, with the remains of B Company's 10 Platoon and D Company's 16 Platoon being surrounded and forced to surrender. It is unclear if any Panzer IV tanks had made it to the anti-tank ditch. The resistance of the NNSH Support Company, D Company and the remains of B and C Companies appears to have been particularly intense here, inflicting heavy casualties on the *10.* and *11. Kompanien* of the *SS-Panzergrenadiere*. Five times the Germans were reported to have assaulted Hill 75 and the anti-tank ditches which D Company of the NNSH were using as trenches. Five times they were driven back, despite heavy supporting fire from the surviving Panzer IV tanks still in action.[45]

At this moment, just after 2030 hours, heavy Canadian RCA field artillery fire finally hit the advance elements of *III. Btl./SS-Pz.Gren.Rgt. 25* as it was locked in combat with the last remains of the NNSH, some of the fire even hitting NNSH positions. The 14th Field Regiment, RCA, after a delay that spanned roughly from the point of the initial Canadian NNSH vanguard advance that morning, was finally firing in support of the 9th Canadian Infantry Brigade.

During this event, some D Company prisoners of the *Waffen-SS* appear to have escaped their captors, who were forced to take cover from the field artillery concentrations. After this bombardment hit the forward *Waffen-SS Züge* in the open, 12 remaining tanks of the SFR attacked, along with the remains of D Company. In this very aggressive counterattack with few forces, the tanks pushed right over some *SS-Panzergrenadiere Züge*, running over some of the Germans as they lay prone in the fields. As the artillery fire from the 14th Field Regiment, RCA FOO teams, continued to engage the Germans, a number of wounded were transported to the rear by the Panzer IV tanks, these most likely from *5. Kompanie*, which had not taken the heavy losses in the same manner as *6. Kompanie*. These tanks were intercepted by *Staf.* Meyer, travelling around the battlefield on a motorcycle-sidecar combination. He ordered the Panzer IVs to counterattack, and they moved off again to continue the firefight north of Buron, the *SS-Panzergrenadiere* there being in trouble and beginning to withdraw.

Strm. Vasold of *9. Kompanie* continues his account, as presented in the Hubert Meyer history:

> We were on the attack in Buron with the remaining Panzers. Again, house-to-house fighting. Many prisoners were taken. We pushed past the edge of the town. Heavy machine-gun fire, we pressed our heads into the ground. There was no possibility of further advance. We had to withdraw again. A Panzer gave us cover fire.[46]

As a result of the heavy RCA field artillery fire and the determined counterattack of the remaining SFR tanks, these being the remains of all three squadrons of the SFR, the *SS-Panzergrenadiere* began to retreat, as well as the Panzer IVs of *5. Kompanie*, through Buron to the vicinity of Authie, which was not under fire from the RCA. What was left of the NNSH D, C and B Companies, also supported by the NNSH Support Company, followed the retreating Germans and pushed into a burning and ruined Buron to find the Germans gone. Too weak to defend the village, the Canadians would abruptly withdraw before dark. During the German withdrawal occurring at the same time, a large number of *SS-Panzergrenadiere* were killed or wounded by RCA field artillery concentrations that were redirected south by the FOO teams. It was at this point that direct contact was broken between the two sides, ending major combat for the day.

Advancing at 1600 hours, at the time the battle near Authie appeared to be going well for Milius's men, the *II. Btl./SS-Pz. Gren.Rgt. 25* of *Stubaf.* Hans Scappini advanced through the wheat fields, their start line being the village of Bitot. This *Bataillon* advanced through and around St Contest to Galmanche and beyond into the fields south-west of Cambes. This *Bataillon* made excellent progress because it faced no opposition in its initial advance. There is little detail that has survived the war due to the destruction of the *II. Btl./SS-Pz. Gren.Rgt. 25 Kriegstagebuch* and the lack of first-hand accounts, but the experience of this unit was almost the exact opposite of *SS-Panzergrenadiere* fighting at Authie and Buron.

Starting from Bitot, *6. Kompanie* of *Hstuf.* Dr Thirey advanced on the left flank to Galmanche. The *5. Kompanie* of *Hstuf.* Kreilein advanced in the centre, right through St Contest and into Galmanche as well, while the *7. Kompanie* of *Ostuf.* Schrott advanced on the right flank towards the left edge of Galmanche. This *Kompanie* pushed into the field south of the Cambes, parallel to the left flank of *I. Btl./SS-Pz. Gren.Rgt. 25*, whose attack and contact with the British 185th Brigade will be discussed shortly.[47]

While the *6.* and *5. Kompanien* of *II. Btl./SS-Pz. Gren.Rgt. 25* halted in Galmanche, the *7. Kompanie*, as mentioned previously, did advance into the fields some distance towards the *SS-Panzergrenadiere* of *2. Kp./SS-Pz. Gren.Rgt. 25*, it also making contact with Anglo-Canadian forces. It was at this point that the tanks of the East Riding Yeomanry of the British 27th Armoured Brigade and British infantry in the way of D Company, the 2nd Battalion, Royal Ulster Rifles (2 RUR) appeared, advancing toward Cambes and its wooded area. This battalion of the British 185th Infantry Brigade had launched its push into the village at roughly 1515 hours. The sudden appearance of British tanks surprised the *Bataillon Kommandeur*, *Stubaf.* Scappini and his headquarters party, which had come to the edge of Galmanche to view the terrain.

Tank fire decapitated Scappini, and *Bataillon* command reverted to *7. Kompanie-Chef Ostuf.* Schrott, who was duly promoted on the arrival of *Staf.* Meyer in his circuit of the regimental positions at the end of the fighting on 7 June. Pulling back to Galmanche as heavy RA field and medium batteries pounded the fields around Cambes and the wooded area, the *II. Btl./SS-Pz.Gren.Rgt. 25* halted and dug in.[48]

The exact role of the group of seven to ten Panzer IV tanks of the *7. Kompanie* during the fighting near Authie and Buron is unclear, but it did lose one tank, Panzer IV '704' of *Oscha*. Radek being a total loss. It appears to have started its advance from Bitot and may have engaged the SFR in a long-range gunnery battle from there in conjunction with the other Panzer IV *Kompanien* and the anti-tank assets of *Pz.Jg.Abt. 200* and other forces of the *21. Pz.Div.* still active in the area. It then followed the advance of *II. Btl./SS-Pz.Gren.Rgt. 25* but was too far back to immediately engage the British tanks that killed the *Bataillon Kommandeur*. The Panzer IV tanks immediately took the British Sherman troop under fire and forced them to pull back.[49]

At roughly 1615 hours and nearly two hours after the attack of *III. Btl./SS-Pz. Gren.Rgt. 25* had commenced near the villages of Franqueville and Authie, the three *SS-Panzergrenadiere Kompanien* of *I. Btl./SS-Pz.Gren.Rgt. 25* under *Stubaf.* Hans Waldmüller began their advance on the villages of Malon and Cambes, the latter being a sprawling series of homes and businesses on a paved road contained within or near a wooded area. Waldmüller, an Eastern Front veteran, had extensive infantry combat experience with the *Leibstandarte*, and had been wounded several times on the Eastern Front.[50]

Pushing north through the fields with *2. Kompanie* on the left flank, *3. Kompanie* in the centre and *1. Kompanie* on the right, the *SS-Panzergrenadiere* advanced towards Cambes, bypassing Malon, which was free of German and Anglo-Canadian forces. The objective that Waldmüller had been given was the village of Anguerny, which was nearly 8.7 kilometres to the north from la Folie, the start line for the *Bataillon*. This was a very ambitious objective over nine kilometres away and would imply that the *SS-Panzergrenadiere* would simply sweep forward and through everything in their path.[51] Even if the *Bataillone* had strong *Artillerie* and tank support, this was an unrealistic goal and could only be achieved if British forces had not occupied Anguerny, which they had. Most of the armoured and artillery support had gone to the *III. Btl./SS-Pz.Gren.Rgt. 25* attacks on Authie and Buron, a battle that was still raging as Waldmüller started his advance.

Pushing forward on the left, *2. Kompanie* of *Ostuf.* Knössel advanced to the left through the village of Malon and encountered no enemy presence. The other two *Kompanien* advanced roughly parallel in the infantry wedge, and soon all three had reached the edges of the wooded area of Cambes, which had its main street run north–south through the village. The idyllic Norman countryside and wooded area exploded into a scene of heavy combat as the first *SS-Panzergrenadiere Zug* pushed north into the woods of Cambes and beyond. It is unclear here if the *Bataillon* was receiving good fire support from *III. Abt./SS-Pz.Art.Rgt. 12* at this point, this artillery unit reporting within its *Kriegstagebuch* that its *7. Batterie* lost radio communications at this time with the *SS-Panzergrenadiere* in the sector.

British tanks of the aforementioned East Riding Yeomanry opened fire with main guns and co-axial machine guns, ripping into the ranks of the *SS-Panzergrenadiere Züge*. The Shermans were also accompanied by the lead platoons of D Company of the 2 RUR, whose soldiers immediately began to fire Bren gun bursts into northern Cambes.

As the tank and infantry fire continued to hit the *SS-Panzergrenadiere*, FOO teams forward with the 2 RUR infantry and ERY tanks observed the first shells from their calls for fire hit the wooded area of Cambes. The shells hit the tops of the many trees lining the main street and the northern section of the village, with horrific results for the *SS-Panzergrenadiere* crouching next to buildings and homes. The shells hitting the treetops would cause an airburst of shrapnel and wood shards to be hurled through the air at terrific speed, lacerating the Germans on the ground.[52] Before this fire hit, some chance encounters did occur with the *Waffen-SS* in the wooded area near Cambes, as it appears the *3. Kompanie* ambushed some Shermans and elements of the 2 RUR D Company that pushed into the wood after the *Waffen-SS* withdrew from the fields. The *SS-Panzergrenadiere* appeared to come out on top, knocking out some Shermans with *Panzerfauste* anti-tank weapons and causing the 2 RUR D Company to pull back. It was then that intense RA field artillery concentrations hit the wooded area. As the casualties inflicted by the tank and artillery fire began to accumulate, the three *Kompanien* made their first withdrawals towards the southern exits from Cambes and into the fields to the south and west after some brief infantry combat. The British RA field artillery fire was just too intense, and the *SS-Panzergrenadier Kompaniechefen* had no solution to the problem.

Support allocated to Waldmüller in the way of armour was measly. This consisted of the five operational Panzer IVs of *8. Kp./SS-Pz.Rgt. 12*, under *Ostuf.* Hans Seigel. These were the only Panzer IVs that had survived the road march, the others having fallen out or under repair on the afternoon of 7 June, as previously noted in Chapter 6. Seigel, who after the war would participate in many battlefield tours and have his recollections reprinted in many books on the Normandy campaign and the *Hitlerjugend*, led his Panzer IV *Zug* cautiously forward, the tanks acting in overwatch while the *SS-Panzergrenadiere* pushed forward in the fields. This was in stark contrast to the battlefield manoeuvres of the *5.* and *6. Kompanien* near Authie, which had charged forward past the infantry.[53]

As the tanks edged forward in the wake of the *SS-Panzergrenadier Kompanien*, they observed heavy medium artillery and naval gunfire, which caused huge explosions in the fields near Cambes and within the village itself. This fire began to hit the positions of the *SS-Panzergrenadiere*, causing some casualties to occur. Looking with his naval binoculars to the east from the cupola of his Panzer IV, Seigel observed camouflaged Panzer IVs of *Pz.Rgt. 22* of the *21. Pz.Div.* observing the advance of the *Waffen-SS*. It was clear to him that there was no activity from the units of the *21. Pz.Div.* to the east near Epron and its surroundings east of the Caen–Douvres north–south railway line. The *21. Pz.Div.* was not attacking. Cognisant of this and the potential threat to his flank the farther north he pushed, it was at this point that Seigel observed what he believed to be *SS-Panzergrenadiere* waving their entrenching tools at his Panzer, indicating enemy presence to the north and signalling for tank support.

Radioing the other Panzer IVs with him to advance, Seigel skirted what the author believes to be the western edge of Malon, and pushed north to the western edge of Cambes, their 7.5cm cannon trained to the north. Moving forward, Seigel drove up to the *SS-Panzergrenadiere* and began to fire at the enemy, though it is unclear from the surviving accounts whether he was engaging British tanks or infantry.

The result for *8. Kp./SS-Pz.Rgt. 12* was a disaster, with one Panzer IV falling out due to a mechanical fault, and Seigel's tank being immobilised by a tree cut down by artillery fire. Further losses were encountered when one Panzer IV was damaged by British tank fire and another lost a track. The last Panzer IV of the force drove into a bomb crater and was immobilised. All this happened in a small area east of Galmanche in a short period of time, effectively removing the tank support allocated to *I. Btl./SS-Pz.Gren.Rgt. 25*.

Faced with the events near Buron and Cambes and the advent of extremely heavy artillery fire along his entire front and a completely open left flank across the Mue river due to the non-appearance of *SS-Pz.Gren.Rgt. 26*, by late afternoon *Staf.* Meyer had been ordered by the *Hitlerjugend Gefechtsstand* to go on the defensive and halt the attack. However, it appears he did not immediately halt the combat, the *Kriegstagebuch* of *SS-Pz.Gren.Rgt. 25* recording that it was not until 2023 hours that *Staf.* Meyer halted the attacks of all *Bataillone*.[54]

This did not stop the Royal Navy from continuing the fight as the late evening wore on. As darkness fell, warships moored off Caen opened fire on multiple targets for an extended period, impairing any continued German operations on the frontage of *SS-Pz.Gren.Rgt. 25*.[55] While Meyer had achieved some success in his attacks, it was only of a temporary tactical nature. The larger result of simply halting the Allies in front of Caen was the more important achievement.

During darkness that evening, the first re-organisations occurred following the battle, *SS-Flak.Abt. 12* being deployed to west of Caen and ordered at 2030 hours to emplace its *Batterien* at Carpiquet airfield and in the vicinity of Cussy and Franqueville. It had seen more intensive combat on this day, its *Batterien* firing forty 8.8cm shells and one thousand and sixty-nine 2cm anti-aircraft shells exclusively at aircraft.[56] After discovering the village of Buron was free of Canadian forces, *III. Btl./ SS-Pz.Gren.Rgt. 25* made the decision to occupy it, but only after the worst of the field and medium artillery and naval gunfire had subsided. In the darkness of the late evening, the *SS-Panzergrenadiere* moved forward from Authie to occupy Buron.

It is not the intent or object of this chapter to go into detail about the extensive war crimes of *III. Btl./SS-Pz.Gren.Rgt. 25* and attached forces following the end of combat as night approached on 7 June. This has been done already in the masterfully researched and written account of the Canadian prisoner of war killings in Normandy by Canadian military historian and former Canadian Forces Judge Advocate General officer Howard Margolian, in his book *Conduct Unbecoming: The Story of the Murder of Canadian Prisoners of War in Normandy*, published in 1998.

However, a summary of events is necessary as it is important to illustrate for the reader the behaviour of the *SS-Panzergrenadiere* in Authie, Buron and the surrounding fields. These events directly support the statement made by the author in the introduction to this work that one of the important sub-factors that led to the defeat of *Hitlerjugend* during this time period is that the *Hitlerjugend* officers and seniors NCOs failed to exercise firm command and control during operations. Despite its long period of training, the *Hitlerjugend* recruits displayed a marked lack of observance of the Geneva Convention in their first operations.

This lack of professionalism exhibited by the *SS-Panzergrenadiere* under the command of the *Bataillon Kompaniechefen* (battalion company commanders) manifested itself in outbursts of murderous rage that saw a multitude of war crimes committed on the eventing of 7 June once combat ended in Authie and Buron. This behaviour illustrated the unvarnished true nature of murderous German National Socialism, and the effects of propaganda the former *Hitlerjugend* had been subjected to since their early teenage years.

This mentality had been reinforced by the approach to combat taken by the junior leaders who were present, which the young *SS-Panzergrenadiere* witnessed, emulated and often exceeded. These veteran junior leaders who had survived two to three years of war by this point had been brutalised by the combat on the Eastern Front in which both sides displayed a complete lack of adherence to the Geneva Convention's rules on prisoner care. This statement is to in no way excuse the events in Authie and Buron, or to endorse the views of *Waffen-SS* apologists. At academic conferences the author has heard the story retold many times that a Canadian infantry platoon commander captured on 7 June had on his person company orders that stated 'no prisoners are to be taken, and this antagonized the Germans'. There has never, to the author's knowledge, been any historical evidence to support this claim, in the way of German or Canadian records or witness statements. Given the speed at which the prisoner-of-war killings began, and the multitude of *SS-Panzergrenadiere* involved, it is highly unlikely any Canadian act or acts spurred them on to 'revenge'.

While the junior leadership at the *SS-Panzergrenadier-Kompanie* level was often a model of brutality, during the events of 7 June it was often the absence of leadership and supervision that arguably allowed some of the worst excesses. It is often overlooked by Anglophone historians that the *III. Btl./SS-Pz.Gren.Rgt. 25* had suffered heavy casualties in the Authie and Buron fighting, and many junior leaders, whose presence influenced the level of discipline among the *SS-Panzergrenadiere* on the battlefield, had been killed or wounded by Canadian defensive fire.

The first war crimes to occur happened in the immediate aftermath of the collapse of Canadian resistance in Authie. Wounded Canadian soldiers of the NNSH C Company were shot or bayonetted in their orchard fighting positions where Captain Fraser of C Company and the A Company platoon had made their stand south of the village. These events were repeated in the positions of A Company north of the village.

The village of Authie in June 1944 was laid out like many French farming villages with a mixture of stone-walled buildings and walled enclosures, often with orchards nearby and the main road leading to other villages running right through the main square. The town square, with its fountain, was surrounded by stone buildings and the D220 road runs right through the square, north to Buron and south to Franqueville. On the western side of the square, there existed a line of trees next to a line of stone buildings. Across the intersection is the town church and graveyard. The scene inside Authie was anything but idyllic on the evening of 7 June – several buildings were on fire, and dead bodies from the combat that afternoon were strewn all over the streets. Emerging from buildings were French civilians: men, women children, and the elderly who had not had a chance to escape in the hours earlier, and who thought the Canadians had liberated them from four years of German occupation and military rule. Within the square and on the exits out of it, the utmost brutality would be exhibited by the *SS-Panzergrenadiere* towards captured and wounded members of the SFR, NNSH, Cameron Highlanders and French inhabitants of the village caught in the wrong place at the wrong time.

Over a period of a couple of hours prior to sunset at 2200 hours, roughly 150 Canadian prisoners of war were rounded up from the fields and in the village. The prisoners were slowly pushed towards the town square, and by last light were gathered there together, assembled most likely by members of *9. Kompanie* or *15. Kp. (Aufklärung)/SS-Pz.Gren.Rgt. 25*, which had arrived on the battlefield that evening.[57] It is unclear from the research of Howard Margolian or archival material researched by the author where exactly the *9. Kompanie Kommandeur* or his senior NCOs were during this phase, and who exactly was 'running the show' within the square.[58]

As the small groups entered the town square, a series of war crimes occurred, carrying on the pattern of events that had begun at the end of combat. The most prominent event was the shooting of a group of eight NNSH soldiers by a group of three *SS-Panzergrenadiere* who conferred about it first in an alley, the event witnessed by a wounded Canadian soldier slumped against a wall.[59] One wounded Canadian soldier was killed by the *Waffen-SS* in a horribly casual manner, and his body was then dragged up the main road and through the square, where it was placed with the body of a second Canadian who had been killed, with the obvious expectation by the Germans that a wheeled or armoured vehicle would crush the bodies.[60] This occurred shortly afterwards, as a *5.* or *6. Kompanie* Panzer IV of *SS-Pz.Rgt. 12* moving south from Buron crushed them, hideously mutilating the bodies under its tracks.[61]

The prisoners, mostly from the NNSH, were told to stand in rows, and orders were barked at them in German that must have sounded very sharp and curt to the Nova Scotians. The *SS-Panzergrenadiere* moved from man to man, stripping everything from them except for their woollen uniforms, belts, boots and underclothing. The search was violent, and immediately the tone was set by the execution by pistol shot of one Canadian who, from eyewitness reports moved his head around in a manner the *Waffen-SS* felt was unacceptable.

Why exactly were the *SS-Panzergrenadiere* so angry and brutal? One can only speculate, but it appears that the most likely reason for their brutality and hair-trigger conduct was because they were shocked at the losses incurred to them by artillery and tank fire in the combat on the north side of Buron. Canadian historian Howard Margolian speculates that it was the twin factors of the heavy losses incurred by the *Waffen-SS*, combined with the prominent destruction of any sort of aura of invincibility or supremacy, which drove the perpetrators of the war crimes to act as they did on the evening of 7 June, these men being primarily from *9.* and *11. Kompanien* of *III. Btl./SS-Pz.Gren.Rgt. 25.*[62]

As this search of the prisoners began, more *5.* and *6. Kompanie* Panzer IV tanks of *II. Abt./SS-Pz.Rgt. 12* began to move back through Authie in order to laager south to refuel and rearm. During this time, much to the horror of the French civilians, a second Panzer IV tank crushed another wounded NNSH soldier, still alive, with its tracks. The French civilians had begun to move out into the street, brutally pushed out of their hiding spaces by the *Waffen-SS* who were searching every building. The French civilians were searched as well, and evidence of any Canadian food or other items given to them was met with brutal beatings. Some *SS-Panzergrenadiere* at this time also began playing with a dead Canadian soldier lying against an ivy-covered wall, moving him into a sitting position, putting a cigarette in his mouth and a wine bottle in his hand.[63]

When the Germans reoccupied Buron during the hours of darkness once they realised Canadian forces had withdrawn, the scenes at Authie were repeated to a certain extent, this time inflicted on a small number of Canadian stragglers who had been taken prisoner. These Canadians were abused by the *SS-Panzergrenadiere* as they were violently rounded up and searched by the *11. Kompanie* of *III. Btl./ SS-Pz.Gren.Rgt. 25*, led by *Ostuf.* Stahl. During the late evening one Canadian soldier who was being searched was discovered to have an object in his pocket. This object could not be removed fast enough for the *SS-Panzergrenadier* searching him, who shot the man in frustration.[64]

Once the searches were complete, large groups of Canadians were marched south. In the semi-darkness, the roads south of Authie and Franqueville were witness to further prisoner killings of a random nature. Marching south in large groups, one case saw several prisoners of war being hustled into a farmhouse and shot. Another group was shot at by a passing marching group of *SS-Panzergrenadiere*, several Canadians suffering bullet wounds. Casual violence occurred as well, as prisoners who could not keep up due to wounds were shot.[65]

Several groups of prisoners were held at the *SS-Pz.Gren.Rgt. 25 Gefechtsstand* of *Staf.* Meyer at the Abbaye Notre-Dame d'Ardenne for a period before being marched south. After a brief interrogation by the *Hitlerjugend* intelligence officer, *Ic. Ostuf.* Doldi, and his escort of *Heer Feldgendarmerie*, most of these prisoners were divided into groups and marched south. The 11 prisoners who remained were beaten and shot to death and buried in the grounds, a mere 20 meters from *Staf.* Meyer's main headquarters building in the Abbaye Notre-Dame d'Ardennes and the *Kommandeur* himself. Marching south, a German truck with Red Cross markings veered into the column, killing and wounding a number of Canadian prisoners. Later that evening, a SFR jeep from Canadian lines took a wrong turn near Les Buissons, and was ambushed by a *Waffen-SS* patrol near Galmanche. One of its occupants, a SFR padre, was killed by the patrol members after his capture by bayonette.[66]

Reviewing the 7 June totals of prisoners of war known to have been executed, the number is 48, if those at Authie, Buron, the Abbaye Notre-Dame d'Ardenne and those killed on the roads are combined. If one includes unverified cases of Germans executing wounded Canadians in slit trenches all over the battlefields of *SS-Pz.Gren.Rgt. 25* immediately post combat, the number of prisoner of war and wounded killings could significantly rise.

This total more than anything else represents a total breakdown in military discipline in the *Waffen-SS* units involved and their embrace of criminality and brutality, especially true for its junior leaders, who in many cases were the lead perpetrators of these crimes.

Analysing the fighting of 7 June and drawing conclusions, one of the most amazing factors of this day, the first in combat for the *Hitlerjugend*, was the lack of Allied artillery fire. This is something important to discuss, as it was only in the late afternoon, and far too late, that the 14th Field Regiment, RCA, provided its first fire support to the NNSH and SFR near Buron. Immediately the impact of this fire was felt on the front lines by the *Waffen-SS*, disrupting their advance further north to Les Buissons and stopping a potential assault on the Stormont, Dundas and Glengarry Highlanders and the NNSH headquarters in the village. Similar British artillery fire hit the elements of *SS-Pz.Gren.Rgt. 25* that had assaulted the British near Cambes, to the east. It appears that it was this lack of fire, more than anything else, which allowed the *Hitlerjugend* to savage the 9th Canadian Infantry Brigade on 7 June, attaining a limited tactical victory in the largest battle on the *SS-Pz.Gren.Rgt. 25* front.

The lack of coordination between the headquarters staffs of the 3rd Canadian Infantry Division, the 9th Canadian Infantry Brigade and the 2nd Canadian

Armoured Brigade regarding the lack of RCA and RA field and medium regiments deployed, or even alerted, to support the dash to Carpiquet displayed a lack of planning ability within Canadian headquarters. It is unfair to blame the divisional Commander, Royal Artillery (CRA), Brigadier Todd, as he had not yet fully taken on a coordinating leadership role with the division on D +1.

The afternoon's fighting is not the only time period in which to fault the performance of the RCA. On its setting out from Villons-les-Buissons on the morning of 7 June, there were not even the briefest artillery concentrations or a small scheduled artillery program to support the NNSH vanguard. This observation is sorely lacking from C.P. Stacey's official history of the Canadian Army's campaign in north-west Europe and from the Royal Regiment of Canadian Artillery's official history of the Second World War, and obviously it is doubtful this type of criticism would have ever been approved. And while the 14th Field Regiment, RCA, is singled out since it had been assigned to support the Canadian armour and infantry on the left flank of the division, the three other Canadian RCA field regiments could have possibly been tasked to provide immediate support, given the emergency the NNSH-SFR vanguard was facing by mid-afternoon.

Both sides on this day claimed to have destroyed a large number of the enemy, the *II. Abt./SS-Pz.Rgt. 12* being no exception. Of course, due to the chaotic nature of combat, exhaustion and human error, not to mention the inability of the regimental *Gefechtsstand* to come to the battlefield to verify claims, the numbers were inflated. Of course, multiple tank crews would claim to have destroyed the same tank and others would claim to have destroyed a tank that Anglo-Canadian forces would later tow away at night to allow it to fight another day.

The Panzer IV *Kompanie* that arguably saw the heaviest combat, *5. Kompanie*, claimed nine Shermans destroyed in Franqueville and Authie. Though taking the heaviest losses, *6. Kompanie* claimed 14 Shermans destroyed as well as three half-tracks and three anti-tank guns in and around Authie. The *7. Kompanie* would claim five Shermans destroyed near Buron. The *8. Kompanie*, lacking its full number of operational *Züge*, could claim only one Sherman destroyed.[67]

What were the long- and short-term effects of these losses? While *II. Abt./SS-Pz. Rgt. 12* had suffered relatively little in the way of personnel losses, the losses of tanks as complete write-offs were a problem. The *Waffen-SS* armoured officers understood new tanks were not plentiful, and the wait to get new tanks straight from Germany was a long one. Thus, for the next roughly two-to-three-month period, what tanks the *Abteilung* did have to fight with were all they would have, and if they were lost, there would be no new ones, or only a trickle of repaired vehicles in small batches. A *Panzerregiment* in 1944 thus could not be handled on the battlefield in a rough or cavalier way, as had been the practice for the *Leibstandarte*, the former home of many of the *SS-Pz.Rgt. 12* officers, in the winter of 1943/44 in Ukraine.

To conclude this chapter, it is a very clear, unavoidable fact that despite their best efforts, the Sherbrooke Fusiliers Regiment were soundly defeated on 7 June. The armoured strength of the regiment, the whole of which deployed for action on the morning of 7 June, was close to its war establishment with an estimated 60 Shermans and 10 Stuart light tanks. The organic and attached anti-tank capability of the NNSH was not insignificant, and this consisted of four M-10 tank destroyers of L Battery of the 3rd Anti-Tank Regiment, RCA, as well as the six 6-pounder anti-tank guns of the NNSH Support Company anti-tank platoon, which were towed by Universal Carriers. The SFR Squadrons were not an insignificant force, and they had trained in England for a significant amount of time prior to Operation *Overlord*. Conversely, despite the SFR receiving a large amount of training and the most up-to-date armour the Western Allies could supply, it was very inexperienced. It had never fought an armoured engagement, or, for lack of a simpler term, a tank battle. While young German crews were also fighting their first battle, the *Waffen-SS Panzerkommandanten* were nearly all veterans of the fighting in Russia and multiple armoured engagements. When the SFR was set upon by German anti-tank guns, mortars, *Artillerie* and the finally the *5.* and *6. Kompanien* of *SS-Pz.Rgt. 12*, it had come up wanting. Because of this failure, the separated NNSH companies, who at the critical point of contact were extremely poorly deployed by the commanding officer of the NNSH, Lieutenant Colonel Petch, were overwhelmed, and except for D Company and the Support Company, were largely destroyed or dispersed.

Examining the Authie–Buron fighting, the NNSH counted 26 dead of its total of 242 casualties, many of these being taken prisoner. The SFR would suffer 63 casualties and lose 21 tanks destroyed and a further 7 damaged. British 185th Infantry Brigade losses on 7 June near Cambes amounted to 31 casualties in the 2 RUR infantry company and 4 Shermans of the East Riding Yeomanry destroyed.[68]

German losses were also heavy, with *III. Btl./SS-Pz.Gren.Rgt. 25* losing 28 dead, 70 wounded and 12 missing. *II. Btl./SS-Pz.Gren.Rgt. 25* lost 21 dead, 38 wounded and 5 missing. The *I. Btl./SS-Pz.Gren.Rgt. 25* would lose 15 dead, 87 wounded and 10 missing. 12 Panzer IVs of *II. Abt./SS-Pz.Rgt. 12* were confirmed total losses, and probably an equivalent number were badly damaged but would return to service.[69]

The organic indirect fire assets of *SS-Pz.Gren.Rgt. 25* had contributed significantly to the weight of fire that rained down on the NNSH and SFR. All three *Bataillone* used three hundred and ninety 8cm mortar rounds, three hundred and fifty-six 7.5cm *I.G.* rounds and one hundred and eighty-five 15cm *I.G.* rounds. Canadian units gave accounts which spoke of mortar fire raining down on them, when in reality it was only a third of what was being fired at them from the smaller calibres, the rest coming from the *Infanterie-Geschütz* howitzers.[70]

Despite this tactical defeat of the 9th Canadian Infantry Brigade vanguard, the outcome of the day's fighting was inconclusive for both sides. Caen and Carpiquet airfield had been denied the enemy, but front lines held by the 9th Canadian Infantry

Brigade as part of the Anglo-Canadian sector of the Normandy beachhead were stronger than ever, and had not been penetrated. At the end of the day on 7 June, a stalemate occurred with the Canadians and British taking up 'Fortress'-style brigade defences, as per their doctrine. The *Hitlerjugend* were forced to do the same and wait for *SS-Pz. Gren. Rgt. 26*, which was very much not according to plan or their supposed doctrine of speed, aggression and the use of maximum armoured force at the critical point. Critically, what was stopping the *Hitlerjugend* continuing the attack was the *Hitlerjugend*.

The *Hitlerjugend* had halted the British 1st Corps advance in front of Caen and the area north-west of it, but it had not been able to break through to the beaches and destroy this sector of the Allied lodgement in occupied France. The division had simply not assembled itself in time and did not have the reserves or resources to continue a 24-hour battle to penetrate the Anglo-Canadian positions at all costs, ably supported by infantry formations from the *Heer*, as their theoretical role on the battlefield had been envisioned by the founders of the *Panzerwaffe* in the pre-war period.

To conclude this analysis of the combat of 7 June between Canadian forces and the *Hitlerjugend*, an encounter battle had been fought that neither side had wanted or been totally prepared to fight. Events had forced *Brig. Fhr.* Witt to commit his division piecemeal in a limited counterattack, certainly not the unified multi-pronged effort that the doctrine demanded. The attempt at using Panzer forces to crush the bridgehead in a quick, hasty attack had failed in the face of an enemy that had overwhelming artillery firepower. Unfortunately for Witt, all three *Bataillone* of *SS-Pz. Gren. Rgt. 25* were now pinned down in defensive *Infanterie* roles which they were not designed for, and they could not quickly be disengaged for further operations without being relieved from their positions at the conclusion of combat on 7 June.

CHAPTER 8

The 7th Canadian Infantry Brigade advances, 7 June 1944

As the battle for Authie raged, the left flank of the *Hitlerjugend* was largely open, and contained only small forces that could at best only temporarily halt an enemy advance west of the Mue river. The regiment intended to take up position there along the RN 13 – *SS-Pz.Gren.Rgt. 26* of *Ostubaf.* Mohnke – had not arrived yet due to the time needed to travel from its assembly area on 6 June and would only have the first elements of its motorised columns arrive in the vicinity of Cheux to the south on the evening of 7 June to link up with reconnaissance elements of *SS-Pz. Aüfkl.Abt. 12* and the *Panzer-Lehr* already in the area.[1]

However, by nightfall on 7 June the Canadians had handily beaten the *Waffen-SS* elements still in transit to the positions they were supposed to occupy.[2] Encountering little to no opposition, the 7th Canadian Infantry Brigade had occupied Putot-en-Bessin, Secqueville en-Bessin, Bray, the twin villages of Norrey-en-Bessin and Bretteville-l'Orgueilleuse and finally La Villeneuve to the east along the paved RN 13. South of this highway was the east–west Caen–Bayeux rail line, which was an excellent defensive obstacle, with a sunken section existing to the immediate west of Putot-en-Bessin that had an overpass built over it.

That morning, the 7th Canadian Infantry Brigade had been ordered to achieve its D-Day objectives by the headquarters of the 3rd Canadian Infantry Division. On the same morning, General Montgomery had verified with British Second Army commander Lieutenant General Dempsey that these objectives were his first priority for the day. Dempsey assured him that was the case, and that the formations of the British 1st and 30th Corps were in motion to capture them.[3]

The Royal Winnipeg Rifles (RWR) had set off from Cruelly at 0650 hours, and shortly afterward had occupied Putot-en-Bessin. Commanded by Lieutenant Colonel Meldram, this unit reached what was designated the left-front bastion facing south for the 7th Canadian Infantry Brigade fortress by 1050 on the morning of 7 June. Thirty minutes earlier the 1st Battalion, the Regina Rifle Regiment, had secured

Bretteveille–Norrey-en-Bessin area straddling the railway line, as well as a bridge over the Mue river at La Villeneuve.[4]

As morning wore on, the fortress position of the 7th Canadian Infantry Brigade solidified, consisting of two infantry battalions forward, RCA Forward Observation Officer (FOO) teams in place, and anti-tank guns of the 3rd Anti-Tank Regiment, RCA, and the British 62nd Anti-Tank Regiment, RA, in support. Heavy machine guns and 3-inch mortars of the Cameron Highlanders of Ottawa were also present, a platoon of this machine-gun battalion being split up amongst the Canadian infantry battalion company positions. A third infantry battalion was also in Secqueville, this being the 1st Battalion, the Canadian Scottish Regiment (Can Scots), along with an understrength armoured regiment of the 2nd Canadian Armoured Brigade, the 1st Hussars (6th Canadian Armoured Regiment).

Putot-en-Bessin was a compact Norman village with a mixture of orchards, homes, small businesses and farm buildings with a series of small lanes crisscrossing it. Roughly 500 metres to the north was the paved RN 13, which crossed the north–south road leading into the village. The village and the area to its south was not ideal tank country, and any sort of armoured attack would be confined to the paved roads and farmers' dirt tracks that led from one village to another.

To the north-east of Putot and the RN 13 was La Ferme La Bergerie, which was located on a small rise, from which the ground along the RN 13 was visible to the west and east. To the west of the La Ferme La Bergerie was high ground near the village of St Croix-Grande Tonne, also located on the RN 13.[5]

RWR CO Lieutenant Colonel Meldram's forward line of defence consisted of all four line companies deployed along the railway line in a linear defence. Dug in west to east from a railway cutting that went over the sunken rail line were A Company, then B Company, C Company, D Company, and finally the carrier platoon deployed to the east to attempt some kind of contact with the neighbouring RRR positions in Bretteville-l'Orgueilleuse. While this deployment offered a strong forward defence and took advantage of the sunken railway line as a defensive barrier, it made an all-around defence that utilised the buildings as bunkers to shelter from artillery fire impossible. Also, being deployed as they were, Meldram did not have a reserve company that was not already engaged in the defence with which to launch a counterattack. And, if a large powerful armoured or infantry force forced its way between the RWR and RRR in Bretteville, the risk of encirclement if attacked from the flank was very real.

The RWR A Company under Major Hodge was dug in on the right flank of the battalion position facing south in and around the Brouay bridge overpass that runs over the sunken Caen–Bayeux railway line, quite close to the neighbouring wooded village of Brouay. Hodge made the decision to send his 7 Platoon of A Company west to establish contact with British infantry units of the 69th Infantry Brigade, none of which had reached the area. In his position, Hodge had at least one 6-pounder anti-tank gun of the RWR anti-tank platoon, as well as a number of Vickers medium machine guns of the Cameron Highlanders of Ottawa covering the Brouay railroad overpass.[6] Next to Hodge was B Company, under Captain Gower, which was dug in on the front right of the village facing south within orchards that are part of the village and with its rear to the most western buildings. Next in line and dug in on both sides of the level railway crossing at Putot was C Company, under Major Jones.

Further east along the rail line was D Company of Major Fulton, dug in within the fields north-east of the village. It had a reasonably good field of fire from its positions and could adequately cover the railway line. In the rear of the four companies and north-east of the village itself was the battalion headquarters of Lieutenant Colonel Meldram. Near the headquarters were the positions of the RWR Support Company minus the guns of the anti-tank platoon, which were forward within the company positions.

After assaulting Juno Beach on 6 June 1944, D-Day, the 1st Battalion, the Regina Rifle Regiment under Lieutenant Colonel Matheson had made steady progress inland, moving from the landing beaches at Courseulles-sur-Mer through the village of Reviers, to a position near Le Fresne-Camilly by nightfall on 6 June 1944.[7] The following day the regiment pushed further south in order to take up its assigned location in its parent 7th Canadian Infantry Brigade's defensive line, 'Oak'.[8] The designated defensive position for RRR, centred on the village of Bretteville-l'Orgueilleuse, was first reached by the vanguard of the battalion at 0730 hours, supported by a troop of Sherman tanks from the 1st Hussars.[9] The individual infantry line companies were not mechanised, and simply marched south into the area. An anti-tank battery of the 3rd Anti-Tank Regiment, RCA, soon joined them, as well as a Vickers medium machine-gun company of the aforementioned Cameron Highlanders of Ottawa Machine Gun Regiment.[10]

Matheson immediately began planning how to deploy his battalion's companies in discussion with his brigade commander, Brigadier Foster of the 7th Canadian Infantry Brigade. His initial dispositions would see his companies take up positions in the area Rots, La Villeneuve, Bretteville-l'Orgueilleuse and Norrey-en-Bessin, dominating the local road network, its villages and prominent geographic features.[11] This was in line with the Anglo-Canadian infantry doctrine circa 1944 which demanded 'defended localities' if a continuously manned defensive line was not possible or feasible.[12] The RCA assets designed to support the 7th Canadian Infantry Brigade fortress were significant, and consisted of the 12th and 13th Field Regiments, RCA, with a total of 48 M7 105mm Priest self-propelled guns deployed in the village of Bray within designated gun position 'Nora', as the 12th Field Group, RCA.[13] West of this and roughly one kilometre north of Putot were the battery positions of the 62nd Anti-Tank Regiment, Royal Artillery (RA), and remaining battery positions of the 3rd Anti-Tank Regiment, RCA.[14] Brigadier Foster also realised that a gap existed on his left flank, facing south from the village of Cairon east of the Mue river to the area east of the twin villages of La Villeneuve and Le Bourg. To fill this gap, a strongpoint was created at the village of Cairon to the north-east with a company of the 1st Battalion, the Canadian Scottish Regiment, a tank squadron of the already weakened 1st Hussars and some attached RCA anti-tank guns, although from which unit the author has not ascertained, but most likely a troop from the 3rd Anti-Tank Regiment, RCA.

Additional forces at this time could not be spared from the 9th Canadian Infantry Brigade in the period after 7 June, as its units were being concentrated for a possible all-out assault to recapture Buron and Authie following its defeat, to be supported by all 3rd Canadian Infantry Division divisional artillery.[15]

Upon their arrival on the morning of 7 June, the forward 7th Canadian Infantry Brigade forces immediately began entrenching themselves to form a brigade 'fortress' in line with Anglo-Canadian doctrine. The area had been studied by the Anglo-Canadian high command and strongpoints were purposefully chosen to defend against the anticipated German armoured counterstroke, using land features such as the Caen–Bayeux railway line as obvious anti-tank barriers.

Immediately facing these formations and the supporting armour of the 2nd Canadian Armoured Brigade on 7 June was very little in the way of German resistance, only small recce parties and remnants of forces that had withdrawn from the *Atlantikwall* being present for the moment. Until more *Hitlerjugend* forces could arrive, *SS-Pz.Gren.Rgt. 25*, now established north-west of Caen east of the Mue, had an open left flank. While *SS-Pz.Gren.Rgt. 26* and the *Panzer-Lehr* columns of vehicles ground their way forward, the present situation was very disconcerting to *Hitlerjugend Kommandeur Brig.Fhr.* Witt and *Staf.* Meyer, among others.[16]

Canadian and British sources are very vague with regard to the contact between the British 69th Infantry Brigade and Canadian forces on 7 June. Any contact that did exist would have been between patrols sent out by the infantry battalions of each brigade, but unfortunately any sort of observation or contact between fighting positions did not exist. French military historian Georges Bernage places the nearest British position on 7 June just north of Loucelles and just west of St Croix Grand Tonne.[17] The British simply had not closed the distance to Putot as of 7 June due to a variety of factors, combat with German reconnaissance forces and stragglers from the *Atlantikwall* being the chief causes.

Further to the west on 7 June, the British 50th Infantry Division advanced out of its front-line positions which had been gained by nightfall the previous day and came close to achieving its list of 6 June objectives. Columns of the British 151st Infantry Brigade reached the river Aure south of Bayeux at 0815 hours, sweeping aside negligible resistance. The neighbouring 69th Infantry Brigade would also advance, but its progress would be halted by a series of obstacles, including barbed wire, minefields and finally a *Luftwaffe* radio station that needed to be subdued. The 56th Infantry Brigade was given the task of clearing the city of Bayeux, and its process was temporarily halted by the jubilation of the city's population, throngs rushing out to see and meet the liberators. All three British infantry brigades involved in the 7 June advance would have had some British 8th Armoured Brigade forces attached to them, and these armoured units provided important support throughout the day to ensure the advance of all columns was successful.[18] Further British advances that day included the clearing of Longues-sur-Mer, an attack on Port-en-Bessin and pushing forward to the British Second Army boundary in the area of the river Drôme.[19]

Many German pockets of resistance remained near the beaches, and British troops had bypassed the worst of these, allowing their vanguards to avoid getting bogged down in clearing every last German from an area. But this left a situation in which follow-on forces would have to often 'sweep' sectors to catch lone German holdouts that had been hiding and refused to surrender to passing Allied columns. The destruction of the thin and brittle German defensive 'crust' that was the *Atlantikwall* had allowed the Anglo-Canadian forces, now past it, to surge forward against little to no resistance, and were now free to capture elusive D-Day objectives and establish brigade-level fortresses against which it was hoped the German armoured reserves would smash themselves to bits.

But if small pockets of Germans were present, it mattered little in comparison to the larger picture, as these forces would soon be overwhelmed by Allied follow-on forces, many of them from the assembling British 8th Armoured Brigade under Brigadier Cracroft. This brigade would begin to concentrate itself in the Martragny area on 7 June for a future push forward to extend the front lines of the British 30th Corps forces. The forces allocated to the British armoured brigade were as follows: the 4th/7th Royal Dragoon Guards, the Sherwood Ranger Yeomanry, and the 24th Lancers armoured regiments of the Royal Armoured Corps (RAC), the 147th Field Regiment, RA, and the 168th Light Field Ambulance. Attached forces from the 50th British Infantry Division included the 61st Reconnaissance Regiment, RAC, the 1st Battalion, the Dorset Regiment, the 280th Anti-Tank Battery, RA, A Company of the 2nd Battalion, the Cheshire Regiment Machine Gun Battalion, and the 86th Field Regiment, RA.[20]

What was happening on the left flank of the *Hitlerjugend* on 7 June? The simple answer is: not enough. The main body of *SS-Pz.Aufkl.Abt. 12* was beginning to concentrate near the village of Audrieu, within the bocage country north-west of Cristot. From this base it was sending out screening forces, some of which would have brief combat with advancing British and Canadian units on 7 June. At roughly 1800 hours French military historian Jean-Claude Perrigault asserts that the first part of the *Panzer-Lehr*, in the way of the lead elements of *II. Btl.(Gepanzert)/Pz.Gren.Lehr.Rgt. 902*, had reached the area just south of the village of Brouay, immediately south-west of Putot.[21] The tactical *Hauptquartier* of *I. SS-Pz.Korps*, attempting to assert control of a situation that was very fluid and made difficult by the seemingly endless delays to German units travelling from one point to another by the ever-present Allied fighter-bombers, had established itself 20 kilometres north-west of Falaise, and at 1600 hours was in contact with the *Panzer-Lehr* command staff.

Ogruf. Dietrich, *Oberbefehlshaber* of the *I. SS-Pz.Korps*, at this time made a momentous decision regarding the arriving *Panzer-Lehr*, given the presence of British forces and their seizure of the initiative to the west. Rather than attack straight north with the *Hitlerjugend*, he ordered *Gen.Lt.* Bayerlein, *Kommandeur* of the *Panzer-Lehr*, to be in position to attack along the Caen–Bayeux railroad toward Bayeux with two *Kampfgruppen* on 8 June. The previous plan for the *Panzer-Lehr* was to have two of its *Kampfgruppen* assemble in the Norrey-en-Bessin-Brouay area, and then attack north after making contact with the *Hitlerjugend*.

Detailed orders would be issued by Bayerlein for 8 June, but these would be rendered useless due to the later direction of Dietrich for elements of the *Hitlerjugend* to fill the void next to *SS-Pz.Gren.Rgt. 25* due to the inability of the *Panzer-Lehr* to move fast enough. One of the assembly areas designated for the *Panzer-Lehr*, that of Norrey-en-Bessin and Bretteville-l'Orgueilleuse, had already fallen to the Canadians that morning. The closest approaching regimental headquarters of the *Panzer-Lehr* was that that of *Pz.Gren.Lehr.Rgt. 902*'s *Oberst* Gutmann, and on the night of 7/8 June, it was still travelling the roads south of Cheux. It, like many *Panzer-Lehr* vehicle columns, had at times attempted to go cross-country to get off the roads and away from the burning wreckage of previous Jabo attacks, with mixed results. The wheeled vehicles got stuck trying to follow the tanks, half-tracks and self-propelled guns that tore up the French farmers' fields, causing even more delays.[22]

The finale to the chaos came when *Gen.Lt.* Bayerlein of the *Panzer-Lehr* was nearly killed by a fighter-bomber attack on the evening of 7 June, he and his staff being forced to stop their car and flee into the ditches, one staff member losing his life to the low-level strafing from Thunderbolts in the process.[23]

CHAPTER 9

The first battle of Caen: The 8 June 1944 attack of *SS-Pz.Gren.Rgt. 26*

As dawn broke on 8 June, any chance for the German *Panzerdivisionen* to easily cut through to the coast in the same manner that the *Kampfgruppe* from the *21. Pz.Div.* had done on 6 June, pushing its way between the Anglo-Canadian forces on Juno and Sword Beaches, had been lost. Additional new Allied combat power, in the form of tanks, guns and personnel, had been landed in the period 6–8 June, meaning only grinding, attrition warfare was a realistic possibility. *Ogruf.* Dietrich, the *Kommandeur* of the *I. SS-Pz.Korps*, appears to have begun to realise this, but the *Oberbefehlshaber* of *Panzergruppe West, Gen.d.Pz.Tr.* von Schweppenburg, was still hopeful some kind of offensive action could be launched, and was soon touring units on the front lines to gain an appreciation of conditions there.

Enough Anglo-Canadian forces were now in place to man a nearly continuous front line, and German units still arriving had to first attempt to form their own defended line before considering concentrating their forces in preparation for a massed attack. In order to attempt to establish a defensive line and at the same time establish conditions necessary for further assaults, arriving *Hitlerjugend* units would be directed to destroy any British Second Army units they found in their planned jump-off positions.

Some opportunities for fluid manoeuvre on 8 June still existed, but mainly for forces of the British 50th Infantry Division and 8th Armoured Brigade west of the Mue, who had ample units to both hold the line and launch determined advances to seize territory to the south. Directly in the path of the *Waffen-SS* units advancing as part of the *Hitlerjugend's* western flank, the Canadians were busy building fortress-like positions for their infantry battalions and supporting arms.

As previously mentioned, the absence of the two *Panzergrenadierregimenter* of the *Panzer-Lehr*, which were yet to arrive, had forced *Ogruf.* Dietrich to adjust his operational plan for 8 June. In the absence of the destroyed *I. SS-Pz.Korps* war diary *Kriegstagebuch* records, the author has concluded that Dietrich ordered *SS-Pz.Gren.*

Rgt. 26, arriving south-west of Caen, into the area initially selected for battlegroups from the *Pz.Gren.Lehr.Rgt. 901* and *902* due to their delayed arrival. *SS-Pz.Gren. Rgt. 26* was to be supported by *SS-Pz.Aüfkl.Abt. 12*, which was ordered to guard the temporarily unguarded western flank of the *Hitlerjugend*. This type of role for the specialised reconnaissance force of the *Hitlerjugend* was one they were capable of, but was also a mismanagement of its resources and potential. However, circumstances deemed it necessary due to the total absence of strong *Panzer-Lehr* forces.

It is unclear exactly where the German higher command, in this case the *I. SS-Pz. Korps*, initially planned, on 7 June, for the *SS-Pz.Gren.Rgt. 26* to be deployed. It will never be known if the regiment was intended to actually be placed on the right of *SS-Pz.Gren.Rgt. 25*. This all became irrelevant when it became apparent that that Mohnke's regiment was needed on the left flank to fill a gaping hole that the absent *Panzer-Lehr* could not fill right away due to its delayed transit.

As discussed in the last chapter, what made the entire matter worse was that the *Panzer-Lehr* tactical *Gefechtsstand* of *Gen.Lt.* Bayerlein had not been adequately informed of events due to total radio silence and the fact that his headquarters was in transit and away from telephone landlines and exchanges. As a result, it was impossible for them to inform their subordinate *Panzergrenadier* units, who in error began to arrive on the night and early morning of 8 June behind the first *SS-Pz. Gren.Rgt. 26* forces, to be discussed shortly, that had beaten them to the area south of Bretteville-l'Orgueilleuse.[1]

Dietrich and his *Chef des Stabes, Brig.Fhr.* Fritz Kraemer, had made the decision to redeploy *SS-Pz.Gren.Rgt. 26* due to military necessity. Because of the communication challenges with Bayerlein, proper instructions to deploy his units did not reach him, and it is possible that even if he had received these orders, he could not have communicated them rapidly enough to stop the first forces of the *Panzer-Lehr* arriving at the wrong place. Because of this, military historians have judged Dietrich a poor *Korpskommandeur*, and highlighted in their accounts that elements of two *Panzerdivisionen* attempted to deploy into the same area. It should also be noted that the severe losses inflicted by Allied Jabo bombing and strafing runs had also resulted in a large number of German radios being rendered inoperable or destroyed, making the command-and-control situation infinitely worse.[2]

Whether within his headquarters in Château La Roche Guyon, 40 kilometres north of Paris, or visiting headquarters at the front, *G.F.M.* Rommel at this point was desperately trying to co-ordinate a mass action between the *Panzer-Lehr, Hitlerjugend* and *21. Pz.Div.* for a three-division push, sometime within the next few days to either drive the Allies into the sea or at least gain the overall initiative.[3] This was impossible at the moment due to Allied air and ground attacks which disrupted travel, assembly and forced the arriving German units into immediate defensive duties and into launching immediate counterattacks.

The advance units of *SS-Pz.Gren.Rgt. 26* of *Ostubaf.* Mohnke, minus the Panther tanks of *I. Abt./SS-Pz.Rgt. 12*, which was still in transit, began filtering into the area west of Caen in the darkness late on the night of 7/8 June. To the west and east of the mass of *SS-Pz.Aüfkl.Abt. 12* at Audrieu, which had established a picket line against advancing British and Canadian forces, no German troops were present to hold off or even delay a British advance from Sword Beach, the majority of the *Atlantikwall* forces in the area having been destroyed by nightfall on 7 June. In the area west and south-west of Bayeux, scattered a *352. Inf.Div.* force was being driven back by US and British forces.

By midnight on 7 June the three *SS-Panzergrenadier Bataillone* of Mohnke's regiment were close to or beginning to assemble in their jumping-off points for offensive operations the next day. As mentioned earlier, Witt had ordered Mohnke to attack at first light on 8 June to both defeat Allied forces in the area and close the gap between *SS-Pz.Gren.Rgt. 25* and the *SS-Pz.Aüfkl.Abt. 12* in Audrieu. Specifically, Mohnke was ordered to capture Putot, Bretteville, Norrey-en-Bessin and Brouay to accomplish this.

Going into more detail, the *Befehl für der Angriff* order issued at 2140 hours on 7 June, which survived the war, was distributed to the *Bataillone Kommandeure* for action on 8 June or whenever their units arrived. The immediate attack objectives were determined by the reconnaissance reports from *SS-Pz.Aüfkl.Abt. 12*, which detected the presence of the 7th Canadian Infantry Brigade. The final attack objectives for the *Bataillone* were quite ambitious, with Bernières-sur-Mer being the final target for the regiment, right in the centre of the Juno Beach landing zone. The document also shows that the *Hitlerjugend* was aware, without having all the details, of possible deployment orders that placed both *Hitlerjugend* and *Panzer-Lehr* units in the same area with the words 'The *Panzer-Lehr* will lift left after arriving' and that *SS-Pz.Aüfkl. Abt. 12* was to secure the left flank of the regiment. The order also stresses that the units must be deployed with all possible speed.[4]

The right flank of the regimental attack was to be carried out by *I. Btl./SS-Pz. Gren.Rgt. 26*, supported by a *Zug* from *13. Kp.(s.I.G.)/SS-Pz.Gren.Rgt. 26* and a *Zug* from *14. Kp.(Flak)/SS-Pz.Gren.Rgt. 26*. The final object for *Stubaf.* Krause, *Kommandeur* of *I. Btl./SS-Pz.Gren.Rgt. 26*, was St Aubin-sur-Mer. The left flank of the regiment's attack was to be executed by *II. Btl./SS-Pz.Gren.Rgt. 26* of *Stubaf.* Seibken, with the same supporting forces as assigned to Krause's *Bataillon*. Its objective was Courseulles-sur-Mer, and its deployment was to be staggered left initially to help shield the flank of *I. Btl./SS-Pz.Gren.Rgt. 26* until more units of the *Panzer-Lehr* arrived in the area west of Audrieu.[5] *III. Btl.(Gepanzert)/SS-Pz.Gren.Rgt. 26* was to initially be the regimental reserve in the area Vendes–Juvigny–St Vaast. Both of the attacking *Bataillone* were ordered to conduct extensive combat reconnaissance, and the time when the *Bataillone* were ordered to open fire was left to the discretion of the two *Bataillone Kommandeure*. The regimental *Gefechtsstand* of Monke and his adjutant, *Hstuf.* Kaiser, was established in Vendes.[6]

In a radio message whose written slip has survived the conflict, *Brig.Fhr.* Witt ordered that the enemy on the front of *SS-Pz.Aüfkl.Abt. 12* were to be thrown towards the Seulles region, in order to make way for a larger division-level attack, to be carried out in conjunction, it was hoped, with the other forces of the *I. SS-Pz.Korps*, these being *21. Pz.Div.* to the east and the advancing *Panzer-Lehr* to the west. To do this, Witt ordered that the SPW 251 half-track equipped *III. Btl. (Gepanzert)/SS-Pz.Gren.Rgt. 26* be possibly subordinated for this purpose rather than staying in reserve.[7]

The finalised initial operational plan called for the *SS-Panzergrenadiere* forces of *SS-Pz.Gren.Rgt. 26* – supported by *II. Abt./SS-Pz.Art.Rgt. 12* and whatever tanks from *I. Abt./SS-Pz.Rgt. 12* managed to appear – to capture three villages along or just north or south of the Caen–Bayeux railway line and the parallel RN 13 paved highway running from Caen to Bayeux. The *I. Btl./SS-Pz.Gren.Rgt. 26* was to capture Norrey-en-Bessin and Bretteville, the *II. Btl./SS-Pz.Gren.Rgt. 26* was to capture Putot, and the *III. Btl.(Gepanzert)/SS-Pz.Gren.Rgt. 26* was to follow the previous *Bataillone* echeloned west, establishing contact with the arriving forces for the *Panzer-Lehr* and those of *SS-Pz.Aüfkl.Abt. 12* already in the area. It was expected, perhaps unrealistically, by the leadership of the *Hitlerjugend* and *SS-Pz.Gren.Rgt. 26*, that the *Panzer-Lehr* was to appear later in the day and secure the area to the west of village of Brouay.

The general terrain in the area must be discussed to explain the limited role armour had south of the Caen–Bayeux railway line. While some open, flat areas did exist near Norrey-en-Bessin and Bretteville, the Putot-en-Bessin and Brouay areas were heavily forested south of the rail line and in places the sunken nature of the railroad provided a significant terrain obstacle. The terrain was broken with hedges, hills and wooded areas, the high points in the area being Hill 99 near Cheux to the south and a rise that ran from this point to Hills 102 and 103 near Cristot to the north-west.[9]

While the *Kriegstagebuch* war diary annexes for the *I. SS-Pz.Korps* in June 1944 have not survived, the operational order for the *Panzer-Lehr* on 8 June did, and it states which objectives were assigned to the *21. Pz.Div.*, the *Hitlerjugend* and the *Panzer-Lehr*, the three main attack forces under the command of *I. SS-Pz.Korps*. The partial reprint (only points 3–5, 8 and 13 being relevant) of the *Panzer-Lehr* operation order from Meyer's *Hitlerjugend* divisional history is as follows:

3) *I. SS-Pz.Korps* with attached *21. Pz.Div.*, *SS-Pz.Div. HJ* [*Hitlerjugend*] and *Panzer-Lehr* will advance from the Caen–St. Croix area into the beachhead and capture the line St. Aubin–Vauvres–Cruelly. It will secure the left flank in line Carcagny–Ellon–Trungy by reconnaissance forces.

4) *Panzer-Lehr* will assemble at 0300 hours in the night of 7 to 8 June in such a manner as it can, on the order of the division, attack in the direction of Courseulles.

12.ᛋ-Pz.Division "Hitlerjugend"
Pz.Gren.Rgt.26

Rgt.Gef.St., den 7.6.44

-Kommandeur-

B e f e h l für den Angriff am 7.6.44
==

1.) Am 6.6.44 zwischen Dives und Ornemündung abgesprungene feindl.
Fallschirmjäger halten in Linie P e t i v i l l e - B a v e n
- R a n v e l l e. Der westl. der Orne seegelandete Feind hat
die Linie B e n o n v i l l e - C r e u l l y - R y e s -
A s n e l l e s im Angriff nach Süden überschritten.
Im Angriffsstreifen des Rgt. wurde festgestellt: Um 12.00 Uhr
2 feindl. Panzerspähwagen 2 km südwestl. 150, feindl. Brücken-
posten 1 km südl. 71, Feindfeuer von 107 auf Straße 122 - 52.

2.) Das Rgt. greift den westl. der Ornemündung gelandeten Feind
rechts an Rgt.25 angelehnt, links mit offener Flanke an und
stößt bis zum Meer durch und nimmt den Ort B e r n i e r e s -
sur Mer.
Die Pz.-Lehr-Div. wird nach Eintreffen links neben 12.ᛋ-Pz.Div.
(dann linker Nachbar des Rgt.26) zum Angriff angesetzt werden.
Zunächst klärt die Pz.Aufkl.-Abt.12 in der linken Flanke auf.

3.) Hierzu stellen sich zum Angriff bereit:
   a. Rechts das verst. I./26 (verst. durch 2 Bttr. II./ᛋ-Pz.Art.Rgt.1
   1 Zug 13./26, 1 Zug 14./26)
   Bereitstellungsraum: C h e u x, St. M a r t i n (ausschl.),
   T e s s e l, B r e t t e v i l l e, R a n r a y.
   Grenze rechts zum Rgt.25: Bachlauf von St. M a u r i e n bis
   zum Zusammenfluß 2 km westl. C o l o m b y, (B a s l y zu I./
   Bahnübergang 800 m westl. St. A u b i n - sur Mer

   b. Links das verst. II./26 (verst. durch 1 Bttr. II./ᛋ-Pz.Art.Rgt.1
   2 Züge 13./26, 1 Zug 14./26)
   Bereitstellungsraum: St. M a r t i n (einschl.), l a C a n d
   R u e, J u v i g n y (einschl.), V e n d e s (einschl.).
   Grenze links zum später angreifenden Pz.-Lehr-Div.:
   C r i s t o t, Höhenrücken bis Straßenkreuz 1 km nördl. P u t o
   Verlauf des Baches bis R e v i e r s (zum II.Btl.), C o u r -
   s e u l l e s - sur Mer (ausschl.).

4.) Trennungslinie zwischen beiden Btl.:
Straßengabel bei St. M a r t i n, l e M e s n i l - P a t r y
(zu II.Btl.), Straßengabel 500 m Straßenkreuz 500 m nordwest
Kirche B r e t t e v i l l e, Straße bis C a m i l l y,
(Straße und Ort zum I.Btl.), M o u l m e a u x (zum I.Btl.),
Westrand B e r n i e r e s - sur Mer.

5.) Die Bereitstellung ist sofort einzunehmen.
Vorderster Rand der Bereitstellung:
Straße 500 m südl. St. M a u r i e n, Straßengabel bei St.
M a r t i n, l a C a n d e - R u e, J u v i g n y.

- 2 -

- 2 -

6.) Bisher unterstellte Teile 16./26 sind sofort nach L a n d e l
l e in Marsch zu setzen und stehen dort zur Verfügung des Rgt.
15.Kp. ist abzulösen und steht ebenfalls mit allen Teilen der
Stabskp. dem Rgt. zur Verfügung.
15.Kp. sammelt in dem Raum B o r d e l - la S e n e v i e -
r y. Besondere Aufklärungsaufträge ergehen noch.

7.) Aufträge:
 a. Verst. I./26 stößt mit Masse durch und nimmt B e r n i e r e s
 b. Verst. II./26, links rückwärts gestaffelt, schirmt mit allen
Kräften den Angriff der Div. gegen den S e u l l e s - Ab-
schnitt ostw. der Linie L u m c e l l e s - St. G a b r i e l
ab, bis Pz.-Lehr-Div. im Angriff die gleiche Höhe erreicht hat.
Enge Verbindung zwischen beiden Btl., sowie zwischen I./26
und Rgt.25 ist möglichst zu halten.
 c. Verst. III.(gp.)/26 (verst. durch 1 Zug(SFL) 14./26) ist Div.
Reserve und steht im Raum V e n d e s (ausschl.), J u v i g -
n y (ausschl.), St. V a a s t und südl. davon zur Verfügung
der Div.
 d. Durch I. und II./26 ist bis Angriffsbeginn intensive Gefechtsaufklärung bis Straße beiderseits Bezugspunkt 7 vorzutreiben.
 e. Feuereröffnung der Art. nach Ermessen der Btl.Kdr.

8.) Mit Angriffsbeginn ist umgehend zu rechnen. Er wird rechtzeitig durch das Rgt. befohlen.
Erfolgte Bereitstellung ist beschleunigt zu melden.
Es muß damit gerechnet werden, daß vor Eintreffen aller Verbände mit dem Angriff begonnen wird.

9.) Nachrichtenverbindungen:
Funk wie bisher. Draht zum II.Btl.

10.) Meldungen sind laufend halbstündl. oder bei besonderen Ereig-
nissen sofort unter Benutzung der Bezugspunktkarte "Fall C"
zu erstatten.

11.) Rgt.Gef.St.: 800 m südl. V e n d e s, später hinter dem
I.Btl.

12.) Krankenkraftwagen-Haltestellen
Herb-südl.-im- Im Waldstück hart südl. J u v i g n y.
H.V.Pl.: im Raum um M i s s y. Ab Missy Beschilderung.

13.) Jedes Btl. stellt sofort einen Ord.Offz. zum Rgt.ab.
Meldung umgehend auf dem Rgt.Gef.St. mit geländegängigen Kfz.

Vom Erfolg des Angriffes, insbesondere unserer Division
hängt im hohen Maße die weitere Entwickelung der Lage ab.

SS-Obersturmbannführer
u. Rgt. Kommandeur

Operation order for the 8 June attack of *SS-Pz.Gren.Rgt. 26* dated 7 June 1944. Intended end state was to liquidate the Juno Beach landing area.[8] Signed by *Ostubaf.* Mohnke. (Vojenský ústřední archiv)

5) To be assembled:

Pz-Lehr.Gren.Rgt. 901 on the right, *Pz-Lehr.Gren.Rgt. 902* on the left. Dividing line Le Mesnil-Patry–Putot (902)–Secqueville (901)–Lantheuil (902) Forward line of assembly; Road to Bayeux.

8) *Pz-Lehr.Aüfkl.Abt. 130* will advance via Villers–Bocage to the north-west and capture the line Le Ducet–Ellon–Trungy and thus secure the left flank of the division. *SS-Pz.Aüfkl.Abt. 12* will link up to the east and secure up to the assembly area of the division. Dividing line: Road Tilly–Bayeux.

13) Division command post will be located in the Cheux area.[10]

The excerpts from the *Panzer-Lehr* 8 June 1944 divisional operation order illustrate that by mid-morning large parts of it were now irrelevant, as German units already in the area by 8 June were involved in heavy combat with Canadian and British forces that had occupied most of locations named in the written order. With the exception of some advance units, the remainder of the *Panzer-Lehr* was also unable to even reach the battle area in time to support in any meaningful way the *Hitlerjugend's* 8 June attacks.

It must be noted that *Ogruf.* Dietrich and his staff were responding to a very dynamic and fluid situation, and attempting to do so as rapidly as possible. The appearance of ad hoc half measures in the way of German countermoves was due to real time pressures, the perceived danger caused by rampant advances of Allied forces, and the threat posed by the gaping hole in the front from the Mue west. In this area the scattered units of the *352. Inf.Div.* were in full fighting retreat from British and US forces driving forward from Omaha Beach in the west and Sword Beach to the north-east of Bayeux.

As discussed earlier, the tanks that were meant to support the future operations of *SS-Pz.Gren.Rgt. 26* were late arriving. For *I. Abt./SS Pz.Rgt. 12*, which had 66 Panther tanks on strength led by *Stubaf.* Jürgensen, the night of 7/8 June was spent slowly crawling along the roads to the battle zone, their progress limited by the tanks having to drive without lights in blackout conditions. On the morning of 8 June, the *Kompanien* were directed to depart their latest waypoint at Maizert at 0930 hours once they had refuelled, but the *1.*, *3.* and *4. Kompanien* would not arrive in the vicinity of Caen until roughly 1600 hours that day.[11]

Moving into its assembly position in Cheux during the night of 7/8 June, the attack of *I. Btl./SS-Pz.Gren.Rgt. 26* in the early hours of 8 June was not a rushed affair. Fire support was planned to be provided by *5.* and *6. Batterien* of *II. Abt./SS-Pz.Art.Rgt. 12*.[12] While the attempt to attack Canadian positions was well planned, it lacked armour to support it. This support was vital if the enemy, the entrenched Canadian infantry of the 1st Battalion, the Regina Rifle Regiment (RRR), was to be overwhelmed. This Canadian battalion had had time, with its attached forces, to fortify its positions and arrange for powerful RCA field artillery support in the way of a series of pre-registered defensive fire (DF) fire tasks.

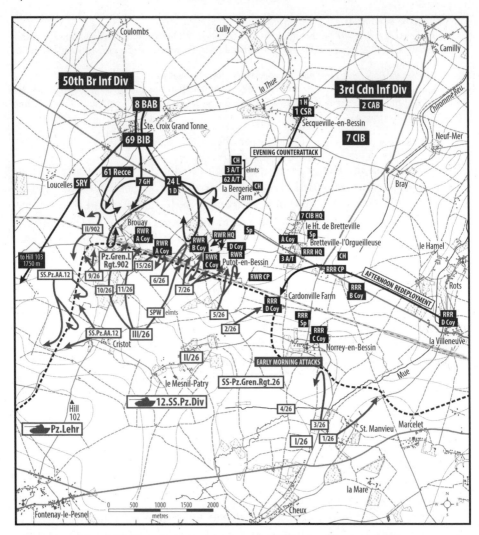

Attack of *SS-Pz.Gren.Rgt. 26*, 8 June 1944. (Map by Mike Bechthold)

Once the *Kompanien* of *I. Btl./SS-Pz.Gren.Rgt. 26* had debussed from their truck transport that had got into their assembly areas, *Stubaf.* Krause, the *Bataillon Kommandeur*, gave his orders to his assembled *Kompaniechefen* (company commanders). The objectives immediately in front of the *Bataillon* were to be seized by silent night attacks; with stealth, speed and determination making up for the very visible lack of *Artillerie* and armoured support. Surprise was doubtful, as it was reported some minor contact with Anglo-Canadian forces had occurred in the area one kilometre north of Vendes.[13]

On the far-left flank, *2. Kp./SS-Pz.Gren.Rgt. 26* was to attack the outskirts of Bretteville by crossing the Caen–Bayeux railway line and pushing into the village. It appears fire support was also to be provided by *SS-Pz.Art.Rgt. 12*, but little to no detail exists on what unit was close enough to give the actual support. In the action that followed, Canadian radio interference stopped the German forward observer teams from calling in or arranging support.[14] This could have been overcome by motorcycle messengers delivering messages to the German *Batterie* locations to the rear – the locations of the objective villages were not subject to change, and something basic in the way of support could have been arranged even if the attack had to be delayed.

After the verbal orders group of Krause, the *Kompaniechefen* then returned to their *Kompanien* in order to give their orders and make final preparations. The *4. (Schwere) Kompanie* divided its assets among the three *SS-Panzergrenadier Kompanien* in order to provide fire support for them when the action commenced. What fire support did actually occur that night for the Germans seems to have come from the 8cm mortars and 7.5cm and 1.5cm *Infanterie-Geschütz* guns allocated to each *Bataillon Schwere Kompanie*. The mortar and gun crews would deploy as far forward as they could safely be, ready to begin firing for as long as the ammunition they brought with them would hold out. While these assets would have to do, they could not perform the same function as the powerful field *Artillerie* of *SS-Pz.Art. Rgt. 12*, which for the moment was only partially deployed to the west supporting *SS-Pz.Gren.Rgt. 25*.

Setting out in the darkness, the three *SS-Panzergrenadier Kompanien* moved towards their objectives in column and then deployed for silent night attacks. In front of them it is important to note there were no reconnaissance forces from the *15. Kp. (Aufklärung)/SS-Pz.Gren.Rgt. 26* or from the nearby *SS-Pz.Aüfkl.Abt. 12* that could give the *Kompaniechefen* and *Stubaf.* Krause an indication of the strength and deployment of Allied forces. Travelling in the dark and exhausted from the extensive route march via truck that was constantly under the threat of aerial attack, the *SS-Panzergrenadiere* officers were not fresh and rested, and neither were their men.[15]

The one advantage of the darkness was the reduced ability of Allied artillery spotters to adjust RCA and RA fire, and the complete lack of Allied fighters. Also, due to Canadian Armoured Corps (CAC) doctrine, Canadian tanks at this time were in laagers, the crews asleep, servicing their tanks or ready in a counterattack role.

The *3. Kompanie Kommandeur, Ostuf.* Karl Düwel, attacked first in the centre, his objective being Norrey-en-Bessin. His point of departure with La Gaule, a village north-west following the road out of Cheux. Moving through this village towards the west of St Manvieu and beyond, he crossed the Mue over one or two bridges, and then pushed onto the slight rise of Hill 63, just north of the Mue and north-west of St Manvieu. Cresting the hill, first contact was made with Canadian outposts forming the outer defences of Norrey-en-Bessin.[16] It was at this point that

RCA field artillery fire was called in on the Germans, and the *SS-Panzergrenadiere* were pinned to the ground in the fields. Canadian RRR outposts were also alert and poured intense mortar and small arms fire on the first Germans they saw, halting the advance of the *Kompanie* on the crest.

Attacking on the left flank towards Bretteville, the advance of *2. Kp./SS-Pz.Gren. Rgt. 26* under *Heer Lt.* Sauer took a circuitous route north-west of Cheux and then north-east, towards the railway line and the southern outskirts of Bretteville. After seizing some railway service buildings, the *Kompanie* halted after news arrived that the *3. Kompanie* had stopped its attack. After suffering some casualties, this *Kompanie* dug in near Ferme Cardonville.[17] The *1. Kompanie* of *Ostuf.* Eggert halted at St Manvieu, its progress also stopped after the *3. Kompanie* had halted.

The primary RRR company in contact, C Company under Major Tubb, had utilised effective artillery support in conjunction with machine-gun and mortar fire to defeat this German assault, conducted at 0300 hours without similar artillery support.[18] Desperate to not let the Allies establish themselves in their beachhead, real or imagined time pressures had spurred the Germans on to attack with little in the way of supporting armour or artillery, utilising their infantry forces piecemeal as they arrived. Initial events portrayed a lack of planning ability as well as patience by the *Waffen-SS* to concentrate the proper resources to accomplish missions. The lack of recent battlefield experience by the *Kommandeur* of SS-Pz.Gren.Rgt. 26, *Ostubaf.* Mohnke, and an initially dismissive attitude towards the Canadian Army by members of his division, may have contributed to this.[19]

Both sides launched frequent patrols on the night of 7/8 June, and these small sections of Canadian infantry and *SS-Panzergrenadiere* clashed with one another in a series of small firefights that went on throughout the night. It is reasonable to assume that neither side slept that night, with periods of time spent not firing across the railway line spent improving fighting positions. The RWR pioneer platoon laid what anti-tank mines it had near the RWR company positions, and on obvious avenues of approach for German vehicles and armour. The Universal and T-16 Carriers of the Support Company, having dropped off their anti-tank guns and mortars, drove around in a sporadic manner, occasionally firing across the railway line in order to disrupt German actions. During the night, the *SS-Panzergrenadiere* did the same except that they did it from fixed MG-42 positions, firing long bursts into the Canadian company positions.[20]

Moving east, it is important to discuss the actions and military operations of some units of the *Panzer-Lehr* on 8 June as well. It can be argued legitimately that the *Panzer-Lehr* on this date did not accomplish anything of significance other than to move its units closer to the battlefield. The majority of its combat units would fail, for the third straight day, to make contact with, or destroy, the enemy. Due to the lateness of its dispatch to the front, it was ordered to travel in large columns by day, and suffered terrible losses as a result, its average speed reduced to a paltry 10–12 kilometres an hour on a roughly 220-kilometre route for most units, interrupted by halts and crushing air attacks by Allied tactical airpower.[21] It may seem stupendous for a reader in modern times to see this average German column speed, given that the average motorist today can travel the route on the same paved country roads in a little over two hours with average commuter traffic. Post-war, Bayerlein stated that on 7 June he had lost 40 trucks carrying fuel and ammunition, that 5 Panzer IVs had been knocked out, and that other losses had included a total of 84 SPW 251s, self-propelled guns and prime movers.[22] The *7. Armee Hauptquartier* had ruthlessly demanded *I. SS-Pz.Korps* drive the divisions forward to the beaches at with the highest possible speed and did not comprehend the impact of the tactical fighter-bombers attacking everything on French highways, bridges and intersections.

The *Hitlerjugend*, while taking a shorter route and having been dispatched to the front earlier, was luckier and managed to get half its division into combat on 7 June. The *Panzer-Lehr*, dispatched later, could only manage to insert *Pz.Aüfkl.Lehr. Abt. 130*, the reconnaissance *Abteilung* of the division, and the *II. Btl.(Gepanzert)/ Pz.Gren.Lehr.Rgt. 902* into the area of operations west of the *Hitlerjugend*. Both, for various reasons, would do such a poor job of halting the British that Hill 103, a significant height of tactical value, was lost to the British 8th Armoured Brigade by nightfall on 8 June. As a result of this a significant threat was posed to the left flank of *SS-Pz.Gren.Rgt. 26*, with the British simply driving into the sector the *Panzer-Lehr* should have aggressively already occupied.

This was a significant failing, and fault can equally be shared by *OKW*, *Hrs.Gr.D* (the future *O.B. West*), *Hrs.Gr.B*, the subordinate sub-*Heeresgruppe* under *Hrs.Gr.D*, *Pz.Gr.West*, and the *Kommandeur* of the *Panzer-Lehr*, *Gen.Lt.* Bayerlein. In the entire Normandy campaign, never did such a powerful German force accomplish so little at a time when action was needed so badly.

Major Willi Welsch's *II. Btl.(Gepanzert)/Pz.Gren.Lehr.Rgt. 902*, one of the two *Panzergrenadier Bataillone* within the *Pz.Gren.Lehr.Rgt. 902*, along with the regimental *Gefechtsstand* vehicles of the headquarters of *Pz.Gren.Lehr.Rgt. 902*, led by *Oberst* Joachim Gutmann, reached Brouay on the morning of 8 June at roughly 0430 hours.[23] As stated previously, the regiment had been ordered into this sector mistakenly due to lack of proper communication between the *Panzer-Lehr*, *Hitlerjugend* and higher headquarters staffs in the frantic and fluid situation of the days immediately after the invasion.

French military historian Jean-Claude Perrigault notes that this *Bataillon* had reached an area of sporadic combat, the remnants of German forces fleeing the coast attempting to hold up the British forces that were active north of the Caen–Bayeux railway line. Mechanised patrols from both *SS-Pz.Aüfkl.Abt. 12* and *Pz.Aüfkl.Lehr. Abt. 130* were operating in the area, and had established observation posts and a small number of anti-tank gun positions. Ordered only to hold the railway line

Caen–Bayeux, a patrol from the *II. Btl.(Gepanzert)/Pz.Gren.Lehr.Rgt. 902* advanced on foot to the railroad cutting bridge north of Brouay and west of Putot-en-Bessin and made contact with British forces. It was here that the division engaged in its first ground combat.

Members of this patrol from *5. Kp./Pz-Lehr.Gren.Rgt. 902*, using a *Panzerschreck* or *Panzerfaust* infantry anti-tank weapon, fired at a light British recce tank near the railway line. This may have been a recce troop Stuart tank from one of the British armoured regiments of the 8th Armoured Brigade, which had been massing its forces to the north-west. It is unclear where exactly *Major* Welsch, the *Kommandeur* of *II. Btl.(Gepanzert)/Pz.Gren.Lehr.Rgt. 902*, had his tactical *Gefechtsstand* set up, but it would most probably have been in one of the buildings in the sprawling village of Brouay south of the railway line. His regimental *Kommandeur, Oberst* Gutmann, had set up his tactical headquarters in a field during the night, but his radio communications led to instant triangulation carried out by the Royal Artillery units to the north, followed by a patrol from an Auster observation aircraft at first light. It is unclear if the Germans were hit by naval or field artillery, but the entire headquarters had moved by mid-morning to the Château Brouay, located to the south of the village.[24]

It appears *Gen.Lt.* Bayerlein had no idea that this was exactly where *SS-Pz.Gren. Rgt. 26* had determined its *III. Btl.(Gepanzert)/SS-Pz.Rgt. 26* of *Stubaf.* Olboeter was to be deployed. On arrival, US military historian Dr Frederick P. Steinhardt states the *II. Btl.(Gepanzert)/Pz.Gren.Lehr.Rgt. 902* found a 'melee occurring between German and hostile troops with leading elements of enemy forces advancing on both Brouay and Le Bas d'Audrieu'.[25] This melee was probably best explained as sporadic encounter combat between the British 69th Infantry Brigade and 8th Armoured Brigade forces and weak forces from one of the aforementioned German reconnaissance *Abteilung* in the area, *SS-Pz.Aüfkl.Abt. 12* or *Pz.Aüfkl.Lehr.Abt. 130*. There were also isolated stragglers from the *352. Infanterie Division* that were being driven back by the rampant British advance.

While a *Heer Gepanzert* (armoured) *Panzergrenadier Bataillon* in the year 1944 did have heavy weapons in the way of a number of 7.5cm-gun equipped SPW 251 half-tracks and Pak 40 7.5cm anti-tank guns in its *Schwere Kompanie*, it was in no way equipped to fight a major tank battle from its position at Brouay and was waiting for the *II. Abt./Pz-Lehr.Rgt. 130* Panzer IV tanks to arrive in order to form battle groups for offensive actions.

What exactly happened later that day, when larger groups of British tanks, presumably from the 24th Lancers, appeared in the area? Very little data is provided in the Normandy historiography of the *Panzer-Lehr* as to details of the battle fought by this *Battalion* and what its overall outcome was. Some maps within books on the fighting near Tilly-sur-Seulles mark the 6th Battalion, the Green Howards (6 GH) infantry battalion of the British 69th Infantry Brigade as being in contact with

Panzer-Lehr forces on 8 June. The author has found no solid evidence that the 6 GH was this far south, and all that remains as a logical possibility is the Stuart or Sherman tanks of the 24th Lancers.

Panzer-Lehr divisional historian Helmut Ritgen, in his work *The Western Front 1944*, states that an *Oberfeldwebel* Gunther, a *Zug* leader within *7. Kp/Pz.Gren.Lehr. Rgt. 902*, reported that, on their arrival, the majority of Brouay was occupied by enemy forces, and whether these were Canadian infantry or British armoured forces is unclear. The resulting firefight forced the Germans on the defensive, and by early morning, shortly after this combat began, a *Kompanie-Chef* conference with *Oberst* Gutmann in the Brouay château grounds was called. Mid-conference, British RA fire killed or wounded several of the attendees, rendering the *Bataillon* largely leaderless and in need of reorganisation.[26] Sometime before this, Welsch had sent a liaison officer, *Oberleutnant* Dibben, to the *Gefechtsstand* of the recently arrived *II. Btl./SS-Pz. Gren.Rgt. 26* of *Stubaf.* Seibken to attempt to discern where the divisional boundary was, something it appears neither *Panzer-Lehr* or *Hitlerjugend* division headquarters had managed to communicate to their regiments due to radio silence and a lack of direction. This said, it must be noted that the travelling *Bataillon* headquarters were difficult to find as they were on the move or just being established.[27]

Adding insult to injury, the situation grew rapidly worse when at some time mid-morning, a group of British tanks, possibly the aforementioned 24th Lancer's recce Stuart 37mm gunned light tanks, chanced upon the château grounds and shot up the parked regimental *Stabskompanie* vehicles, many of them the vital SPW 251 command variants and radio truck vehicles, causing further chaos and damage. During this tank rampage the German *Panzergrenadiere* reportedly scurried for their lives in every direction before the British tanks withdrew. Nothing within the very scant historical records of this event gives the impression that the *Panzergrenadier Kompanien* and the *Schwere Kompanie* were deployed defensively or in cooperation with *Pz.Aüfkl.Lehr.Abt. 130* or *SS-Pz.Aüfkl.Abt. 12* reconnaissance forces in the area. Neither does it appear that the towed 7.5cm Pak 40 anti-tank guns engaged the enemy, apart from one account of a lone 7.5cm Pak 40 anti-tank gun attached to *5. Kp./Pz-Lehr.Gren.Rgt. 902* firing at British tanks on the Brouay village railroad overpass bridge between Brouay and Putot-en-Bessin sometime during the morning. This speaks to poor leadership, poor deployment of the *8. (Schwere) Kompanie* heavy weapons, and the fact that the troops were exhausted and not expecting contact, never mind roving groups of tanks from the British 8th Armoured Brigade.

Events took an even worse turn for the Germans as the morning went on and combat was occurring to the east along the railway line between the RWR and newly arrived *II. Btl./SS-Pz.Gren.Rgt. 26*, whose operations will be discussed shortly. Reportedly, an Auster RA artillery spotter observation aircraft appeared over the château grounds near Brouay, and heavy RA artillery fire and naval gunfire was directed at this target area, destroying more vehicles and inflicting heavy casualties on the German *Panzergrenadiere*. One of the casualties was *Oberst* Gutmann, who was badly wounded in the artillery strike. After taking over the *Pz.Gren.Lehr.Rgt. 902* himself, *Maj.* Welsch appointed *Hptm.* Muller to take over the now disorganised and poorly deployed *II. Btl.(Gepanzert)/Pz.Gren.Lehr.Rgt. 902.*[28]

A short time later, the first elements of *III. Btl.(Gepanzert)/SS-Pz.Gren.Rgt. 26* arrived in the former positions of the *Heer* troops, who had vacated the area. This *Bataillon* had stopped for the night at Fontenay-le-Pesnel and had been ordered to close the gap between *SS-Pz.Aüfkl.Abt. 12*, arriving or in place near Audrieu, and *II. Btl./SS-Pz.Gren.Rgt. 26*, approaching Le Mesnil-Patry that night. The *SS-Panzergrenadiere*, moving into Brouay, reportedly found parts of bodies hanging from trees and vehicles utterly destroyed by British bombardments, a sort of moonscape of craters existing on the château grounds. What exactly became of the *Panzer-Lehr Bataillon?* It was found dug in on the north-west corner of Brouay, still south of the railway line. It had rapidly moved its position away from the destruction being inflicted on the Brouay village area before the first troops from *III. Btl.(Gepanzert)/SS-Pz.Gren.Rgt. 26* of *Stubaf.* Olboeter had pushed patrols into the area by mid-morning.[29]

Before this chapter discusses the main combat engagement on 8 June, the battle of Putot-en-Bessin, we must consider what were the intentions of the *Hitlerjugend* and the opposing British forces to the west of Brouay? While Canadian forces of the 7th Canadian Infantry Brigade were firmly entrenched within their fortress by nightfall on 7 June, the British forces to the west within the 30th Corps sector planned to unleash an armoured drive south on the afternoon of 8 June. From their concentration area near Rucqueville–Martragny, discussed in the last chapter, the British 8th Armoured Brigade was readying the attached 61st Reconnaissance Regiment of the 50th Infantry Division to drive south on route 'Congo', in order for it to push onto Hill 103. This route would take this force south just to the west of the positions of *SS-Pz.Aüfkl.Abt. 12*. A Squadron of the 24th Lancers armoured regiment, with infantry support, was ordered to advance south then east along the RN 13, linking up with the 7th Canadian Infantry Brigade and exploiting any openings in the German lines to advance south on route 'Isel', this planned route travelling through Brouay to Cristot and Hill 102.

While the 8th Armoured Brigade was preparing to send these first forces forward, what was occurring on the front of the British 69th Infantry Brigade holding the line in front of them to the south? By mid-afternoon 7th Battalion, the Green Howards (7 GH), had reached a position to the north-west of Putot-en-Bessin and Brouay, the scene of fierce fighting to be described later in this chapter. It is likely that it did not advance further because of a lack of situational awareness and the need to stay on the right side of the British 30th Corps–1st Corps boundary. The 6th Battalion, the Green Howards (6 GH) had advanced to near St Leger-Locales in the west, where three tanks of the supporting attached squadron of the 4th/7th Royal Dragoon Guards, including a RA Observation Post (OP) tank from the 147th Field Regiment, RA, were shot up by what were recorded as '88s'. It is unclear which German unit was firing on them. By 1600 hours the 4th/7th Royal Dragoon Guards tanks had captured Loucelles, and by midnight had entered Le Bas D'Audrieu.[30]

By midday on 8 June *SS-Pz.Aüfkl.Abt. 12* was deployed just north-west of Hill 102 and its most southern position was just east of Hill 103. Rather than being on the top of Hill 103, or in a reverse slope position near its height, it appeared the Germans had completely neglected to occupy it at all as evening approached, possibly to keep their positions hidden from the British tanks. The large number of wooded areas, orchards and extensive hedges that divided the famers' fields helped hide the *Waffen-SS* reconnaissance troops from British observation.

It is indicative of the poor military situation that the *Hitlerjugend* found itself in, that *Stubaf.* Bremer of *SS-Pz.Aüfkl.Abt. 12* was forced to use his reconnaissance battalion to attempt to hold ground on 8 June. This was due to the lack of *Panzer-Lehr* forces that had actually made it to the front and taken up some kind of position to establish a continuous front line. The employment of the *Abteilung* should have been in front of units of *SS-Pz.Gren.Rgt. 25* or *26*, carrying out ongoing reconnaissance missions in order to find weak points in the front for *Hitlerjugend* armoured forces to exploit.

This was not the case, and this unit was pinned in place due to the fact that the *Hitlerjugend* had a completely exposed left flank, something the 7th Canadian Infantry Brigade had exploited on 7 June and the British 8th Armoured Brigade would exploit on 8 June, pushing south into the area Le Bas D'Audrieu, Audrieu and Hill 103.[31] The commander of the British 8th Armoured Brigade, Brigadier Cracroft, was to unleash his brigade's three armoured regiments and attached forces from the 50th British Infantry Division to push south in the direction of Villers Bocage, the town being the objective he had been directed to secure. His advance on 8 June would be aided tremendously by the continued inability of the *Panzer-Lehr* to reach a position to the west of the *Hitlerjugend*, allowing the British tanks to push forward into an open gap to the west of Brouay.

Bypassing the *Hitlerjugend* forces to the east and pushing on to the heights of Hill 103 at last light, the tanks of the Sherwood Rangers Yeomanry captured a high feature of significant tactical value from which the surrounding area could be observed. Accompanying the tanks was A Company of the Cheshire Regiment, who then dug in to help defend it. These forces were strengthened by the arrival of the 288th Anti-Tank Battery, RA, which established positions for its anti-tank guns in the wooded areas covering the height.[32]

To the east, the positions of *SS-Pz.Aüfkl.Abt. 12* were in a rough line south-west of *9. Kp.(Gepanzert)/SS-Pz.Gren.Rgt. 26*, its parent *III. Btl.(Gepanzert)/SS-Pz.Gren.*

Rgt. 26 now fully deployed from Brouay to a position just north of Cristot, where the positions of *SS-Pz.Aüfkl.Abt. 12* began. Its main strongpoints on 8 June consisted of the *2. Panzer-Spähkompanie* dug in north of Cristot, and to the south-west the *3. Aufklärung Kompanie*, which was dug in around the Ferme Les Hauts Vents farm, just east of Hill 103.

Now that events west of Putot have been examined, this chapter can now discuss the heavy fighting in the village of Putot to the east, which went on all day on 8 June. Arriving on the night of 7/8 June and slowly filtering into the area just south of the village, first German contact was made with Canadian forces by a motorised scouting party from *II. Btl./SS-Pz.Gren.Rgt. 26* or the *15. Kp.(Aufklärung)/SS-Pz. Gren.Rgt. 26* at roughly 0630 hours. As the Germans edged close to the Caen–Bayeux railway line and its paved road overpass, they immediately received heavy small arms fire from members of A Company of the Royal Winnipeg Rifles (RWR). A 6-pounder anti-tank gun of the RWR anti-tank platoon fired into the small column of German vehicles, knocking out the lead Panzer III light tank that had been assigned to the *Stabskompanie* of *SS-Pz.Gren.Rgt. 26*, causing the Germans to pull back. It has never been determined by the author what the other vehicles in this party were, possibly Schwimmenwagens jeeps from the reconnaissance *15. Kp.(Aufklärung)/SS-Pz.Gren.Rgt. 26*.

By 0630 hours, the sporadic combat to the east between *I. Btl./SS-Pz.Gren.Rgt. 26* and the Canadian forces had been going on for several hours and there was no chance of a coordinated surprise attack by both forward *SS-Pz.Gren.Rgt. 26 Bataillone*, with the forces of *Stubaf.* Siebken of *II. Btl./SS-Pz.Gren.Rgt. 26* having barely arrived on the front lines at this stage.

Knowing this, Seibken allowed time for his forces to assemble and called a proper orders group during which he would issue direction to attack Putot with *6.* and *7. Kompanien* of *II. Btl./SS-Pz.Gren.Rgt. 26*, with its *8. (Schwere) Kompanie* providing fire support and anti-tank defence. The *5. Kompanie* would remain in reserve initially. At this time, Seibken knew two things: he did not have armoured support in the way of tanks and he had limited anti-tank capability if he encountered Canadian or British armour ready to aid in the defence of Putot. It is unclear if he had fire support from *SS-Pz.Art.Rgt. 12*, and if he did have it, how much.

He did have the unplanned support from some elements of the *Panzer-Lehr* that had arrived near Brouay. Contact had been made with the *II. Btl./SS-Pz.Gren.Rgt. 26* staff by various *Panzer-Lehr* units of *Pz.Gren.Lehr.Rgt. 902*. The *9. Kp.(Geschütz)/Pz. Gren.Lehr.Rgt. 902* was present in the south, and its 15cm *Infanterie-Geschütz* howitzers under the command of *Hptm.* Hennecke would be employed during the course of the day to help bombard Canadian positions.[33] It was also reported that a *Zug* of *II. Btl.(Gepanzert)/Pz.Gren.Lehr.Rgt. 902* fought with Seibken's troops that day, and that some indirect fire support was also provided from what could have possibly been the *8. (Schwere) Kompanie* of *II. Btl.(Gepanzert)/Pz.Gren.Lehr.Rgt. 902*.

Following the *Bataillon Kommandeure* orders group in the early morning, Canadian and possibly British artillery fire began in earnest on the German positions south of the railway line, positions that were certainly given away by the combat on the left and right of Seibken's newly arrived *Bataillon*. Returning to his *Kompanie Gefechtsstand*, the *Kompanie-Chef* of *6. Kompanie, Ostuf.* Schmolke, found it a smoking ruin due to a surprise RA or RCA field artillery concentration, this artillery bombardment wounding and killing several officers of the *Stabskompanie* and the *Züge*. Counter-battery fire also occurred during the day, a gun of *5. Batterie, II. Abt./SS-Pz.Art.Rgt. 12* being destroyed by RCA shellfire.[34]

Sometime between 0700 and 0800 hours, both *6.* and *7. Kompanien* of *II. Btl./SS-Pz.Gren.Rgt. 26* pushed forward north from the wooded areas and across the railway line. Pushing on the right flank attacking the positions of B and C Companies of the RWR was *Ostuf.* Schmolke of *7. Kompanie*. On the left, attacking the railway overpass position of A Company of the RWR, was *6. Kompanie* of *Lt.* Henne, a *Heer* transfer. Using gaps in the fields of fire of the RWR positions, both *Kompanien* managed to push forward and to eventually surround the platoons of the RWR companies using aggressive infantry tactics that were supported by a number of SPW 251 half-tracks of the neighbouring *III. Btl.(Gepanzert)/SS-Pz.Gren.Rgt. 26*, using their MG-42 machine guns and 7.5cm cannon on the Canadian RWR infantry positions.

By late morning, A, B and C Companies of the RWR were encircled or had groups of German *SS-Panzergrenadiere* effectively firing into their positions from all directions. By this stage, due to technical failure and the heavy combat, all wireless communication from company headquarters to Lieutenant Colonel Meldram's battalion headquarters was impossible.

A Company of the RWR, being less the one platoon that was covering northern Brouay to the west, had been badly weakened by this decision to detach it. While Lieutenant Battershill was doing a good job at defending the buildings of Brouay north of the rail line with the help of Royal Navy naval gunfire against elements of *II. Btl.(Gepanzert)/Pz-Lehr.Gren.Rgt. 902*, it was not available for the main battle that would see the RWR largely defeated as a fighting force.[35] Battershill would also be aided by the gunfire of F Battery of the 62nd Anti-Tank Regiment, Royal Artillery, which fired south at anything coming over the railway line.[36]

Major Hodge, the A Company commander, realised by mid-morning that he needed to break out of his encirclement, as his men were taking fire from the flanks and behind their positions. Germans near the railway underpass rallied as the Canadians left their fighting positions, and utilising three to four SPW 251 half-tracks, managed to block any escape routes north or west. Canadian accounts noted that these 'self-propelled guns' effectively fired into the RWR company remnants until Hodge called to his men to surrender.[37] It is unclear to the author what happened to the RWR Support Company 6-pounder anti-tank platoon guns, and whether all of these guns had been knocked out or overrun by this point.

The fighting was also intense in front of the RWR B and C Company positions, and both *SS-Panzergrenadiere Kompanien* fought their way forward in the battle that raged all morning and would see these two Canadian infantry companies defeated. In 2018, the author gave a presentation at an academic conference that speculated that the RWR were overcome by an assault that did include the involvement of a significant number of armoured vehicles. It has never been properly documented exactly what role in the fighting was played by *III. Btl.(Gepanzert)/SS-Pz.Gren.Rgt. 26*, entirely equipped with SPW 251 half-tracks. *Hitlerjugend* division historian Hubert Meyer states they were left to the rear in Fontenay-le-Pesnel, and that the members of the *9., 10.* and *11. Kompanien* marched forward into Brouay at the same time as the fighting was going on in Putot. The author believes that the first-hand accounts of RWR veterans which state that a number of armoured vehicles were present are correct, and that these SPW 251 half-tracks, mistaken for tanks as they were heavily camouflaged, did take part in the fighting and did cross the railway line into Putot. Also, a number of SPW 251s were involved after the fighting to retrieve and evacuate Canadian prisoners of *II. Btl./SS-Pz.Gren.Rgt. 26* once the village fell to the Germans.

It is also the viewpoint of the author that a small number of 7.5cm-cannon equipped SPW 251/9 half-tracks stood off and provided fire support, which allowed the *SS-Panzergrenadiere* of *II. Btl./SS-Pz.Gren.Rgt. 26* to break into the perimeter of the RWR companies, forcing a large number of those who were not wounded in the fighting to surrender when they ran out of ammunition. It is not inconceivable that these SPW 251 half-tracks could also have come from *SS-Pz.Aüfkl.Abt. 12*.

The fate of C Company, deployed near eastern Putot in an orchard beside the village's buildings, is the best example of the heavy involvement of the SPW 251, either from *SS-Pz.Aüfkl.Abt. 12* or *III. Btl.(Gepanzert)/SS-Pz.Gren.Rgt. 26*, that arguably decided the battle in Putot. At a climatic point in the battle, as *7. Kp./SS-Pz.Gren.Rgt. 26* was working to encircle C Company, an SPW 251 is reported to have driven right into the Canadian company perimeter, spraying all the fighting positions with heavy machine-gun fire from two MG-42s mounted on the vehicle. It was at this point that resistance in the C Company positions collapsed, and men who had not been killed or wounded already began to surrender.[38]

It is impossible to say conclusively how much of a role the SPW 251 half-tracks from *III. Btl.(Gepanzert)/SS-Pz.Gren.Rgt. 26* or possibly *SS-Pz.Aüfkl.Abt. 12* played in the fighting. Unfortunately for the purposes of gaining historical insight, the *Kommandeur* of *III. Btl.(Gepanzert)/SS-Pz.Gren.Rgt. 26*, *Stubaf.* Erich Olboeter, died in combat in September 1944, and *Stubaf.* Bernard Seibken was executed by the British in January 1949 for war crimes.

Thrown into combat last, what is often overlooked or not mentioned in overviews of the Putot battle is that Major Fulton's D Company of the RWR did successfully fight off the attack of *5. Kp./SS-Pz.Gren.Rgt. 26*, led by *Ostuf.* Gotthard, committed mid-battle by *Stubaf.* Seibken to complete the destruction of the RWR. Having a greater field of fire in the open fields east of the village and north of the railway line, the soldiers of D Company used their Bren guns effectively to beat back the German assault through sheer force of firepower. While the *6.* and *7. Kompanien* had employed infiltration and utilised the ground effectively to approach and surround A, B and C Companies of the RWR, it appears this one effort and its repulse was enough for the *SS-Panzergrenadiere* of *5. Kompanie*, who would not attempt to push over the railway line again. D Company was aided in its defence by the parts of the RWR Support Company platoons still in action. This last stronghold was strengthened by the arrival of Lieutenant Colonel Meldram's tactical headquarters, the remains of Support Company and stragglers and escapees from the surrendered A, B and C Companies. They were also joined by a lone platoon of B Company, which had been placed in reserve in the rear of the village, to the north of the remainder of its parent company. Why this platoon never advanced or was never ordered forward to join the fight to fend off the *Waffen-SS* as the rest of the company was being destroyed is unclear. At the height of combat, this meant that B Company had only fought with two platoons against the full force of the *Waffen-SS* assault.[39]

As the battle was raging, a strange event occurred in the *II. Btl./SS-Pz.Gren.Rgt. 26 Gefechtsstand* of *Stubaf.* Seibken in Le Mesnil. A wounded *Panzer-Lehr Artillerie* officer, *Hauptmann* Graf Clary-Aldringen, was brought into the headquarters. Wounded and in shock, he frantically began to tell the story of his capture and escape from British forces to the west, saying again and again 'the English kill the prisoners'. In a shocking display of naivety or ignorance as to where the front line was, the command staff of the *Gefechtsstand* of *Pz.Art.Rgt. 130* had parked their vehicles and gathered on what they thought was an unoccupied rise, Hill 103, just west of Audrieu and the positions of *SS-Pz.Aüfkl.Abt. 12*, to recce on foot the area they were about to deploy into. They were then set upon by two armoured cars of the British Inns of Court reconnaissance regiment and taken prisoner before they knew what was happening. Since this was long before the Sherwood Rangers Yeomanry would arrive to capture Hill 103, the area was largely uninhabited by both sides. Ordered to withdraw via radio, the British patrol seized the one-armed Eastern Front veteran *Oberst* Luxenburger, and ordered he ride on the outside of the vehicle. When he refused, he was beaten unconscious and bound to one of the armoured cars. It appears from multiple accounts, *Hitlerjugend* divisional historian Hubert Meyer's being one of the most famous, that the rest of the party, standing in the field next to the British recce armoured car crews, were machine gunned by Besa and Bren gun fire.[40] Luxenburger was then killed when the armoured car he was tied to was knocked out by the German Pak 40 7.5cm anti-tank gun in the area from *SS-Pz.Aüfkl.Abt. 12*. It is unknown to what effect the frenzied report of the prisoner killings had on the *Waffen-SS*, or if word of the incident quickly made its way to the *Gefechtsstand* of *SS-Pz.Gren.Rgt. 26 Kommandeur, Ostubaf.* Mohnke.

At the moment of victory in Putot in the early evening, as combat was winding down and contact lost with remaining RWR soldiers who had escaped to the east through the village and into the D Company positions to hold as a final stronghold, the *SS-Panzergrenadiere*, many of whom were lying wounded in the fields, saw the cloud of dust from the west down the RN 13. Much to the dismay and surprise of the *SS-Panzergrenadiere*, this dust was kicked up by British tanks. Never were the Panther tanks of *I. Abt./SS-Pz.Rgt. 12*, the first of which were approaching Caen at this very moment, missed more.

Pushing south-east on the RN 13 that afternoon were B and C Squadrons of the 24th Lancers, along with some Stuart light tanks from their recce troop. These forces were intent on pushing forward south on route 'Isel' to the east of Brouay. The British tanks planned to cross the overpass bridge over the Caen–Bayeux railway line in an attempt to reach Hill 102, an important tactical feature near Cristot. The remainder of the 4th/7th Royal Dragoon Guards, with the 1st Battalion, the Dorsetshire Regiment attached, planned to push south as a mobile reserve in between this force and the aforementioned Sherwood Rangers Yeomanry force pushing south on the left flank via route 'Congo' to Hill 103. Brigadier Cracroft, commander of the British 8th Armoured Brigade, was confident the day's advance would be just as easy as that on 7 June, and that the only opposition to be expected were the scattered groups of retreating Germans from the *352. Inf.Div.* and *716. Inf.Div.* Cracroft hoped to easily push aside any opposition and be able to consolidate his forces on the twin points of Hills 103 and 102 before nightfall, and expected the infantry forces of the British 69th Infantry Brigade, some of which were close by, to possibly help him do so.[41]

Arriving in a column of armour from the west after a series of heavy RA field artillery concentrations, B and C Squadrons of the 24th Lancers advanced into the unprepared and exhausted *Waffen-SS* forces in and near the western edge of Putot. B Squadron would drive right up to the village and its orchards before it realised it was in the midst of a large number of Germans. Once contact with the *SS-Panzergrenadiere* had been made, the tank commanders and other crewmembers who had their heads sticking out of the hatches began to receive small arms fire, some of it coming from *SS-Panzergrenadiere* who had climbed trees as well as installed themselves in the village's buildings. To the terror and surprise of the wounded *Ostuf.* Schmolke, he was captured by a tank crew who loaded him onto the back of their Sherman and drove off. In total, roughly 40 *SS-Panzergrenadiere* – some wounded – were taken prisoner during the combat as the British tanks simply drove into their positions. Terrified and surrounded by the large number of tanks, many Germans from *6. Kompanie* simply surrendered, this act illustrating the myth of frenzied, fanatical German *Waffen-SS* resistance. Some German anti-tank fire from

Brouay and near Putot-en-Bessin was encountered by the British, who without infantry support decided to withdraw back to the RN 13 after a period of exchanging fire and taking prisoners.

While the *5.* and *6. Kompanie* attempted to continue to consolidate their newly won positions in the village after the tank raid, they realised the heavy weapons that had been supporting them were now on the wrong side of the railway line, and the mortar bombs and artillery ammunition that had supported the fighting all morning long were now very depleted. To wrestle mortars, Pak 40 7.5cm anti-tank guns and other weapons forward would take time, and Seibken's exhausted men at the same time had to handle a large number of Canadian prisoners and wounded from both sides. During this time SPW 251 half-tracks crisscrossed the battlefield, attempting to move weapons and evacuate wounded and prisoners. Many of these drove over Canadian anti-tank mines.

As all this was occurring to the north-west of the captured RWR positions on the afternoon of 8 June, it is the author's conclusion that an extremely unfortunate incident of friendly fire occurred to the north of the RN 13 at Ferme La Bergerie. In the works of Canadian military historians Mark Zuehlke, Marc Milner and others, a contact with German armour was reported to have occurred against the Anglo-Canadian Ferme La Bergerie (Bergerie Farm) strongpoint, created as a right rear-flank position of the 7th Canadian Infantry Brigade fortress. A heavy exchange of fire did occur, and one of the two Allied officers involved in this action received the Military Cross (MC) for acts of bravery in combat. The following paragraphs attempt to raise some points regarding the incident, and illustrate that there were no German tanks in the area during this time.

To guard against German armour outflanking Putot, the 7th Canadian Infantry Brigade had installed two 6-pounder anti-tank guns from the 3rd Anti-Tank Regiment, RCA, as well as two 17-pounder anti-tank guns from the British 62nd Anti-Tank Regiment, RA, both of which were placed in support of the 7th Canadian Infantry Brigade. Also present were several Vickers medium machine guns of the Cameron Highlanders of Ottawa Machine Gun Battalion. Altogether, this strongpoint was bristling with weaponry and ready to inflict heavy losses on whatever approached it.

During the afternoon, the defenders of the strongpoint, which was dug into a high point near the farm buildings, observed tanks to the west cresting a high point in the fields near the RN 13, which is south of the farm. In the account the tanks were first seen crossing over the rail line to the south and moving north towards the RN 13. Against the initial wishes of the officers present, the men of the strongpoint opened up prematurely when the tanks were still at long range, and several Vickers medium machine guns and some anti-tank guns were knocked out in the resulting firefight which raged for a significant amount of time. The Anglo-Canadian position also received heavy field artillery fire, causing more casualties. During this time, the Canadian and British anti-tank gun crews and machine gunners claimed four enemy tanks knocked out.

There are three main reasons why the author believes that this was, unfortunately, not a battle between Anglo-Canadian forces and the Germans, but a tragic case of friendly fire in which both parties, the Anglo-Canadian anti-tank positions and what actually were British Sherman or Stuart tanks, fired extensively at one another at a range that did not allow for positive identification, causing casualties and equipment and vehicle losses on both sides.

The British and Canadian gun crews fought from their positions against what they believed to be a group of nine to ten tanks, which were identified in their accounts as both Panzer IV and Panthers. Examining the historical record, while German SPW 251 half-tracks and eight-wheeled armoured cars were in the area, no German tank forces were recorded as pushing past the RN 13. However, as far as German records can testify, the only possible tank unit close enough to launch a reconnaissance across the railway line was *II. Abt./Pz.Lehr.Rgt. 130*, and the records of this unit very pointedly note that no tanks pushed north of the Château Monts, located 16 kilometres away near the modern village of Monts-en-Bessin.[42] This *Abteilung* had been directed to deploy in this area with *Pz.Pio.Lehr.Btl. 130*, the SPW 251 half-track equipped combat engineer *Batallion* of the *Panzer-Lehr*, and to await further orders for future operations, according to the *Panzer-Lehr* divisional order of 8 June, which has survived.[43] The commanding officer of *Gepanzert Gruppe Schonberger*, the armoured battlegroup of *II. Abt./Pz.Lehr.Rgt. 130*, *Major* Wilhelm, Prinz von Schönburg-Waldenburg, had the exhausted tank crews camouflage themselves in the woods on the château grounds and wait all day for orders that never came. This unit effectively missed the entire battle to the north. Due to the German orders on radio silence, and the lack of any kind of reliable means of communications, the Panzer IV tank crews languished all day long, when they could have been deployed en masse in the Putot–Bretteville–Norrey-en-Bessin area in a manner similar to *II. Abt./SS-Pz.Rgt. 12* north of Caen on 7 June. This was evidence of German military failure in the early stage of the Normandy campaign, and another example of the utter waste and misemployment of what was one of the best German armoured forces in Normandy.

All German *SS-Pz.Rgt. 12* Panzer IVs, the only tanks available to the *Hitlerjugend* at this point, were east of the Mue in anticipation of another renewed Canadian drive on Buron on 8 June. The Panther tanks of *I. Abt./SS-Pz.Rgt. 12* had not reached the area yet. It is unlikely that the tanks reported by the Ferme Le Bergerie strongpoint were German SPW 251 half-tracks or armoured cars of *SS-Pz.Aüfkl.Abt. 12*, as the accounts of the Anglo-Canadian anti-tank and machine gunners recount the tanks 'swinging their guns in their direction'.

In the account of the 24th Lancers, the British armoured unit in the area that day, while pushing down the RN 13 just east of St Leger, they received heavy anti-tank fire, and one Stuart light tank was knocked out. The British are recorded as firing intensively at anti-tank guns and calling in artillery on what they believed to be a German position. It is not stated within the very sparse detail in the 24th Lancers' war diary entry for 8 June where this German position was. The Lancers reported no German tanks in the area, though they did encounter anti-tank gun fire that could have come from 7.5cm SPW 251/9 half-tracks. There were also some Pak 40 7.5cm towed anti-tank guns from *8. Kompanie* of *II. Btl./SS-Pz.Gren.Rgt. 26* under *Hstuf.* Fasching in the area that may have fired at them near Putot.

Lastly, Ferme La Bergerie is almost directly to the north of Putot and a distance north of the RN 13. Looking at the map provided in the RWR divisional history, *Named by the Enemy*, the line of sight to the railway line is blocked by a series of orchards to the west and north-west of Putot village, and there are more woods to the west in front of Brouay. The only place the armour could have crossed is on the Brouay railway cutting bridge, which was, till just before noon, held by A Company of the RWR at the time of the firefight. Given this data, it would have been impossible for the RCA, RA and Cameron machine gunners to 'see' the 'tanks' cross the rail line.

The terrible conclusion the author comes to is that the RA and RCA anti-tank gunners and Vickers medium machine-gun crews fought a long-range firefight against most likely the recce troop of the 24th Lancers, knocking out one Stuart and damaging others, and received tank and RA field artillery fire in return. The two groups were too far away from each other to properly identify one another, and in the resulting firefight the anti-tank gunners and medium machine-gun crews kept firing until nearly all their gun positions were destroyed. Seeing the position destroyed, which it was, and the guns silenced, it is reasonably accurate to assume the British armour pulled back, not wanting to risk more casualties. This conclusion is one that had been already explored and discussed in online internet Normandy forums, that it was a truly unfortunate and tragic incident. It is also unfortunate that this account was printed and reprinted in many Canadian military history works, and that no German or French sources appear to have been consulted.

Immediately prior to the arrival of the British tanks on the western flank of the former RWR positions, all Canadian prisoners who could walk were marched to the rear of the former company positions. The RWR prisoners, taken when large numbers of A, B, and C Company personnel surrendered, would suffer varying degrees of treatment at the hands of the *Waffen-SS* in the days to follow. The amount of SPW 251 traffic was intense in the former positions of the RWR on the afternoon of 8 June, and many of these vehicles were used to transport Canadian prisoners over the railway line and back toward Le Mesnil-Patry, the *Gefechtsstand* of *II. Btl./SS-Pz.Gren.Rgt. 26.*[44] Many of these prisoners, whether marching back south on the roads or taken in vehicles to the rear, reported after the war a considerable number of self-propelled guns and other armoured vehicles. This was likely the mass of the entirely mounted *III. Btl.(Gepanzert)/SS-Pz.Gren.Rgt. 26* with its SPW 251 half-tracks as well as other vehicles from *SS-Pz.Aüfkl.Abt. 12.*

The personnel losses inflicted on the Royal Winnipeg Rifles had been very high, totalling 256 in all. Of these, roughly 175 were prisoners of war, most of whom were able to walk. It is estimated by the author that, from eyewitness accounts, a number of wounded still in their fighting positions were executed as the *SS-Panzergrenadiere* swept the battle site. The prisoners taken on the afternoon of 8 June were divided by the Germans into three groups. Roughly 100 men, most of them from A Company of the RWR, had been removed as a large group from the battlefield, and marched immediately south to the *Gefechtsstand* of *SS-Pz.Gren.Rgt. 26* in Le Haut-de-Bosq. A second group of prisoners of roughly 40 men was taken to the *II. Btl./SS-Pz. Gren.Rgt. 26 Gefechtsstand* where *Stubaf.* Siebken treated them reasonably well according to the Geneva Convention. A further group of roughly 25 to 26 men was transported south on what appears to be SPW 251 half-tracks and unloaded when the half-tracks met a party from *SS-Pz.Aüfkl.Abt. 12.* This later group contained Major Hodge, the commander of the surrendered RWR A Company.[45] It was in the area immediately south of the Putot battle zone that the first organised group executions of Canadian prisoners of war by the *SS-Panzergrenadiere* of both *SS-Pz. Gren.Rgt. 26* and *SS-Pz.Aüfkl.Abt. 12* began.

At roughly 1400 hours that day, the *SS-Pz.Aüfkl.Abt. 12 Gefechtsstand* was located within the Audrieu château grounds. Three Canadians were separated from the group of 25 to 26 men and were shot after a brief interrogation by *Stubaf.* Gerd Bremer. Among the three was Major Hodge. This was followed by a second group of three killed on the château grounds a short time later. Roughly two hours later at 1630 hours, a group of 13 were shot. All had been briefly interrogated, and with their usefulness at an end or with no information obtained, *Stubaf.* Bremer had them killed. Rather than focusing on utilising the combat power of *SS-Pz.Aüfkl.Abt. 12* to interdict British progress to the tactically important Hill 103 to the west or the village of St Pierre, threatened by British forces by nightfall, Bremer had prioritised interrogating and then shooting helpless prisoners. This is indicative of the mentality of select officers taken from the *Leibstandarte.* It is unclear exactly how events had changed them in the USSR, but this experience and Nazi indoctrination had appeared to have robbed them of their humanity and military professionalism.[46]

Following these executions and the previous combat with British forces to the west of *SS-Pz.Aüfkl.Abt. 12*, at 2000 hours a tremendous Royal Navy naval gunfire bombardment of the Audrieu and Cristot areas began. This destroyed the former village, and at 2100 hours fire shifted to the château, the *Gefechtsstand* of the *Abteilung.* This fire wounded the *Abteilung Kommandeur, Stubaf.* Bremer, who had to be evacuated after turning over command to *Hstuf.* von Reitzenstein.[47] A number of vehicles were destroyed, and the *Abteilung* pulled back its positions to the line Château Brouay–Cristot–Ferme Les Haut Vents.

In the semi-darkness on the evening of 8 June near Le Mesnil-Patry the afore-mentioned group of 40 RWR prisoners were marched south from the *II. Btl./SS-Pz. Gren.Rgt. 26 Gefechtsstand*. The column was stopped by a staff car coming from the south, and the NCO in charge of the prisoners spoke with an officer in the staff car, who reportedly was very agitated. Post-war postulations suggests that this officer could have been *Ostubaf.* Mohnke. After a large armoured column passed, this most probably the newly arriving Panther tanks of *2. Kp./SS-Pz.Rgt. 12* heading for new *SS-Pz.Aüfkl.Abt. 12* positions in order to support them, the group of prisoners were made to sit in a field. Suddenly, a SPW 251 half-track driving by abruptly stopped. The guards, joined by several *SS-Panzergrenadiere* from the half-track, shot the prisoners sitting in the field with MP-40 submachine guns, killing 35 of them. Five Canadian prisoners of war managed to escape.[48]

Moving back to events in Putot, Brigadier Foster, commander of the 7th Canadian Infantry Brigade, decided in late afternoon that a major counterattack would have to be mounted with his immediate reserve, the 1st Battalion, the Canadian Scottish Regiment (Can Scots), with tank and field artillery support. It was apparent at this point that large portions of the RWR had been overrun and destroyed, and what was left was now in a final defensive perimeter to the east of the village. The survivors – D Company, parts of the Support Company, and the forward tactical headquarters of the RWR – were all that was left to Lieutenant Colonel Meldram.[49]

A significant amount of time passed before contact was made with the Can Scots, it being 1830 hours by the time Foster arrived at the headquarters of the battalion in Secqueville-en-Bessin to speak with Lieutenant Colonel Calbedu, the commanding officer of the Can Scots. Foster ordered him to launch the attack in no less than two hours, before last light. Support had been promised in the form of a squadron of 1st Hussar tanks, which would drive in from their harbours in Secqueville-en-Bessin to the north, and fire support which would be provided from the two RCA field regiments, the 12th and 13th, from their positions at Bray.[50]

Calbedu decided the La Bergerie farm woods, still in Canadian hands and the site of the possible unfortunate friendly fire incident just north of the RN 13, would be his battalion start line for this counterattack. His objective would be to drive the German forces in Putot over the Caen–Bayeux railway line, restoring the original lines of the brigade fortress. The Secqueville-en-Bessin–Putot road would be the centre axis of advance for the infantry company commanders and right flank protection would be provided by the 1st Hussar tank composite A and B Squadron, led by Major White. Moving on the left flank would be the Can Scots carrier platoon. Attacking right of the road looking south would be D Company, led by Major McEwan, and left of the road looking south would be A Company, led by Major Plows. Following D Company would be the reserve C Company of Major Crofton. B Company, deployed at Bray to hold it against possible German attacks, would that afternoon be ordered to conduct a forced march to follow on in the path of A Company at the best possible speed. A battery of the 62nd Anti-Tank Regiment, RCA, would be moved in with the anti-tank forces of the Can Scots Support Company to quickly consolidate in Putot if all went well on the initial assault.

The indirect fire plan would also see the Cameron Highlanders of Ottawa, whose forces were deployed all over the 7th Canadian Infantry Brigade front, join in to use some of its 4.2-inch mortars to fire smoke to cover the infantry as they marched at a walking pace south from the start line north of the RN 13.[51]

This was a risky plan with regard to flank protection. While the Canadians believed there were British forces in front of Brouay, there were actually only scattered patrols, the 24th Lancers armoured group and other recce forces having departed the area by this stage. Luckily, what was there by early evening, the *III. Btl./SS-Pz.Gren.Rgt. 26* of *Stubaf.* Olboeter, had no tank support. What was left of the *II. Btl.(Gepanzert)/Pz.Gren.Lehr.Rgt. 902* had had its *Bataillon Gefechtsstand* destroyed by naval gunfire and a British tank raid, and was scattered and needed to be reorganised. Under artillery fire, the *Waffen-SS* in Brouay were not aggressively directed to attack Putot from the west or be ready to support the *II. Btl./SS-Pz. Gren.Rgt. 26* of Seibken to resist a potential Canadian counterattack. Worst of all, no communication existed with the *II. Abt./Pz.Lehr.Rgt. 130* and its Panzer IV tanks due to the German-imposed policy of radio silence. The first tanks of *I. Abt./SS-Pz. Rgt. 12*, which had arrived by this point to the east of Le Bourg and La Villeneuve, had not been directed forward to aid Seibken or help defend Putot. The German command and control over forces in the area was a shambles, and at the heart of this lack of control was *Ostubaf.* Mohnke, who seems to have been totally overwhelmed by the challenging situation on the battlefield, and who seems to have been unable to communicate effectively with *Panzer-Lehr* forces.

The RCA fire support plan started at 2030 hours, and the start line for the attack appears to have been the RN 13. Moving purposefully behind a wall of artillery fire, with the 1st Hussar tanks on their flank, the two lead companies pushed into Putot and began to clear buildings. Resistance from the Germans was not fierce, and in the face of the very heavy artillery fire the *Waffen-SS* begin to pull back, some bursts from German MG-42 positions inflicting infantry losses on the Can Scots. Still having their heavy weapons on the wrong side of the railway tracks, the 6. and 7. *Kompanien* were not prepared to defend what they had recently conquered and were overwhelmed by the RCA field artillery and mortar fire. D Company of the Can Scots took very heavy casualties from machine-gun fire, but pushed over the railway overpass halfway to Brouay. This company was so weakened during the fighting that it was later amalgamated with A Company.[52] Once the village was cleared, the Can Scots established an all-around defence and dug in for the night, their defences strengthened by the Can Scot Support Company heavy weapons which were then deployed in the village.

To summarise the actions of the *SS-Pz.Gren.Rgt. 26* up to the early evening of 8 June in the Brouay–Putot-en-Bessin–Bretteville-l'Orgueilleuse–Norrey-en-Bessin sector, a firm defensive front had been established along the railway line Caen–Bayeux and south of Norrey, and one Canadian infantry battalion had been nearly destroyed. However, *Waffen-SS* failures near Norrey-en-Bessin and Bretteville had seen some *SS-Panzergrenadiere* casualties incurred for marginal gains, and the positions of the RRR remained unchanged. Lack of coordination with armour and more importantly, artillery, had condemned the attack of Mohnke to failure. Simply waiting for all the right elements to be in place rather than hastily throwing the whole regiment into combat would have given the enterprise a much better chance for success. A suitable starting point cleared of the enemy for a concentrated multi-*Panzerdivision* push had not been created, as the Canadians still held the 'Oak' line. The new front line above the *SS-Pz.Gren.Rgt. 26* stretched along the railway line just north of a line Brouay–Cristot–Les Hauts Vents to St Pierre.

The efforts of the *I. Btl./SS-Pz.Gren.Rgt. 26* of *Stubaf.* Krause had been largely frustrated, in large part to heavy RCA field artillery fire. While the Germans had engaged in heavy combat, their front line had not changed, and *SS-Pz.Gren.Rgt. 26* was entrenched in a static defence by the evening of 8 June. Following the failed surprise early morning attack, the deployment of *I. Btl./SS-Pz.Gren.Rgt. 26* was scattered, with *1. Kompanie* slightly east of St Manvieu, *3. Kompanie* just north of the same village and *2. Kompanie* in Ferme Cardonville near Le Mesnil-Patry. The *Bataillon* hardly appeared to be a concentrated force, its commander at this stage being hard-pressed to merely hold the frontage he had been assigned, never mind move his *SS-Panzergrenadier Bataillon* forward in a concentrated manner to attack a specific objective.

II. Btl./SS-Pz.Gren.Rgt. 26 had succeeded initially in its infantry combat but by nightfall it had taken a considerable number of casualties and achieved little in the way of territorial gains. In response to the temporary loss of Putot and the near destruction of the RWR, Canadian forces had delivered a ferocious counterattack which regained the village, and inflicted further casualties on *II. Btl./SS-Pz.Gren. Rgt. 26*. To the west, the *SS-Pz.Aüfkl.Abt. 12* had experienced some combat, but it had retained its positions and defended the flank of the *Hitlerjugend* in the face of a British advance to the west against a lack of supporting forces from the *Panzer-Lehr*. The absence of the Panther tanks of *I. Abt./SS Panzer Regiment 12*, intended to be attached to *SS-Pz.Gren.Rgt. 26* but not yet in the battle zone due to lack of fuel, most certainly influenced events. The entrenched 7th Canadian Infantry Brigade infantry had thwarted Mohnke's progress in a convincing manner, again using massed artillery fire as the 'stopper'.[53]

It should be noted that as of midday on 8 June 1944, the activities and dispositions of *I. Btl./SS-Pz.Gren.Rgt. 26* were the last thing on the mind of its regimental commander, *Ostubaf.* Mohnke. The battle in Putot, raging all day on 8 June and involving the *II.* and parts of the *III. Btl./SS-Pz.Gren.Rgt. 26*, had fully occupied Mohnke's attention. The amount of pressure which came from the regimental higher command for Krause's *Bataillon* to capture Norrey-en-en-Bessin or any RRR positions is debatable. Certainly nothing was coordinated with his counterpart to the east, *Staf.* Meyer, the commander of the neighbouring *SS-Pz.Gren.Rgt. 25*, who slept for large portions of the afternoon and evening of 8 June 1944.[54] Mohnke was also travelling constantly to monitor the progress of the fighting, trying to establish contact with the *Panzer-Lehr*, and was strangely enraged when the commander of *II. Btl./SS-Pz.Gren.Rgt. 26* sent back many Canadian prisoners to his regimental headquarters after the Putot battle against his wishes. Tragically, many of these would later be murdered as prisoners of war.[55]

On the evening of 8 June, *Gen.d.Pz.Tr.* von Schweppenburg, *Oberbefehlshaber* of *Pz.Gr.West*, arrived at the Château La Cain, five kilometres north of Thury-Harcourt, to establish his headquarters and attempt to gain control over the chaotic situation unfolding at the front. This had to be done quickly if he was to be able to mass the bulk to two *Panzerdivisionen* to launch a powerful and decisive thrust for the coastline, as he had been ordered to do, using the *I. SS-Pz.Korps* for this purpose. While he had operational control of the eastern sector of the *7. Armee*, he was still dependent on its staff for logistics and rear area administration. The administrative and logistical limits of *Pz.Gr.West* and its ability to function as a fully-fledged equivalent to an *Armee* headquarters were very apparent at this stage.

The planned attack of von Schweppenburg was to utilise the *Panzer-Lehr* to attack on the west side of the Mue, with the *Hitlerjugend* and the *21. Pz.Div.* attacking from their current positions west of the Orne. This area was good tank country in which to deploy the armour of each division, and a successful attack might penetrate the front of the Anglo-Canadian front and create a military crisis, forcing the Allies on the defensive and containing the bridgehead.[56]

But this attack, as well as many other German plans during the Normandy campaign, was to be dashed due to mounting Allied pressures forcing the Germans on the defensive and postponing their plans, again and again. On 8 June the obvious absence of the *Panzer-Lehr* had completely derailed any coordinated action, and the need for its proper deployment forced the German high command to accept delays.

As a result, the planned attack was pushed to 10 June, and only the two divisions to the west of the *21. Pz.Div.* would take part. It is doubtful on 8 June that von Schweppenburg had any reason to be confident that the attack could ever take place, as the *Oberbefehlshaber* of *H.Gr.B.*, *G.F.M.* Erwin Rommel, had intervened on this date to direct the *Panzer-Lehr* to attack towards Bayeux with all due haste, dragging its forces into an isolated attack not coordinated with its neighbours.[57] Events such as these, mated with endless delays, forced reactions to Allied operations, and a general lack of infantry to hold the front line in the place of his precious *Panzerdivisionen*, were destroying his plans and limiting his ability to impose his will on events.

The first battle of Caen: The 8–9 June 1944 attack on Bretteville-l'Orgueilleuse

There were no major Canadian offensive operations that occurred on 8 June immediately north of Caen or east of the Mue. Realistically, *SS-Pz.Gren.Rgt. 25* was in no position to continue any kind of offensive operation without major reinforcement. Attempting to link up with the *SS-Pz.Gren.Rgt. 26* of *Ostubaf.* Mohnke and alleviate the gap between the two *SS-Panzergrenadierregimenter*, Meyer devised with *Ostubaf.* Wünsche a plan for an armoured night assault from the east, along the Caen–Bayeux highway on the town of Bretteville-l'Orgueilleuse, set to begin late on 8 June. The capture of this town would bring about the isolation of Norrey-en-Bessin, which would also have to fall eventually for the *Hitlerjugend* to establish a solid line running along the Caen–Bayeux railway line.

In a series of spectacular, yet minor, small unit actions over the timeframe 8–9 June that would begin with the night assault on Bretteville – the subject of this chapter – the 7th Canadian Infantry Brigade forces would fight off several *Waffen-SS* attacks that would fail miserably in the face of a determined infantry, anti-tank and field artillery defensive effort. In Bretteville, Canadian infantry and supporting forces would fight an all-night battle against a seemingly unstoppable force of Panther tanks and light infantry that pushed into the town itself, yet they were forced to withdraw due to lack of infantry strength.

Within the historiography of the Normandy campaign, the battle of Bretteville-l'Orgueilleuse, fought over the night of 8/9 June 1944, is viewed as one of the most outstanding small unit actions of the Second World War.[1] The victorious night-time defensive battle of the 1st Battalion, the Regina Rifle Regiment (RRR), against an armoured battlegroup of the *Hitlerjugend*, is a well-known event in Canadian military history. Canadian authors Marc Milner, Mark Zuehlke and Oliver Haller have all presented narratives of the night-time battle, but largely from a Canadian perspective.[2] Apart from the first-hand accounts of *Staf.* Kurt Meyer in his autobiography *Grenadiers* and within the *Hitlerjugend* divisional history of Hubert Meyer, there is little detail on the German side of this engagement. The ability to gain a fuller picture of the night-time encounter has recently become more attainable with the widespread dissemination of the Normandy *Kriegstagebuch* war diaries of *SS-Pz.Rgt. 12* and newer works by French military historians.[3]

The failure of the *Hitlerjugend* attack on the village of Bretteville-l'Orgueilleuse and its surrounding area on the 8/9 June 1944 was not exclusively due to poor planning, inexperience, lack of coordination and inadequate infantry support. Though secondary sources for the battle state that these factors were present in abundance, the main reason for failure was the German confidence in mutated armoured tactics that were successfully used by the *Waffen-SS* on the Eastern Front.[4] This argument has been presented by Marc Milner in his work *Stopping the Panzers*, but little exists in the Normandy historiography in the way of a detailed discussion of these tactics or their practitioners.[5] By supplying greater detail on this particular battle and German armoured tactics, this chapter can provide historical insight into how and why initial German armoured attacks floundered in the face of strong Anglo-Canadian resistance in June 1944.

These rough tactics, though proven successful during 1943 German operations in Ukraine, violated established German armoured doctrine that propagated the use of all arms, especially infantry support, artillery and airstrikes, to conduct operations. The Russian enemy, so familiar to the Germans, fought in an entirely different manner than Anglo-Canadian forces. The lack of available resources confronting both sides in Ukraine often negated the ability to use artillery preparatory fire to reduce enemy defences. Often, groups of German tanks with limited infantry present could achieve battlefield objectives using shock and surprise on the vast steppes, where in depth Red Army anti-tank and artillery forces were often absent.[6] These conditions were not present in Normandy, to the dismay of the Eastern Front veterans of the *Waffen-SS*. The failure of the *Waffen-SS* commanders to recognise the need for greater preparation and by default, larger and more powerful resources, doomed their early operations to failure.

The greatest victory in Ukraine achieved by the two German protagonists mentioned in this chapter, then-*Sturmbannführer* Kurt Meyer and Max Wünsche, at the time both *Abteilung Kommandeure* within the *1. SS-Panzergrenadierdivision Leibstandarte SS Adolf Hitler*, occurred on 23 February 1943 when their combined forces successfully attacked the village of Paraskowejewskije. This victory resulted in Meyer, the senior officer commanding the mixed *Kampfgruppe* involved, being awarded the Oak Leaves to the Knight's Cross, a significant award for battlefield bravery within the *Wehrmacht*. In this operation *Kampfgruppe* Meyer, consisting of part of parts of *I. Abt./SS-Pz.Rgt. 1* under Wünsche and the *SS-Pz.Aufkl.Abt. 1* under Meyer, attacked the Ukrainian village from two directions. The *Panzerabteilung Kompanien* with their Panzer IV tanks flanked the village while Meyer attacked down its main road. As a participant in the attack, *Obersturmführer* Georg Isecke recalled that it was a complete success:

With two Panzer *Kompanien*, we pursued the enemy to the east and north-east and destroyed him. Our own Panzer crews suffered no wounds to personnel and only light damage to the equipment. Our thrust hit the Russian divisional headquarters precisely. The [Russian] division commander was reported killed, and their first officer of the general staff was taken prisoner.[7]

There were many such attacks made by the *Kampfgruppen* of the *Leibstandarte* in the winter and spring of 1943 in Ukraine, and the successes achieved solidified the soundness of these armoured tactics in the minds of the *Waffen-SS* commanders that had executed them. While certainly not in accordance with approved textbook German armoured tactics, Meyer and others had made do in situations where they had little in the way of resources on the vast expanses of the Ukrainian steppes.

Transferred to the west in the spring of 1943 to help form the *Hitlerjugend*, Meyer, Wünsche and other *Waffen-SS* officers retained an appreciation for these tactics and encountered nothing to change their minds in the relatively placid training environment of Belgium and France in the months leading up to the Allied invasion. Unfortunately for these newly promoted, now regimental commanders, they did not gain any experience whatsoever fighting the Western Allies in Italy or Sicily, nor did they understand the great gulf in operational tactics practised by the Commonwealth armies and the Russians.

The Germans possessed significant strengths during their attack on Bretteville-l'Orgueilleuse during the night of 8/9 June 1944, but accompanying weaknesses ultimately assured their failure during the resulting close-quarters fighting. Attacking with an overabundance of armour on hand, including a *Batterie* of six Wespe 10.5cm self-propelled guns to accompany two under-strength *Kompanien* of Panther tanks, the infantry which was needed to construct a well-balanced battlegroup was not present.[8] Further weaknesses in the assault forces' infantry contingent included weak leadership, lack of coordination with the armour, poor start line positions and a lack of numbers. Also, completely missing from the German plan was an effective preliminary artillery barrage to supress the defensive capabilities of the Canadians. This was in part to effect or facilitate surprise, which had been vital to Meyer's success in Ukraine, and secondly, there is no evidence that he utilised his regimental staff to organise such support. It is quite possible he saw no such need during a night attack.

These factors would be ruthlessly exploited by a powerful Canadian combined arms force that dealt with the small attacking German infantry force that sought to follow in the tracks of the Panther tanks. Most of the Anglo-Canadian defenders were inexperienced in battle, despite a small number of officers having gained combat experience in Italy and North Africa, however they were extremely well trained, and this level of training within the 3rd Canadian Infantry Division had been gained during two and half years in southern England. This factor allowed many of the division's units to perform at a high level in their first battles.[9]

During the early afternoon of 8 June, *Staf.* Meyer, fresh from his successful 7 June counterattack on the 9th Canadian Infantry Brigade near Caen, conferred with *Brig. Fhr.* Witt on the topic of his next objective. Witt directed Meyer to assist *SS-Pz. Gren.Rgt. 26*, then heavily engaged in battle in Putot to the west, in clearing the localities of Norrey-en-Bessin and Bretteville-l'Orgueilleuse.[10] Meyer decided that he would seize Bretteville-l'Orgueilleuse in a night attack, cutting off Norrey-en-Bessin, which could then be tackled by the *I. Btl./SS Pz.Gren.Rgt. 26* at its leisure. Despite not reaching the invasion beaches the previous day, Meyer was confident that overall victory against the landings could still be achieved, regardless of factors such as Allied air superiority. As previously noted, *Ostubaf.* Mohnke was heavily occupied by events in Putot, and could not attend this meeting.[11] In a brief encounter at roughly noon, Witt had also met with *G.F.M.* Rommel, *Oberbefehlshaber* of *H.Gr.B.* As Canadian military historian Terry Copp recounts, Witt 'reported that one panzer battalion was waiting for dusk to attack Bretteville-l'Orgueilleuse and Norrey-en-Bessin. The intent was to secure a start line for a multi-divisional thrust to the coast'. The divisions involved in this future would be the *21. Pz.Div.*, the *Panzer-Lehr* and the *Hitlerjugend*. Rommel approved Witt's upcoming small operation and then quickly left the divisional *Gefechtsstand* in Venoix.[12]

As of the afternoon of 8 June, a significant gap still existed between the frontline positions of *SS-Pz.Gren.Rgt. 25* and *SS-Pz.Gren.Rgt. 26*. The right wing of the newly arrived forces of *SS-Pz.Gren.Rgt. 26*, *I. Btl./SS-Pz.Gren.Rgt. 26* was centred on Saint-Manvieu–Norrey-en-Bessin, 6.5 kilometres from other German forces.[13] In the eastern *SS-Pz.Gren.Rgt. 25* zone, a makeshift western flank of weak divisional support *Kompanien* was strung out in a line roughly from Franqueville to Gruchy north–south.[14] This gap was a dangerous weak point, and the overall German front line distance needed to be shortened. Also, the Bretteville-l'Orgueilleuse–Norrey-en-Bessin Canadian position was a dangerous salient that needed to be dealt with. By taking Bretteville-l'Orgueilleuse, Meyer would eliminate the gap in his division's front, shorten it at the same time and secure the start line for further attacks.[15]

Continuing to plan with the *Kommandeur* of *SS-Pz.Rgt. 12*, *Ostubaf.* Wünsche, Meyer then set about assembling his task force. He was extremely short of infantry reserves. All that could be spared was the reconnaissance *15.(Aufklärung) Kompanie*. This was a lightly armed force equipped with Volkswagen Schwimmenwagens (amphibious jeeps), motorcycles, staff cars and a few light trucks. It was led by *Hstuf.* von Büttner.[16] Numbering near 100 men, it had nowhere near the capability of a fully equipped *SS-Panzergrenadier Bataillon*, three of which would be the standard force required today within Western armies (3:1 ratio) for the task of successfully attacking a battalion-sized enemy strongpoint. Attached to this small infantry force was an overabundance of armour in the way of roughly 25 operational Panther tanks of the *1.* and *4. Kompanien*, led by *Hstuf.* Berlin and Pfeiffer, and accompanied by *Stubaf.* Jürgensen, the *Abteilung Kommandeur*.[17] The last two *Kompanien* of the

Abteilung were to the west and east. The last to arrive in Caen, the *2. Kompanie*, would be inserted that night near the Parc de Boislande, which would see the Panther tanks take up positions near its château, ready to support *SS-Pz.Aüfkl.Abt. 12* secure Hill 102, just to the south of its main positions.[18] The *3. Kompanie* would initially be sent to the village of Authie north of Caen on its arrival to help shore up the defences of *SS-Pz.Gren.Rgt. 25*.

There was nothing new about conducting a night attack involving tanks for Wünsche or Meyer, who had practised night attacks multiple times in the USSR during the winter of 1943. Although German armoured doctrine relates: 'Offensive operation in fog or dusk could be necessary if it serves to destroy an already shaken enemy and cause them to disintegrate completely', the enemy in this case was not shaken, nor were they about to disintegrate.[19]

Much has been made regarding the number of tanks involved in the German attack, with many sources differing on the number. As previously noted, the *Abteilung* only had 66 Panthers on hand at the time of the invasion versus its authorised level of 79 tanks, and not all *Kompanien* were up to strength.[20] A 1 June 1944 readiness report from the division states that of 50 Panthers on hand at that point, 48 were combat ready, a readiness rate of 96 per cent.[21] While considering this figure it must be reflected that the tanks were brand new, combat operations had not begun and long route marches had not occurred. Also present was the six-vehicle strong *2. Bttr./ SS-Pz.Art.Rgt. 12* with its Wespe self-propelled guns. This force was led by acting *Batterie-Chef Ustuf.* Hoke. Additional armoured fighting vehicles included at least one Czech 38(t) 20mm Flakpanzer (anti-aircraft tank) of the *Pantherabteilung Flak Zug*.

Neither Berlin or Pfeiffer had any recent combat experience, and while Berlin was completely untested in actual operations, only Pfeiffer had combat experience near Kharkov with *6. Kp./SS-Pz.Rgt. 1* during the winter fighting there in 1943 as parts of the *Leibstandarte*. Berlin in the meantime had served in various *Abteilung* and regimental staff positions in *SS-Pz.Rgt. 1* before his arrival within *SS-Pz.Rgt. 12*.[22]

While Meyer should have taken care to further coordinate his operations by holding an orders group with the nearby infantry commanders of the *I. Btl./SS-Pz. Gren.Rgt. 26. Kompanien* nearby or contacted a liaison officer, no evidence exists that he did. The involvement of these *SS-Panzergrenadier* units bordering his objective would potentially be vital to his success or failure. Also, no evidence can be found regarding any sophisticated German indirect artillery fire plan or organised artillery support for the operation.[23]

Stubaf. Wünsche, meeting with the Panther *Kompanien* commanders late in the afternoon of 8 June, briefed them on the upcoming attack on Bretteville-l'Orgueilleuse and clearing the Le Bourg–Rots area due east of the village.[24] He made it clear to them they would be the vanguard of the attack. The allocation of 25 operational Panthers and the Wespe *Batterie* to take a small village was a massive allocation of armoured resources for the task at hand, especially by German 1944 standards. This may have been in part to mitigate the weakness in the accompanying infantry forces and the poor performance to that point of *I. Btl./SS-Pz.Gren.Rgt. 26*, which had been badly repulsed in its attack on Norrey-en-Bessin the previous night.

The final armoured objective decided by Wünsche, and Meyer was to secure the high ground north-west of Bretteville, Hill 68, after supporting the *SS-Panzergrenadiere* in clearing the village area of enemy resistance. The H-Hour of the attack was decided for 2130 hours, partially to negate the Allied air threat and partially to achieve surprise at last light with the violent swarming of armoured vehicles onto the objective as per German armoured doctrine.[25] Several German *Panzerkommandanten* and *SS-Panzergrenadiere Zug* leaders conducted recces of the Canadian dispositions near the Mue in the late afternoon of 8 June 1944. These movements were observed by the Canadians, who noted the positions and amount of armour moving in the area. Short but violent artillery bombardments, these being 'concentrations' in RCA artillery terminology, were called in on the Germans on several occasions that afternoon. These were directed by the Royal Canadian Artillery (RCA) Forward Observation Officer (FOO) from the 13th Field Regiment, RCA, assigned to B Company, RRR, Lieutenant O'Brennan.[26]

The area of Bretteville and Norrey-en-Bessin defended by the RRR was made up of flat, open beet and wheat fields and was broken up by dense tree lines. All the buildings were constructed of stone masonry, making each one a potential bunker. Around the villages were walls 2.5 meters tall that posed significant barriers to armoured movement or infantry assault. South of Bretteville-l'Orgueilleuse was the Caen–Bayeux railway line, which ran slightly north-west.[27] On his arrival in the area, Lieutenant-Colonel Matheson sited his headquarters in the centre of Bretteville. RRR A Company of Captain Ron Shawcross was positioned in the village itself and encircled the battalion headquarters located near the village church.[28] B Company, with its new commander, Major Eric Syme, was initially positioned in the neighbouring village of Rots to the east, but by the evening was pulled back to the open fields broken by tree lines south of the railway line near Bretteville-l'Orgueilleuse, with its positions facing south-east.[29] C Company under Major Tubb was firmly entrenched in Norrey-en-Bessin in an all-around defence and had repulsed a *SS-Pz. Gren.Rgt. 26* attack the previous night. D Company, under its new commander Captain Brown, was initially placed in La Villeneuve, south-east of Rots, but was withdrawn at the same time as B Company. Its new defensive position was south-west of Bretteville-l'Orgueilleuse at Cardonville Usine (Cardonville factory), a flax factory north of the east–west railway line. This walled-in compound had an orchard beside it and contained the flax production facility.[30]

Interspaced within the RRR positions were the 6-pounder anti-tank guns of RRR Support Company's anti-tank platoon, and one complete battery (94 Battery with two troops) of the 3rd Canadian Anti-Tank Regiment, RCA, also with 6-pounder anti-tank guns. In accordance with Anglo-Canadian doctrine, each gun's field of fire interlocked with other nearby anti-tank guns to provide maximum firepower on any enemy attacking armour.[31] The total strength for the RRR company positions was 14 6-pounders, an impressive amount of firepower. These were supplied with discarding sabot ammunition, which was more than adequate for penetrating all German panzers apart from the frontal armour of the heavier Panthers and Tigers.[32]

The 6-pounder anti-tank gun was a formidable weapon that could fire rounds at 2,000 ft/second (610 meters per second) and had an accurate, flat trajectory. It also had a total of 90-degree traverse and could fire up to 12 rounds per minute. It was very mobile, easily manhandled into position and could be towed by a jeep or the tracked Universal Carrier. Further support was given by at least two platoons of A Company, the Cameron Highlanders of Ottawa machine-gun battalion, with their Vickers medium machine guns. At least one medium machine gun was assigned to each company position. 6- and 17-pounder anti-tank guns from the 3rd Anti-Tank Regiment, RCA, and British 62nd Anti-Tank Regiment, RA, were still positioned to the north-west of Bretteville-l'Orgueilleuse in depth at Ferme La Bergerie, but it is unclear if they partook in the night-time battle due to their near destruction by the aforementioned possible friendly fire incident described in the previous chapter.[33] Support in the way of indirect field artillery was supplied by the 12th and 13th Field Regiments, RCA, who were on call to carry out pre-planned defensive fire missions.[34] Each regiment had a full complement of 24 M7 Priest 105mm self-propelled guns and each RRR company position had an RCA FOO assigned to it.

As a result of the increased German activity in the east during the afternoon of 8 June, Lieutenant Colonel Matheson expected an armoured assault to be launched imminently and placed his battalion on high alert.[35] Of interest and ignored in previous accounts of this battle is the proximity of the 7th Canadian Infantry Brigade headquarters during the battle. No more than 100 meters from the headquarters of Matheson was the headquarters of Brigadier Foster, located in the hamlet of Haut de Bretteville, attached to the northern part of the village.[36] Even though Canadian infantry had held Bretteville-l'Orgueilleuse in force for more than a day, two bizarre incidents occurred at roughly noon on 8 June. First, a German dispatch rider on a motorcycle, ignorant of German and Canadian positions and who held the village, was shot and killed by the battalion commander, Lieutenant Colonel Matheson, as he attempted to drive past the battalion headquarters near the church. Shortly afterward, a German Volkswagen Kübelwagen staff car drove up with a driver who dismounted and began to curiously look around. A PIAT infantry anti-tank weapon was fired at the vehicle, and he was killed. These incidents have been recounted in various accounts as occurring in midst of the night-time battle that night, when in fact it is much more likely they occurred during the day. This appreciation is supported by the testimony of the former commanding officer of the 13th Field Regiment, RCA, who while present in Matheson's headquarters observed the Kübelwagen event.[37]

As planned, at 2130 hours the Meyer/Wünsche armoured group began to advance from their assembly point at Saint Germain-la-Blanche Herbe.[38] As the Panthers assembled, no indirect artillery barrage to support their attack was fired, which was in direct violation of established wartime German combined arms armoured doctrine, which states: 'In spite of all their firepower, tanks are dependent on the support of extensive indirect fire'.[39] Doctrine was followed, however, with regard to basic *Zug* (platoon) tactics, with the Panther advance to contact being conducted in staggered formation on the paved RN 13.[40] Passing through Franqueville and driving west, the Panther tanks entered the hamlet of La Villeneuve, divided from the neighbouring Le Bourg by the highway, and encountered no resistance.[41] *Stubaf.* Jürgensen, the *Abteilung Kommandeur*, then established his advanced headquarters there, taking no part in the initial combat that followed. The lead *4. Kompanie* reached this hamlet at approximately 2140 hours with the *SS-Panzergrenadiere* of the *15. Kp./SS-Pz.Gren. Rgt. 25* riding on the rear engine decks. The *Kompanie* reconnaissance Volkswagen Swimmenwagens and motorcycles had been mostly left in the rear, though some were present. *Hstuf.* Pfeiffer, in one of the lead Panthers, then ordered *4. Kompanie* into column formation and with himself in the lead crossed the village bridge over the Mue, his *Kompanie* followed by the tanks of *1. Kompanie* under *Hstuf.* Berlin. On exiting the village of La Villeneuve west of the Mue, wedge formation was resumed with *4. Kompanie* on the north of the RN 13 and *1. Kompanie* to the south, the tanks roaring through the open fields during last light at 35 kilometres per hour. *Hstuf.* von Büttner, the *Kommandeur* of *15. Kompanie*, rode on the engine deck of one of the lead *4. Kompanie* tanks with his command staff. Meyer was himself riding in a motorcycle-sidecar combination near Wünsche's Befehlspanther (Panther command tank) on the main highway.

Anticipating an attack from this direction, the RRR carrier platoon with its tracked Universal Carriers of Support Company and two Cameron Highlanders Vickers machine-gun crews had been dispatched by Colonel Matheson to form a reinforced combat outpost to the east of Bretteville-l'Orgueilleuse. Placing themselves 200 meters east of the village near a rise along the RN 13, they had good fields of fire in a slight reverse slope position. Matheson wished to detect and possibly disrupt any attack with these forces in a manner like that which occurred near Norrey-en-Bessin on the night of 7/8 June. His plan was to utilise this reinforced combat outpost position to do so, in accordance with Anglo-Canadian infantry defensive doctrine.[42] But the attack on Norrey-en-Bessin the night previous did not include Panther tanks, and to what extent this grouping could be supported by the B Company positions south of the railway line is unclear.[43] The Germans were rapidly approaching this improvised skirmish line at 2145 hours, by which time the Canadians had not yet completed digging in. Eight 6-pounder anti-tank guns of K Troop, 105 Battery of the 3rd Canadian Anti-Tank Regiment, RCA, temporarily attached to 94 Battery to form a composite battery, appear to have been sited both south and north of the

RN 13 highway in support of the carrier platoon position.[44] The Canadians, on high alert, were ready for the Germans.

At this point first contact was made. The lead Panthers, coming over the rise present in the corn fields east of Bretteville-l'Orgueilleuse along the RN 13 highway, stopped to observe on this crest. These Panthers, one of them, Panther '404' commanded by *Hstuf.* Pfeiffer, received a violent volley of Canadian heavy machine-gun and anti-tank fire.[45] Thus began the first phase of the battle of Bretteville-l'Orgueilleuse that lasted from 2145 to 2330 hours and consisted of a high intensity firefight between the Panther *Kompanien* and the Canadian defenders as the Germans advanced on the village from the east and manoeuvred to the south. This firefight was to destroy most of the outlying combat outposts of the RRR carrier platoon and Cameron Highlander machine-gun crews, but miss the B Company south of the railway line. During the process, more than one Panther tank was destroyed or disabled, and heavy casualties were inflicted on the accompanying *SS-Panzergrenadiere* by the ferocity of Canadian defensive fire.

On receiving the first Canadian volley of anti-tank rounds and medium machine-gun fire, *Hstuf.* Pfeiffer ordered the rest of *4. Kompanie* forward and ordered the village buildings be set on fire to expose Canadian positions in the fading light. Taking

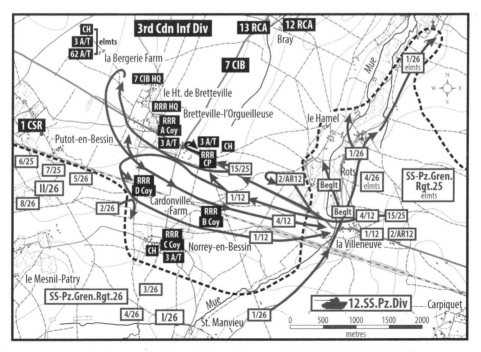

Attack on Bretteville-l'Orgueilleuse, 8/9 June 1944. (Map by Mike Bechthold)

casualties in their positions on the rear hulls of the tanks, the *SS-Panzergrenadiere* dismounted and began to follow the tanks on foot. Panther '404', the *Kompanie-Chef* vehicle, destroyed what German sources reported as a lone Canadian Sherman tank located at the entrance to the village after a short firefight. It is unknown to what Canadian armoured regiment this tank belonged, but it was not an artillery observation vehicle.[46] It has been incorrectly reported that at this point Pfeiffer's tank was hit and set ablaze shortly afterward by a Canadian anti-tank gun.[47] There is no evidence this occurred. Another Panther, '427' of *Uscha.* Hartmann, was certainly destroyed and did burn out. Canadian field artillery fire from both the 12th and 13th Field Regiments, RCA, also joined the battle with defensive fire tasks, hammering the Germans.[48] The war diary of the 12th Field Regiment, RCA, describes the 'firing of DF (Defensive Fire) and DF SOS tasks as well as Mike (Regimental) and Uncle' (Division) -level targets, involving large numbers of RCA artillery pieces, practically 'all day and all night'.[49]

The *1. Kompanie* Panther tanks, moving west to the south of *4. Kompanie*, also encountered the anti-tank guns and machine guns and joined in the intense firefight. Roughly twenty-five Panthers in total engaged the RCA anti-tank gunners who were outnumbered by at least three-to-one odds. The Panther tanks' machine-gun and cannon fire raked positions of the outlying RRR carrier platoon, and then drove right over it, destroying six Universal Carriers in the process.[50] Any Canadian survivors of this onslaught ran south to the B Company positions, the advancing Panthers pushing forward in the semi-darkness.

A small number who were not killed or wounded did not manage to escape and were taken prisoner. Regina Rifle Regiment veteran Bert Adams stated in a personal account, reprinted in Gordon Brown and Terry Copp's *Look to your Front...Regina Rifles: A Regiment at War 1944–1945*, that as a stretcher-bearer party member, he searched the former overrun positions of the RRR carrier platoon and other supporting forces at the combat outpost on the RN 13 to Caen days after the 8/9 June combat. In a ditch he reportedly found several members of the RRR carrier platoon, without weapons, facedown and shot. Three to four of this group were carrying prayer books and many had obvious signs of automatic weapons being used on them at close range. It appeared to the stretcher-bearer party retrieving the bodies that the executed prisoners had been arranged in this manner by the Germans after being captured, and given time to pull out their prayer books. It is unclear who committed the executions, but it appears that *15. Kompanie SS-Panzergrenadiere* following on foot after dismounting from the Panther tanks would have swept through the positions after the firefight had been won by the Panthers and they drove forward to the first buildings of Bretteville-l'Orgueilleuse.[51]

During this first portion of the firefight the German tankers also claimed to have destroyed or disabled four anti-tank gun positions near Bretteville-l'Orgueilleuse with high explosive rounds, utilising fire and movement in the semi-darkness. The

Panther crews were fighting in accordance with their armoured doctrine, which stated 'When it comes to taking position and opening fire, targets are to be destroyed in rapid succession, following by a prompt change in position'.[52] All the 6-pounders of K Troop, 105 Battery of the 3rd Anti-Tank Regiment, RCA, were thus silenced, vastly reducing the defensive anti-tank capability of the Canadians.[53]

To rectify this inequality, the remaining RCA gunners of G Troop, 94 Battery began to manhandle their 6-pounders to face east to engage the Panthers.[54] Positioned to defend the remainder of the village, the crews frantically manoeuvred their guns to orientate them to the south and east and took up the fight.[55] The Panther crews, now bunching up in front of the village in the semi-darkness, were following their doctrine that stated: 'Limited intervals are needed in darkness as that visual contact can be maintained'. But by maintaining this close formation in the limited visibility of the burning village, they did not adequately disperse in the face of enemy fire. It was difficult for tactical spacing distances to be judged by the *Panzerkommandanten* in the low light of the late evening, and the crew's focus was on engaging the anti-tank guns. During this point in the battle the six Wespe 10.5cm self-propelled guns also entered the fray. They appear to have taken up positions on the rise or behind it, and engaged some Canadian anti-tank and infantry positions with some success. At this point during the firefight many Panther tanks were being hit with anti-tank shells, some multiple times. It appears Wünsche, now joined by Jürgensen, then ordered the Wespe self-propelled artillery back to the village of Rots after they had fired several salvos, fearing they would be lost to the anti-tank fire.[56] It is estimated they returned and re-crossed the Mue before midnight, having only lost a Volkswagen Kübelwagen and suffering a small number of casualties. It can be concluded that their direct contribution to the battle was minimal.

With the entrance to the village looming up in front of them with its one street, as mentioned previously the mass of *4. Kompanie* Panthers was now bunched up in front of the objective. This made things easier for the Canadian RCA anti-tank gunners targeting the Panthers and the RRR machine gunners who engaged German infantry near the tanks. The attached *SS-Panzergrenadiere* of the *15. Kompanie* during this period took heavy casualties as they attempted to dismount and fight their way on foot to the first buildings, which the Panthers had now reached. Unseen by the Panther tank crews, A Company riflemen in the village ignored Panthers to concentrate on engaging the following *SS-Panzergrenadiere*, as per the direction of the RRR commander, Lieutenant-Colonel Matheson. The *15. Kompanie Kommandeur, Hstuf.* von Büttner, was killed during the initial part of the firefight, he and his command team being shot off the rear deck of a Panther. Also shot was the driver of the motorcycle combination which *Staf.* Meyer was riding. The motorcycle itself was destroyed, the fuel tank explosion briefly setting Meyer's uniform on fire. After recovering, Meyer at this point was still able to move on foot and communicate with the *SS-Panzergrenadiere* junior leaders, but he had no access to a wireless net to control or influence the armoured group except by running up to the Befehlspanther of Wünsche.[57] His ability to lead and influence the battle at this point was temporarily diminished.

At this point in the battle, just before midnight, whatever advances the *SS-Panzergrenadiere* of *15. Kompanie* had made towards Bretteville-l'Orgueilleuse had stalled due to the defensive fire of the RRR A Company positions in the village along the main street, the RN 13. The Germans found themselves pinned down in the ditches on each side of the highway, this being the only cover, apart from treelines bordering fields. They were suppressed by defensive small arms fire from the Canadian infantry positions that were difficult to locate and silence in the semi-darkness. While the Panthers could churn through the Canadian positions, in the darkness each individual fighting trenches could not be identified and engaged by the crews.

Despite having lost wireless communication with the 7th Canadian Infantry Brigade headquarters shortly after the German attack began, RRR battalion head-quarters stood firm and continued to direct the fight as best it could. The darkness was the friend of the A Company soldiers fighting from the buildings and fields as the Panther crew commanders could only see by the light of the burning buildings. The RCA anti-tank gunners also continued to fire, refusing to be suppressed by the Panther cannon and machine-gun fire. RCA Sergeant Dumas of G Troop, 94 Battery, moved a 6-pounder from one position to another, firing it singlehandedly from his position along a Bretteville-l'Orgueilleuse hedgerow, reportedly hitting at least four Panthers.[58] RCA Bombardier Askin also got a damaged 6-pounder working again and reportedly hit at least three Panther tanks.[59] Vital to the efforts of the RCA 6-pounder crews were the actions of RRR rifleman Frank Wolfe, who fired 2-inch mortar magnesium illumination flares all night, blinding the Panther crews and exposing the tanks positions to the anti-tank guns.[60] While German doctrine insisted 'signal flares, parachute flares or haystacks set on fire by gunfire will assist the tanks in locating the objective', a similar effort was being directed against them by Canadian 2-inch mortar crews. Firing magnesium flares all night, they were determined to blind the tank crews.[61] Each 2-inch illumination round had a parachute attached, which lengthened the illumination effect.[62]

Wünsche, after watching his armoured group bombard Bretteville with all available weapons for at least 90 minutes, shortly before 2330 hours ordered a thrust into the village when he perceived Canadian defensive fire to be weakening. This began the second phase of the battle, lasting from 2330 to 0200 hours, which consisted of determined German armoured and infantry thrusts into and past the village of Bretteville-l'Orgueilleuse from the east and south. These assaults were successfully repulsed by the Canadian defenders, who managed to continue to inflict high armoured and infantry losses on the Germans.

On reaching the eastern entrance to the village, the *I. Zug* of *4. Kompanie*, led by Panther '418' of *Uscha*. Muhlhausen, began to push up the main street, followed by another Panther. The *II. Zug* pushed left of the village while the *III. Zug* remained in depth. As the two Panthers began their attempt to push down the main street, Meyer reorganised the *15. Kompanie* forces to continue the assault. He assigned command of the *Kompanie*, now vastly reduced from its original 100 men, to *Ustuf.* Reinhold Fuss, commander of the *15. Kompanie I. Zug*. Meyer's new order for the surviving *SS-Panzergrenadiere* was as follows: *I. Zug* was to assault right along the east–west road and *II. Zug*, under *Ustuf.* Fehling, was to assault left. Both *Zug* objectives were the church of St Germaine, located at the heart of the village. *III. Zug* under *Hscha.* Boigk was to be in depth for the assault.[63]

Shortly after Panther '418' approached the RRR battalion headquarters and the positions of A Company, it was hit at short range by a round from a Canadian PIAT (Projector, Infantry and Anti-Tank) hand-held infantry anti-tank weapon. It was then hit several more times by PIAT fire and then drove over a necklace of Type 75 anti-tank grenades. This final explosion rendered it immobile, its track broken.[64] The Panther crew was then shot as they attempted to dismount, and the burning hulk then blocked traffic. Seeing this, the following second Panther began firing on the houses nearby the first Panther, accidentally hitting it and setting it on fire.[65] Wünsche was thus forced to abandon his attempt to drive right through the village and ordered the remaining Panther tanks of *4. Kompanie* to pull back and regroup to the east of Bretteville-l'Orgueilleuse.

Shortly after or at the same time Panther '418' was destroyed, the re-formed *SS-Panzergrenadiere* of *15. Kompanie* launched their planned attack. The *I. Zug* managed to fight its way to the centre of town after an intense small arms battle, but with only 6 of the original force of 30 men. The *II. Zug* was stopped in its advance on the left flank by Bren light machine-gun fire and pinned down, having run into the positions of A Company, RRR, near the left side of the eastern village entrance.[66] During both these advances A Company, RRR, put up fierce resistance with all available weapons. Despite reaching the centre of the town and entering the church, a reduced *I. Zug* party led by *Ustuf.* Fuss could not control the area and only a few members of this group would evade eventual death or capture. On reaching the church all they could do was hold on and await another push by the Panther tanks into the village. This armoured support never arrived.

On observing the *4. Kompanie* Panthers pull back to regroup, Canadian morale and resistance surged. It is unclear why this occurred, but the Canadian soldiers sensed the Germans were withdrawing and an opportunity to aggressively open fire was present. The regrouped *4. Kompanie* responded to the increased Canadian fire by firing high explosive 7.5cm rounds and machine-gun fire into the burning village from the south and onto suspected Canadian positions, causing further fires.[67] This second sporadic bombardment by the Panthers lasted an estimated 45 minutes and must have not been too intense, as the Panthers only carried 79 rounds, half of which were high explosive *Panzergranate* shells. *1. Kompanie* under *Hstuf.* Berlin was still engaging targets on the southern portion of the village at this point, having previously advanced on the south side of the RN 13.

Following the failed drive through the village, at 0045 hours, *4. Kompanie* was then ordered to bypass the village to the south and capture the high ground north-west of Bretteville-l'Orgueilleuse along the RN 13 west of the village. After *4. Kompanie* passed its position in its drive west, *1. Kompanie* was directed to continue to try to crush resistance from the south-west and try to press into the village from this direction. *4. Kompanie* travelled at high speed in wedge formation with turrets at 45 degrees. It was led by *III. Zug*, with the *II. Zug* echeloned right and the *I. Zug* echeloned left. As the mass of tanks bypassed the village to the south, they were silhouetted by the fires raging in the village and again received heavy anti-tank gun fire. Despite receiving many hits, the *4. Kompanie* Panthers drove past the western entrance to the village and again straddled the RN 13. They then drove west onto the high ground to the north of village of Putot, west of Bretteville-l'Orgueilleuse. It is stated within the *I. Abt./SS-Pz.Rgt. 12 Kriegstagebuch* war diary that after reaching Hill 68 to the north of Putot, the Panthers 'came to a halt and occupied what they describe as a high feature' on which no enemy activity was detected.[68] *4. Kompanie* then assumed an all-around defensive position.[69] While they did drive further north-west, they must have not driven too far, for they never encountered Anglo-Canadian anti-tank positions north of Putot.

At 0045 hours, just as *4. Kompanie* was pushing south and bypassing the village to reach the Hill 68 high ground, the *1. Kompanie* was ordered to push south, then north, to fight their way into the village from the south-west. To get into position, some Panther *Züge* travelled as far south as Norrey-en-Bessin in their route and were observed by the C Company, RRR defenders, but not engaged in the dark. The *I. Zug* of *1. Kompanie*, however, pushed too close to the southern portion of Bretteville and was illuminated, receiving heavy anti-tank fire which hit all three tanks in this *Zug* simultaneously. Panther '116' burned out in this exchange, '115' was severely damaged, but '117', commanded by *Uscha.* Rust, managed to survive despite taking many hits. The still mobile but damaged '115' Panther picked up the crew of '116' and withdrew back with the third Panther to the east of Bretteville-l'Orgueilleuse, there meeting up with the *Kompanie* commander *Hstuf.* Berlin.[70]

Shortly after this, an *II. Zug* Panther of *1. Kompanie*, commanded by *Ustuf.* Teichert, managed to push right into the village from the south, but almost immediately was immobilised by PIAT and anti-tank fire. To save Teichert and his crew, a force of three *III. Zug* Panthers pushed into Bretteville from the west to pick up the dismounted crew. A second Panther, tactical number unknown, was then destroyed by anti-tank gun fire in this attempt. Fighting furiously, the Panther crews suppressed the Canadian positions enough to rescue the crew and retrieve

Teichert's Panther, which was towed away.[71] Following this a tank of *III. Zug* was badly damaged by anti-tank fire, its turret cupola being shot off.[72]

Following a period of fighting in the village which lasted until 0200 hours, the remaining Panthers of *1. Kompanie* withdrew from the village surroundings. It is unclear as to whether Wünsche or Berlin ordered the *1. Kompanie* to disengage and pull back to the south-west, or whether they pulled back due to their losses in the village itself. Wünsche mistakenly felt that the village had been sufficiently suppressed at this time to allow the remaining *SS-Panzergrenadiere* of *15. Kompanie* that were in the area to go in and 'mop up'. Regardless, the remains of *1. Kompanie*, less the *I. Zug* which had withdrawn, regrouped near the orchard of the Cardonville Usine complex shortly after 0200 hours.

Following these actions, a third phase of the battle took place between 0200 and 0630 hours. With the Panther *Kompanien* holding new positions near Cardonville Usine orchard and Hill 68, several sporadic clashes occurred. These involved renewed German piecemeal infantry assaults into Bretteville-l'Orgueilleuse and a surprise encounter for the German tank crews near Cardonville Usine. Neither of these clashes involved coordinated or even combined tank and infantry action, something noticed even by the Canadian defenders.[73] This was followed by a determined German infantry assault on the flax factory compound itself later as dawn broke, curiously without armoured support. None of these actions were decisive or resulted in favourable results for the German forces, the Canadian defenders continuing to hold on and resist all attempts to evict them from their positions. Daylight would see the Germans withdraw for good from the battlefield at approximately 0630 hours.

Beginning at roughly 0200 hours and sometime after the failed *15. Kompanie* two *Zug* assault into Bretteville-l'Orgueilleuse, another set of bizarre incidents occurred in the village. First, two light trucks full of German *SS-Panzergrenadiere* arrived in the centre of the village at roughly 0300 hours. This may have been the previously in-reserve *III. Zug* of *15. Kompanie*. The first truck was destroyed by the RRR A Company infantry with PIAT bombs. The second truck reversed out of the village at full speed.[74] Lastly, at roughly 0315 hours, a German anti-aircraft 20mm 38(t) Flakpanzer moving through the village was destroyed in front of the burning hulk of Panther '418', also by PIAT bombs fired from the second storey of a building. These reckless attempts speak to a possible mistaken German belief that only small pockets of Canadian resistance were remaining in the village.

As previously noted, at approximately 0100 hours, six *1. Kompanie* Panther tanks, their number minus those withdrawn or destroyed earlier, assembled in an all-around defence near the orchard of Cardonville Usine, their engines idling. Thinking the flax factory compound free of Canadian troops, they were totally unaware of D Company RRR, led by Captain Brown, who was charged with defending it. The RRR riflemen maintained total silence to not alert the German tank crews. The gunners present within the attached RRR anti-tank platoon 6-pounder section also kept silent, uneasy at the prospect of alerting the Panthers and starting a firefight that they potentially could not win.

The uneasy co-existence of the infantry and Panthers was broken shortly after 0230 hours when a RRR D Company rifleman shot down members of a dismounted Panther crew.[75] The Panthers then drove off and poured concentrated fire into the factory buildings, supressing the RRR riflemen and anti-tank gunners. At this point, had any German *SS-Panzergrenadiere* forces arrived, it is highly likely Cardonville Usine would have fallen. None arrived as the Panthers raged, forcing Captain Brown and Company Sergeant Major (CSM) Jackson to hunker down in the main flax factory building. Without supporting infantry, the tanks could not evict D Company, even though they did incur significant casualties on the Canadians. By staying calm and remaining in their positions, D Company withstood a deluge of high-explosive and machine-gun fire.

By 0400 hours an effective stalemate had occurred in Bretteville-l'Orgueilleuse, Cardonville Usine and the general vicinity. Any further German infantry assault into the village of Bretteville-l'Orgueilleuse was impossible, and the RRR and RCA soldiers inside the village could not destroy the Panthers due to the darkness and distance they were away from Canadian positions. Established German armoured doctrine was very clear in stating: 'The tanks have to function as the fire bases while the infantry takes the vanguard role in the assault'.[76] Wünsche led the Panther group in a manner entirely opposite to this maxim, attempting to replace the missing infantry with tanks to try to force the assault to succeed. Also, neither German heavy artillery nor supporting mortar fire was present, and the Panthers were forced to attempt to fulfil this role as well. Supporting the RRR throughout the battle in Bretteville-l'Orgueilleuse were the RCA field artillery regiments of the 3rd Canadian Infantry Division. These forces consisting of the 12th and 13th Field Regiments, RCA, were based near the village Bray, two kilometres to the north. A large portion of their support in the six hours of battle so far had been given to RRR A and B Companies in Bretteville-l'Orgueilleuse. Despite all of Matheson's efforts, he was nearly totally out of contact with RRR D and C Companies.[77] The field telephone lines had been cut by Panther tank tracks.

Quoting Canadian military historian Mark Zuehlke: 'Having committed too few infantrymen, Meyer was unable to support the Panthers properly'.[78] Seeing the ineffectiveness of the Panthers, at 0350 hours Wünsche, possibly directed by Meyer, attempted one last time to turn the tide of events by driving to the vicinity of Norrey-en-Bessin to attempt to contact *3. Kompanie* of *I. Btl./SS-Pz.Gren. Rgt. 26*, in the hope of rallying these infantry forces for a continued assault. No *SS-Panzergrenadiere* could be found.[79] As his Befehlspanther was receiving heavy Canadian fire, he quickly drove back to the area east of Bretteville-l'Orgueilleuse. Despite making an utmost effort for the better part of six hours, Meyer and Wünsche then met at 0430 hours and made the call to pull all forces back to the vicinity of the twin villages of La Villeneuve and Le Bourg, their start points.

On hearing the radio command to withdraw, both Pfeiffer and Berlin moved their *Kompanien* back.[80] While driving back from Hill 68, the *4. Kompanie* again received heavy anti-tank fire near the edge of Bretteville-l'Orgueilleuse. Panther '425' was penetrated by 6-pounder anti-tank fire and burned out, wounding its commander, *Uscha.* Hiller. To add insult to injury, Wünsche on his return to La Villeneuve was hit by fragments from a Canadian anti-tank round as he dismounted from his command Panther.[81] The intelligence log of the 13th Field Regiment, RCA, mentions engaging tanks over open sights at 0545 hours with 105mm M67 anti-tank rounds, but it is unclear if this fire came from an M7 105mm Priest or a 6-pounder anti-tank gun. German accounts of the action do not specify the sources of the anti-tank fire.[82] On arrival in La Villeneuve, the weakened Panther *Kompanien* reorganised themselves and took up securing tasks facing west.

In an inexplicable conclusion to the third and final phase of the battle, sometime after the withdrawal of Meyer and Wünsche, the *2. Kompanie* of *I. Btl./SS-Pz. Gren.Rgt. 26* finally made an attempt to attack Cardonville Usine, illustrating the complete lack of coordination with Meyer or the Panthers.[83] Captain Brown, the officer commanding (OC) of D Company of the RRR, was put under extreme pressure by this assault that was by Canadian accounts very close to success when barely beaten back by fire from all available machine guns and very timely RCA artillery support.[84] To decisively beat back the attack, Lieutenant-Colonel Matheson, now finally in touch with Brown via radio, called in 105mm artillery fire from the 13th Field Regiment, RCA. This fire landed virtually on top of Canadian positions but effectively drove the attackers back into their start lines.[85] Why the Germans waited until first light and the Panthers' withdrawal before making their move is beyond comprehension. It illustrates a complete lack of any planning between Meyer, Wünsche, Mohnke and *I. Btl./SS-Pz.Gren.Rgt. 26* of *Stubaf.* Krause. RRR D Company, now reduced to roughly 50 men due to extensive casualties during the earlier Panther bombardment and the morning battle, had prevailed again.[86]

Final German casualties of the Meyer–Wünsche armoured force were 91 total casualties and 31 dead, the majority being in the *15. Aufklärung Kompanie* of *SS-Pz. Gren.Rgt. 25.* The *I. Abt./SS-Pz.Rgt. 12* lost five Panther tanks as total write-offs: '427', '425', '418', '116' and an unknown fifth vehicle. Panther Tanks '115', '128' and others were badly damaged, some having to be towed away from the battlefield.[87] One 2cm 38(t) Flakpanzer built on the tracked Czech 38(t) chassis was also destroyed, as well as at least one motorcycle combination and one truck. In the hapless *I. Btl./ SS-Pz.Gren.Rgt. 26*, total casualties were 61, with 12 *SS-Panzergrenadiere* being killed.

Canadian losses in the 3rd Anti-Tank Regiment, RCA's 94 (Composite) Battery, included 17 missing, 5 killed and 5 wounded, almost all from K Troop, which had been overrun along with the RRR carrier platoon. At least eight Universal Carriers were destroyed, and one was captured by the Germans. Accounts differ as to how many anti-tank guns were lost, but a reasonable estimate would be a half-dozen. A

Company of the Cameron Highlanders of Ottawa suffered 11 killed and 10 wounded or missing. The 1st Battalion, the Regina Rifle Regiment, suffered 42 killed in the period 8–9 June and suffered an unknown number of wounded.[88] French military historian Georges Bernage lists its total Canadian casualties as approximately 150 men for the 8/9 June night-time battle. Among these are what appear to be several soldiers shot after capture.[89] In addition, an unknown number of Canadian jeeps and trucks were destroyed.

Throughout the time the RRR held out at Cardonville Usine, Norrey-en-Bessin and Bretteville-l'Orgueilleuse, no relief force of Allied armour arrived to support the unit in the thick of its six-hour battle against vastly superior armoured forces. No information has been found to establish if this option was ever considered by the 7th Canadian Infantry Brigade headquarters staff. The Anglo-Canadian armoured practice of 'harbouring' in the hours of darkness forced the RCA units, Cameron machine-gun crews and infantry forces of the RRR to fight it out the best they could without tank support. In response to RRR headquarters' inquiries regarding armour reinforcement, the terse response from 7th Canadian Infantry Brigade headquarters was that 'tank support would arrive at dawn'.[90] To the average solider during a firefight with multiple Panther tanks, and considering that said firefight lasted six hours, these words were cold comfort. That the brigade headquarters, with multiple Panthers nearby within 100 meters, did not force the issue speaks to a steadfast reluctance to rapidly commit Canadian armoured reserves. The concept of night employment of armour appears to have been very much anathema to senior Canadian commanders but, given the circumstances, its employment could hardly have made matters worse for the RRR defenders.[91]

In conclusion, this chapter has sought to provide an improved historical understanding of the early German armoured assaults on the Normandy bridgehead, and to illustrate why these ad hoc assaults often met with failure. The defeat of the German armoured battlegroup occurred largely due to the failure to properly exercise established armoured doctrine and allocate correct infantry and artillery resources to the operation. Though stronger German infantry forces were present to the south near Norrey-en-Bessin and Cardonville Usine, little if any coordination was made with them. Everything depended on the assault of weak *15. Kompanie* to succeed. This failure in planning was compounded by a complete lack of heavy artillery fire support, despite German armoured doctrine stating, 'In spite of all their firepower, tanks are dependent on the support of extensive indirect fire'. The lack of a decisive impact made by the large group of Panthers illustrates the limitations of direct fire support.[92] The Canadian commander of the 7th Canadian Infantry Brigade, Brigadier Foster, remarked that no attempt was made to exploit the flanks of the RRR battlegroup.[93] Rather than avoid the strongpoint of Bretteville-l'Orgueilleuse altogether, a wiser option would have been to bypass it. Meyer's attempt to use shock and armoured firepower was met by an equally determined foe who exploited the

German weaknesses present to the maximum. To quote Hubert Meyer, divisional historian of the *Hitlerjugend*:

> The daring surprise attack by the small Meyer/Wünsche *Kampfgruppe* had scored a significant initial success. The enemy had been manoeuvred into a very difficult situation. However, because of the lack of German infantry, full advantage could not be taken of the situation. The tactic of surprise, using mobile, fast infantry and panzers even in small, numerically inferior *Kampfgruppen*, had often been practised and proven in Russia. This tactic, however, had not resulted in the expected success against a courageous and determined enemy, who was ready for defence and well-equipped.[94]

CHAPTER 11

The first battle of Caen: The 9 June 1944 attack on Norrey-en-Bessin

Taking up events on the western flank of the *SS-Pz.Gren.Rgt. 26* frontages by mid-morning on 9 June, the line of German *SS-Panzergrenadiere Kompanien* positions on or near the Caen–Bayeux railway line had not changed since the *II. Btl./SS-Pz. Gren.Rgt. 26* of *Stubaf.* Seibken had been driven out of Putot and *I. Btl./SS-Pz.Gren. Rgt. 26* of *Stubaf.* Krause had been halted multiple times near Norrey-en-Bessin. The positions of *III. Btl.(Gepanzert)/SS-Pz.Gren.Rgt. 26* of *Stubaf.* Olboeter and the *SS-Pz.Aüfkl.Abt. 12* of *Stubaf.* Bremer were slightly more fluid, the area to the west near Brouay and south-west near Cristot still in the process of being occupied by British and German forces that were pushing into the area, the *Waffen-SS* watching anxiously for powerful elements of the *Panzer-Lehr* to establish a strong front to the west, reducing the danger to their flank.

In the village of Cheux, seven kilometres to the south of the front lines, daybreak had found a tense atmosphere in the regimental *Gefechtsstand* of SS-Pz.Gren.Rgt. 26. The continuous operational failings of the first *Bataillon* of the regiment, *I. Btl./SS-Pz.Gren.Rgt. 26*, had made the situation very frustrating for regimental *Kommandeur, Ostubaf.* Mohnke. This *Bataillon* had performed very poorly in the period 8–9 June 1944 despite strong armoured support, this largely due to a lack of coordination, strong Canadian infantry defences and powerful Anglo-Canadian field artillery support. The 7th Canadian Infantry Brigade forces arrayed against it had inflicted heavy casualties on two of its four *Kompanien*.

Amongst the losses was the *Kompanie-Chef* of *2. Kompanie, Leutnant* Robert Sauer, a *Heer* transfer posted to the *Hitlerjugend* and killed in the early 9 June fighting. The remains of the *Kompanie*, now led by *Ustuf.* Kühl, was still dug in around the farm buildings of Cardonville, the neighbouring Cardonville Usine flax factory buildings being the stronghold of D Company of the RRR. *3. Kp./SS-Pz.Gren.Rgt. 26*, now led by *Hscha.* Kaiser, was still in its position south of Norrey-en-Bessin in the wooded area, opposite C Company of the RRR.[1]

1. Kp./SS-Pz.Gren.Rgt. 26 had installed itself in the twin villages of Le Hamel–Rots on the Mue and was the only *Kompanie* of *I. Btl./SS-Pz.Gren.Rgt. 26* to succeed in its mission during 8–9 June. It had pushed through the largely undefended area east of the RRR positions to clear Le Bourg and La Villeneuve, and then pushed north into the twin villages of Le Hamel and Rots. Now this *Kompanie* was somewhat isolated, and the situation had forced the divisional *Gefechtsstand* of the *Hitlerjugend* to detach the divisional *Begleitkompanie* headquarters' escort company to deploy north-east of the *3. Kompanie* positions near Norrey-en-Bessin, effectively making Le Bourg, La Villeneuve and its nearby château a stronghold in order to maintain a link with the forces in Rots and Le Hamel. The entire regiment was overextended, attempting to hold the line like a *Heer Infanterie-Division* with fewer forces and little reserves. It was attempting to still carry out offensive operations on a reduced scale, but was forced to take away units that were holding the front lines or reserves to do this. The Anglo-Canadian forces opposing them were not bothered by this situation and had reserves in place with which to carry out attacks and counterattacks, while the units holding the front simply kept on holding their fighting positions and prepared to fight off attacks. The Anglo-Canadian forces selected for operations in the period 7–11 June could carry out attacks was because they were, to a certain extent, 'fresh'. This was a condition not present in the German units, who after a period of time on the front lines and after experiencing incessant Allied fighter-bomber attacks and artillery strikes, were exhausted.

The remainder of the battered *4. Kp./SS-Pz.Rgt. 12* with its Panther tanks under *Hstuf.* Pfeiffer had been deployed to help defend the possession of the Le Hamel–Rots 'salient'. Parts of the *Kompanie* with some tanks were in Rots and others were in Le Bourg–La Villeneuve in order to counter any Anglo-Canadian advances from Bretteville to the west or Bray to the north-west, While some other Panther tank *Kompanien* had been very active around Bretteville-l'Orgueilleuse and Norrey-en-Bessin and would continue to be during the course of the day, these forces would remain under the command of *Ostubaf.* Wünsche, not *Ostubaf.* Mohnke. It is unclear if there was even the most basic attempt at coordination or communication with the forces of *SS-Pz.Gren.Rgt. 26*, whose forces would have to be involved for any real success to occur. *Ostubaf.* Mohnke did not have even one Panzer *Kompanie* attached to his regiment, and the forces operating out of Le Bourg–La Villeneuve in the period 8–9 June, were strictly under the control of Wünsche and Meyer.

In the early morning of 9 June, the Panther tank equipped *3. Kp./SS-Pz.Rgt. 12* was relieved in its positions near Authie by the Panzer IV tanks of *7. Kp./SS-Pz.Rgt. 12*. As the Panthers drove off to the south-west in the direction of La Villeneuve and Le Bourg, they observed a Panzer IV take a direct hit by RCA artillery fire, the tank bursting into flames. This very well could have been the event in which *Ustuf.* Hartfied Zick, a *Zug* leader, was reported killed on 9 June.[2]

This Panther *Kompanie*, being near full strength, was earmarked for a new local attack for that afternoon, yet another attempt to secure the start line for further larger operations to turn the eastern flank of the 7th Canadian Infantry Brigade. Moving south of Authie, the tanks travelled in broad daylight with wide-spaced intervals, crossing the bridge on the Mue river and entering Le Bourg and later La Villeneuve at roughly 1000 or 1100 hours. Here it would have encountered the harried and exhausted figure of *Ostubaf.* Wünsche, would have been conferring with *Stubaf.* Jürgensen, the *Kommandeur* of *I. Abt./SS-Pz.Rgt. 12*, on the next planned move. *Staf.* Meyer would arrive later to help oversee this upcoming operation.

The morning of 9 June also saw an abortive attempt by *II. Btl./SS-Pz.Rgt. 26* and possibly parts of *III. Btl.(Gepanzert)/SS-Pz.Gren.Rgt. 26* to drive back the 1st Battalion, the Canadian Scottish Regiment (Can Scots) from Putot. A and D Companies of Can Scots, dug in forward near the railway line, the scene of the disaster for the Royal Winnipeg Rifles, began to receive what they reported as heavy tank fire from dug in or camouflaged tanks south of the railway line. Supported by the 6-pounder anti-tank guns of the Can Scot Support Company and medium machine guns of the Cameron Highlanders of Ottawa, the companies remained in their positions as further fire support was provided by the RCA FOO teams located with the battalion. In response to the German fire and observed movement by the *SS-Panzergrenadiere* near the railway line, intensive RCA field artillery fire was brought down on *II. Btl./SS-Pz.Gren.Rgt. 26*, forcing its troops away from the area of shellfire.

After this brief action, the remainder of the day was used by the *Kompanien* of *II. Btl./SS-Pz.Gren.Rgt. 26* to reorganise itself under the direction of *Stubaf.* Seibken, *Kommandeur* of *II. Btl./SS-Pz.Gren.Rgt. 26*. During this time heavy harassing shellfire continued to fall, and the *Kompanie-Chef* of 5. *Kompanie*, *Ostuf.* Goddard, was killed when a shell hit his *Kompanie Gefechtsstand*. His place was taken by *Ustuf.* Rinne, formerly of *I. Zug*. A lot of time also had to be taken to re-organise 7. *Kompanie*, its *SS-Panzergrenadiere* being forced to disperse during the heavy RCA shellfire of 8 June during the evening counterattack of the Can Scots. During 9 June many small, scattered groups rejoined the *Kompanie*, having taken refuge with other units during the fighting.[3] The Can Scots in the 8–9 June period took a total of 125 casualties, 45 of these being killed and another 80 wounded in the counterattack and later German attempts to destroy their positions.

The main event of the day to the east of Putot would be one of the last massed *Abteilung*-level attacks by *SS-Pz.Rgt. 12* in Normandy, the ones in the future being largely defensive counterattacks. The well-known attack of 3. *Kp./SS-Pz.Rgt. 12* against Norrey-en-Bessin, supported by 1. and 4. *Kompanien* of *I. Abt./SS-Pz.Rgt. 12*, is one of the most prominent historical events within the historiography of the 3rd Canadian Infantry Division during its battles of June 1944.

Who exactly ordered or organised the attack is difficult to ascertain, but it appears the driving force was the *Kommandeur* of *SS-Pz.Rgt. 12, Ostubaf.* Wünsche. Given that the *Hitlerjugend* had no prospect of resupply of replacement tanks for the immediate future, the attack was a shockingly rash waste of resources that were poorly employed in a clumsy attack with little regard for its flanks against a prepared anti-tank defence.

Prior to the arrival of the *3. Kompanie* tanks in Le Bourg and La Villeneuve, the *1. Kompanie* Panther tanks of *Hstuf.* Berlin had moved out first, moving south of La Villeneuve by crossing under its nearby railway bridge in order to be in position to act as a flanking force for *3. Kompanie*, and to be ready to attack southern Norrey and a nearby château's grounds at the same time.

The *3. Kp./SS-Pz.Rgt. 12* was in position by mid-morning near the La Villeneuve advanced tactical *Gefechtsstand* of *Stubaf.* Jürgensen. Moving back and forth to avoid Canadian RCA field artillery harassing fire, Panther '318' broke down with damage to its final drives, the sole mechanical failure of the day. The movement of the Panthers was under fire right from the start near La Villeneuve, which was described in German accounts as being naval gunfire from warships off the invasion beaches. Canadian military historian Marc Milner suggests it's possible this fire came from the British 79th Medium Regiment, RA.

What exactly the *3. Kompanie* hoped to achieve with exposing their flank to the treeline near the rail line south of Bretteville to attack Norrey-en-Bessin from the east is difficult to understand, as Wünsche would have understood the area would very likely be bristling with anti-tank guns following the attack of the Meyer–Wünsche force the previous night. *Heer Hptm.* Lüdemann, acting *3. Kompanie Kommandeur*, would in effect completely ignore this threat in his tactical planning, presenting the thin side hull and turret armour of the Panthers to the Caen–Bayeux RN 13 highway and treelines where Allied Sherman tanks, M-10 tank destroyers or 6- or 17-pounder anti-tank guns were possibly sited.

Amazingly, no recce was completed, despite the assets of the *SS-Pz.Aüfkl.Abt. 12* being very close by, and the dismounted remnants of *15. Kp.(Aufklärung)/SS-Pz. Gren.Rgt. 25* being part of the proposed assault force and still having potential access to their motorcycles and VW Schwimmenwagen if need be. The officers and NCOs of *3. Kp./SS-Pz.Rgt. 12* were moving forward blindly, as they did not have the experience in the area which other parts of the *Hitlerjugend* who had fought there recently had. It could be best described as a blind charge forward against Norrey-en-Bessin and the C Company, RRR positions, while in plain view of other Canadian defences that included anti-tank guns.

The Canadian tank reinforcements requested by Brigadier Foster for his 7th Canadian Infantry Brigade forces had arrived, as promised, at dawn. These were replacement tanks destined for the Fort Garry Horse (FGH) and the 1st Hussars, who, following the fighting 8–9 June were directed with their crews to

Bretteville-l'Orgueilleuse and positions close to the railway line. There was a total of twelve tanks, two troops of three from each regiment. While the 1st Hussar replacement tanks were crewed from the personnel of C Squadron of the 1st Hussars, it is unclear which squadron from the FGH had supplied the crews for their replacement tanks. The crews could have come from all three squadrons.

Further back in the area south of Gold and Juno Beaches was the newly arrived independent British 4th Armoured Brigade, located in Colomby-sur-Thaon as a counterattack force should the German Panzers break the Canadian line along the Mue. This was a danger, as only very weak forces were located there, the area of the stream being between the 7th and 9th Canadian Infantry Brigade fortresses. In Bray, north-west of Rots, the RCA 12th Field Group gun position of 'Nora' was under pressure due to German harassing fire in the way of mortar and artillery fire hitting the battery positions of the 12th and 13th Field Regiments, RCA.

Also in and around Bray were several batteries from the 2nd Royal Marine Armoured Support Regiment, these being the S, T, X and Z Batteries equipped with 95mm-gunned Centaur tank fire support vehicles. These had been deployed in the area to defend it against infantry or armoured attack if needed.[4]

A sizeable number of German Panther tanks would see action on 9 June 1944. During the attack on Norrey-en-Bessin, the *3. Kompanie* deployed a total of twelve Panthers in three *Züge*. This is probably very close to the number of operational *3. Kompanie* Panthers that left Le Neubourg on 6 June 1944.[5] A full company war establishment would have been seventeen Panthers, with five in each *Zug* and a Panther each for the *Kompanie-Chef* and *Kompanie-Trupp* leader. On 1 June 1944, the *Hitlerjugend* strength return for that date reported that the *3.* and *4. Kompanien* had 17 Panther tanks each and the *2. Kompanie* only had 10.[6] Ten more Panthers had been delivered by 6 June, strengthening the *2. Kompanie* and finally getting the *1. Kompanie* some tanks of its own, it having been trained on others up to this point.

It is accurate to assess the Panther tanks involved in the operations on 8–9 June 1944 as being mechanically reliable in combat, despite coming off a recent 140km road march in difficult circumstances. In reviewing accounts of this action, there is only one mention of a Panther breaking down or being abandoned in combat due to a mechanical fault, this being Panther '318' of *3. Kompanie*, which fell out due to final drive issues just before the attack was to get underway.[7] This would have given the *Kompanie* a starting strength of 13 tanks. It is unclear where the other tanks were, and some may have been transferred to other *Kompanien*.

At 1200 hours the attack of *I. Abt./SS-Pz.Rgt. 12*, with *3. Kompanie* leading the way, began, with the *SS-Panzergrenadiere* of *15. Kp./SS-Pz.Gren.Rgt. 25*, who were still in the area, again following the Panthers on foot as they drove off towards Norrey. Supporting the attack, and for the most part excluded from many historical accounts for the fighting, were both *1.* and *4. Kp./SS-Pz.Rgt. 12* with all available Panther tanks providing fire support to suppress Canadian forces in Norrey-en-Bessin, the railway station, surrounding farms and providing flank support for the main thrust by the up-to-strength *3. Kompanie*. Artillery support was to be provided by *5.* and *6. Batterien* of *II. Abt./SS-Pz.Art.Rgt. 12*. It is unclear how effective this fire on RRR positions was.[8] However, the counter-battery artillery fire each side subjected the other to was intense. The *II. Abt./SS-Pz.Art.Rgt. 12 Kriegstagebuch* entry for 9 June mentions that the *Batterie Kommandeur, Ustuf.* Kilching, was wounded due to shellfire, his place taken by *Ustuf.* Zärtner.[9]

The actual fighting of the German forces as summarised in the unit war diaries is very different in some areas than what is presented in Canadian secondary sources and by Canadian military historians. The main objective of the attack, despite very few available records on who planned or ordered it, was the destruction of Canadian forces in Norrey-en-Bessin in the same manner that had been attempted in Bretteville-l'Orgueilleuse, albeit in broad daylight rather than during a pitch-black night. *1. Kompanie*, on the left flank, would support the advance of the *3. Kompanie* from a hull-down position east of Norrey-en-Bessin. Its primary task was to bombard the church tower in Bretteville-l'Orgueilleuse with all gun tubes, the tower being, in German eyes, the obvious location for an RCA FOO team.

The *4. Kompanie* of *Hstuf.* Pfeiffer would provide flank security for the *3. Kompanie* advance by guarding the entry to La Villeneuve and engaging Canadian positions if possible.[10] Its strength had been reduced from the number that had driven into and around Bretteville-l'Orgueilleuse on the night of 8/9 June, and the operational Panthers were deployed on the wood-line near the Château Rots and the RN 13. Their guns were oriented towards Bretteville-l'Orgueilleuse and Bray, these being Canadian strongholds on the left flank of the 7th Canadian Infantry Brigade.

While the *1.* and *4. Kompanien* had taken losses during the fighting in Bretteville-l'Orgueilleuse and near Norrey-en-Bessin on the night of 8/9 June, they were back fighting by noon the following day, their previous battle ending by roughly 0800 hours on the morning of 9 June. The crews of both these *Kompanien* must have been exhausted, and perhaps this is the reason for their supporting the main attack launched by *3. Kompanie*. They were also fighting on the same exact battlefield they had just left, and despite its exhaustion and potential low ammunition and fuel supplies, it may have been beneficial for the stronger *4. Kompanie* to make the main foray against Norrey-en-Bessin near noon on 9 June.

What of the infantry in the area? Was the *15.(Aufklärung) Kompanie* the only infantry support provided for the attack to clear the village? The actions of *I. Btl./SS-Pz.Gren.Rgt. 26*, its battalion *Kommandeur* and staff are largely unknown for this day. Was it intended to closely attack with the Panthers? If it was, it certainly did not happen to any great degree. It is possible the *SS-Panzergrenadiere* were readied to advance, but seeing the outcome of the *3. Kp./SS-Pz.Rgt. 12* attack, which will be discussed shortly, they probably returned to their positions.

Just prior to the advance of the *3. Kompanie*, the tanks of *1. Kompanie* under *Hstuf.* Berlin did fire a barrage of high-explosive rounds at the church steeple from their hull-down positions east of Norrey-en-Bessin and south of the railway line, destroying it. It was felt that this position was surely inhabited by an aforementioned RCA FOO team, something the author has not been conclusively able to determine. The *3. Kompanie* tanks also took part in this direct fire effort, resulting in the complete destruction of the steeple with high-explosive rounds. The *1. Kompanie* tanks were also under harassing RCA artillery fire that morning, a fact made apparent by the death of a crewmember from Panther '126', who was killed while outside the tank in La Villeneuve.[11]

Moving in column until they cleared the railway underpass, *3. Kp./SS-Pz.Rgt. 12* advanced, 12 Panthers strong, assuming attack formation as they lined up their three *Züge* for their assault on Norrey-en-Bessin. On the left flank facing west, and furthest south, was *I. Zug* of *Ustuf.* Bogensberger; in the centre was *II. Zug* of *Ustuf.* Alban; and on the right flank facing west and closest to the railway line on his right was the *III. Zug* of *Ustuf.* Stagge. *Hptm.* Lüddemann was somewhere in the centre with a *Kompanie-Trupp* Panther, either '304' or '305'.[12]

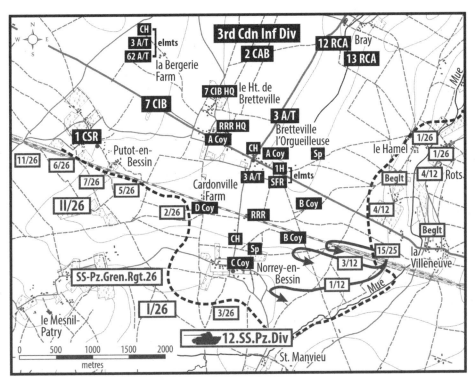

Attack of *I. Abt./SS-Pz.Rgt. 12* on Norrey-en-Bessin, 9 June 1944. (Map by Mike Bechthold)

Losses to the advancing *3. Kompanie* were very heavy when contact was made with Canadian forces, these primarily being RRR and 3rd Anti-Tank Regiment 6-pounder anti-tank guns and the 12 tanks of the FGH and 1st Hussars, ready in ambush positions near Bretteville. According to German accounts of the action, the location of and what was present in the Canadian firing positions were largely unknown and is referred to as 'anti-tank gun fire'. Within five minutes the tank and 6-pounder anti-tank gun fire from the camouflaged positions in the tree lines just south-east of Bretteville-l'Orgueilleuse and north-west of the railway line had destroyed six Panthers, these being Panthers '325', '328', '335', '336', '337' and '338'. Tanks '327' and '329' of the *II. Zug*, trailing the other two *Züge*, were badly damaged but made it back to the railway cutting and escaped under their own power.[13] These tanks were then either towed or driven to the *3. Kompanie I-Trupp* (repair) location where they were repaired over the next few days. French military historian Stephan Cazenave mentions at least two or three tanks were sent to the rear for repairs following the action.[14]

The withdrawal after the losses that occurred over a very short period to *3. Kompanie* saw the remaining tanks firing blindly and backing away at the best speed they could manage to get out of the kill zone of the Canadian reinforcement tanks and the anti-tank guns. They would reverse back to the railway underpass, firing as they went. Heavy RCA field artillery fire was recorded as hitting the German positions and their axis of advance from the moment they emerged from the railway underpass.[15]

The burning hulks of the *3. Kompanie* tanks, often with dead crew members inside or badly wounded lying on the ground just beside them, would burn and smoulder for the rest of the day. The crews of the destroyed Panther tanks that managed to bail out were subjected to intense infantry fire, and many of the wounded had to be carried or crawl along a sunken road next to the railway line in order to get back to the shelter of the railway underpass. There was a Bren gun position manned by members of either C or B Company of the RRR in a lineman's cottage along the rail line, and these soldiers allowed the mass of tanks to pass without firing, obviously to avoid being killed by Panther tank fire. Once all the Panther tanks had left the vicinity, the RRR section in the lineman's cottage opened up with rifle and Bren gun fire, inflicting casualties on German motorcyclists and tank crew attempting to withdraw on foot.

Uscha. Hermani, one of the *Panzerkommandanten* that had bailed out, threw two or three hand grenades into the cottage, killing or wounding the Canadian Bren gun team. This allowed the German tank crew survivors to continue to walk or be carried along the rail line back to the underpass.

After the six Panthers were destroyed, German motorcycles, carrying out various tasks from passing messages to who was left in command of the surviving tanks to trying to rescue the worst of the wounded, raced onto the battlefield east of

Norrey-en-Bessin and Bretteville-l'Orgueilleuse near the railway line, some using the sunken road that ran parallel to the scene of the Panther ambush. One of the motorcycle trips involved the *3. Kompanie* medic in a first-hand account, to be related shortly, and another involved a motorcycle messenger passing a message to the command Panther, presumably to *Hptm.* Lüdemann, bizarrely after the action had taken place and the Panthers were in the middle of withdrawing back to their starting point under fire. There is also a mention within Canadian accounts of the battle of a prisoner execution during the German withdrawal, with one Canadian soldier of B Company, RRR, being shot to death and another wounded by a German officer near the railway line after being discovered and captured near their observation post.[16]

All of the German motorcycle forays into the battlefield took place under extremely heavy infantry small arms, mortar and field artillery fire, the Canadian RCA FOO teams with the RRR now benefitting from the light of day. The wounded tank crewmen, of which there were a significant number, were trying to keep pace with the withdrawing tanks and using the cover of the raised rail line for shelter as they evaded small arms fire. The more badly wounded were picked up by the German motorcyclists with their sidecars and brought back to the Le Bourg and La Villeneuve areas to be transported further back to medical clearing stations. The rest of the crewmen walked, shuffled or ran back to the railway underpass, each step being further away from the RRR small arms fire.

In this account, reprinted from the Hubert Meyer divisional history, the then-*Uscha.* Alois Morawetz, in a post-war narrative, provides the most detailed first-hand account of the attack on 9 June 1944. In this account, a *Hitlerjugend* medic from *3. Kp./SS-Pz.Rgt. 12* who went forward to save or assist the wounded from the *Kompanie* was killed as he went to transport wounded back to the attack's starting point. It is certain now from this account that he was most likely killed by the RRR soldiers within the railroad lineman's cottage, before *Uscha.* Hermani killed or wounded them with hand grenades. This account shows the horror and reality of Second World War infantry and armoured combat. The author has chosen to reprint this account from Meyer's history due to this being the best recorded account of the attack and its aftermath:

> We crossed the rail line Caen–Bayeux and through an underpass, turned right and took up positions on a back slope. The 12 Panthers were lined up next to each other at a right angle to the rail line. My vehicle sat on the right flank, close to the rail embankment. *I. Zug* under *Untersturmführer* Bogensberger was on the left. *II. Zug* under *Untersturmführer* Alban was in the centre. *III. Zug*, led by *Untersturmführer* Stagge, was deployed on the right. *Hauptmann* Lüddemann, sat somewhere in the middle. The time was approximately 12:30 hours. In front of us it was relatively quiet. There were almost no fighter-bombers in the air, as was usual for noontime. A short time later we set out through the slowly rising terrain. After approximately 500 metres we reached completely open and level terrain, meadows and fields. Half left ahead of us lay Norrey-en-Bessin. I was driving approximately 20–50 meters to the left of the rail line. It

ran through a gully, beginning at a lineman's cottage. On the left edge of the gully was probably a hedge, which provide us with some cover against being spotted. The whole *Kompanie* drove as a body, at high speed and without any stops, in a broad front. When the left flank was just outside the village, the order came in 'Wartesaal' (waiting room) swing to the left! (Wartesaal was the code name for our *Kompanie*). I ordered my driver to go at full speed and pull slightly to the left. Until then we had not experienced any resistance. Approximately 100 metres ahead was a railroad station where some movement could be spotted. I was driving approximately 30 metres ahead of the *Kompanien* in a slow left turn, in order not to fall behind. At that moment, after a muffled bank and a swaying as if the track had been ripped off, the vehicle came to a stop.

It was quiet inside the vehicle. I thought we had driven over a mine. When I looked to the left to check the situation, I happened to see the turret torn off the Panzer driving on my left flank. The same moment, after another minor explosion, my vehicle began to burn. The machine gun ammunition caught on fire and there was a crackling noise like dry wood burning. Since we were to push into the town, I had closed the turret hatch moments before. I tried, without success, to open the turret hatch. I could only lift it with the spindle but could not swing it out. Paul Veith, the gunner sitting in front of me, had apparently been seriously injured by fragments from the hit. Veith did not move. I tried for a long time with all my energy to swing out the hatch. I was only successful when I tried different height settings on the lift crank. It had probably been damaged by the hit. I jumped out, fell on the rear, and was unconscious for short time. Then I saw flames coming out the open hatch as if from a blowtorch. I got up and tried to jump off. However, I could not keep my balance and landed, head-first, on the ground. I do not know how long I lay there. Then I got to my feet and saw to my left, along the same line as my vehicle, other burning Panzers. Among them was Stagge's. Approximately 200 to 400 metres behind the Panzer, I spotted the sidecar motorcycle of our medic, *Unterscharführer* Gose. I walked towards it. Members of the crews from the other knocked-out Panzers also arrived there. They were burned, without exception, in their faces and hands. In the meantime, we had noticed that the whole area was under infantry fire, the medic's driver [*Unterscharführer* Hartling] was trying to start the motor again. It had stalled after taking a hit to left cylinder head. After a few tries, the motor started again. Gose glanced at the men standing about, and, since I was the apparently worst burnt, he put me in the sidecar. We turned around and drive back. After a few meters, Gose, who sat in the rear seat, dropped backwards off the moving motorcycle. I drew the driver's attention to this since he had not noticed it. We drove on another 200 meters or so back to the lineman's cottage, there we stopped. I kept the motor running, using both my hands on the twist grip, while the driver made his way forward to the medic. After approximately ten minutes the driver came back and told me that Gose did not have a chance. He had been critically wounded in the stomach. The remaining five Panzers were now withdrawing, firing rapidly. When I left with the motorcycle drive from the lineman's cottage in the direction of La Villeneuve, the Panzers were approximately at the same line as the cottage. Seven of the twelve [actually six] attacking Panzers were left at the front. From what I can remember, all seven were on fire. We made it back to La Villeneuve. I think we met some men of the *Kompanie* baggage train near a restaurant. The motorcycle driver left me there and returned to the front to pick up more wounded. As I learned in the late afternoon at the main dressing station, 15 of the 35 crew members from the knocked-out Panzers had been killed. The rest, with few exceptions, were wounded, almost all with burn wounds.[17]

While the Panthers that took part in the attack did not fail mechanically and were very much ready for action, the 9 June attack on Norrey-en-Bessin was a spectacular tactical reverse due to the action of the RRR anti-tank guns and the FGH and 1st Hussar tanks with accurate defensive fire that easily penetrated their weak side turret and hull armour. As reflected in the table below, a total of six, not seven, Panthers were lost near Norrey-en-Bessin over the course of the day as complete write-offs, and a further three were badly damaged.

3. *Kompanie* Panther tanks destroyed on 9 June 1944[18]

3. *Kompanie* Panthers	*Panzerkommandeure*
325	*Ustuf.* Alban
328	*Uscha.* Krahl
335	*Ustuf.* Stagge
336	*Uscha.* Brandt
337	*Uscha.* Morawetz
338	*Uscha.* Hermani

Many accounts state that the *15. Kp.(Aufklärung)/SS-Pz.Gren.Rgt. 25* was accompanying the attack of the Panthers and was present on the battlefield. If this was true, and they did leave Le Bourg, no mention of their presence is given by either the motorcyclist or the Panther crews in their accounts of the ambush of *3. Kompanie*. If an advance was made, it appears it was stifled rather quickly by RCA artillery fire. The presence of the *SS-Panzergrenadiere* would have been invaluable for evacuating the wounded tank crewman and securing the area, especially in light of an RRR outpost in the lineman's cottage, in which a Bren gunner managed to fire on motorcyclists and the wounded tank crewmen. It is very likely that the *SS-Panzergrenadiere* were rapidly outdistanced by the *3. Kompanie* advance and were reduced to trudging along, the tanks far out in front. It is very probable that the *SS-Panzergrenadiere* of *15. Kp./SS-Pz.Gren.Rgt. 25* did their best, but were exhausted following the fighting on the night of 8/9 June and were probably suppressed nearly immediately by RCA shellfire that the tank crews managed to shrug off as they advanced at high speed.

While the *3. Kompanie* attack of *SS-Pz.Rgt. 12* is the focus of Canadian military historical accounts of the action, *1. Kompanie* under *Hstuf.* Berlin also moved forward in the attack, not just firing at the church steeple, and this event is ignored by anglophone historians. After moving south via the railway underpass from La Villeneuve, it appears to have driven further south, out of the way of the *3. Kompanie*, which was going to attack parallel to the railway line. It appears the *Kompanie* moved into a low piece of ground in which it was hidden from sight, and when the attack began, its Panther tanks had to climb a rather steep hill in order to take part in the attack, moving against southern Norrey-en-Bessin.

The Panthers, breaking out into open country, advanced towards the Norrey-en-Bessin Château grounds and its woods, and came into contact with Canadian positions. Heavy anti-tank gun fire was encountered by the crews, and it appears the Panthers aggressively engaged at least two anti-tank gun positions in the C

Company RRR positions, which they managed to destroy, at least one being dramatically driven over by a Panther tank. According to French military historian Stephan Cazenave, an estimated total of 11 Panthers of *1. Kompanie* were in action. During the action, Panther '126' was badly damaged by anti-tank gun fire, but its driver, *Strm.* Wittköper, managed to drive the damaged tank back to the German line to the east.[19]

Also supporting the attack was *4. Kp./SS-Pz.Rgt. 12*, which moved up to the treeline outside of the Rots–Le Bourg–La Villeneuve area to support the attack with fire and suppress the RRR and its attached forces in Bretteville-l'Orgueilleuse. Due to the slight rise in the ground on the Bretteville-l'Orgueilleuse–Caen road and the trees planted to each side of it, this rise being the site where the night previous the *4. Kompanie* had destroyed the Ottawa Highlanders, RRR and 3rd Anti-Tank Regiment, RCA, blocking position, they could only have been able to see a partial view of Bretteville-l'Orgueilleuse. This lack of vision from Rots was brought to the attention of *4. Kompanie* in shocking fashion early that afternoon as combat with the Panthers of *3. Kompanie* was occurring. An anti-tank gun in Bretteville fired on Panther '417', its shots penetrating the turret and killing the turret crew, including the *Panzerkommandant, Uscha.* Martin Voss.[20] The Panther subsequently burned out.

Following the destruction of Panther '417', several Panthers of *4. Kompanie* managed to locate the anti-tank gun position, it being on the RN 13, and destroy it. During the firefight, in which possibly other RCA anti-tank guns were involved, another Panther, '404', was hit and damaged by several rounds that impacted its frontal armour. Despite heavy damage to his tank and the death of his radio operator, the wounded tank driver managed to reverse Panther '404' behind a slight rise and out of danger. Damaged tanks were later towed away to be repaired and survive to fight another day. These losses and the those from the previous night during the fighting around Bretteville-l'Orgueilleuse had seriously depleted the number of operational combat-ready Panthers within *4. Kompanie*. Critically, the combat force *Hstuf.* Pfeiffer would later be able to muster to attempt to drive back a mixed Anglo-Canadian assault force on 11 June, an event to be discussed later in this book, had been significantly weakened.[21]

Following the firefights near Norrey, contact with Canadian forces near northern Norrey would not be broken until 1430 hours when the last of Lüdemann's *3. Kompanie* tanks had driven back under the railroad underpass. The surviving tanks of *3. Kompanie* had fired off a tremendous number of rounds, attempting to engage in long-range firefights with the Canadian tanks and anti-tank guns in southern Bretteville-l'Orgueilleuse.[22] This is something they did not do successfully, and no Canadian tank losses appear to have occurred.

Having completed its mission of attempting to support the attack by *3. Kompanie*, which was intended to push right into Norrey-en-Bessin village proper and destroy C Company of the RRR, *Stubaf.* Jürgensen ordered by radio the *1. Kompanie* tanks that had advanced towards the woods near the Norrey-en-Bessin Château to return back to their start line, following the damaged Panther '126' that had already withdrawn back to the areas just south of La Villeneuve. It is likely that the *1. Kompanie* Panthers reached the railroad bridge after the surviving *3. Kompanie* tanks had crossed under it.

The wounded tank crews from *4.* and *3. Kompanie* were evacuated through La Villeneuve and Le Bourg east towards Caen and the German rear area. As was typical of tank casualties taken on both sides during the fighting in Normandy, most of the wounded suffered from burns to their faces, heads and hands. The leather surplus U-boat clothing some of the crews wore into combat saved them from serious burns on other parts of their bodies, but exposed areas of the body were almost always burned. The ammunition and fuel within the Panther, just like on the Sherman and Panzer IV, ignited immediately in most cases. Only the fastest of crewmen managed to evacuate their stricken tanks without burns. The cruelty of war inflicted further harm on the wounded from the 9 June fighting near Norrey-en-Bessin, when the ambulances moving the wounded to the south from Le Bourg and La Villeneuve were strafed by Allied fighter bombers, despite the Red Cross markings on the roofs of the vehicles.[23]

Looking past the casualties of *SS-Pz.Rgt. 12*, the losses to *SS-Pz.Gren.Rgt. 26* in the period 8–9 June had been severe, and totalled 30 killed (1 officer, 3 NCOs, 26 men), 53 wounded (2 officers, 8 NCOs, 43 men) and 16 missing (2 NCOs, 14 men).[24] This total of 99 was significant, and nothing had been achieved that could significantly be counted as a military success, other than the establishment of a strong front south of Bretteville-l'Orgueilleuse and Norrey-en-Bessin, and the temporary capture of Putot-en-Bessin, which was then lost on the same day of its capture. Canadian RCA field artillery fire continued to be overpowering, and due to counterbattery fire, the *I. Abt./SS-Pz.Art.Rgt. 12* had to change its positions, moving from the *SS-Pz.Gren.Rgt. 25* sector to Carpiquet airfield and later Fontenay to escape counterbattery fire and support operations on the western *Hitlerjugend* flank.[25] The one success had been the securing of the Rots–Le Hamel area and the Mue river valley, which was undefended by the Canadian forces.

And what to the west, in the sector of *III. Btl.(Gepanzert)/SS-Pz.Gren.Rgt. 26* and *SS-Pz.Aüfkl.Abt. 12* on 9 June? Little enemy action on 9 June was encountered by these units, and other than harassing artillery fire and some long-range tank firefights, there were no major events. Having arrived late on 8 June, it is reported that the *2. Kp./SS-Pz.Rgt. 12* with its Panther tanks took up position on the château grounds close to Fontenay-le-Pesnel. Little information is available on the initial fighting of the *2. Kompanie* when it reached the Château de Boise and its wooded area and then pushed forward, other than it fought some minor actions near or on Hill 102 and reported knocking out three Shermans on the neighbouring Hill 103, the rise to the immediate west of the *SS-Pz.Aüfkl.Abt. 12* positions.[26]

A significant reverse was suffered by the *Panzer-Lehr* on this date with the forces of the British 50th Infantry Division forcing their way into the village of St Pierre, immediately to the west for the *Hitlerjugend* line running north–south from Brouay to the new positions of the *Panzer-Lehr.* The 8th Battalion, the Durham Light Infantry (8 DLI), with tanks of the 24th Lancers and field artillery from the 147th Field Regiment, RA, in support, forced its way into the village. German forces were then defeated in house-to-house fighting, the *I. Btl.(Gepanzert)/Pz.-Lehr.Gren.Rgt. 901* being driven back.[27] In the subsequent British battalion's consolidation process, two troops of the 288th Battery, RA, arrived to help fortify the village, whose possession would see heavy combat in the immediate future.[28]

The first battle of Caen: The 10 June 1944 attack of *SS-Pz.Pio.Btl. 12* on Norrey-en-Bessin

Saturday, 10 June was another day of intense combat between German and Canadian forces, centred again on the familiar battleground of the village of Norrey-en-Bessin. By this point, it was largely an impregnable fortress due to the support given by the RCA in the way of anti-tank guns and field artillery batteries ready to fire on German forces. This day would see the newly arrived *SS-Panzerpionierbataillon 12* of the *Hitlerjugend* attack the village in the early morning hours from the south without armoured support, and be repulsed with heavy losses due to Canadian defensive infantry, mortar and field artillery fire.

This attack would be another tactical failure for the *Hitlerjugend*, and this last assault had the same characteristics of the previous failed German operations, in that they seemed rushed and lacking in coordination. It was as if Meyer, Wünsche and Mohnke were scraping together whatever was available unit-wise as it arrived and throwing it against the enemy, all with *Brig.Fhr.* Witt's approval. This enemy, the 7th Canadian Infantry Brigade of the 3rd Canadian Infantry Division in its fortress positions, was now experienced in defensive fighting, knowledgeable of *Waffen-SS* tactics and was backed by powerful RCA field artillery forces, ready to deliver heavy fire against any available target for a sustained period.

This day would mark the last German attempt, at the battalion level, to gain the battlefield initiative and improve German positions at the expense of the Anglo-Canadian forces before a large, *I. SS-Panzerkorps*-level attack by at least three *Panzerdivisionen* could be executed. German commanders, *Gen.d.Pz.Tr.* von Schweppenburg in particular, were now anxious to launch this long-awaited coordinated attack. That they were willing to ignore Allied tactical air superiority speaks to a sense of urgency considering the ongoing race to see who could rush more divisions and other formations to the front, one that the Germans were losing at a rapid rate as more Allied forces landed on the beaches.

One of the least studied events of the German–Canadian bridgehead battles, the attack of *SS-Pz.Pio.Btl. 12* on Norrey-en-Bessin would be the third direct attack on the village, after the half-hearted attack by *I. Btl./SS-Pz.Gren.Rgt. 26* on the early morning of 8 June and the subsequent major assault on 9 June by *3. Kp./SS-Pz.Rgt. 12* with other forces in support. Some brief contact with the defences had occurred in the overnight 8–9 June battle with the *I. Abt./SS-Pz.Rgt. 12* forces as it assaulted Bretteville-l'Orgueilleuse, but this was incidental.

The attackers, *SS-Pz.Pio.Btl. 12*, had not yet been committed to battle and as stated were the last *Bataillon*-sized unit of the *Hitlerjugend* to reach the front lines. The combat engineer battalion of the division, it was in many ways equipped and structured as a *SS-Panzergrenadier-Bataillon*, its first *Kompanie* being equipped with SPW-251 engineer variant half-tracks and its *4. (Schwere) Kompanie* being equipped with infantry heavy weapons.

Even though the village had been defended since 7 June by only C Company of the RRR and a few attached heavy weapons from the RRR Support Company, it had successfully withstood the previous attacks due to the excellent support the Canadians received from the RCA field artillery and the extra anti-tank forces attached to its all-around defence. Its commander, Major Tubb, had performed well in coordinating the defence, his platoons being well positioned to support one another from the houses and orchards of the village. The defence was also active in that it had been carrying out a program of manning forward observation posts and patrolling.

The divisional commander, *Brig.Fhr.* Witt, had ordered this latest attack. *Gen.d.Pz. Tr.* von Schweppenburg, who had recently visited the regimental *Gefechtsstand* of *SS-Pz.Gren.Rgt. 25* at the Abbaye Notre-Dame d'Ardenne, had acknowledged the need to remove the stronghold of Norrey-en-Bessin to the south-west and had likely reminded Witt to redouble efforts to eliminate it. As has been mentioned previously, its presence as a salient in German lines impaired the future offensive operations of both *SS-Pz.Gren.Rgt. 25* and *26*.

It was envisioned by the German high command that at this point in time the *Panzer-Lehr* would be taking over a larger frontage up to the Mue river, and as it continued to move into the western battle space of the *Hitlerjugend* the *Waffen-SS* would have less front line to be responsible for. This would allow the *Hitlerjugend* to concentrate its forces in a smaller area for a future *I. SS-Pz.Korps* counteroffensive.[1] That the newly arriving *Panzer-Lehr* would be faced with powerful British forces in the immediate future, and that it was already overstretched and on the verge of being overpowered, seems to be something that the German *Pz.Gr.West* and *I. SS-Pz. Korps Hauptquartier* overlooked or failed to appreciate.

As mentioned previously, the attack of *SS-Pz.Pio.Btl. 12* was, like the preceding German attacks by the *Hitlerjugend* in this sector over the previous days, uncoordi-nated in that it lacked an adequate support by all arms in order to overwhelm the

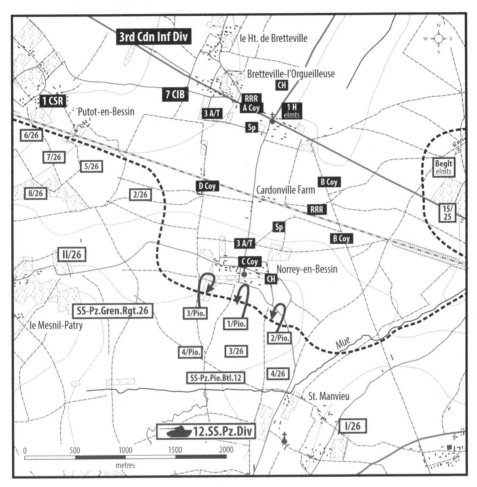

Attack of *SS-Pz.Pio.Btl. 12* on Norrey-en-Bessin, 10 June. (Map by Mike Bechthold)

Canadian defenders. While there was no armour present to lead this attack, possibly due to the poor results of the 8/9 June night attack on Bretteville and that the exhaustion of the Panther *Kompanien*, it does appear *6., 8.* and *9. Batterien* from *II.* and *III. Abt./SS-Pz.Art.Rgt. 12* were slated to support this effort. As this was planned to be a night attack, it is unclear how effective the indirect fire support provided could be as it could not be adjusted. Little detail is recorded regarding the actual effect of the supporting German artillery fire in the *SS-Pz.Art.Rgt. 12 Kriegstagebuch*.[2]

However, for this attack the *Waffen-SS* did have local superiority in infantry numbers; these being three-to-one odds in the way of three fresh *SS-Panzerpionier Kompanien*, ready to attack the beleaguered C Company, RRR defenders. This infantry attack would have to move fast enough to close with and overwhelm the defenders before major Canadian RCA field artillery support in the way of defensive fire tasks could be called in on the Germans. The Germans now understood that field artillery and naval gunfire were the most powerful Anglo-Canadian defensive forces opposing them on the Caen battlefield.

At 0430 hours, it was reported that the three *Artillerie-Batterien* supporting the attack fired a total of seven field artillery concentrations on Bretteville-l'Orgueilleuse and Norrey-en-Bessin.[3] The assembly point for the attackers prior to the attack was just south of Norrey-en-Bessin within the positions of *3. Kompanie* of *I. Btl./SS-Pz. Rgt. 26.* The *2. Kp./SS-Pz.Pio.Btl. 12*, under *Ostuf.* Kuret, was to attack on the right flank, while *1. Kompanie* under *Oblt.* Toll, a *Heer* officer, was to push forward in the middle and *3. Kompanie* under *Hstuf.* Tieke was to attack on the left flank. *Ostuf.* Bischoff, the *Kommandeur* of *4. (Schwere) Kompanie*, deployed his 8cm mortar *Zug* within the *3. Kompanie* positions on the left flank.[4]

Attacking at 0500 hours, the three *SS-Panzerpionier Kompanien* attacked in what appears to have been a staggered formation rather than one straight start line running east–west. Creeping forward quickly in the half-darkness towards southern Norrey-en-Bessin as the last German artillery shell was fired, the *SS-Panzerpioniere* attempted to get into the positions of the RRR riflemen before they could react. The Canadians, however, allowed the *SS-Panzerpioniere* to get close, and then, like a thunderclap, mortar rounds and field artillery fire in the way of RCA defensive fire tasks hit them in the open fields south of the village. This bombardment was then joined by rifle, Bren gun, and Vickers medium machine-gun fire as the platoon positions of the RRR opened up on the Germans, who were driven to the ground or into hedges and wooded areas as the indirect and direct fire hit them. It is unclear from accounts if any RRR 6-pounder anti-tank guns participated in the fighting, as accounts do not describe their use and the accuracy of the anti-tank guns would be poor in the darkness without the use of flares.

The *SS-Panzerpioniere* were forced to creep and crawl back to their starting points apart from *Oblt.* Toll's *1. Kompanie*, which used a sunken road south of the village to get closer to the Canadian trenches. From this position they attempted to reorganise themselves and set up MG-42 positions. Attacking again from this closer location, the *SS-Panzerpioniere* were thrown back by intense small arms fire, Toll being hit in the process.

Casualties were heavy, not just in the way of *SS-Panzerpioniere*, but also in the number of junior leaders and officers killed and wounded. The *Bataillon* surgeon, Dr Zistler, attempted to save the fatally wounded *1. Kompanie Kommandeur, Oblt.* Toll, but could not save the *Heer* officer who had been assigned to the *Hitlerjugend* because of a lack of officers and junior leaders.

As the latest example of inconclusive fighting near Norrey-en-Bessin dragged on into the day for the *SS-Panzerpioniere* with no appreciable result other than the loss of lives and an extended firefight, the divisional leadership of the *Hitlerjugend* exhibited frustration not only with battlefield events but with challenges in the way of order and discipline exhibited in the rear areas. The divisional *Gefechtsstand* was forced to issue an order to all *Hitlerjugend* formations and units concerning the breakdown of military discipline amongst the supply units of the regiments. *Brig.Fhr.* Witt's written order stated that all personnel found by officers to be lacking discipline with regards to dress and deportment, or found to fail to salute officers or be guilty of other misdemeanours, were to be rounded up immediately and punished severely.[5]

It seems unclear exactly why even some weak armoured forces, such as an understrength Panzer *Kompanie*, were not added to Müller's force for the early morning attack. It was not as if they were uncomfortable operating at night, and they had fought near Norrey-en-Bessin in the previous days. It is understandable that *Pantherabteilung Kompanien* were not involved, as they had lost a significant number of tanks in the area recently and were exhausted. There are many potential reasons for this, ranging from engine noise taking away the *SS-Panzerpioniere* element of surprise, the dangers of negotiating Canadian anti-tank minefields, and possible concerns regarding unacceptable losses to *SS-Pz.Rgt. 12* and the fact that no replacement tanks were available. Also, not mentioned in Canadian accounts is the heavy Jabo air activity over the battlefield, strafing and bombing the Germans. The *Flak Zug* of *SS-Pz.Art.Rgt. 12*, in heavy action this day, shot down both a USAAF Mustang and a Thunderbolt.[6]

However, the most likely reason for the lack of German armour in the Norrey fighting was that this day saw nearly the entire *SS-Pz.Rgt. 12* conduct road moves in the early morning hours of darkness to strengthen the threatened left flank of the *Hitlerjugend*. The *1.* and very much weakened *3. Kompanien* of *I. Abt./SS-Pz.Rgt. 12* conducted a road move away from Le Neuborg and La Villeneuve at 2300 hours the previous day, driving 15 kilometres to take up position near Fontenay-le-Pesnel, joining the nearby *2. Kompanie* and leaving what was left of *4. Kompanie* to defend the Rots-Le Hamel salient with weak *SS-Panzergrenadiere* forces. These two *Kompanien* were in position by daybreak and camouflaged all their Panther tanks in an assembly area just north of the Tilly-sur-Seulles–Caen road.[7] On this day there is also the first mention of the *Aufklärung Zug* of *I. Abt./SS-Pz.Rgt. 12* in German accounts, and it is assumed that at least three of these tanks joined the two *Kompanien*, both of which had lost tanks in the 8–9 June fighting near Bretteville-l'Orgueilleuse.[8]

Not excluded from this armour redeployment, the complete *II. Abt./SS-Pz.Rgt. 12* conducted a night road move from their assembly areas near Buron and south of Cambes to Fontenay-le-Pesnel, a move of roughly 13 kilometres. This move was completed by 0600 hours, and bizarrely, while moving into their new assembly areas, the Panzer IV *Panzerkommandanten* would have literally driven right past the raging infantry battle to their north at Norrey-en-Bessin as they passed through St Manvieau. Once it arrived in its new location, *II. Abt./SS-Pz.Rgt. 12* began preparations to carry out counterattacks against anticipated British offensive operations, which did occur as foreseen by the Germans and will be studied in the next volume of this series. What was left in the way of operational and damaged Panzer IVs under repair within *7. Kompanie* were transferred to *6. Kompanie* on this day, the *Abteilung* now restructured with *5., 6., 8.* and *9. Kompanien*, all of which were still not at full strength despite this reorganisation.[9]

At 0900 hours, the *Kriegstagebuch* of *II. Abt./SS-Pz.Rgt. 12* records that Anglo-Canadian artillery forces had indeed identified the *Gefechtsstand* of the *Abteilung*, which came under surprise heavy field artillery concentrations from RCA and RA forces to the north. As a result, it had to be moved from Fontenay-les-Pesnel south, down the Fontenay–Rauray road to a safer location away from the radio triangulation or aerial observation efforts of the Allies. This may have been a critical event during the day, as during the move the *Batterien* could not support *SS-Pz.Pio.Btl. 12* at this time, it being involved in heavy infantry combat near Norrey-en-Bessin.[10]

Further action occurred at 1515 hours, when the *Gefechtsstand* of *Ostubaf.* Mohnke of *SS-Pz.Gren.Rgt. 26* made the request for Panzer support against British armour approaching from the north-west nearing the German-held Hill 102 near Audrieu. While the *5.* and *6. Kompanien* were kept in readiness, the Panzer IVs of the *8.* and *9. Kompanien* drove to Hill 102 and assumed hull-down positions to secure the area, their guns pointing to the west and north-west for an extended period. No British assault materialised, although two British soldiers were captured in the area. At 1730 hours a *Stabskompanie* Panzer IV of *5. Kompanie*, Panzer IV '553', was recorded in the *Abteilung Kriegstagebuch* as burning out, but it is unclear why this occurred and whether Anglo-Canadian artillery fire was the cause.

In conclusion, the attack on the morning of 10 June was the last real attempt by the *Hitlerjugend* to gain the initiative and remove the blocking position of Norrey-en-Bessin–Bretteville-l'Orgueilleuse from its front line, in order to create the right conditions for the division to attack north as part of the planned three-*Panzerdivision* attack by *I. SS-Pz.Korps*. The combat power of the *SS-Panzerpionierbatallion*, which was not insignificant, could not take a single village defended by one infantry company of the RRR. There is no real reason why parts of *SS-Pz.Rgt. 12*, though battered from the previous fighting, could not have deployed in a support role to try to 'shoot in' – using the Canadian Armoured Corps parlance – the *SS-Panzerpioniere*. Even if one half-*Kompanie* of Panthers had been made available, possibly some progress could have been made against the C Company RRR and its attached forces.

The *Waffen-SS* idea that somehow night attacks, surprise and stealth would achieve success was rooted in Eastern Front combat experience and tactics that still prevailed within the division, despite recent early morning coups de main failing in Norrey-en-Bessin on the morning of 8 June and failing in Bretteville-l'Orgueilleuse in the early hours of 9 June. It seems that the lessons learned from these battles were not passed to the newly arrived *SS-Panzerpionierbatallion 12* or were ignored by its officers, the advantages of a combined arms attack during daylight with Panzers also being rejected. What role *SS-Pz.Gren.Rgt. 26 Kommandeur Ostubaf.* Monke had in influencing his area of operations is unknown, and the refusal to commit more forces from his regiment to the fight as dawn turned to mid-morning speaks of a regimental command team that was quite content to let the *SS-Panzerpioniere* fail.

Because of these factors, the attack on the morning of 10 June was the last, and the most pathetic, of the *Hitlerjugend* attempts to gain the battlefield initiative in the period 7–11 June 1944. It was poorly executed and the C Company, RRR, forces managed to use this engagement as an opportunity to inflict heavy infantry casualties on the attacking Germans that could not be replaced. The losses of 28 dead, 42 wounded and 10 missing were made all the worse by the death of the *1. Kompanie Kommandeur Oblt.* Otto Toll, a Knight's Cross recipient with considerable combat experience, for absolutely no gain.[11]

To the north-east, for the aforementioned *SS-Pz.Gren.Rgt. 26* forces in the Rots–Le Hamel salient, the 10 June was also a day of combat, and constant vigilance was needed against the Allied strongholds of Bray and Bretteville-l'Orgueilleuse. These two Anglo-Canadian fortresses to the north-west and south-west, respectively, of Le Hamel, posed a constant threat to the Germans. Movement from Bray this day saw a Royal Marine Centaur fire support tank mounting a 95mm gun emerge from the village, it being engaged by both *SS-Panzergrenadiere* of the *15. Kp.(Aufklärung)/ SS-Pz.Gren.Rgt. 25* and Panther '438' commandeered by *Uscha.* Berkert, an experienced tank commander. The Centaur burnt out after being hit, the Germans observing the crew escaping from the burning tank.[12]

10 June would see further intense combat on the left flank of the *Hitlerjugend*, focused on the village of St Pierre, just west of the *SS-Pz.Aüfkl.Abt. 12* positions. Attacking at dawn, the *I. Btl.(Gepanzert)/Pz.Lehr.Gren.Rgt. 901* managed to re-take the village. Fighting back, at 1130 hours a British counterattack by 8th Battalion, Durham Light Infantry (8 DLI) forces supported by tanks and very heavy field and medium artillery fire as well as naval gunfire retook parts of the village, but failed to drive the Germans completely out.[13] To the north-east, long-range firefights would continue with the forces of *SS-Pz.Aüfkl.Abt. 12* and the Panther tanks of *2. Kp./SS-Pz.Rgt. 12*, these forces firing on the British 1st Battalion, the Dorsetshire Regiment (1 Dorsets) and British armour on Hill 103.

This date would see one further disaster at last light, not just for the *Hitlerjugend*, but for the operational prospects of all *Panzerdivisionen* on the eastern section of the Normandy bridgehead front. On this date, one of the most effective and powerful tactical air raids of the Normandy campaign occurred. The raid by RAF B-25 Mitchell bombers and swathes of RAF fighter-bombers was launched on the evening of 10 June on the *Hauptquartier* of *Pz.Gr.West*, located in and around the château at La Caine, six kilometres north-west of Thury-Harcourt and 20 kilometres south-west of Caen. The 61 B-25 medium bombers from several RAF squadrons would drop 220 kilograms of bombs from an altitude of 4,000 metres. Following this bombing run,

40 RAF Typhoon fighter-bombers also hit the location. Surprisingly, the château was relatively unscathed, but the area around it was rendered a moonscape. *Gen.d.Pz. Tr.* von Schweppenburg would survive with wounds, but his headquarters vehicles were destroyed and a large number of casualties were inflicted on the headquarters staff, these being vitally important high- and mid-level *Heer Generalstabsoffiziere* who were indispensable for German military operations in Normandy.[14]

CHAPTER 13

The first battle of Caen: Actions on the right flank, 8–11 June 1944

The villages of Norrey-en-Bessin and Bretteville-l'Orgueilleuse had not fallen to Witt despite the best efforts of his former Eastern Front fighters, these being the regimental *Kommandeure Staf.* Kurt Meyer and *Ostubaf.* Wünsche, whose approaches to battle had radically different results than those experienced in the USSR. What was needed as soon as possible was for infantry battlegroups from nearby *15. Armee Infanterie-Divisionen* to arrive in the sector north of Caen, allowing the *Hitlerjugend* to reorganise its forces away from the front lines for later assaults, to be carried out with other armoured reinforcements in order to make headway in pushing back the British and Canadian territorial gains to this point. This had not occurred, and the *SS-Pz.Gren.Rgt. 25* of *Staf.* Meyer was being employed in a strictly defensive role, very much like a German *Infanterie-Division* from the First World War, complete with elaborate bunkers, communication trenches and even the beginnings of more anti-tank ditches dug by French civilians held at gunpoint in Buron. The mobility of the regiment was squandered, and it was now pinned in place, to be pummelled by Anglo-Canadian air strikes, artillery fire, naval gunfire and armoured and infantry assaults, launched in a set-piece fashion.

The area north of Caen had in some ways become Flanders in 1916, with the difference being that more and more British reinforcements were landing on the invasion beaches by the hour. The reinforcement race, so important to both sides, was being won by the Allies, the Germans simply being unable to rapidly deploy their forces due to poor previous deployment choices and the effective implementation of the Allied 'Transportation Plan' campaign of air interdiction of all German movement and destruction of all transport infrastructure. The Germans were also loath to abandon their very strong Pas-de-Calais defences, and many in the German high command still thought the Normandy landings were a ruse. Having no such transport problems in the English Channel, the build-up of the British Second Army went on unabated. The biggest threat to its success was poor sailing weather in the way of high seas, the Allies still fully exploiting their total naval and air supremacy.

Due to real or imagined-time pressures to attain cleared start lines for the *Hitlerjugend* to participate in the proposed multi-division counterattack of *I. SS-Panzerkorps*, the division had so far been guilty of attempting the hasty tactics of the Eastern Front, which against often unprepared or poorly supported Red Army forces were successful. Here, however, on the approaches to Caen, they had not been successful, and the power of the RCA and RA field artillery and anti-tank units, and the defensive resilience of the Anglo-Canadian infantry and armoured forces, had proven too much for the hasty and uncoordinated *Waffen-SS* armoured thrusts.

The front line of the *SS-Pz.Gren.Rgt. 26* had not been straightened out, and the powerful defensive abilities of the 3rd Canadian Infantry Division, most notably supported by coordinated artillery strikes, had become brutally apparent to its regimental *Kommandeur, Ostubaf.* Mohnke. What was worse than the failures on the German side were the repeated attempts to continue the same type of attack, with the expectation that the results would be different. Despite the knowledge that the losses in tanks and men were not going to be replaced, Mohnke, Meyer, Wünsche and others had simply thrown their units at the Canadians again and again, expecting a different result but approaching the problem in the same manner. The learning process for the *Hitlerjugend* in these first few bloody days of combat must have been tremendously painful for its *Kommandeure*. This was the new way of war, one very different from the one on the wind-swept steppes of Ukraine.

Things were not going well either for the neighbour of the *Hitlerjugend*, the *21. Pz.Div.* of *Gen.Maj.* Feuchtinger. After the failure of its 6 June attack, it had largely gone over to the defensive due to the fact that it, like the *Hitlerjugend*, was now the only force holding the front lines in the total absence of *Heer* infantry formations. One half of the *21. Pz.Div.* was facing the British 3rd Infantry Division, and the other half was facing the British 6th Airborne division east of the Orne. Its frontage was nearly 10 kilometres wide in places.[1] Instead of being held in reserve for a counterattack or powerful assault, the *21. Pz.Div.* was simply holding the line and seeing its strength dwindle daily. The endless Anglo-Canadian medium and field artillery harassing fire, supported by periods of naval gunfire, would bleed the *Panzergrenadiere* units of the division dry in the month of June. What was continuing to occur, and had happened to the *Hitlerjugend* in the period 7–8 June, was beginning to occur for the *Panzer-Lehr* to the west and the *21. Pz.Div.* to the east. These divisions were intended for offensive operations and aggressive counterattacks if they were on the defensive. The role of simply holding the line in the *Heer* was reserved for the *Infanterie-Divisionen*. The obviously very challenging reality was that none had arrived to replace the now virtually destroyed *716. Infanterie-Division*.

The front of *SS-Pz.Gren.Rgt. 25* was relatively static following the events of 7 June. The absence within the division of *SS-Panzerjäger-Abteilung. 12* meant that the division was without its dedicated anti-tank asset, and whatever towed anti-tank guns it held were limited to those assigned to the *SS-Panzergrenadiere Batallione*. The 8.8cm dual-purpose Flak guns of *SS-Flak Abt. 12* were thrust into this role by the *Hitlerjugend*, its *Batterien* being deployed near enough to the front line to fire at long range at vehicles or movement. As of 8 June, the *1., 2.* and *3. Batterien* of *SS-Flak Abt. 12* were in new firing positions within the *SS-Pz.Gren.Rgt. 25* sector to deal with any Allied tank squadrons that appeared. Bolstering the anti-aircraft defensive effort to the south, *4. Batterie* took up new positions at 0900 hours with its *II.* And *III. Zug* near Carpiquet airfield. Air activity in the clear French summer weather continued unabated, with all German forces reporting strong Jabo fighter-bomber activity all along their fronts and along main supply routes. At 1530 hours on 8 June a Typhoon was shot down by *4. Batterie*. To the north, a Thunderbolt was downed at 1543 hours by *1. Batterie*, and at 2142 hours, a B-26 Marauder bomber was shot down at last light by the same *Batterie*.[2] There appears to have been heavy firing by all units of *SS-Flak.Abt. 12* this day, with 45 8.8cm, 108 3.7cm and 1,000 2cm shells consumed.[3] The Flak units were not alone in being pushed into an anti-tank role. The *Kompanien* of *II. Abt./SS-Pz.Rgt. 12* were placed on standby to support the *SS-Panzergrenadiere* if large numbers of Anglo-Canadian armour appeared.

Artillery support for *SS-Pz.Gren.Rgt. 25* during the timeframe 8–11 June continued to be primarily provided by *III. Abt./SS-Pz.Art.Rgt. 12*, whose *Batterien* were sited on the north-west and western outskirts of Caen.[4] This artillery unit did not have the near limitless supply of ammunition of the Allies for harassing and speculative fire, and had been forced to begin to ration its limited stocks of shells for defensive purposes. Strict orders had to be issued by the Germans to save ammunition for actual Anglo-Canadian attacks when they materialised. Because of this, special artillery missions were planned, in which maximum effectiveness was to be achieved from the limited numbers of shells stockpiled in each *Batterie* position. For the German *Artillerie*, *Infanteriegeschütz*, mortar and Flak gun crews firing in an indirect role, defensive tactics worked out with the *SS-Panzergrenadiere* officers focused on bombarding attacking Anglo-Canadian forces in their assembly areas or former German-held objectives that had fallen. If British or Canadian infantry and armour were getting ready to attack or were in the process of consolidation, a pre-planned defensive indirect fire-strike could be enacted on this predefined target.

While fighting raged to the east on the front of the *SS-Pz.Gren.Rgt. 26*, minor skirmishes occurred to the north of Caen on 8 June 1944. The village of Cambes was the scene of these encounters between British 2nd Battalion, the Royal Ulster Rifles (2 RUR) and German patrols in the following days after the battle on 7 June.[5] On this date the *I. Btl./SS-Pz.Gren.Rgt. 25* had dug in within the open fields and small wooded areas just to the west of La Bijude, which is east of the north–south D7 paved road running into Caen. This *Bataillon* had only temporary observation posts or patrol bases in Cambes, which was quite densely wooded and a no-man's land that *I. Btl./SS-Pz.Gren.Rgt. 25* did not seek to occupy due to the severity of the Allied artillery fire. It used the period of inactivity following the 7 June fighting to strengthen its positions and monitor the wooded areas north of Cambes that were held by forces of the British 3rd Infantry Division.[6] Almost all accounts of the British 185th Infantry Brigade on this date talk about Cambes and the wooded area of 'Cambes Wood'. What is not made clear is that the village and the wooded area were one, and the French paved road, D7, that ran parallel to Cambes was very tactically important.

The *I. Btl./SS-Pz.Gren.Rgt. 25* was not the only German *Bataillon* that guarded the approaches to Cambes. On its left was the *II. Btl./SS-Pz.Gren.Rgt. 25*, which was dug in to positions in the village of Galmache, south-west of Cambes. To the east, the forces of the *21. Pz.Div.* held and defended La Bijude, and it was possible to site anti-tank weapons and tanks that could fire directly from this village right down the connecting road into Cambes. Thus, any armoured vehicles attempting to drive into northern Cambes and push south on the main road would immediately fall under German anti-tank fire.

On 8 June the field and medium regiments of the Royal Artillery were very active, with harassing fire laid down on all identified *Hitlerjugend* positions. At roughly midday, a probing attack was launched by the British on the area marking the boundary between the *II. Btl./SS-Pz.Gren.Rgt. 25* and *I. Btl./SS-Pz.Gren.Rgt. 25*. The attacking force of two infantry companies forward was supported by Sherman tanks. It is likely that this attack, not recorded in British or Canadian accounts, was ordered to probe the German positions.[7] Two 7.5cm Pak 40 anti-tank guns, detached from the *4. Kp.(Schwere)/SS-Pz.Gren.Rgt. 25*, went into action immediately, knocking out several tanks. Added to this fire was long-range MG-42 machine-gun bursts and mortar fire, which went some way to causing the attack to stall. The British then withdrew, and the Panzer IV tanks of *III. Zug* of *8. Kp./SS-Pz.Rgt. 12* led by *Uscha.* Drebert which had been dispatched to aid the *SS-Panzergrenadiere* returned to their readiness positions to the south.[8] Heavy British RA medium and field artillery fire then rained down on the German positions on the front lines and to the south, unfortunately killing and wounding some of the Panzer IV crews that had dismounted. It did not cause heavy casualties for the *SS-Panzergrenadiere*, as they had spent most of the morning of 8 June improving their positions by building bunkers and digging communication trenches. These were very much needed, as at 1658 hours a very heavy fighter-bomber Jabo attack went in just south of Cambes, a large number of aircraft bombing and strafing the German positions.[9]

In the aftermath of this probing attack, the Commanding Officer (CO) of the 2nd Battalion, the Royal Ulster Rifles (2 RUR), carried out a reconnaissance near Cambes with the CO of the 33rd Field Regiment, RA, Lieutenant Colonel Hussey, in order to gain information on how to best attack the objective from a planned start line south of the village of Anisy. This was needed to determine what areas could be pre-registered for field artillery concentrations and defensive fire tasks. The attack plan called for two squadrons of the British 27th Armoured Brigade's East Riding Yeomanry (ERY) with its Sherman tanks to provide tank support for an infantry assault. Powerful indirect fire support was to come from all three field artillery regiments of the British 3rd Infantry Division as well as an RN cruiser assigned to provide naval gunfire.[10]

The German defences at the *Bataillon* level depended on heavy weapons that were temporarily attached to front line positions. The heavy weapons of *4. Kp.(Schwere)/ SS-Pz.Gren.Rgt. 25* were deployed within the *1., 2.* and *3. Kompanie* positions with good fields of fire; the 8cm mortar crews had pre-registered targets, and the 7.5cm Pak 40s were ready in their camouflaged and dug-in positions. The defences of the neighbouring *II. Btl./SS-Pz.Gren.Rgt. 25* to the west in Galmanche were arranged in a similar manner and oriented towards possible Canadian and British routes of advance.

Further to the west, the positions of *Ostubaf.* Milius's *III. Btl./SS-Pz.Gren.Rgt. 25* and attached forces had been steadily improved in the timeframe 7–8 June. Bunkers were installed in Buron, Gruchy and Authie and fields of fire for the MG-42 machine guns in the sustained fire role were created by cutting down wheat in the fields during the hours of darkness. Initial work was also begun, using the forced labour of French civilians, on enlarging the anti-tank ditches slightly north of Buron to thwart any armoured attacks from Les Buissons, the most obvious start point for attacking Canadian forces of the 9th Canadian Infantry Brigade. Some tank activity was spotted north of Authie and Buron at 1110 hours, but this never resulted in a major attack.[11] This village was now referred to by the Canadian units as 'Hell's Corners' due to periods of German mortar, *Infanterie-Geschütz* and *Artillerie* fire from the *Waffen-SS*. The front near Buron on 8 June saw very little in the way of large-scale combat, it being quiet apart from some harassing artillery fire fired by both sides. On 8 June it was recorded all three *Bataillone* of SS-Pz.Gren.Rgt. 25 consumed 120 8cm mortar rounds, 210 15cm *I.G.* rounds, and 200 7.5cm *I.G.* rounds.[12]

Most of the Panzer IV *Kompanien* stayed near the final positions they had occupied at the close of 7 June fighting, apart from some manoeuvring to emplace themselves in the best ambush positions or out of sight of the enemy and its artillery spotters in the way of the RA and RCA FOO teams. Some reinforcement of these *Kompanien* did occur on 8 June, as tanks that had not arrived in time for combat on 7 June due to breakdowns or other causes rolled into the Caen area. As a result, the tank strength of the *II. Abt./SS-Pz.Rgt. 12* grew by the evening of 8 June, and that night 67 Panzer IVs were recorded as on strength. This would be the maximum strength of the *Abteilung* during its time in Normandy. But because of combat, repairs and tanks still arriving in the battlefield, just a small number of tanks were reported serviceable for all five *Kompanien*.

II. Abt./SS-Pz.Rgt. 12 total Panzer IV losses and operational tanks up to nightfall on 8 June 1944[13]

	Total losses up to 8 June 1944	Operational tanks on 8 June 1944
Abteilung Stab	—	3 Panzer IVs
5. Kompanie	3 Panzer IVs	6 Panzer IVs
6. Kompanie	4 Panzer IVs	6 Panzer IVs
7. Kompanie	4 Panzer IVs	—
8. Kompanie	1 Panzer IV	5 Panzer IVs
9. Kompanie	—	10 Panzer IVs

The situation regarding the number of unserviceable tanks due to mechanical breakdown and tanks under repair from battle damage reflects the impact of the combat on 7 June and the long distance covered in the march to Caen. Those Panzer IVs which were still en route to the *Abteilung*, or under repair, are shown in the following table.

Panzer IVs of *II. Abt./SS-Pz.Rgt. 12* under repair or in transit from repair or route march locations on 8 June 1944

	Panzer IVs in transit or in repair
Abteilung Stab	—
5. Kompanie	—
6. Kompanie	7 Panzer IVs
7. Kompanie	13 Panzer IVs
8. Kompanie	11 Panzer IVs
9. Kompanie	6 Panzer IVs

Relief in the way of a short break from the front-line deployment arrived on 8 June for the *5.* and *6. Kompanien* elements that were still deployed forward following the combat on 7 June with the aforementioned arrival of the Panthers of *3. Kp./SS-Pz. Rgt. 12*. These Panthers, under command of the ill-fated *Heer Hauptmann* Lüdemann, who would go on to suffer a terrible defeat on 9 June near Norrey-en-Bessin, took up readiness positions near Authie and were immediately subject to harassing RCA artillery fire. Luckily, only Panther '337' of *Uscha*. Alois Morawetz suffered slight damage. A FOO team in a camouflaged Bren Gun Carrier within Canadian lines to the north near Les Buissons had observed the arrival of the Panthers and taken them under fire.[14]

9 June 1944 was a day of heavy action for the *II. Abt./SS-Pz.Rgt. 12*, and this action has historically been largely ignored by Canadian historians, as the focus of their accounts lies with the destruction of the *3. Kp./SS-Pz.Rgt. 12* Panther

tanks near Norrey-en-Bessin. Holding the line south of the 9th Canadian Infantry Brigade of the 3rd Canadian Infantry Division, the Panzer IV tanks of *II. Abt./ SS-Pz.Rgt. 12* were tasked on this date to act as a quick reaction anti-tank force and were arranged defensively as follows. The depleted *7. Kp./SS-Pz.Rgt. 12*, with only four operational tanks at the start of the day, was deployed north of Gruchy. Also facing the 9th Canadian Infantry Brigade was the *5. Kompanie*. Equally weak, it was redeployed north of Buron in the morning with eight (though the author believes it was actually six) Panzer IVs. The *6. Kompanie*, also near half strength, was redeployed north-west of Authie with nine tanks. As the numbers indicate, the *Abteilung* had taken losses, and while some vehicles were under repair, the capability of the Panzer IV *Kompanien* to engage in extensive armoured battles and carry out effective counterattacks had been sharply reduced.[15]

The infantry positions of *SS-Pz.Gren.Rgt. 25* on this date were still static, and the *SS-Panzergrenadiere* took time when not under artillery fire to work to improve their positions.

On 9 June extremely heavy artillery fire was recorded at times by all German units in the front-line north of Caen.[16] This artillery fire took the form of light harassing fire that went on for long periods and also surprise artillery concentrations on observed German positions. Air activity over the front of *SS-Pz.Gren.Rgt. 25* continued to be heavy, and strong Jabo attacks were recorded as having occurred during the day. By 1100 hours on 9 June, the *1.* and *3. Batterien* of *SS-Flak Abt. 12* were pushed forward in anti-tank roles with their 8.8cm Flak guns, and German newsreel footage of the *Hitlerjugend* in the days following the 7 June fighting shows an 8.8cm Flak artillery piece firing at Canadian or British positions in the distance.[17] There appears to have been little to no Allied air activity on 9 June, the *Batterien* of *SS-Flak.Abt. 12* recording little in the way of ammunition expenditure.[18]

On 9 June, tank firefights with Canadian armour and anti-tank guns began during mid-morning, when the Panzer IVs of *5. Kompanie* knocked out two Canadian anti-tank guns. At 1100 hours, the Panzer IV tank commanders, using their binoculars, observed a force of roughly 13 Fort Garry Horse (10th Canadian Armoured Regiment) Canadian Shermans emerge from Les Buissons, and begin to advance south-west on Vieux Cairon, the tanks moving without infantry support. *Hitlerjugend* divisional historian Hubert Meyer states the tanks passed in sight of the positions of *II. Btl./SS-Pz.Gren.Rgt. 25* near and around Galmache, and the Pak 40 7.5cm anti-tank guns in this area immediately opened fire at long range. He states these guns, which had proven deadly during the initial part of the 7 June fighting, were again very effective. Six Shermans were reported immediately knocked out, and hits on others were recorded, some tanks careening wildly on the battlefield to escape back to Les Buissons.[19] The *Kriegstagebuch* of *II. Abt./SS-Pz.Rgt. 12* states five Shermans were knocked out, and it is likely the Panzer IVs near Buron in camouflaged ambush positions helped knock out some of these tanks. Meanwhile, the artillery fire from the RA and RCA continued unabated. A *7. Kompanie* Panzer IV of *Ustuf.* Zick was knocked out by a hit to the driver's hatch, the crew being badly wounded. A company-level attack by the Stormont, Dundas and Glengarry Highlanders, aimed at Vieux Cairon in order to neutralise the German *Artillerie* spotters located there, was forced back to Les Buissons. Canadian accounts state a *Batterie* of German 8.8cm guns was present in the village, but research for this book has found no German accounts of gun positions there. At 1210 hours an interesting event is logged in the *SS-Pz.Gren.Rgt. 25 Kriegstagebuch* war diary. *Staf.* Meyer was asked to call the divisional *Kommandeur, Brig.Fhr.* Witt. It is next noted in the war diary that four Germans had been found within Rots by a reconnaissance patrol, all shot in head, and some with wounds bandaged from earlier injuries. It is unclear what effect this had on the Germans, or if it influenced future prisoner-of-war executions that took place within the *SS-Pz.Gren.Rgt. 25* sector.[20]

To the north-east of the Buron, on 9 June, the aforementioned assault planned the day previous was made on the village and wooded area of Cambes by the 2nd Battalion, the Royal Ulster Regiment (2 RUR) of the British 185th Infantry Brigade, supported by A and B Squadrons of the 27th Armoured Brigade's East Riding Yeomanry armoured regiment.

Artillery support for this assault to clear Cambes, as stated previously a no man's land fought over by patrols from either side, was provided by an RN warship and RA field and medium regiments. A diversionary artillery bombardment was made by an RA field artillery regiment to try to divert German attention to the Lébisey Wood area to the east, its batteries firing on the wooded area briefly to fool the Germans into thinking that a possible assault would occur there.[21]

The finalised British plan for attack was for the lead A and B Companies of the 2 RUR to advance from the start line near the village of Anisy just to north-west of Cambes, less than three kilometres away via a road running south. After taking the first northern part of the wood, it was planned that C and D Companies were to leapfrog past A and B Companies and capture more of the strung-out wooded area that contained the village and the paved road that wound its way through it.

The tanks of A and B Squadron East Riding Yeomanry, operating to the rear on each flank, were to advance behind the infantry and to support them once they reached the village area. Four AVREs tanks of the Royal Engineers, as well as RA Observation Post (OP) tanks with wooden guns, were to be part of the armoured advance, ready to help destroy bunkers or direct field artillery fire to suppress enemy positions.

As per Commonwealth infantry tactical doctrine, following the successful capture of the objective, it was planned that the 2 RUR Support Company would advance quickly to prepare it for an all-around defence as the infantry companies dug in following combat. Advancing at 1515 hours from Anisy, a series of RA artillery concentrations were fired on the wooded village area to suppress *Waffen-SS* fighting outposts. The British indirect fire support programs were given a five-minute boost by the fire of the British RN Cruiser HMS *Danae*, which fired for five minutes with its powerful six-inch guns on suspected German positions.

Moving through the fields, A and B Companies made rapid progress, quickly covering the ground to the right and left of the farm track from the start line at Anisy to the wooded area of Cambes. There was a ridge 1,000 yards from the wooded border of the village, and despite the infantry companies and their platoons being fully crested in full view of the German defenders to the south and west of the village, they pressed on through German long-range MG-42 machine-gun fire, 8cm mortar bombardments and *Artillerie* defensive fire tasks. However, when the dismounted 2 RUR companies, attacking on a roughly south-eastern axis, reached the crest, German indirect fire became much heavier. The 2 RUR A Company of Major Tighe-Wood took many losses in the way of section and platoon commanders, but pressed on. B Company of the 2 RUR also took many casualties, but it was not stopped either, and pushed forward with continuous momentum.

Despite the heavy fire from the Germans, the first two British infantry companies reached their immediate objectives for the first phase of the attack and consolidated. Behind them the two following companies passed through their positions in the wooded area and between buildings, using the main road through Cambes as their axis. D Company of Captain Montgomery and C Company, led by Major de Longueil, also pushed forward into the southern portions of Cambes. It is clear from the 2 RUR war diary entries that while the Germans had the village's wooded area and its approaches under fire on the late afternoon of 9 June, there was not even a small *SS-Panzergrenadiere* presence in the village, allowing the British troops to advance quickly. This was part of the Germans' defensive plan.

Once the British were in the village, German artillery fire intensified once again, with airbursts occurring due to mortar and artillery rounds hitting trees and exploding in the air. This fire was very effective, causing heavy casualties that included the commanding officer of the 33rd Field Regiment, RA, who was forward acting as a FOO. It also killed Major D. M. Brooke, a 113/114th Field Battery commander in the same regiment and the nephew of the British Chief of the Imperial General Staff, General Sir Alan Brooke. A mounted FOO officer operating with one of the East Riding Yeomanry squadrons was also killed when he attempted to drive his RA OP Sherman tank with its wooden main gun into Cambes down the main street, it being hit by anti-tank fire from La Bijude. The four-tank strong troop of Royal Engineer AVRE vehicles, also moving into Cambes down the main route to engage and destroy any fortified buildings or bunkers the 2 RUR companies may have encountered, was knocked out in the same fashion as the RA OP tank. One by one its vehicles were destroyed, either by direct or indirect artillery fire.[22]

The indirect fire was provided by the *Batterien* of the *III. Abt./SS-Pz.Art.Rgt. 12* and the attached mortars of the two *SS-Panzergrenadiere Bataillone* dug in south and slightly west of Cambes.[23] This was not a short bombardment, but a planned defensive strategy by *SS-Pz.Gren.Rgt. 25*, using the indirect assets of *I.* and *II. Btl./ SS-Pz.Gren.Rgt. 25* and the *Artillerie Batterien* supporting the regiment. With the large British assault force within the planned kill zone, the maximum fire that the Germans could muster was laid down on them for the better part of five hours, inflicting heavy casualties.

In this period, 2 RUR suffered at total of 193 casualties, with 44 of these being killed.[24] It is unclear how many East Riding Yeomanry (ERY) tanks with A and B Squadrons were lost as total write-offs, but it was a significant number. The *Waffen-SS* were not the only ones firing on the British advance into Cambes. The tanks of *Pz.Rgt. 22* of the *21. Pz.Div.* as well as other anti-tank assets of the same division fired on the British infantry and tanks from east of the D7 paved road into Caen. These tanks had observed a small group of British armour at roughly 1600 hours, and by firing intensively at it, managed to knock out two tanks. Once the larger battalion-level British attack aimed at Cambes went in, the tanks of the ERY squadrons supporting it were engaged heavily once again by the tanks of *Pz.Rgt. 22*, firing from La Bijude in ambush positions. The Panzer IV crews reportedly managed to knock out 15 British tanks.

The Shermans of the two ERY squadrons were also visible to the *SS-Pz.Rgt. 12* Panzer IV tanks, watching the fields north of Cambes from the south-west. These tanks were from the *8.* and *9. Kompanien*, and were ready to fire in ambush positions. During the afternoon and evening, these tanks fired intensively on what British troops and armour they could observe. In the sector of *8. Kompanie*, one Sherman was reported immobilised by Panzer IV fire. In the same firefight, *9. Kompanie* tanks reportedly knocked out three Shermans and three British anti-tank guns that were being brought forward to Cambes, hit by their fire from the south-west.

It is unclear what German casualties were suffered this day, and if any German *Waffen-SS* units outside of minor forward outposts were destroyed by the British. One prominent loss that did occur was due to long-range British artillery fire. In La Folie, south of La Bijude, the *Kompanie-Chef* of *7. Kp./SS-Pz.Rgt. 12*, *Ostuf.* John, was killed by a British RA artillery shell as he climbed out of his Panzer IV.[25]

In British accounts of their push into Cambes, no mentions of prisoners are made. It does appear that many anti-tank and Flak gun crews also opened fire at British armour from long range, taking advantage of the ability to shoot right down roads that went through Cambes as fields of fire. Later that evening, the 2nd Battalion, King's Own Scottish Borderers (2 KOSB), was brought in to reinforce the eastern flank of the 2 RUR, as a German counterattack was feared by the British 185th Infantry Brigade. This attack never materialised, and the British infantry battalions dug in or continued to improve their positions.

The only close contact recorded by the *Waffen-SS* near Cambes is presented in the *Hitlerjugend* divisional history by Hubert Meyer, which notes that the *16. Kp.(Pionier)/SS-Pz.Gren.Rgt. 25* had a detached *Zug* dug in on the eastern right flank of the *I. Btl./SS-Pz.Gren.Rgt. 25*. Several British tanks manoeuvred close to the trenches of the *SS-Panzerpioniere* and drove into and over the positions of these troops, some minor combat occurring. In close-quarter fighting, a tank was destroyed by a magnetic mine before the British tanks pulled back due to heavy *Pz.Rgt. 22* fire from La Bijude.

To summarise the fighting of 9 June north and north-west of Caen, the town of Cambes was abandoned to the British 3rd Infantry Division's 185th Infantry brigade, but a company-strength assault on Vieux Cairon from Les Buissons by the 9th Canadian Infantry Brigade was beaten off.[26] In both battles, extremely heavy artillery fire was exchanged, causing casualties on both sides, but far more on the Anglo-Canadian side.[27]

The front was solidifying, in defiance of German attempts to maintain the initiative and continue to push their armoured assaults forward on their western flank. As the fighting slowly wound down for the night, preparations were made to march the entire *II. Abt./SS-Pz.Rgt. 12* west 15 kilometres to the Fontenay–Le Pesnel sector in the light of imminent British offensive operations.[28] There it would join the remainder of *SS-Pz.Rgt. 12*, and both *Abteilungen* would fight together. The forces of *SS-Pz.Gren.Rgt. 25* would be left to their own devices if another large Canadian armoured assault was to be pushed forward. Luckily, this never occurred as the fighting was moving west across the Mue. Personnel losses on 9 June for *SS-Pz.Gren.Rgt. 25* totalled 23 killed, 40 wounded and 21 missing, many of these from the fighting in Bretteville-l'Orgueilleuse on 8–9 June.[29]

10 June saw increased activity in the hours of darkness; the *Kriegstagebuch* of *SS-Flak.Abt. 12* records that at 0300 hours there was redeployment of some parts of the *Abteilung*, the *1. Batterie* deploying on either side of the village of Cussy where they were to take up an active anti-tank role with their 8.8cm guns, with two positions established on either side of the village. The *I. Zug* of *4. Batterie* was also redeployed, with new positions just south of Carpiquet airfield. This day brought renewed heavy air and ground activity for the *Abteilung* following the relative uneventfulness of 9 June. 10 June required an early start from *Staf.* Meyer, *Gen.d.Pz. Tr.* von Schweppenburg arriving at 0455 hours in order to view the battlefield from the towers of the Abbaye Notre-Dame d'Ardenne. Still intent on launching a multi-*Panzerdivision* attack, it is unclear if Schweppenburg found the visit to be positive, *Staf.* Meyer likely reporting that his regiment was fully occupied with the defensive duties required for it to hold its ground up to the Mue, even deploying *14. Kp.(Flak)/SS-Pz.Gren.Rgt. 25* into the defences at Authie.[30] All the *Bataillone* of the regiment were heavily involved in building fortifications, *7. Kp./SS-Pz.Gren. Rgt. 25* near Galmanche taking care to not dig in close to the buildings.[31] 1100 hours saw the *2. Batterie* of *SS-Flak.Abt. 12* shoot down a Spitfire, and at the same time forward units of the *Abteilung* in the anti-tank role observed 46 enemy tanks near the front of *III. Btl./SS-Pz.Gren.Rgt. 25* just north of Buron. 1615 hours saw

2. Batterie shoot down a second Spitfire, another successful result of their defensive anti-aircraft fire that day. Ammunition consumption continued to be voracious for the *Abteilung*, with 217 8.8cm shells, 150 3.7cm shells and 3,508 2cm shells being fired.[32]

At the same time as static warfare was setting in on the front of *SS-Pz.Gren.Rgt. 25*, the British Second Army was convinced it would be fighting a huge tank battle soon in the area immediately south of Sword Beach. British Second Army intelligence had informed its commander, General Dempsey, that the German salient north formed by the counterattack of the *SS-Pz.Gren.Rgt. 25* on 7 June towards Sword Beach was a likely jumping-off point for a massive German armoured attack, if one was to be launched in the next few days. The *Luftwaffe* Douvres radar station bunker complex, still besieged at this point, reported hundreds of British tanks, most of them from the aforementioned independent 4th British Armoured Brigade, moving into a concentration area around and just north of Anisy. The *III. Btl./SS-Pz.Gren. Rgt. 25* also observed the tanks, some of them in the vicinity of Vieux Cairon that evening, this resulting in German *Artillerie* fire being called in on them at 2200 hours.[33] Dempsey had directed Lieutenant General Crocker, commander of the British 1st Corps, to be prepared to crush any major German armoured attacks. Henceforth, nearly 400 tanks were concentrated in just a small area in the heights near the Douvres–La Deliverance area, ready to repel any German undertaking. The Allied 21st Army Group commander, General Sir Bernard Montgomery, was quoted in communication with his chief of staff:

> We are very strong now astride the road Caen–Bayeux [road Caen–La Deliverance] about the junction of 3 Div and 3 Canadian Div, and if the enemy attacks he should be seen off. I have 400 tanks.

No kind of German attack would or could be launched at this time, and the materiel and personnel strength of the British 1st Corps in the area was approaching an overwhelming level considering the limited strength of *SS-Pz.Gren.Rgt. 25* and the Panzer IV *Kompanien* still in the area. Worse still for the Germans, the Panzer IV *Kompanien* were planning to depart west to be ready to counter future operations of the British 30th Corps. Soon, all that would be left for an anti-tank defence would be the heavy and light flak guns of *SS-Flak Abt. 12* and the anti-tank guns of the *SS-Panzergrenadiere Kompanien*. With these massive British and Canadian armoured forces in the Anisy area on 10 June, it is interesting to note that had the 3rd Canadian Infantry Division attacked with this armoured support, it is an absolute certainty that all the ground lost on 7 June could have been recaptured in the course of the day. This attack never came, benefitting *SS-Pz.Gren.Rgt. 25* defensively in a way that the divisional *Kommandeur* of the *Hitlerjugend*, *Brig.Fhr.* Witt, never could.

The night of 10/11 June would see intensive patrolling launched after midnight by Brigadier Cunningham's 9th Canadian Infantry Brigade forces. From Les Buissons, the Stormont, Dundas and Glengarry Highlanders would utilise two companies, B and A, to conduct fighting patrols against suspected German forward outposts. B Company patrolled between Les Buissons and Vieux Cairon and swept a series of farm buildings referred to as Le Vey, roughly 1600 meters north of Vieux Cairon. No Germans were found, and this was possibly simply too far north for even the most forward outposts of *SS-Pz.Gren.Rgt. 25*. If it was not, the well-hidden Germans must have let the Canadians, operating in company strength, pass by.[34]

C Company of the Highland Light Infantry of Canada (HLI), led by Major Hodgkins, had a more ambitious undertaking planned on this date. With the attached 18th Field Company, RCE, in support, its three platoons of roughly twenty-five men each were to push into the outskirts of Buron, destroying anything they found. This was a raid rather than a fighting patrol. This expedition proved much more eventful for the Canadian infantry, as near the first buildings of Buron several Germans were encountered and killed, and other German positions engaged. The *III. Btl./SS-Pz. Gren.Rgt. 25* forces in the village forward outpost responded with heavy MG-42 machine-gun and mortar fire. Amazingly, the HLI soldiers returned more or less with their platoons intact, suffering only two wounded.[35]

On 11 June, daylight brought with it heavy aerial activity over the front of *SS-Pz. Gren.Rgt. 25* and the *Batterien* of *SS-Flak Abt. 12* forces which were supporting it with an active anti-aircraft defence. The focus of German and Canadian commanders on this date was on the fighting to the east, centred on Hill 102 and the village of Le Mesnil-Patry. The *Kriegstagebuch* of the *Abteilung* notes the location of the *Abteilung Gefechtsstand* at Verson, 4.5 kilometres south-west of Caen. It is unclear if it moved, as the previous location is unknown to the author. At 0915 hours *1. Batterie* shot down a Spitfire, and at 1032 hours a Mustang was downed by *4. Batterie*. Events at 1555 hours saw what was recorded as a Tomahawk shot down by *1. Batterie*, but this was probably a Typhoon as there were no Tomahawks serving on the Normandy front with the RAF 2nd Tactical Air Force or the USAAF 9th Air Force. Ammunition consumption was again heavy, with 113 8.8cm, 418 3.7cm, and 1,532 2cm shells fired.[36] Help would be arriving in the way of reinforcements for the Flak anti-aircraft battle over Caen to assist the *Hitlerjugend*, these forces being in the way of *Luftwaffe Flak Regiment 39*. This would not be all. Deploying near to the *Batterie* positions of *III. Abt./SS-Pz.Art.Rgt. 12* would be the first elements of *Werfer-Regiment 83*, a *Heer* formation, as well as the *1. Batterie* of *SS-Artillerie Abteilung 101*, the *Korps*-level heavy *Artillerie* unit with its powerful 21cm Mörser 18 mortars.[37]

Following the arrival of darkness on 11 June, both sides north and north-west of Caen settled in for an extended period that would end with the massive Anglo-Canadian Operation *Charnwood* attack on 8 July 1944, which would see *SS-Pz. Gren.Rgt. 25* driven from its positions and the entire northern Caen Bridgehead collapse under Anglo-Canadian pressure.

The first battle of Caen: The defence of Le Mesnil-Patry and Hill 102, 11 June 1944

The fighting on the left flank of the *Hitlerjugend* in June was especially fierce and saw the near destruction of the 6th Canadian Armoured Regiment, the 1st Hussars, during a tank and infantry battle near between Norrey-en-Bessin and Le Mesnil-Patry, and a smaller but no less intense infantry and tank firefight on the divisional boundary with the *Panzer-Lehr*, near Hills 102 and 103. The *Hitlerjugend* had by this stage gone on the defensive, never to attempt to gain the battlefield initiative again, excluding defensive actions and battalion-sized counterattacks during the Normandy campaign.

Moving west to east, the fighting on 11 June in the sector of *SS-Pz.Aüfkl.Abt. 12* and *III. Btl.(Gepanzert)/SS-Pz.Gren.Rgt. 26* saw the British attempt to assault the positions of both high points in order to support a larger push by British 50th Infantry Division forces near Tilley-sur-Seulles to the west. The British would use units of the 69th Infantry Brigade to carry out these assaults.

The day would begin inauspiciously for *SS-Pz.Aüfkl.Abt. 12*, dug in against British forces that were now pouring into the area to its west. The *Abteilung* was intent on protecting the left flank of the *Hitlerjugend* against continuous British operations aimed south, whose main objective was to capture the high ground around Villers Bocage, near 17 kilometres south-west of the former *SS-Pz.Aüfkl.Abt. 12* stronghold of Audrieu. The key to later capturing this town was to first seize the major road hub of Tilly-sur-Seulles to the west, defended by the forces of the finally arrived mass of the *Panzer-Lehr*, who had begun establishing a line during the period 8–9 June. During the morning hours, *Brig.Fhr.* Witt arrived with his entourage of staff officers and bodyguard from the divisional *Gefechtsstand* at Venoix and issued decorations to the reconnaissance soldiers for their military deeds in the last few days fighting. With him was *Stubaf.* Bremer, returning to the front after having received medical treatment for his wounding by heavy British artillery fire, which had occurred after he had the group of Canadian prisoners executed at the château near Audrieu.

Bremer was also reinstalled as *Abteilung Kommandeur* by Witt as part of his visit. His presence was very much needed, as the *Abteilung* had suffered heavy officer and junior leader losses and needed every experienced leader it could get.[1] While *SS-Pz.Aüfkl.Abt. 12* was secure in its positions, it must not be ignored that this was not the role for which it was intended, taking on the defensive task of an infantry *Grenadier-Battalione*. In reality it was a mechanised reconnaissance battalion, and needed to be employed as such, carrying out reconnaissance tasks or light screening roles on the flanks of an armoured attack. As it was, it was holding the line because of the desperate lack of German *Infanterie-Divisionen*, and, like the rest of the *Hitlerjugend*, *21. Pz.Div.*, and *Panzer-Lehr* forces, it was only growing weaker against a powerful enemy that was getting stronger by the moment. *SS-Pz. Aüfkl.Abt. 12* was not a powerful unit and did not have the defensive power of an *SS-Panzergrenadier Bataillon*. Its defensive strongpoints in the hedges near Cristot were sparsely manned, and while the *Abteilung* had some heavy weapons, it could not fight an extended tank battle or withstand a powerful infantry assault supported by artillery and armour. As mentioned previously, late on 8 June the *2. Kp./SS-Pz. Rgt. 12* under *Ostuf.* Gaede arrived with its Panther tanks to strengthen the defences.

The headquarters for the British 69th Infantry Brigade received a visit from the divisional commander of the British 50th Infantry Division, Major General Graham, at roughly 0715 hours. The orders received by the brigade were for it to attack and push further south, clearing out German positions near Brouay and Cristot. As these attacks were going on, forces that had taken St Pierre, defeating elements of *I. Btl. (Gepanzert)/Pz.Gren.Lehr.Rgt. 901* in the process in a bitter battle – which is out of the scope of this book to discuss – were to be relieved.

The commander of the British 69th Infantry Brigade, Brigadier Knox, directed the 6th and 7th Battalions, the Green Howards (6 GH and 7 GH), to carry out attacks on Brouay and Cristot, and Brigadier Cracroft of the British 8th Armoured Brigade directed that the 5th Battalion, the East Yorkshire Regiment (5 EYR), was to relieve the 1st Battalion, the Dorsetshire Regiment (detached from the British 231st Infantry Brigade), who were holding onto the beleaguered height of Hill 103 with the Sherwood Rangers Yeomanry. Only one infantry battalion, the 6 GH, would be provided with tank support from the 4th/7th Royal Dragoon Guards armoured regiment. The 7 GH would not have any tanks in support of their operation to bring the remaining parts of Brouay under British control, specifically the sprawling parts of the village and its wooded area.

The areas near both Cristot and Brouay were very poor tank country, and nothing like the flat, open fields next to Caen that had excellent visibility for long-range tank engagements. The complete opposite was true for the area near Cristot and tanks from both sides nearly drove into each other on occasion during the resulting day's fighting in the wooded areas crisscrossed by bocage hedges that divided one French farmer's fields from the other.

Before the H-Hour specified by Major General Graham arrived, some reconnaissance patrols from either side were sent out with tank support, these encountering each other in the bocage. As a result of these meeting engagements, some casualties were suffered by the *Hitlerjugend*. A later patrol sent to establish contact between the *2. Panzerspähkompanie* and the *4. Aufklärung Kompanie*, both of *SS-Pz.Aüfkl. Abt. 12*, spotted a large British tank assembly area west of the Ferme Les Haut Vents farm. In response, the nearby *2. Kp./SS-Pz.Rgt. 12* was alerted to potential tank attack, driving into ambush positions in order to engage the British at the best possible range in the bocage.[2]

A renewed attack by the British on *SS-Pz.Aüfkl.Abt. 12* began at 1720 hours, and this attack was led by two squadrons of the 4th/7th Royal Dragoon Guards, B Squadron attacking on the left flank and C Squadron attacking on the right. One 6 GH Green Howard company followed each squadron, C Company on the left and B Company on the right, the tanks pushing slowly through the bocage. The terrain itself was broken by hedges, wooded areas and slightly rising and falling terrain. C Squadron managed to push into Cristot itself, but the infantry following the Shermans was forced to ground due to heavy MG-42 fire. German reports on this action speak of the *3.* and *4. Kompanien* of *SS-Pz.Aüfkl.Abt. 12* being overrun by the determination of the British attack. At this time a desperate call was made by the *Abteilung Gefechtsstand* for *Artillerie* fire to be placed on the British stronghold of Hill 103. This did not occur for unknown reasons.[3] The Germans did however fight back against the tanks, with seven being reported knocked out with hand-held infantry anti-tank weapons, and one by a German anti-tank gun at the centre of the village.[4] Once this lead tank of the squadron was knocked out in the village, the rest of the B Squadron tanks decided they could not push further without closer infantry support. On the right flank pushing slightly south of Cristot, C Squadron also reported losing a number of tanks in quick succession due to a *2. Kp./SS-Pz.Rgt. 12* counterattack that developed involving at least a *Zug* of Panthers, these knocking out the Shermans as they crossed an open area west of the village. Due to heavy infantry casualties as a result of *SS-Pz.Aüfkl.Abt. 12* MG-42 fire that came from a machine-gun pit located in the curve of the road leading to Cristot, the 6 GH infantry companies pulled back, followed by the tanks. This withdrawal occurred despite the MG-42 machine-gun position in question being knocked out by 6 GH Company Sergeant Major (CSM) Stanley Hollis of D Company, who had won the Victoria Cross earlier on Gold Beach.[5] At 2000 hours if was reported that groups of the German *Aufklärunger* reconnaissance soldiers, under *Ostuf.* Bucheim, *Ustuf.* Wienecke and *Oscha.* Cargol had done their part to push the British back, and following the British withdrawal, regained their old positions.[6]

The German treatment of prisoners after the battle was very brutal. A 4th/7th Royal Dragoon Guards tank crew that bailed out was captured. All four crew members were rounded up and taken back to a hedge surrounded by trees that was a *Waffen-SS* fighting position, with a Panther tank located nearby. On being marched to the hedge, two crewmen, one of whom was wounded, were executed for failing to keep pace or other unknown reasons. Once in the location, the other two were interrogated by their captor, not for battlefield information on British forces, but as to whether they were Canadian. As this was going on, the *SS-Panzergrenadiere* within the hedge, some wounded themselves, alternatively screamed for the captor of the two British crewmen to shoot them, while at the same time demanding he find out if they were Canadian. Luckily, they survived and were later marched to the rear to join other British prisoners.[7]

Near 2000 hours, a determined German counterattack was launched by the 5. and 8. *Kompanien* of *II. Abt./Pz.Lehr. Rgt. 130*, its Panzer IV tanks pushing near the summit of Hill 103. This attack would not succeed due to anti-tank gun fire from St Pierre and the hill itself, the tanks being forced to withdraw after the death of the *Abteilung Kommandeur*, the German aristocrat *Major* Wilhelm, Prinz von Schönburg-Waldenburg, his Panzer IV turret taking a hit from anti-tank fire. This event was witnessed by the personnel of *SS-Pz.Aüfkl.Abt. 12*, who had been made aware of the impending attack three days before it was due to be executed, and who were not impressed when it failed.[8]

While the 6 GH and its supporting tanks engaged combat with the *SS-Pz. Aüfkl.Abt. 12* and a *Zug* of *2. Kp./SS-Pz.Rgt. 12* from roughly 1830 hours on, it is somewhat unclear when a northern simultaneous supporting attack was made by the 7 GH. In their attack on Brouay from the north, they would have to overcome the *SS-Panzergrenadiere* of *III. Btl.(Gepanzert)/SS-Pz.Gren.Rgt. 26*, which had dug in within the wooded area. Attacking with two companies forward, the 7 GH lead platoons were heavily machine gunned and mortared as they attempted to manoeuvre on and just beyond the Caen–Bayeux railway line. On the left, one company was driven to ground by German defensive fire and forced to withdraw, and the other on the right was pinned down 100 meters south of the rail line for a period before it managed to extricate itself once darkness fell.

Losses from both attacks were fairly light on the German side. Compared to the losses inflicted on German units in the days previous, the *III. Btl./SS-Pz.Gren.Rgt. 26* suffered one killed and four wounded *SS-Panzergrenadiere* in this attack.[9] The losses were far more severe to the south, indicating the determination with which the 6 GH pushed forward their attack with the tank support from the 4th/7th Royal Dragoon Guards. *SS-Pz.Aüfkl.Abt. 12* lost 26 killed in the fighting on 11 June, with a further 16 being wounded and 5 counted as missing. *2. Kp./SS-Pz.Rgt. 12* lost five wounded in the fighting. Due to intensive RA shelling the *Gefechtsstand* of *I. Abt./SS-Pz.Rgt. 12*, and the readiness positions of *5. and 9. Kp./SS-Pz.Rgt. 12*, nearby but not directly involved in the fighting, suffered five wounded and five missing.[10]

British casualties suffered during the 11 June combat with *SS-Pz.Aüfkl.Abt. 12* and *III. Btl.(Gepanzert)/SS-Pz.Gren.Rgt. 26* were heavy, with 6 GH suffering a total 250 casualties on this date.[11] Within the ranks of the 6 GH, the company commanders of A and C Companies were killed, and the deputy commander of B Company also fell. The brief action at Brouay to the north would cost the 7 GH 27 killed, 30 wounded and 10 missing.[12] While it is unclear to the author how his death occurred, the battalion commander of 5 EYR also was a casualty in the fighting as this battalion moved up to strengthen the defence of Hill 103. This may have been from German artillery fire placed in support of the *II. Abt./Pz.Lehr. Rgt. 130* attack.[13] At least 12 Shermans were lost from the 4th/7th Royal Dragoon Guards in the fighting.

Moving on to action on the 7th Canadian Infantry Brigade front, at 0400 hours on the morning of 11 June, the commanding officer of the 1st Hussars (6th Canadian Armoured Regiment), Lieutenant Colonel Colwell, returned to the regimental headquarters of his armoured regiment with news that an attack on German positions to the south was to occur within 24 hours, and it would involve the regiment. As this was plenty of time to prepare, the squadrons continued with their daily schedule of maintenance in their harbours. All the action that was anticipated by the officers of the 1st Hussars for the immediate future was possibly providing tank support for the regiments of the 8th Canadian Infantry Brigade. The regiment had been briefed on the neighbouring operation of the 46 Royal Marine Commando (46 RMC) and the Fort Garry Horse to the east to clear the villages along the Mue, but the 1st Hussars were not to be involved. This operation was slated to commence that morning and will be discussed in detail in the next chapter. The upcoming operation for the 1st Hussars, as briefed to Lieutenant Colonel Colwell, was one that would see the regiment attack south and west of the 7th Canadian Infantry Brigade front lines. It was hoped this push would see the capture of the village of Le Mesnil-Patry and the high ground near the town of Cheux, immediately south of Norrey-en-Bessin.

On 10 June, B Squadron of the 1st Hussars had been reconstituted at the village of Cairon, with 20 new and repaired Shermans with replacement crews arriving courtesy of the 25th Canadian Armoured Delivery Regiment. Many of these new Canadian Armoured Corps (CAC) personnel were discovered to lack appropriate training, and some were sent back to the rear echelons. Including repaired tanks, this new armoured vehicle delivery brought the strength of the regiment up to 76 tanks, 15 vehicles overstrength. It is unknown how many of these tanks were the 17-pounder equipped Fireflies and 37mm-gunned Stuart light tanks intended for the 1st Hussars recce troop.

By 0800 hours, urgent news reached the 2nd Canadian Armoured Brigade that the situation had radically changed; the attack due to be carried to be carried out by the 1st Hussars which had been planned for 12 June was to be moved up, as operations to the west involving the British 30th Corps demanded that pressure be applied immediately on the Germans. It was hoped this attack would support the unfolding British operations to the west, where the British 30th Corps' 7th Armoured

Division and 50th Infantry Division were attacking elements of the *Panzer-Lehr* near Tilly-sur-Seulles. These formations were attacking on a broad front using very liberal amounts of armour, infantry and artillery to batter their way forward in the bocage country west of the Canadian front. These were the first moves of the British 30th Corps's Operation *Petch*, which would eventually be referred to historically as the battle of Villers-Bocage. The relentless British attacks would eventually pierce the lines of weak German *352. Infanterie-Division* remnants and outflank elements of the *Panzer-Lehr*, creating a crisis that German armoured reserves would be forced to deploy to resolve. This battle will be discussed in the second volume of this series.

British Second Army Commander General Sir Miles Dempsey felt that the 12 June operation could help draw German reserves away from Tilly, and ruthlessly directed the 3rd Canadian Infantry Division to push the operation forward, demanding that an attack begin no later than 1300 hours. Inexplicably, during the next hours, no warning order reached the 1st Hussars or their designated infantry support for this operation, the Queen's Own Rifles of Canada (QORC). Also, the decision was also taken at this time, either by the 2nd Canadian Armoured Brigade Commander Brigadier Wyman, or the Commander, Royal Artillery (CRA) for the 3rd Canadian Infantry Division, Brigadier Todd, that artillery support for the attack would not be provided due to the haste of the operations and the lack of planning time.

Continuing this chaotic planning cycle, and ignoring the time needed by both units to issue orders for the actual attack, the orders group delivered by the 2nd Canadian Armoured Brigade headquarters would occur at 1100 hours and take roughly an hour. This would allow for only two hours for the battalion, company and squadron commanders to carry out their own planning, recces and orders groups. This was far too short a time for the Canadian infantry and armoured officers involved. There was not even time to properly coordinate with the 7th Canadian Infantry Brigade, their defensive positions including a minefield the Hussar tanks would have to pass through to attack their objective. To top off this impossible situation, during the final orders group for the 1st Hussar squadron commanders, it was realised the unit they had to pass through, 1st Battalion, the Regina Rifle Regiment (RRR), knew nothing about the upcoming operation.

As detailed in the 2nd Canadian Armoured Brigade orders group held at 1100 hours and attended by the armoured and infantry regimental commanders, the attack was to push south with its vanguard being the 1st Hussars B Squadron, with D Company of the Queen's Own Rifles of Canada (QORC) riding on the rear engine decks of the Shermans. Advancing directly behind the Shermans of B Squadron, C Squadron of the 1st Hussars was to push slightly west and secure the right flank of the advance as B Squadron advanced forward to the high ground near Cheux, Hill 100.[14] A Squadron of the 1st Hussars, with the headquarters troop attached, was to follow in reserve. Following the armoured charge forward and the hoped-for destruction of the German infantry strongpoints, the dismounted A, B and C companies of the QORC would fight their way forward with A Squadron of the 1st Hussars, the Hussar B and C Squadrons now forming a 'firm base' at Le Mesnil-Patry and the high ground next to it to fight off any German countermoves.

Disturbingly, it appears from the war diary entries and first-hand accounts that the recce troop of the 1st Hussars, with its 11 Stuart light tanks, was not involved in any kind of recce role or assigned any task during the operation. Also, it must be observed that not one forward observation officer (FOO), either in an RCA OP Sherman or Bren gun carrier, would accompany the advance, and no artillery creeping barrage or concentrations on German positions had been planned. It is also unclear if any defensive fire (DF) fire tasks had been planned by the field regiments or if the RCA chain of the command within the 3rd Canadian Infantry Division had been alerted or included in the planning. In the definitive history of the Royal Artillery and Royal Canadian Regiment of Artillery in Normandy, Will Townend and Frank Baldwin's *Gunners in Normandy*, there is little to no information given on this significant Canadian armoured operation. It is unclear if any indirect fire, other than that from the RRR or QORC mortar platoons, was given to support advance of the entire 1st Hussars armoured regiment, which fielded roughly 60 tanks on 11 June, the lead squadron carrying an infantry company reported to be 105-men strong.[15] The remainder of the dismounted QORC companies were slated to follow in the wake of the tanks on foot to consolidate with the tank squadrons in Le Mesnil-Patry after they had charged forward.

The German defensive front's left flank consisted of positions filled by the *Kompanien* of the *SS-Pz.Pio.Btl. 12* east of Le Mesnil-Patry and within the village itself. These positions were part of the larger *III. Btl.(Gepanzert)* and *II. Btl./SS-Pz. Gren.Rgt. 26* positions that formed the left flank of the *Hitlerjugend*. This flank was triangular in nature due to British advances to the west. It ran from Le Mesnil-Patry in the east to the village of Brouay in the north, then south to Cristot. To the west and just south of Hill 103, which had fallen to the British 8th Armoured Brigade on 8 June, were the most eastern units of the *Panzer-Lehr*, the *Bataillone* of both *Pz.Gren.Lehr.Rgt. 901* and *902*.

Very disturbingly, this amount of combat power deployed to achieve the 2nd Canadian Armoured Brigade's objective of the high ground south of Cheux was not anything near what was needed to effectively attack and eradicate German resistance south of Norrey-en-Bessin. While the entire 1st Hussars armoured regiment was to take part in the operation, very little in the way of infantry, artillery or combat engineer support was attached to support the attacking Canadian Shermans. Infantry combat power would definitely be needed to support the tanks and to hold what ground was to be captured. As reported by Major Tubb of C Company of the RRR, the only indirect fire in support of the operation he witnessed was the QORC mortar platoon, which set up its mortars next the C Company RRR headquarters, and would fire intensively to attempt to support the attack.[16]

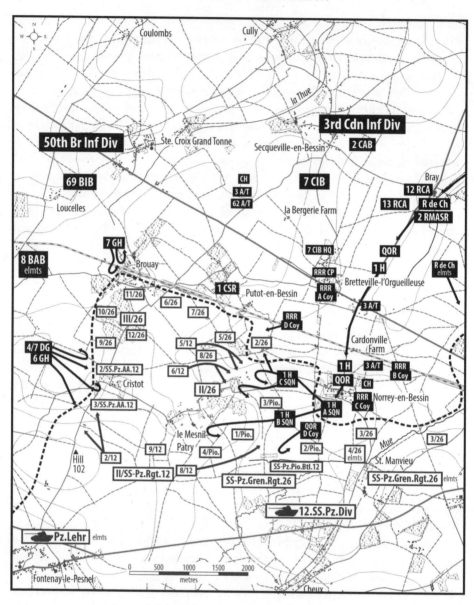

11 June attack on Le Mesnil-Patry. (Map by Mike Bechthold)

As illustrated by the above map, showing the major events for the fighting near Le Mesnil-Patry, the German *SS-Pz.Pio.Btl. 12* positions east of the village were arranged in depth with the *Bataillone Gefechtsstand* near Hill 63. The *SS-Panzerpioniere* were at this stage combat experienced, and the *Bataillone* under *Stubaf.* Müller had worked hard to create a strong defensive position with a number of bunkers. The *SS-Panzerpioniere* were well equipped with *Panzerschreck* infantry anti-tank weapons, as well as all other *Infanterie* weapons found within a German *Panzergrenadier Bataillon*. Its officers were experienced in repelling tank attacks given their past combat in the USSR, and the *SS-Panzerpioniere* were ordered to let the tanks past before engaging the infantry during an enemy attack. While some German positions were in open fields, others were near wooded areas and in ditches next to farming tracks used by tractors and horse drawn wagons in peacetime. All were extensively camouflaged, and the *Kompanien* headquarters positions were well entrenched. To the rear of the *Bataillone* position a small number of Pak 40 7.5cm anti-tank guns were emplaced, as well as 8cm mortars, 7.5cm *l.I.G.* and 15cm *s.I.G.* howitzers from the *Schwere Kompanien* of *I.* and *II. Btl./SS-Pz.Gren.Rgt. 26* and *SS-Pz.Pio.Btl. 12*. A number of MG-42 positions were sited forward and in depth within trenches in the fields and within hedgerows.

Near noon on 11 June the German positions in the village of Le Mesnil-Patry to the south-west of Norrey-en-Bessin were on the alert. Tank and vehicle noise had been noticed, and the *Nachrichten* signal *Zug* of *SS-Pz.Gren.Rgt. 26* had alerted all regimental units as well as *SS-Pz.Pio.Btl. 12* that an Anglo-Canadian operation coming out of Bretteville-l'Orgueilleuse was imminent. On 8 June near Brouay, a Canadian Bren Gun Carrier had been knocked out, and from it the Germans had retrieved maps marked with code words for towns, village, routes and geographical features such a rivers and hills. For an unknown reason, in the period 7–11 June these code words, issued 'in clear' during Canadian radio transmissions, had amazingly continued to be used. This in no small part helped alert the Germans defending the area from south of Norrey-en-Bessin to Le Mesnil-Patry.[17]

The approach march of the 1st Hussar tank squadrons to their start line was indicative of the hopeless position which the headquarters of the 2nd Canadian Armoured Brigade had put the 1st Hussar Commanding Officer Lieutenant Colonel Colwell in, and illustrated the lack of detailed planning for the operation. Leaving the town of Bretteville-l'Orgueilleuse, the tank squadrons then proceeded in column, creating clouds of dust on the road over the rail tracks, past the Cardonville Flax Factory and into Norrey-en-Bessin. The tanks, nose to tail, were forced to drive on one track into the village due to the heavy anti-tank minefield laid by the RRR and the Royal Canadian Engineer (RCE) field companies on the ground between Bretteville-l'Orgueilleuse and Norrey-en-Bessin, as well as to steer around a knocked-out Panther tank in the area south of the first town.

Thankfully, there was no sustained German artillery fire, and as previous stated, the *Batterien* of the *Pz.Art.Rgt. 130* of the *Panzer Lehr* and *SS-Pz.Art.Rgt. 12* of the *Hitlerjugend* were now down to their last shells and suffering from a severe ammunition shortage due to the unexpected levels of consumption in the Normandy fighting up to this point.

Once in Norrey-en-Bessin, the situation became worse for the Canadians. There were over 60 Shermans involved in the move, in a column stretching from Bretteville-l'Orgueilleuse to the railway line, with B Squadron of the 1st Hussars carrying the three platoons of D Company of the QORC on their engine decks. This spectacle was observed by the bewildered Canadian RRR C Company members in their trenches and nearby anti-tank gun crews. Haltingly, the column entered the village, forming a perfect target for *Luftwaffe* ground attack aircraft or a German artillery bombardment. Luckily, no German aircraft were able to penetrate the airspace west of Caen at this time, and the 1st Hussars avoided any kind of aerial attack.

A witness to the 1st Hussar and QORC infantry column traversing Norrey-en-Bessin was Major Tubb, RRR C Company commander and the victor of the past day's defensive battles. The crossroads at the centre of the village contained a 90-degree turn with stone buildings surrounding it. The columns of B and then C Squadron tanks, with infantry riding on the first group, had to make a hard right turn to then exit the village in order to get through a gap in the western anti-tank minefield which had been laid by C Company and the RCE engineers in the previous days to defend against further German armoured incursions.

As the column was in the midst of the village, German artillery and mortar fire finally rained down, destroying several buildings. What was delivered in the way of German indirect fire consisted of a 10-minute concentration of field artillery fire from *II. Abt./SS-Pz.Art.Rgt. 12* and 8cm mortar rounds from the *SS-Panzergrenadiere Schwere Kompanien* to the immediate south.[18] This surprise bombardment startled the Sherman drivers and several tanks crashed into buildings and walls, one tragically crushing a Queen's Own soldier against a wall as the rear hull of a Sherman tank swung around attempting to make the turn.[19] The artillery and mortar fire of the Germans also hit the building holding the company stores of the RRR C Company, with food, fuel and ammunition being destroyed in the fire that resulted.[20] The noisiness of the tanks and the dust which they generated in the summer heat would have now been noticed by the Germans, and reports would have also been passed to the regiment *Gefechtsstand* of *SS-Pz.Rgt. 26* at Cheux. With this many vehicles involved, halts were inevitable, and the resulting traffic jam on the roads around Bretteville-l'Orgueilleuse had slowed the attack down, allowing the alerted Germans to prepare defensively.

And the worst was yet to come. Giving the Germans even more warning, the tanks had to negotiate a small opening in the western Canadian minefield, part of a larger one laid in front of Norrey-en-Bessin in a semi-circular pattern. This made it difficult to exit the town, badly impairing the ability of the 1st Hussars to deploy their squadrons for the attack on their start line, which was the western edge of Norrey-en-Bessin.

The RRR C Company of Major Tubb, deployed in and around the village with attached RCA forward observers and anti-tank gun crews, could do nothing to help and had not been notified of the armoured column going right through their positions. Tubb reportedly first found out about it after returning from lunch with the RRR battalion commander and seeing the columns of tanks with mounted infantry coming out of Bretteville-l'Orgueilleuse. The RRR riflemen and NCOs could only shout information about the enemy to the lead tank commander in B Squadron of the 1st Hussars and the Queen's Own platoon and section commanders on the decks of the tanks as they passed. What of the QORC Support Company? Some of it by this time had entered Norrey-en-Bessin, and the mortar platoon commander, on his own initiative, began immediately firing from a position in the north-west of the town into the wheat fields to the west of the town with its 3-inch mortars, in an attempt to provide some basic fire support.[21]

The 11 June was a bright summer day and the fields of wheat south, in the vicinity of Le Mesnil-Patry, appeared open. Moving past the western exit from Norrey-en-Bessin through the minefields, the B Squadron tanks shook out into troop formation and approached the lines of *SS-Pz.Pio.Btl. 12* on their immediate left as they pushed forward, with more positions manned by personnel from *II. Btl./SS-Pz.Gren.Rgt. 26* to the west. The axis of attack for the B Squadron tanks was the road from Norrey-en-Bessin to Le Mesnil-Patry. On making contact with the German positions, this event being marked by the tank commanders seeing Germans huddled in trenches and within fields as the tanks advanced at speed, the Canadian armour immediately opened fire.

The response to this fire was a fusillade of MG-42 and Pak 40 7.5cm anti-tank gun fire, which began to knock out and destroy Shermans and literally shoot the QORC infantry off the rear decks in a Canadian reenactment of the German attack on Bretteville-l'Orgueilleuse on the night of 8/9 June. While the B Squadron tanks began to aggressively destroy the fighting positions of the *SS-Panzerpioniere*, they also suffered their first losses due to long range anti-tank gun fire.[22] The 7.5cm Pak 40 anti-tank guns were from the *Schwere Kompanien* of *II. Btl./SS-Pz.Gren.Rgt. 26* and *SS-Pz.Pio.Btl. 12*, and were engaging the Canadian tanks from camouflaged positions.[23]

Without armoured support, the *Waffen-SS* began to be overwhelmed by the tank assault, the Shermans traversing their tracks on their dugouts and firing point blank into their bunkers and trenches. While the German *Panzerfaust* infantry anti-tank weapon was not yet available in large numbers on the Normandy front in June, the *Panzerschreck*, or 'tank terror', a German version of the ubiquitous US 'Bazooka', encountered in 1943, was. The Germans used this as well as magnetic mines to destroy or attempt to disable the 1st Hussars' Shermans overrunning their positions. While the German *SS-Panzerpioniere* and *SS-Panzergrenadiere* bravely attempted to destroy the tanks, these were acts of desperation. There was no escape from the rampaging effect of the coaxial, hull and main 75mm guns of a full squadron of Shermans firing at once.[24]

At approximately 1645 hours, the *Kriegstagebuch* entry for *II. Abt./SS-Pz.Rgt. 12* records reports coming in of an Allied tank attack with accompanying infantry on the positions of *II. Btl./SS-Pz.Gren.Rgt. 26* and *SS-Pz.Pio.Btl. 12*. The entire Panzer IV *Abteilung* was alerted, and by 1700 hours the *Kriegstagebuch* entry for 11 June states all four *Kompanien* readied their Panzer IVs for action and moved forward. There were two group of German tanks involved in the counterattack by *II. Abt./ SS-Pz.Rgt. 12*. *Stubaf.* Prinz directed that *5.* and *6. Kompanien* were to attack directly east as a northern group, skirting Le Saullets and its wooded orchard areas to the north. Supporting this attack, the *8.* and *9. Kompanien* were to attack directly east as well as in part of a southern group, forming a second pincer. It was planned that these two pincers were to converge, destroying the Canadian armoured thrust and driving any remnants back to Norrey-en-Bessin, which was exactly what occurred.

The Panzer IVs, moving independently in *Züge* groupings, only came into contact with B Squadron of the Hussars initially, as C Squadron would only enter the battlefield later. All the B Squadron vehicles were caught manoeuvring within the *Waffen-SS* bunker line in the fields, firing into the German fighting positions. The positions of the two *Waffen-SS Bataillone* were seemingly engulfed with Allied tanks, these vehicles driving about literally on top of the German positions.

As the German tanks closed in, the *8.* and *9. Kompanien* appear to have been engaged in combat before the other two *Kompanien*, and inflicted heavy losses on the 1st Hussars. Six Shermans were destroyed in quick succession, the B Squadron commanders' tank of Captain Harrison being one of those lost.

Ignoring the vulnerability of their vehicles in comparison to the heavier Panther tanks in the *I. Abteilung*, the *8. Kompanie* of *II. Abt./SS-Pz.Rgt. 12* under *Ostuf.* Seigel appears to have been in the thick of the fighting, and paid the price, with its three Panzer IVs being lost after they pushed too close to Norrey. This *Kompanie* did however destroy 10 Shermans and what it recorded as four General Lees. In this battle, there were no M3 Grants, the British Army designation for the M3 General Lee, in action with Canadian forces, and it is unclear to the author what these tanks were. The *9. Kompanie* of *II. Abt./SS-Pz.Rgt. 12* was also in the thick of the combat, its crews destroying seven Shermans for the loss of one Panzer IV.[25]

Following some initial success earlier in the battle, the *Kompanie-Chef* Panzer IV of *Ostuf.* Hans Seigel tank was destroyed by Canadian tank fire. The below account of *Ostuf.* Jeran, an *8. Kompanie* Panzer IV commander present in the battle, relates the unfortunate turn of events, as originally presented within the Hubert Meyer divisional history. His account reflects the speed at which tanks crews on both sides of the conflict had to react in order to survive in the kill or be killed environment of a tank battle at close quarters:

> As we rolled forward, and when we halted for an observation stop, I recognized from the agitated gestures of some *Grenadiere* [*SS-Panzergrenadiere*] who were pointing in the direction of the enemy with their spades that acute danger was facing us. 'Ready for action!' On this order, the

hatches for the three Panzers closed as by themselves. The gun barrels were wound down to firing elevation. Anti-tank shells were loaded on the move. A hedge was still obstructing our vision of the enemy on the left. When the hedge suddenly disappeared and the lead Panzer was already in the midst of our own infantry, several Shermans were spotted rolling at a dangerous distance toward us through the orchard of a farm. We had driven right in front of their barrels and were showing them our vulnerable flanks. 'Enemy tanks from the left – 9 o'clock-200 – open fire!' This was all the *Chef* of the 8. [*Kompanie*], who was also the *Kommandant* of the point Panzer, could do. But nothing else was required. The months-long drills and battle experience of the crews had now proved themselves. The driver jerked the Panzer IV to the left, bringing it into firing position. Even before the fighting compartment ventilation fan, crucial to the survival of the crew, got to full speed, the closest enemy tank had been hit. Within a minute or so, four or five Shermans were burning. Only the last one, which had worked its way to 100 meters on the far left, brought sweat to the commander's brow. It had only just been spotted as it was already swinging its turret toward us. 'Enemy tanks, hard left – 10 o'clock – 100.' Barrel was turning toward barrel, muzzle against muzzle. Looking through the guns sights, they [the barrel muzzle brakes] were now close enough to touch. For another blink of an eye, the gunners may have aimed the cross hairs of the gun sights at each other. Then came a blow, a flash of fire from the breech of the gun, the cartridge dropped into the sack, and the enemy tank exploded!

Only now could the other two Panzer [IVs] close in. They had stood behind the hedge, unable to observe what had happened right before our eyes. Even before our infantry was ready to storm ahead, the three Panzers drove past the burning tanks and between the fruit trees to our own main line of resistance. As we were advancing, the command Panzer IV knocked out two more Shermans from a distance of 1,200 meters. They had tried to get away.

The enemy was retreating and in considerable confusion. It was important to take advantage of their situation. The other two Panzers were ordered to follow, staggered to the left rear, and to push through a field of wheat at full speed without stopping. Once they reached a bordering row of trees and a hedge, 1,600 meters away, they were to halt. During the advance, the command Panzer came under anti-tank fire from a line of trees on the right. The command Panzer informed the crew through the throat microphone: 'Pak fire from the right!' Once again, the driver reacted immediately. He pulled the Panzer around into firing position. And now a duel of fire started. After five exchanges, our Panzer took fire from a second or even third anti-tank gun [these were actually 1st Hussar tanks]. The crew bailed out, regrettably, without the radio operator who had fallen victim to the hit on the right front. The Panzer was in flames, and fire from all kinds of weapons covered the spot where it had been knocked out. The two other tanks had also stopped to fire and had been hit. They were stuck approximately 800 meters to the rear.[26]

In this engagement, the German tanks had followed the now-withdrawing 1st Hussars tanks and what was left of the QORC infantry northward, and had made contact with A Squadron 1st Hussar tanks at virtually the entrance to Norrey-en-Bessin. On seeing the carnage ahead, the A Squadron officer commanding had been directed to establish a defensive position in front of the village to halt a German counterattack if one appeared. These tanks had knocked out the 8. *Kompanie* Panzer IVs once they entered their kill zone. More cautious, the remaining *Kompanien* of II. Abt./SS-Pz. Rgt. 12 had suffered light losses and inflicted heavy casualties on Canadian forces. Regardless of the light German losses, all tanks were desperately needed by *II. Abt./ SS-Pz.Rgt. 12*, as no new ones were scheduled to arrive at the front for the *Abteilung*. This was a situation sharply in contrast to the 1st Hussars, who had received 20 replacement tanks and new crews on 10 June, the day previous to this battle and four days after the losses of D-Day had occurred, reflecting the tremendous speed of tank replacement in the British Commonwealth armies by 1944.

C Squadron of the 1st Hussars was still traversing Norrey-en-Bessin when the first tanks of B Squadron were exiting the village and shaking out in the fields to the west. During this time German *Artillerie* from the *Batterien* of *II. Abt./SS-Pz. Art.Rgt. 12* and the mortars and 7.5cm and 15cm *Infanterie-Geschütz* howitzers within *SS-Pz.Gren.Rgt. 26* continued their bombardment of the village, creating chaos as some buildings began to collapse due to shellfire. Seeing this occur, the commanding officer of the 1st Hussars, Lieutenant Colonel Colwell, decided to take action. With his command tank to the rear of the column as part of the RHQ regimental headquarters troop, he attempted to bypass Norrey-en-Bessin to the west, through a famer's field. He had only gone about 100 meters when his tank hit a Canadian anti-tank mine. Dismounting from his stricken tank, Colwell returned to the streets of Norrey-en-Bessin, desperately directing traffic to get the tanks onto the battlefield and through the chokepoint.[27] It is unclear if he mounted another tank or stayed in his command tank, but he remained on the regimental and brigade radio nets and still attempted to exert some control over the battle, one that was largely out of his hands once B and C Squadrons drove out of Norrey-en-Bessin.

C Squadron finally escaped Norrey-en-Bessin, and its first tanks immediately came into contact with wounded B Squadron tanks crews on foot and small groups of QORC infantry that were withdrawing back in the direction of Norrey-en-Bessin, these from some of the first tanks to be destroyed by German anti-tank fire. The fields were full of the noise of battle coming from the area dead ahead, as the B Squadron Shermans were still fighting the German infantry and the arriving Panzer IV tanks. It would take an extended period for the tanks of B Squadron to be nearly entirely destroyed, and during the last part of this period, C Squadron made its appearance on the battlefield.[28]

Commanded by Major Marks, the tanks of C Squadron pushed to the immediate north of what was left of B Squadron. Nearly all of these tanks were now flaming wrecks on the battlefield, some even making it into the town of Le Mesnil-Patry before being destroyed. Contact was made with more bunker lines of the German *SS-Panzerpioniere* and *SS-Panzergrenadiere* at roughly 1615 hours.[29] The decks of a small number of C Squadron tanks held the overflow of some QORC platoon sections that could not fit onto the B Squadron tanks. Reporting fire from their right flank, from the immediate north of Le Mesnil-Patry and in the direction of British forces, Lieutenant Colonel Colwell made radio contact with the 2nd Canadian Armoured Brigade headquarters, who advised him not to fire back in this direction as it was assumed this fire was potentially from British armour supporting the 69th Infantry Brigade attack going on near Brouay. What was actually happening was the German *8.* and *9. Kompanien* of *SS-Pz.Rgt. 12* were now advancing from that direction, making firing halts in order to continue the destruction of the Canadian armoured attack.

Orders were immediately passed down to Major Marks to cease fire in this direction as it was assumed that British armour was firing on them in error. Attempting to do his best in an unfortunate series of events that illustrated poor planning and command and control, Major Marks ordered that recognition flags be flown from the tank wireless antennas, he himself even crawling out of the turret to do so. As this was occurring the Panzer IV and Pak 40 7.5cm anti-tank fire intensified, and the first of many C Squadron tanks began to be knocked out, some of them burning immediately.[30] Ironically, Major Marks' C Squadron command tank would be one of the only three to four surviving tanks from C Squadron to manage to make it back to the safety of Norrey-en-Bessin.[31]

An RCA FOO party at the outskirts of Norrey-en-Bessin, not attached to the attacking force but seeing this spectacle unfold, had its wireless set fail at the exact time it was needed, and despite the FOO's best efforts, contact with his parent 12th Field Regiment, RCA, battery could not be established. Though small, this historical evidence shows there were some desperate efforts to attain RCA field artillery support. Seeing his unit in heavy combat from his position in Norrey-en-Bessin, Lieutenant Colonel Colwell did attempt to have further forces committed to the attack, these potentially being the tanks from the Fort Garry Horse (FGH) and the rest of the QORC infantry companies marching forward and not yet in combat.

It was planned that a second QORC company would ride on the tanks to help the 1st Hussar squadrons consolidate on the high ground near Cheux and in Le Mesnil-Patry. A Company, under Major Dalton, was to ride on the decks of the 1st Hussar A Squadron Shermans to get onto the objective. Seeing plumes of smoke from the burning Shermans in the field ahead of him immediately to his west, Dalton ordered his company to dismount as the A Squadron tanks deployed in the front of the village in their aforementioned defensive line. As previously discussed, this squadron had deployed in an attempt to cover the retreat of what remained of the two destroyed squadrons and defend the village. Only a small number of tanks, four of them from C Squadron, managed to return to the western exit of Norrey-en-Bessin. A Company of the QORC did attempt to push forward briefly, but heavy defensive MG-42 fire forced it back.

Returning the way they had come, the tanks of A Squadron, followed by a small number of surviving tanks from C Squadron and the regimental headquarters, rallied in Bray. They had had to drive again through Norrey-en-Bessin, still under shellfire, and had to make the same 90-degree turn, this time left. Despite the carnage inflicted on the 1st Hussars, the QORC A, B, and C and Support Companies were still largely intact, and would later reorganise themselves in Bretteville-l'Orgueilleuse.[32]

An amazing event occurred immediately after the last Sherman and QORC infantry retreated to the safety of the Norrey-en-Bessin perimeter. *Hitlerjugend* divisional historian Hubert Meyer reports in his divisional history of the *Hitlerjugend* that Canadian ambulances drove onto the field, and, flying white flags with red crosses, began to pick up the wounded. The author assumes these were jeeps, or lighter truck ambulances, as they would be the only vehicles which could swiftly manoeuvre in the fields. Meyer records that this event went on for a solid half hour, with the German and Canadian sides holding their fire as the Canadian stretcher bearers, medics and drivers went about their duties, a stretcher bearer standing on the running boards of the jeeps and ambulances holding a large Red Cross flag.[33]

The losses to the 1st Hussars were staggering for their one-day tank battle. The 1st Hussar A, B and C Squadrons had lost 59 men as casualties, and 11 others were captured or missing. A total of 37 Shermans were lost on this day, a number of Sherman Fireflies among the larger number of Sherman III and Sherman DD short-gunned 75mm models destroyed. As horrific as the danger of a death by fire or explosion was, the tank crews were very good at getting out of their machines quickly. And considering each of the 37 tanks had a crew of 5, the losses, when compared to what a Canadian infantry battalion in similar combat might lose, were light.

German armoured losses in the way of Panzer IVs were also light, and the armoured counterattack had been near flawless in its execution. Only the *8. Kompanie Zug* commanded by *Ostuf.* Seigel with its three tanks had been knocked out, and one of the Panzer IVs was later recovered and repaired. The losses to the *SS-Pz.Pio.Btl. 12* were far worse, as they took the brunt of the Canadian armoured and infantry attack. One officer, one NCO and 27 *SS-Panzerpioniere* were killed. Two officers – one being the *Bataillone* Doctor, Dr Zistler – and three NCOs and forty-five *SS-Panzerpioniere* were wounded. Five *SS-Panzerpioniere* were recorded missing.[34] The tanks had run amok and right through the German positions, destroying many bunkers with direct fire and turning their treads over the trenches of others.

Losses to *I.* and *II. Btl./SS-Pz.Gren.Rgt. 26* included 18 men killed, 32 wounded and 1 missing. Ferme Cardonville, held by part of *2. Kp./SS-Pz.Gren.Rgt. 26*, was overrun during the battle, something left out of Canadian histories, the previous accounts of the attacks and maps just showing *II. Btl./SS-Pz.Gren.Rgt. 26* and *SS-Pz. Pio.Btl. 12* positions. Many SS-Panzergrenadiere were killed as the 1st Hussar tanks shot up the positions of this *Kompanie* near Ferme Cardonville just west of Norrey-en-Bessin and Bretteville-l'Orgueilleuse, which had held its bunkers and dugouts since the first abortive attack of 8 June.[35] Three SPW 251s were also shot up when a small number of Shermans from B Squadron managed to enter the centre of Le Mesnil-Patry before being knocked out. It is unclear if they were attached to *III. Btl.(Gepanzert)/SS-Pz.Gren.Rgt. 26.*

The failure of the 3rd Canadian Infantry Division, Commander, Royal Artillery (CRA), Brigadier Todd, to organise or force the RCA field regiments to implement a rudimentary fire plan to support the 1st Hussars and QORC forces and thus suppress the German defenders in the area, these being *SS-Pz.Pio.Btl. 12* and *II. Btl./*

SS-Pz.Gren.Rgt. 26, was very unfortunate for the two Canadian regiments involved. This oversight allowed the Germans to react quickly to the tank onslaught, which they had seen coming for some time due to the events in Norrey-en-Bessin, and to employ what weapons they had in the way of infantry *Panzerschreck* and 7.5cm Pak 40 anti-tank guns in the initial part of the battle effectively. Though the German bunker lines were badly shot up as some troops of 1st Hussars thoroughly worked over the area, the German *SS-Panzergrenadiere* and *SS-Panzerpioniere* managed to hold on, at least long enough for the calvary to arrive in the way of *II. Abt./SS-Pz. Rgt. 12*. The employment of virtually all operational *II. Abt./SS-Pz.Rgt. 12* tanks allowed the Germans to knock out the majority of the Shermans they encountered, and defeat D Company of the QORC.

Some other events in the battle also worked in the Germans' favour. The incident of the Canadian tank commanders thinking a friendly fire incident with neighbouring forces was taking place – an incident which never occurred – worked wonders at a critical moment to halt Canadian tank fire and allow the German Panzer IV gunners to work undisturbed, firing shot after shot into the mass of Canadian Shermans. This tragic event for the 1st Hussars speaks to the level of unpreparedness and lack of planning that so desperately impaired Canadian fortunes. This event, coupled with a serious lack of field artillery, mortar and naval gun fire or tactical air strikes on German lines, fatally weakened an already weak attack, with just one infantry company and two tank squadrons involved in attacking powerful dug-in infantry forces that outnumbered the Canadian infantry in the initial attack.

Excellent German communications, battlefield initiative by junior leaders and ability to concentrate forces at a critical point allowed for a successful defensive outcome to be achieved. While the accounts of Hans Siegel imply the defensive effort was solely that of several tanks of the *8. Kompanie* of *II. Abt./SS-Pz.Rgt. 12*, the defensive victory hinged on the massed employment of nearly all the *II. Abt./SS-Pz. Rgt. 12* tanks in the area from several *Kompanien*. It was this fire that annihilated B Squadron, inflicted heavy casualties on C Squadron and effectively destroyed D Company of the QORC. *Stubaf.* Prinz, the Commander of *II. Abt./SS-Pz.Rgt. 12*, was recommended by the regimental *Kommandeur*, *Ostubaf.* Wünsche, for the Knight's Cross for his actions that day. In his award submission, Wünsche states Prinz effectively organised the rapid response of his *Abteilung*, which threw the Canadian assault back and managed to inflict heavy casualties on the attackers, recapturing Le Mesnil-Patry in the process (though it was never completely in Canadian hands).[36]

As would be observed in later Canadian operations, the practice of attacking with minimum force an enemy or objective that required maximum force was unfortunately employed, with devastating results. Brigadier Wyman, the lead planner of this attempt at supporting the British advance to the west, was primarily responsible for the outcome. Described accurately by Canadian military historian John A. English in his work *The Canadian Army and the Normandy Campaign* as a 'disgraceful affair', the determination of the 1st Hussars tank crews and the QORC infantry could not replace the absent artillery support needed for this attack.[37]

While the *Waffen-SS* did achieve some tactical victories amongst its defeats in the period 8–11 June, these were tarnished by the continuation of the barbaric practice of prisoner executions by *SS-Pz. Gren. Rgt. 26.* On 9 and 11 of June, two groups of three more prisoners each were executed, this time directly on the orders of regimental *Kommandeur Ostubaf.* Mohnke, who on both occasions demanded it. Despite the resistance of the *II. Btl./SS-Pz. Gren. Rgt. 26 Kommandeur Stubaf.* Seibken and his headquarters staff, who went to the length of communicating with the *Ia Stubaf.* Meyer on the matter, Mohnke determinedly saw the executions carried out. It is unclear if these executions, some of which were carried out on wounded Canadians soldiers, occurred as some sort of bizarre reprisal for the British *Oberst* Luxenburger *Panzer-Lehr* incident, but it cannot be ruled out.

The first battle of Caen: The defence of and withdrawal from Rots and Le Hamel, 11 June 1944

As the combat raged on the western front of the *Hitlerjugend* during late afternoon on Sunday 11 June 1944, a separate, twin Anglo-Canadian operation would be launched with the purpose of eliminating a significant salient held by weak German forces that jutted into the front of the 3rd Canadian Infantry Division. Due to the defensive stance of the Canadian forces in the period 8–10 June, this salient had been permitted to remain. While not equivalent to the armoured engagement that would occur to the west near Le Mesnil-Patry in the late afternoon, the operation to clear the salient encompassing the Mue river, and the villages along it, would see some intense infantry and armoured combat. An Anglo-Canadian battlegroup would launch a determined all-day drive south that at first encountered weak resistance that later turned ferocious. This resistance would later be overcome due to Canadian and British resilience and determination to see opposition crushed in the central Rots–Le Hamel twin village area.

Leading up to the Rots–Le Hamel area there was a series of villages along the Mue. These were La Barbiere, Cairon and Rosel. Each was a cluster of buildings in a small area, in comparison to the sprawling twin villages of Le Hamel and Rots, with Le Hamel on the west side of the Mue river and Rots on the eastern bank. Both villages in 1944 were actually a series of buildings lining the two roads that ran on either side of the river.[1] Almost invisible from the air, the banks of the Mue were surrounded by wooded areas, orchards and fields enclosed with hedges.[2] Due to the depth of the Mue, vehicles were required to cross it via bridge, and two small bridges connected Le Hamel to Rots, one in the north, and another in the south. These were not large bridges, but small one-lane stone constructions under which the Mue flowed.[3] Importantly, a Sherman or Panther tank could cross one, barely. The French civilian population of the Rots area pre-war was roughly 1,000, and those who had not fled by early June were now used to hiding in cellars and basements from the seemingly never-ending artillery fire, fighter-bomber overflights and the presence of the *Waffen-SS* in their homes and on the streets. The northern tip of the main street in Rots contained the church square, and the southern tip contained the school buildings and mayor's office as landmarks.

Approximately one kilometre away were features that the reader will now be familiar with from the events of the past chapters; past the extended line of buildings that was Rots and Le Hamel to the south were the twin villages of Le Bourg in the north and La Villeneuve in the south, divided by the RN 13 Caen–Bayeux paved highway running through them in a north-west direction. South of this was the Caen–Bayeux rail line, the scene of extended combat for *SS-Pz.Rgt. 12* and *SS-Pz. Gren.Rgt. 26*, running parallel to the paved highway approximately 200 meters south. Just to the north-west of La Villeneuve and Le Bourg on the west bank of the Mue was the Château de Rots manor house, with its wooded grounds surrounding it. To the east of Rots was a high point, Hill 63, which was part of an area of open fields that were unoccupied by either German or Canadian forces, and stretched 2 kilometres to the village of Gruchy, which was garrisoned by a small contingent from *III. Btl./SS-Pz.Gren.Rgt. 25*, as well as parts of *14. Kp.(Flak)/SS-Pz.Gren.Rgt. 25* and *16. Kp.(Pionier)/SS-Pz.Gren.Rgt. 25*.[4]

The German defences on the northern tips of Le Hamel and Rots were not strong. It was only to the south-west of Norrey-en-Bessin that the German line held by *SS-Pz. Gren.Rgt. 26* became more continuous with the remaining two *SS-Panzergrenadiere Kompanien* of *I. Btl./SS-Pz.Gren.Rgt. 26* dug in south and west of the village. To the west were the *Kompanien* of *SS-Pz.Pio.Btl. 12* and *II. Btl./SS-Pz.Gren.Rgt. 26*.

Looking back at the events of 8–9 June and the fighting in and around Bretteville-l'Orgueilleuse and Norrey-en-Bessin, the Rots–Le Hamel area had been occupied against little to no Allied opposition by *1. Kp./SS-Pz.Gren.Rgt. 26* on 8 June as part of a general advance by *I. Btl./SS-Pz.Gren.Rgt. 26*. This had occurred when the front lines of the 7th and 9th Canadian Infantry Brigades were still somewhat fluid as they were establishing their brigade 'fortresses'. During this period Canadian and German efforts were focused on the possession of the villages to the south-west, these being Brouay, Bretteville-l'Orgueilleuse, Putot-en-Bessin and Norrey-en-Bessin. Rots and Le Hamel were largely unimportant in the days previous, as both sides wrestled for the aforementioned localities.

Only weak German forces had established positions in Rots, and any prospects for the Germans of an effective defence were limited at best. A dangerous gap affecting the German defences was that from Rots in the west to the positions at Gruchy, 2.5 kilometres to the east. These open fields, with Hill 63 east of Rots being the highpoint, were completely open and could be used by Allied forces to bypass Rots and attack Le Bourg, potentially cutting off *1. Kp./SS-Pz.Gren.Rgt. 26* in the process. These fields were also excellent tank country, and while *Hitlerjugend* tanks and

8.8cm Flak guns near Franqueville and Gruchy could engage targets at long range, the country was wide open. The danger of anti-tank fire was potentially the only reason these open fields were not used for 8th Canadian Infantry Brigade operations.

All this said, Rots was very vulnerable, its defences weak and it was exposed on either flank, its only defensive advantage from an attack from the west being the Mue, which acted as a barrier against enemy tanks and infantry. The question of why *Brig. Fhr.* Witt or *Ostubaf.* Mohnke had not prudently withdrawn German forces from Le Hamel and Rots to consolidate them with others around Le Bourg–La Villeneuve is puzzling. If attacked by powerful Anglo-Canadian brigade-sized forces, it was almost certain that they would either be destroyed or overwhelmed. *Ostubaf.* Mohnke had, logically, given up any notion of pushing further up the Mue river valley given the events of 8–10 June in Putot, Norrey-en-Bessin and Bretteville-l'Orgueilleuse.[5]

The only explanation for keeping the position at Rots, however illogical, was to attempt to keep the line of the *Hitlerjugend* 'straight' in a south–west line from Gruchy in the east to Rots in the west. But the open gap of 2.5 kilometres west of Gruchy made this effort pointless. Whichever way one looked at it, the *Hitlerjugend* on 11 June was occupying too large a defensive sector, in a static role it was not designed for, and it completely lacked any sort of meaningful organic reserves to carry out any counterattacks. If the small village of Rots was to be attacked, its defenders would be on their own.

As of 11 June, the area north of Le Hamel and Rots contained at most a few isolated German forward outpost positions. In Vieux Carion, a small number of combat outposts with a handful of *SS-Panzergrenadiere* intended to provide an early warning role were held by part of a *Zug* from *16. Kp.(Pionier)/SS-Pz.Gren.Rgt. 26*. It made sense to the British high command that it needed to be eliminated if future successful Anglo-Canadian offensive operations were to be enacted. A second motivation would be to solidify the Canadian front line against further German offensive operations if additional enemy reinforcements were to arrive. This was a real concern to the leadership of the British 1st Corps during this early stage of the fighting for the Normandy bridgehead. Observing that it was only held by weak German forces, the British had concluded that the time had arrived to snuff out this German mini-salient. It was also necessary to further isolate the defenders of the *Luftwaffe* Douvres radar station, their extensive above and below ground concrete emplacements still holding onto hope that a German armoured thrust would come and save them.

On the morning of 11 June, the forward positions within Le Hamel and Rots were occupied by *1. Kp./SS-Pz.Gren.Rgt. 26* complete with what appeared from accounts to be three *Züge*, with one being *Schwere* (heavy). This *SS-Panzergrenadiere* force was led by *Ostuf.* Gröschel, in command in the place of *Hstuf.* Eggert.[6] One *Zug* was located on the northern part of Rots and its positions were strengthened by the presence of two 7.5cm Pak 40 anti-tank guns, detached from the *4. Kp.(schwere)/*

SS-Pz.Gren.Rgt. 26. The remaining two *Züge* were deployed on the west side of the Mue, in the northern part of Le Hamel. One of these two was the heavy *Zug* and contained more heavy weapons than the usual allocation of MG-42 machine guns.

Additional forces to the south consisted of the remainder of the *Zug* from the *16. Kp.(Pionier)/SS-Pz.Gren.Rgt. 26*, the regimental combat engineer *Kompanie*, whose position is unclear in accounts but whose location is believed by the author to have been in the south of Rots. The previously discussed divisional escort *Divsionsbegleitkompanie*, occupying a position in depth, was dug in within several locations, these being the Rots Château grounds, Le Bourg and La Villeneuve. From these positions, it could protect the rear of the *1. Kp./SS-Pz.Gren.Rgt. 26* positions on the front lines to the north, guard against any incursions from Bray and Bretteville-l'Orgueilleuse, and though small, act as a ready reserve.

The western base of the Rots salient to the west of Le Bourg and La Villeneuve was also partially held by another force that was not part of *SS-Pz.Gren.Rgt. 26*. On the RN 13, the *15. Kp.(Aufklärung)/SS-Pz.Gren.Rgt. 25*, reduced by casualties after the heavy combat in Bretteville-l'Orgueilleuse, was still assuming defensive positions. Like *4. Kompanie* of *SS-Pz.Rgt. 12*, there was series of contacts with opposing forces on 11 June, one of which saw a MG-42 machine-gun team from its *III. Zug* manage to set an Allied tank that had emerged from Bretteville-l'Orgueilleuse on fire with tracer rounds. Seeing it on fire and begin to burn when something flammable ignited on the rear deck of the tank, the *Aufklärung SS-Panzergrenadiere* then managed to shoot some of the crew when they attempted to bail out of the tank.[7]

Supporting the *SS-Panzergrenadiere* was an artillery forward observation team from *III. Abt./SS-Pz.Art.Rgt. 12*, whose *Batterien* were emplaced near Caen, roughly 5 kilometres to the south-east. How much ammunition the *Batterien* of the *III. Abt./SS-Pz.Art.Rgt. 12* had to fight a sustained counter-battery gunnery duel with Allied forces, and to bombard their infantry and tank concentrations, is difficult to say. It could not have been excessive, given the fighting of the previous days.

The most powerful and key element of the German defence was the Panther tank *Kompanie*, which was emplaced within the village in staged positions, this being the now battle-hardened remnants of *4. Kp./SS-Pz.Rgt. 12*. The total number of Panthers was not more than eight or nine out of an initial establishment of roughly fourteen, with some of the vehicle losses that occurred during the Bretteville-l'Orgueilleuse fighting having been repaired and sent back into action. It was not at full strength when it went into action on the night of 8/9 June in Bretteville-l'Orgueilleuse, and it was not at full strength now.

It appears from accounts that it was organised into two *Züge*, I. and III./4. Kp./SS-Pz.Rgt. 12, and was still led by *Hstuf.* Hans Pfeiffer. The vehicles were deployed at key points to work with the Pak 40 7.5cm anti-tank guns to provide an anti-tank defence, covering key intersections and parked beside buildings in ambush positions. Pfeiffer himself and another Panther were located, it appears, on a highpoint near

A *Waffen-SS* guard handing back paybooks to Canadian prisoners of war, June 1944. With the *Deutsche Wochenschau* newsreel cameraman present, there was little chance of brutality towards the prisoners, but this could change when he stopped filming. (Critical Past)

Brig. Fhr. Fritz Witt speaking with *Ostubaf.* Max Wünsche regarding ongoing operations at the *Hitlerjugend Gefechtsstand* at Venoix on 8 June. (Bundesarchiv Bild 146-1984-031-19A, via Wikimedia Commons)

A photo taken at the same time as the image above it, this time including *Staf.* Kurt Meyer, *Kommandeur* of *SS-Pz. Rgt. 25*. As seen in the photo, Meyer was a relatively short man. (Bundesarchiv Bild 146-1989-099-06, via Wikimedia Commons)

A Panther tank of *1. Kp./SS-Pz.Rgt. 12* photographed during the June fighting. The crew is at readiness with the *Panzerkommandant* in the turret with his headset and throat microphones on, and the cover off the hull ball-mount MG-34 machine gun. (A. Gullachsen collection)

A 7.5cm Pak 40 anti-tank gun being manhandled by its *Hitlerjugend SS-Panzergrenadier* crew, June 1944. (Alamy Stock Images)

A *Hitlerjugend SS-Panzergrenadiere* patrol ready to depart friendly lines, June 1944. (Alamy Stock Images)

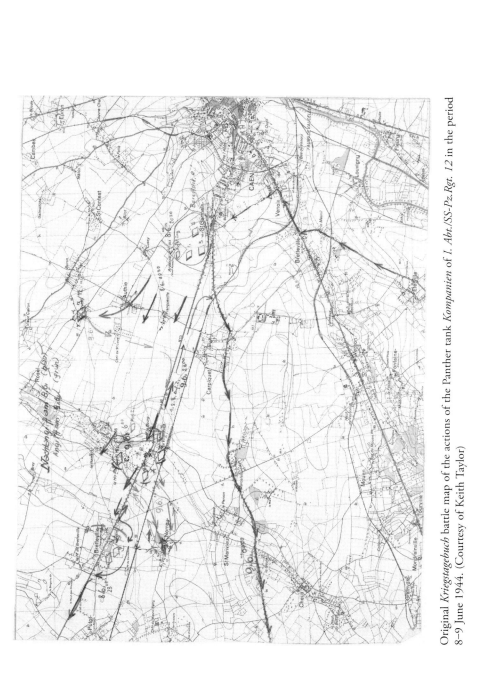

Original *Kriegstagebuch* battle map of the actions of the Panther tank *Kompanien* of *I. Abt./SS-Pz.Rgt. 12* in the period 8–9 June 1944. (Courtesy of Keith Taylor)

Photo of the RN 13 through the western portion of the heavily shelled village of Bretteville-l'Orgueilleuse, with the destroyed Panther '418' on the right some time after the fighting on 8/9 June 1944. (Image courtesy of the National Army Museum, London. NAM 1975-03-63-18-64)

Overturned Panther of *1. Kp./SS-Pz.Rgt. 12* post fighting in Bretteville on 8/9 June 1944. (Imperial War Museum. IWM CL 398)

Speaking in La Villeneuve immediately before the 9 June attack on Norrey by *3. Kp./SS-Pz. Rgt. 12* are, from left: *Stubaf.* Jürgensen, *Ostubaf.* Wünsche, *Stubaf.* Krause and *Staf.* Meyer. Note that *Ostubaf.* Wünsche has a head wound due to shrapnel from Canadian anti-tank gun fire. (Bundesarchiv via Wikimedia Commons)

Wünsche, Meyer and Witt convene after the 8/9 June fighting at the *Hitlerjugend* divisional headquarters at Venoix. Again, note the bandaged head wound on Wünsche. (Bundesarchiv Bild 146-1988-028-25A via Wikimedia Commons)

The remains of the *3. Kp./SS-Pz.Rgt. 12* Panther tank hulks after their disastrous attack on Norrey-en-Bessin on 9 June. They were later used as targets by passing Anglo-Canadian tank units on their way to the front. (Libraries and Archives Canada MIKAN 3226737)

Hitlerjugend SS-Panzergrenadiere in a fighting position in bocage country, photographed in June or July 1944. (A. Gullachsen collection)

Panther tanks of *3. Kp./SS-Pz.Rgt. 12* driving through La Villeneuve on 9 June 1944 prior to their attack on Norrey. (Wikimedia Commons)

Photo of *Ostubaf.* Mohnke of *SS-Pz.Gren.Rgt. 26* at an awards ceremony in mid-June 1944 issuing Iron Crosses to *SS-Panzergrenadiere* of *SS-Pz.Gren. Rgt. 26.* This is how he would have appeared during the 8 June 1944 fighting and subsequent prisoner executions. (A. Gullachsen collection)

Hitlerjugend SS-Panzergrenadiere photographed near a Panther tank in June 1944. (Alamy Stock Images)

An *SS-Panzergrenadiere* MG-42 team near a French château, June or July 1944. (Archiva Panstwowe via Wikimedia Commons)

Brigadier Harry Foster of the 7th Canadian Infantry Brigade and Lieutenant General John Crocker of the British 1st Corps with destroyed Panther '435'. This photo was taken some time after the fighting in Rots. (Courtesy of Keith Taylor)

SS-Hauptstürmfuhrer Hans Pfeiffer, *Kompanie-Chef* of *4. Kp./SS-Pz.Rgt. 12*, who was killed in the turret of his Panther tank during the fighting in Rots, 11 June 1944. (A. Gullachsen personal collection)

British prisoners of war, guarded by the *Waffen-SS*. The British prisoners are from 46 Royal Marine Commando. (Bundesarchiv_Bild_101I-738-0276-05A, via Wikimedia Commons)

the middle of Rots, just west of Hill 63, which gave them a limited overwatch ability from a hull-down position. Each Panther was heavily camouflaged with vegetation, their crews ready in ambush positions with their best fields of fire to the north and north-west, covering the road to Lasson from Le Hamel. It was the crews of these tanks and the combat power they brought that would determine whether a successful defence of Rots could be enacted or not.[8]

The battle of the *4. Kp/SS-Pz.Rgt. 12* was confused from the start, and it is only through the determination of *Hstuf.* Pfeiffer that he was able to use his weak *Kompanie* effectively to put up the resistance it did in the fighting that was to follow. He had made a tactical mistake in the deployment of his *Kompanie* by placing the Panthers in exactly the wrong direction, facing west, when they were needed on the northern perimeter to meet the actual Anglo-Canadian attack on Le Hamel from the north on 11 June.

According to the research of French and Hungarian military historians Stephan Cazenave and Norbert Számvéber, and the review of primary documents, it appears half of the strength of the *Kompanie*, roughly five Panthers, was deployed near the western exit of La Villeneuve, with another two just to the north covering the north-west and western approaches to the château at Rots, in ambush positions looking west. The remaining three, including Pfeiffer's *Kompanie-Chef* Panther '405', were located in reserve positions near Rots or La Villeneuve, although it is unclear where.[9] This deployment was viewed as logical, as powerful Canadian recces with Sherman tanks, and surprise RCA field artillery and anti-tank fire, had come from the direction of the Bray–Bretteville-l'Orgueilleuse road. This area was the Canadian rear left flank of the 7th Canadian Infantry Brigade fortress in the Putot–Norrey-en-Bessin–Bretteville-l'Orgueilleuse triangle of villages. Canadian activity on 10 June indicated an attack would be directed against La Villeneuve or Rots from this flank.[10] Hence, the defensive focus of the German forces was not north, but west. Unfortunately for the Germans, the actual main attack would come not from the direction of the Bretteville-l'Orgueilleuse–Bray road to the west, but right down the Mue river road from Rosel, to the north-east of Rots. No Panthers were deployed within or very close to the front line of the *1. Kp./SS-Pz.Rgt. 26* with its three *Züge*, influencing the tactical defeats on it that would follow.

The mission given to *Hstuf.* Pfeiffer and his *4. Kp./SS-Pz.Rgt. 12* by the *Gefechtsstand* of *I. Abt./SS-Pz.Rgt. 12* on 11 June was as follows: 'Secure the Rots–Le Bourg [La Villeneuve] line together with the *Grenadiere*, that is on the left flank at Le Bourg, with five tanks of the *Kompanie*, and on the right flank on the western side of Rots with two tanks; securing in the south-western, western and north-western direction.'[11]

The readiness level of *4. Kp./SS-Pz.Rgt. 12* was low and it desperately needed to be withdrawn from the front for rest and to conduct vehicle maintenance. It had suffered heavy vehicle and personnel losses in the Bretteville-l'Orgueilleuse fighting on the night of 8/9 June and had been shelled intensively in its ambush screening positions on 9 June. The *Kompanie* had either been marching, fighting or on alert each day since 6 June. The harassing RA and RCA field artillery fire sometimes went on 24 hours a day, and during daylight, if there was good flying weather, Allied fighter-bombers would be constantly overhead. Tanks often had to constantly change positions to counteract the impact of Allied radio triangulation that would result in artillery fire if they used their onboard radios to communicate with the *Kompanie-Chef, Hstuf.* Pfeiffer. Its crews were suffering from extreme sleep deprivation and in some cases hallucinations. To be effective in combat, each crew member had to be alert, responsive, vigilant and ready to act as part of a team. Anything less could lead to the tank being slow to react during combat and taking a hit from an anti-tank gun or tank and being destroyed, the crew possibly burning to death or having body parts shot off by penetrating anti-tank solid shot. In Normandy, whichever tank saw the enemy first was often victor in tank-versus-tank duels, with shorter combat ranges in wooded or bocage areas negating the long-distance gunnery advantages of the better German tank cannons.

Also, the tank crews, despite their best attempts, were not adept at night combat, and luckily very little of this took place during the fighting in Rots. At or near Carpiquet airfield, the *Kompanie* had come across a *Luftwaffe* storage facility with high octane aviation gasoline and used it to fuel up the Panthers. While it did not damage the engines, the exhaust flames from the motor exhaust at high engine RPMs created a flame one meter high, providing a great target for Allied anti-tank and tank gunners.[12]

The *1. Kp./SS-Pz.Gren.Rgt. 26* of *Ostuf.* Gröschel had not seen any combat to this point and had not encountered British or Canadian infantry or tanks. It had been shelled intensively in the period 9–10 June, something that will be discussed within this chapter. While the German forces were seemingly well equipped and had not suffered heavy casualties apart from the Panther *Kompanie*, they were not a fresh, fully equipped *SS-Panzergrenadiere Battalione* or an up-to-strength *Panzerabteilung*. As stated earlier, apart from the *Pioniere Zug* and the *Begleitkompanie* to the south near the Rots château near La Villeneuve, there were no powerful reserves available to be thrown in to save Gröschel and Pfeiffer if Allied forces were to attack in strength. It was a situation ripe for disaster.

The orders for the 8th Canadian Infantry Brigade to attack and clear Rots and Le Hamel were received from the headquarters of the 3rd Canadian Infantry Division on 10 June. In response, the commander of the 8th Canadian Infantry Brigade, Brigadier Blackader, working with his staff, formulated the following plan of attack. The 46 Royal Marine Commando (46 RMC), subordinated to the brigade for this operation, would attack directly south from the village of Rosel on the Mue with a squadron of Fort Garry Horse Sherman tanks in support. Following the successful attack, Le Régiment de la Chaudière and the North Shore (New Brunswick) Regiment, the 8th Canadian Infantry Brigade forces held in reserve, would move in forces to consolidate the brigade's hold on the Rots–Le Hamel sector and form a brigade fortress with armoured support. To support the 46 RMC drive south along the Mue, a force from the Regiment de la Chaudière would launch a diversionary probing patrol near Le Hamel during the day.[13]

The preparatory fire to soften up the German defences and harass the defenders over the period 9–10 June had been intense, with RCA and RA medium and field artillery units firing timed concentrations on the villages. Their efforts at times had been interrupted when their full support was required to combat German offensive operations to the west on the front of the 7th Canadian Infantry Brigade as it struggled against the attacks of *SS-Pz.Gren.Rgt. 26.* and *SS-Pz.Rgt. 12.* This artillery effort was matched by intense activity by Allied fighter-bombers, ready to pounce on any dismounted or vehicle movement in the twin villages.

The 46 RMC, a light infantry battalion-sized unit, was one of several transferred from the Royal Navy Marine Division in 1942 to become commandos in the British Army Special Service Brigades, with each of the latter brigades fielding several of these types of units. Previous service by the commandos included a series of daring amphibious raids in 1942 on the defended ports of occupied France. The establishment strength of the unit on paper was 464 officers and men, and it is estimated that on 11 June it went into battle with roughly 420 of all ranks. 46 RMC contained six troops that were in fact the equivalent to weak British Army infantry companies, with fewer heavy weapons. These troops were equipped primarily with light handheld weapons, in striking contrast to a regular motorised British Army infantry battalion that also contained a carrier, mortar, anti-tank and pioneer platoon. As mentioned earlier, these platoons together formed a Support Company to radically enhance the combat power of its four infantry line companies. The British Army infantry battalion of 1944 was entirely motorised and contained light armour in the way of its tracked Universal Carriers and a number of trucks. The Royal Marine Commandos had none of these things, the commando possessing only the most essential vehicles and heavy weapons. The marines did not even wear steel helmets, preferring berets. While it was an all-volunteer, highly fit, motivated elite marine light infantry unit, it was a special purpose force not designed to attack an entrenched enemy supported by Panther tanks, artillery and anti-tank guns in broad daylight. The question of why it was employed to spearhead this attack must be asked – especially when the largely intact 8th Canadian Infantry Brigade was ready to fight and had mostly not seen heavy combat since D-Day. Though it would eventually prevail, the 46 RMC would suffer high losses in the day's battle.

Armoured support for the assault that was to come from A Squadron of the Fort Garry Horse, led by its officer commanding (OC), Major Harry Blanshard. One of the three regiments of the 2nd Canadian Armoured Brigade, the FGH was close to full strength on 11 June, having not seen heavy combat since the Juno Beach assault. A Squadron fielded a total of 17 Shermans for the operation, two short of its war establishment strength. Only one of these tanks was a 17-pounder gunned Firefly variant. There were five three-tank troops, totalling fifteen tanks, and two squadron headquarters tanks, commanded by Major Blanshard and Captain Goodman.[14]

Providing artillery support to the light infantry force was the newly arrived 191st Field Regiment, RA, of the 4th Army Group, Royal Artillery (4 AGRA), the corps-level field and medium artillery formation of the British 1st Corps. This field regiment was placed in support of the operation with its 532, 533 and 534 Batteries, RA, all equipped with towed 25 pounders.[15] It had just arrived in Normandy on 9 June and was delegated to provide support for 8th Canadian Infantry Brigade operations along the Mue.

Also placed in support was one troop of Royal Canadian Engineers (RCE). Little information has been gathered on the role of the attached RCE field engineer troop, and it is unclear if they were mounted in Universal Carriers for the advance or marched along with the marines.

Somewhat ignored in the writing on Rots, Royal Marine historian Si Biggs states a number of Centaur tanks from the 2nd Royal Marine Support Regiment of the Royal Marine (RM) Armoured Support Craft Group supported the 46 RMC attack. This armoured group was split into two regiments, one assigned to support the British 50th Infantry Division and one to support the 3rd Canadian Infantry Division. The 5th (Independent) RM Armoured Support Battery was subordinated to the British 3rd Infantry Division for these operations, with three troops equipped with Centaur fire support tanks mounting 95mm howitzers.[16] As these tanks are not mentioned in the later fighting, it is possible that they were ordered west shortly after the operation began to Bray to help defend the 12th and 13th Field Regiments, RCA, whose battery positions were located there. A map created by Royal Marine historian Keith Taylor shows the entire 2nd Royal Marine Support Regiment travelling to Bray on 11 June, and not part of the Mue clearance operation.[17]

Orders had been received by the 46 RMC at 2100 hours on 10 June to clear the Mue river area from Barbiere to Rots with attached forces. With the mass of the Royal Marine troops assembled in the fields near the village, by 0615 the first Fort Garry Horse (FGH) tanks rolled up, and columns were formed for the advance.[18]

The operational plan for 46 RMC was to have four main parts. Phase one called for the clearing of the road from the village of Barbiere to the small, wooded area nearby. The second phase called for the clearing of the village of Vieux Cairon. The third phase demanded the clearance of the twin villages on either side of the Mue, Rosel and Lasson, and the last phase was to see the clearing of Le Hamel and Rots by evening. If conditions permitted, a final advance to the area of Le Bourg and La Villeneuve, bisected by the RN 13, was to be attempted.

The 46 RMC commander, Lieutenant Colonel Hardy, was at this time completely unaware of how many Germans were holding the Rots–Le Hamel area to the south and in what strength. Just prior to his clearing operation getting underway, Hardy did request a recce patrol into the area of these two villages from the headquarters of the 8th Canadian Infantry Brigade.

This task fell onto Le Regiment de la Chaudière under Lieutenant Colonel Mathieu, whose C Company, under its OC Major Sevigny, dispatched an infantry section to the area of the twin villages of Rots and Le Hamel. This patrol set out early morning through the fields, a risky undertaking in the half-darkness. The Germans in the area let the patrol enter what could only be Le Hamel, and then ambushed it, wounding nearly all its members except for its commander, Corporal Desbiens. He managed to escape due to fire support from another Chaudière infantry section nearby, the Chaudière mortar platoon, and fire from a battery of the 13th Field Regiment, RCA. This regiment luckily had a FOO party attached to the Chaudière elements near Bray. To undertake this task in the early morning rather than the pitch-dark night was unfortunate, and four Chaudière infantrymen who were badly wounded and left in Le Hamel were later found having been shot at close range and bayoneted, yet another war crime committed by the *Hitlerjugend*.[19]

It is unclear from primary sources and books written on the fighting when the official H-Hour for the 46 RMC attack was, but it is known that the advance began shortly after 0800 hours, with the FGH tanks in the lead. It is then unclear if they were joined at this time by the aforementioned small number of Centaur tanks of the 2nd Royal Marine Armoured Support Regiment. The Centaur troops consisted of four tanks and a Royal Marine Observation Post (OP) Sherman tank, all of which had the distinctive 360-degree markings on the turret to help dismounted troops communicate with the tank commander on where to lay his gun towards the enemy.[20] The armoured columns drove slowly at a pace that matched the dismounted Royal Marines, the lead Shermans ready to pour fire into any enemy positions on receiving a prearranged signal from the dismounted troops, this being flares fired in the direction of a suspected enemy positions.

Advancing along the main road, the first phase of the 46 RMC clearing operations near Barbiere was completed by 1100 hours. No. 1 Troop for the Fort Garry Horse A Squadron, led by Lieutenant Rushford, led the column's advance on the road from La Barbiere to Vieux Cairon, a very wooded area in places. The road began to wind as it encountered the Mue and there were several small bridges that the tanks had to cross. The OC of A Squadron, Major Blanshard, nearly had his tank topple off one of the bridges, temporarily slowing the progress of the column.[21] This Sherman was recovered by another tank, and soon managed to successfully traverse the bridge.

Once the column was going again, the advance was led by Lieutenant Jefferies of No. 5 Troop of the FGH A Squadron. Very little in the way of opposition was encountered, with only a small group of possibly either German *Artillerie* spotters from the *716. Infanterie Division* or *Pioniere* of *SS-Pz.Gren.Rgt. 26* being overwhelmed and captured. These isolated groups surrendered after the lead Sherman tank troops fired at Vieux Cairon in unison. Attempting to fight from dugouts, the Germans had been trapped by the tank fire, which made escape through the open fields around the village impossible. Some German mortar rounds were fired from the south at the Royal Marines and FGH tanks as they manoeuvred to surround and overcome the German positions, but this fire was ineffectual. Soon resistance stopped, and those Germans not killed or wounded surrendered to the Royal Marines.

After this brief combat and once the tank columns were reformed, the second phase of the advance began. The armoured and infantry force broke in two, with one column advancing on Lasson on one side of the Mue and the remaining forces on the other advancing on Rosel. The dust from the large number of armoured vehicles was noticed by the Germans, who had further small outposts forward in the vicinity of Rosel and Lasson. Accordingly, German artillery fire rained down on the Anglo-Canadian columns, effectively halting them from 1130 to 1245 hours just past Vieux Cairon as they attempted to advance.[22] It is unclear if any casualties in the way of personnel or vehicles were suffered.

About the same time as the columns departed from Vieux Cairon, German accounts recorded post war by the *Waffen-SS* defenders of Rots and Le Hamel mention another contact on the morning of 11 June, when members of the *IV. (Schwere) Zug* of *1. Kp./SS-Pz.Gren.Rgt. 26* observed the appearance on the Lasson–Le Hamel road to the north of the Le Hamel of what appeared to be a sole Sherman or Sherman RA Observation Post (OP) tank with two artillery observers sitting on the turret. This could have been either a FOO party from the 191st Field Regiment, RA, which had gone ahead, or the troop leader from the attached RM Centaur troop. What exact time this occurred is uncertain, but it would have had to have been after the clearing of Rosel and Lasson.

While a German 7.5cm Pak 40 anti-tank gun located near the northern edge of Le Hamel could not get a clear shot at it, a tripod mounted MG-42 of the *Schwere Zug* did fire at the tank, forcing it to retreat. Following this engagement, a very heavy RA or RCA field or medium artillery concentration was brought down on the forward defenders of Le Hamel and Rots, which suppressed the *SS-Panzergrenadiere*. It appears this artillery fire occurred several hours before the actual main 46 RMC attack on the two villages.

To the north, the Anglo-Canadian columns began a rapid advance again at 1320 hours. A small infantry ambush of the leading FGH tanks occurred near Rosel, the next small village with a cluster of buildings. In response, Major Person, the senior 191st Field Regiment, RA, FOO team leader attached to the tank column, called down a Royal Artillery Mike Target, utilising the entire regiment for a short heavy concentration of fire on Rosel and surrounding woods.

Once the timed artillery concentration ended, the marines with tank support successfully cleared the village of Rosel, taking several *Waffen-SS* members who could not escape fast enough into the nearby wooded area prisoner. Whatever remaining *Heer* or *Waffen-SS* that were in the area fled, and no further resistance was encountered. Three quarters of the operation was now completed, and the tank and infantry columns had not encountered serious German resistance to this point. Both Rosel and Lasson were cleared by roughly 1500 hours.[23] While some marine casualties had been incurred, the tanks of A Squadron had been employed successfully without suffering any losses. Both columns now reformed together on the west bank of the Mue.

Approaching Le Hamel, the column halted, and a final orders group was called by Lieutenant Colonel Hardy of 46 RMC. This orders group was held in a water mill just north of Le Hamel and occurred in the afternoon just after the village of Rosel had been cleared. Assembled within this building were all six troop commanders and headquarters officers from 46 RMC and officers of the FGH A Squadron. The plan for the final attack of the day was for the 46 RMC's A and B Troops on the western bank of the Mue to secure the start line just to the north of Le Hamel in the area of the north–south road of the village, supported by a timed RA field artillery concentration fired on this area. Once this area was secured, a second artillery concentration was planned to be fired into Le Hamel, and the Marine S and Y Troops, supported by three Shermans of the No. 4 Troop of the FGH A Squadron, were to begin their assault. It was planned to clear northern Le Hamel first, followed by a push east to secure the first (northern) bridge into Rots. The Marine S Troop, attacking south on the left side of the main road running south into Le Hamel with a troop of tanks in support, was to clear the area south, the Chemin du Hamel road. Y Troop, following the advance of S Troop, was to clear any remaining areas of resistance in northern Le Hamel and then push east on the Chemin de la Cave street past the first, most northern bridge over the Mue and into Rots.[24]

Once these two attacks by S and Y Troops were complete, follow-on forces in the way of A and B Troops, with the FGH No. 2 and 3 Troops and the two headquarters tanks in support, were to be ready to push into Rots proper. B Troop was to attack behind a column of FGH tanks and push right into the centre of Rots, with A Troop following behind. Once the centre of the sprawling village was secured, both troops were to continue the advance south, if possible, to Le Bourg and La Villeneuve, the twin villages being the final objectives.

A separate platoon-sized force from the Marine A Troop at this point was to push though the fields to the east of Rots and flank Le Bourg and La Villeneuve from that direction, hopefully causing the *Waffen-SS* defenders to consider themselves outflanked and to withdraw.

For A Squadron of the FGH it was at this point that the fog of war badly impaired their battle. As his squadron approached Le Hamel, Blanshard received what he believed to be a message from the FGH regimental headquarters ordering him to send back the No. 1 and 5 Troops to the FGH regimental headquarters laager. Amazingly, he complied with this order, which could have come from a *Hitlerjugend Nachrichten* (signals) section. He could have easily stated at this point that all his troops were

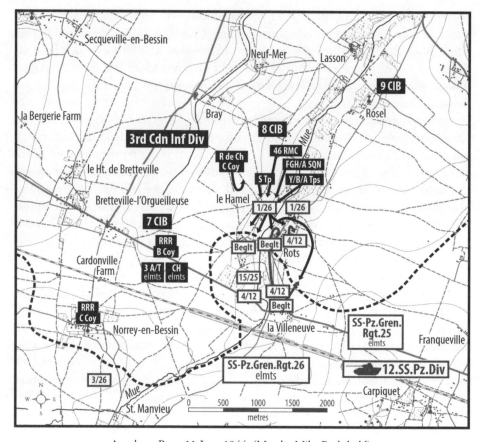

Attack on Rots, 11 June 1944. (Map by Mike Bechthold)

engaged in combat, something they very shortly would have been. Without firing a shot, the Germans observed a total of six Shermans depart the way they had come up the road on the west side of the Mue. This still left Blanshard three tank troops and the headquarters troop. It is very unclear if the RMAS Centaur troop was present at this stage, but regardless the armoured force was weakened by this event, making the future fighting arguably tougher for the Royal Marines.[25]

Following Lieutenant Colonel Hardy's Orders Group, a further regrouping occurred in which two columns of tanks and marines were established, one behind the other, for the pushes aimed at reaching the outskirts of Le Hamel on the west bank of the Mue and the other over the bridge into Rots. Moving first, the No. 4 Troop of A Squadron led the charge into the outskirts of Le Hamel at close to 1800 hours. At this point the first large RA field artillery concentration was fired on the area north of the village.

When the dust cleared and the Germans emerged from their foxholes and bunkers, dismounted Royal Marines in large numbers were seen assembling near the Mue beside the mill on the west side of the river. German observers counted at least 12 Canadian Shermans assembling in their troops just north of Le Hamel. Driving forward as if on a training exercise, the tanks poured concentrated fire into the first buildings of Le Hamel, shooting them up with high-explosive shells and machine-gun fire.

As the tanks edged closer, still firing, heavy German 8cm mortar and MG-42 fire was immediately encountered by S and Y Troops of 46 RMC. The German defenders deployed on the north edge of Le Hamel consisted of rough line of dugouts and fortified houses with *I. Zug* and parts of the *IV. (Schwere) Zug*. In front of these positions were two lines of barbed wire. Slightly south of the *SS-Panzergrenadiere* positions on the west bank of the Mue was one of the two Pak 40 7.5cm anti-tank guns.[26]

It was at this time that the marines, on receiving the order, charged forward and moved quickly through the fields, yelling as they passed the tanks. S and Y Troops of 46 RMC ran forward line abreast, S Troop on the left near the Mue, Y Troop opposite it on the right through the waist-high wheat fields. The former troop had the Mue and a dense hedgerow bordering the road near the Mue that confined its movements on its left flank. On reaching the barbed wire that the *Waffen-SS* had erected across the fields, the marines crossed it without difficulty. Once S Troop passed the wire obstacles, which did not significantly obstruct its progress, it reached and cleared several German fighting dugouts, surprising the defenders with the speed of its advance. The tanks brought up the rear and were soon driving down the main road, clearing Le Hamel of its German defenders and finally coming to rest at a point approximately 600 meters past the first farmhouse of Le Hamel.

Just as the columns of tanks and infantry were first observed by the Germans near Le Hamel, it appears sometime after 1700 hours *Hstuf.* Pfeiffer ordered the Panthers of *4. Kp./SS-Pz.Rgt. 12* to redeploy to meet the threat. Due to the loss of tanks within the *Kompanie* and the previous disintegration of its *Züge* due to the fighting in Bretteville-l'Orgueilleuse on 8–9 June, this meant the German Panthers often arrived and fought alone, rather than in a *Zug* of three to four tanks. Pfeiffer could only do his best, and hope some tanks positioned near the highway on the left flank could travel north quickly to the vicinity of Le Hamel and Rots fast enough to intervene and repel the Anglo-Canadian force bearing down on *1. Kp./SS-Pz. Gren.Rgt. 26*.

In a series of events that happened quickly, it appears the speed of the Royal Marine thrust into the German lines with the help of the FGH tank attacks caused the positions of the *I. Zug*, the Franke group, on the left flank of the *1. Kp./SS-Pz. Gren.Rgt. 26*, to disintegrate. Suddenly the Germans broke, the *SS-Panzergrenadiere* running to get away from the Shermans and swarms of marines closing on their positions. The tanks had been allowed to get too close to the Germans too quickly, and now were driving into their positions. In short order, the Germans were overrun.

With S Troop pushing down the Le Hamel road and clearing more and more buildings, Y Troop, now to its right rear facing south, had caught up to a point just west of the first group of farmhouses and the T-junction there leading to the first bridge over the Mue. Pushing east across the path of S Troop, the marines of Y Troop advanced past the farmhouses, engaged some leftover Germans and then pushed over the bridge into Rots, advancing a short distance towards the first T-junction on the Rots north–south road. After Y Troop had pushed a distance into Rots, it halted and dug in within the fields and buildings south of the T-junction of the main north–south road leading through the village.

Following quickly behind, B Troop of 46 RMC advanced, following the Shermans of the FGH as they drove up the sunken road after the first bridge, the La rue de la Cavée, which led to the T-junction, one direction leading north to the church square, and the other direction south to the school and mayors' office. The spire of the Catholic church loomed above the heads of the FGH tank commanders as they followed the road in column, roaring into the confined area to no initial German resistance.[27]

Suddenly a German Pak 40 7.5cm anti-tank gun fired at the Shermans as they reached the main road, and two Shermans from A Squadron were quickly knocked out. This fire did not stop the other FGH tanks, and they began to rapidly and systematically use their co-axial and hull machine guns to fire at everything surrounding them as they pushed into the confines of northern Rots with No. 2 troop in the lead with its Firefly.[28]

After the tanks turned left at the T-junction and moved north to the church square up the main road, *Waffen-SS* resistance came to life, with the *SS-Panzergrenadiere* shooting and throwing grenades from the buildings at the B Troop marines behind the tanks as they drove down the narrow streets. As the lead FGH tank moved toward the church square, it was hit by some kind of anti-tank weapon that started a small fire on its rear engine deck. Stalling momentarily, it then sprang back to life and pushed forward. This was either the tank of FGH Sergeant Crabb or Captain Goodman, both of which would later have their tanks destroyed next to the church.[29]

The German resistance in Rots, initially being centred around the *SS-Panzergrenadiere* of *III. Zug*, the Ludwig group, rushed from the northern edges of the village to the church square and began to offer resistance. As this was occurring, the fighting was going poorly for the remaining elements of the *IV. (Schwere) Zug*, with its forces in Rots being driven south along the main road by groups of marines pushing towards the school and town hall. *Oscha*. Hahn, its *Kommandeur*, was forced south to the second Mue bridge and the nearby position of the second 7.5cm Pak 40 anti-tank gun, where he began to rally his men and take up new positions near the Mue. The Royal Marines, quickly following, engaged in hand-to-hand combat with German

Züge.[30] Hahn attempted to direct some of his men to help manhandle the second German Pak 40 7.5cm anti-tank to a new position to engage the tanks, but the amount of small arms fire was too much, and this effort had to be abandoned.

He also briefly attempted to launch a diversionary attack to aid the *I. Zug* across the Mue in Le Hamel, who appear to have been totally overrun by the British troops and Canadian tanks in Le Hamel, and this also failed. *Ustuf.* Gross, the *I. Zug Kommandeur*, had become separated from his men in the Le Hamel melee, and managed to be rescued during some point in the later fighting by *Uscha.* Hahn. It was at this stage approaching 1800 hours, and it can be fairly said that the northern outskirt of Rots was now a scene of heavy combat for the FGH and the Royal Marine B Troop. All of Le Hamel on the west bank of the Mue had now fallen to the one FGH tank troop and accompanying Royal Marine S Troop. In one of the last actions in Le Hamel, a Pak 40 7.5cm anti-tank gun was knocked out near the main road, the commandeered Italian truck acting as its prime mover also being set ablaze.

Where exactly were the Panthers at this time? Their lack of the involvement in the defence to this point had allowed the Canadian tanks to push into Rots. The poor tank country, consisting of twisting French lanes running through the sprawling village of Rots, broken up by wooded areas, had completely negated the Panthers' range advantage which they gained by their 7.5cm KWK 42 L/70 tank cannon. The Panther tanks had been poorly deployed to the rear and while they were covering certain tactical intersections within Rots, had not been able to intervene to save the *SS-Panzergrenadiere* from the quick advance of the FGH tanks when their help was desperately needed.[31]

As more Sherman tanks pushed into the church square, they began to back up towards buildings and the church so as to have a better field of fire and to avoid being attacked from the rear. From these positions they began to fire in all directions at the *SS-Panzergrenadiere*, many of whom were in upper levels of homes and places of business.

It was at this point that two German Panthers, in ambush positions near a farm with the church on their right, opened fire on the main group of FGH tanks that were now gathered and firing on the German *SS-Panzergrenadiere* in the church square. *Strm.* Hans Kepler of the Panther '426', which was lying in an ambush position at an intersection near the church, recalled in Hubert Meyer's divisional history:

> Around 1930 hours the Canadians launch repeated attacks after heavy artillery bombardments. We are laying in an ambush position, well camouflaged, near a farm. The church is to our right. After a heavy bout of artillery fire 10 to 12 Sherman tanks [most likely the two troops and the headquarters Shermans, equalling 8 tanks] attack us frontally. Ecki Stuhldreher, our gunner on Panzer '426', under the command of *Hscha.* Heinz Lehman, opens fire on an approaching formation of Shermans, and Stuhldreher knocks out four or five of this group. The others, turn away. In retaliation the enemy tanks concentrated horrific fire on us. Our infantry suffers severe losses. The village is attacked once more. Our Panzers of *III. Zug* fight it out with the

> Shermans and infantry who have broken through. Our Panzers of *I. Zug*, amongst them the
> command Panzer, are holding a slight rise.[32]

Rttf. Eberhard Wenzel of Panther '438', fighting alongside '426', recalls that the
number of Shermans destroyed was fewer, much closer the figure that the FGH A
Squadron accounts state were lost in the first action in the town centre. *Rttf.* Eberhard
Wenzel recalled in Keith Taylor's *The Waist-High Cornfield*:

> I remember being on the outskirts of the village. I am a gunner in Panzer '438' positioned
> next to Stuhldreher's Panzer '426' and together we opened fire on some attacking Shermans,
> certainly destroying four tanks, maybe more, and damaging several more. We change position
> several times, I lose sight of Stuhldreher's Panzer. The enemy tanks pull back under the fire of
> our Panzers.[33]

Both of these first-hand accounts detailing the first ambush of the FGH tanks that
entered Rots via the first bridge make it appear as if the battle was in an open field,
rather than the tight village streets of Rots. This in-close fighting resulted in battle
conditions that favoured whoever managed to get off the first shot of their main
gun, and the limitations and advantages of both side's tank guns were negated here
due to the extremely close range of the engagements.

The Panthers, aggressively moving forward and firing from ambush positions in
intersections or side streets, began to take an immediate toll on the group of Shermans
in action near the town square. Lieutenant McPherson, Lieutenant Goodman, and
Sgt. Crabb of A Squadron all had their tanks destroyed in short order. The crews
for the most part managed to bail out but were subjected to immediate small arms
fire from the *SS-Panzergrenadiere* in the buildings.

A Troop of 46 RMC, after following B Troop across the first bridge, was confronted
by a Panther that was manoeuvring on the streets near the T-junction. Coming
under tank fire, A Troop's commander, Major Burton, had his force dig in within
the orchards near the buildings, its contribution to conquering Rots coming to a
halt for the moment.

In an extremely unfortunate incident, a liaison officer from the Fort Garry Horse
to the 2nd Canadian Armoured Brigade unexpectedly drove right over the first
bridge into the church square, the Humber armoured car being hit by Panther tank
fire and bursting into flames. Tragically, the driver and liaison officer were killed
instantly in this incident.

In the face of the heavy German anti-tank fire, Major Blanshard ordered via
radio that those Shermans tanks that were still operational, including the Firefly
of Sergeant Strawn located in the north of Rots, should withdraw away from the
hotspot of German resistance in the church square. In the chaos of the heavy German
fire, Sergeant Strawn became disoriented in the tight streets due to his turret being
traversed, and drove in the wrong direction in his attempt to follow the tank of
Major Blanshard. Strawn drove out of Rots south and eventually into La Villeneuve,

held by part of the *Hitlerjugend Begleitkompanie*. In a wild charge that saw a point-blank exchange with Panther '435' that he set on fire, Strawn's Sherman careened wildly to the south in an attempt to escape, unfortunately away from Allied lines. Its escape was only stopped when the Firefly was shot up by another Panther tank in the centre of La Villeneuve. Sgt. Strawn managed to evade capture, but some of his crew were killed when the tank was destroyed, or were hit by small arms fire when they bailed out.

It was at this time, roughly 2000 hours, that the Germans launched a counter-attack, with two *Züge* of the *Begleitkompanie*, supported by a handful of Panther tanks led by *Hstuf.* Pfeiffer. The *SS-Panzergrenadiere* were led by *Hstuf.* Gutum, who attacked with the infantry component of the headquarters escort *Begleitkompanie*. The remainder of this unit was left in La Villeneuve, Le Bourg and the grounds of the Château Rots. At this point, some effective use of *Panzerfausts* was made by the scattered members of the *IV. (Schwere) Zug* in central Rots, and *Uscha.* Gross of *I. Zug* was reported to have knocked out a Sherman by firing the infantry anti-tank weapon at it in the close confines of the village streets.

Hstuf. Pfeiffer, observing this infantry counterattack from the high point next to Rots next to the battle-damaged Panther '426', realised that personal action needed to be taken to support the *Begleitkompanie* soldiers. Charging forward downhill into battle with his *Kompanie-Chef* Panther '405', he is joined shortly afterwards by Panther '435' of *Ustuf.* Günther Deutscher, the *III. Zug Commander*. Soon Pfeiffer reached the main road of Rots leading to the church square, and there engaged several Shermans that were still shooting up the positions of the *SS-Panzergrenadiere* and had not withdrawn. Knocking out three of them, Pfeiffer then pushed further ahead, dangerously entering the street between two buildings, which limited his ability to traverse his turret. His advance was a particularly gruesome event for the Royal Marines and the *SS-Panzergrenadiere* watching, as the tracks of the Panther crushed dead and wounded British and German soldiers alike, the screams of the victims drowned out by the tank engine and the clatter of the tracks.

In this fighting it is unclear how many more Sherman tanks were destroyed, but the few which remained in the church square at this stage withdrew. The German tanks' onboard weapons were used against the marines, who were fighting just as hard against the Germans at close quarters, and as a result dead and wounded from both sides littered the streets. The dramatic appearance of the Panther, backed by the *Begleitkompanie* elements that attacked from the south and pushed north-east through the village, turned the tide temporarily for the Germans. Some 40 Royal Marine prisoners were reportedly taken prisoner, though later 46 RMC records stated the number of the missing as 35.[34] Rallied, the survivors of the *1. Kp./SS-Pz.Gren.Rgt. 26* fought on with the *Begleitkompanie SS-Panzergrenadiere*, and attempted to push the marines back.

Disturbingly, at this point the Royal Marines and some FGH tank crewman from destroyed or disabled tanks observed groups of *SS-Panzergrenadiere* moving around on the battlefield, at times stopping to shoot wounded Royal Marines and FGH tank crew members.[35] Previously having hidden in buildings, Germans ran into the street to stand beside the Panthers as they fired on the Royal Marines. Progress was made by the Germans, as the FGH tanks and Royal Marines were forced back and the German attack pushed northward, clearing the northern part of Rots from west to east.

Observing the see-saw fighting and the impact of the Panther tanks under *Hstuf.* Pfeiffer, Lieutenant Colonel Hardy made the decision to regroup his forces around those FGH tanks which had survived, to attempt a second push. From the location of his tactical headquarters near a farmhouse north of Le Hamel, Hardy gathered what Royal Marine officers he could, and reorganised their efforts. Returning to action with several tanks, the FGH aggressively pushed into Rots a second time with the surviving Royal Marines of B Troop. It appears the FGH tanks operated in two groups, one of which was No. 4 Troop under Lieutenant Curtain. This troop skirted the western side of Rots along the Mue to cut off the Germans at the rear of the village. The other, commanded by Captain Goodman of the FGH A Squadron Headquarters Troop, determinedly pushed once again into the town square.

The battered Royal Marine B Troop under Captain Docwra, supported by elements of the Y and A Troops, at this point rallied and counterattacked in a determined manner, forcing the *SS-Panzergrenadiere* of the *1./SS-Pz.Gren.Rgt. 26* and the *Begleitkompanie Züge* onto the defensive. The Royal Marines would not give up, and following the Shermans, engaged the Germans with all weapons.

As the main body of Royal Marines still in action fought to take control of northern Rots and its church square from the Germans, a detachment of B Troop that had been assigned to carry out the wide left-flanking operation through the fields to attempt to infiltrate into La Villeneuve from the east set off on foot. Moving into the fields in column, they left the firefight behind them in the evening light as they moved south. This party, led by Lieutenant Hart, had been ordered to do this as part of a wider effort to surround Le Bourg and La Villeneuve with elements of A and B Troops. Running into superior German forces near Le Bourg, it would later be forced to surrender.

As darkness approached, the battle reached its turning point. Examining events, it is plausible to suggest that the tide of battle in the late evening turned with the FGH tanks attacking from several directions, which resulted in the death of the *4.Kp/SS-Pz.Rgt. 12 Kompanie-Chef, Hstuf.* Pfeiffer, who was arguably leading the defence of Rots. This would be the decisive act in the fighting, and this incident would influence the *Waffen-SS* decision to withdraw from central Rots south towards La Villeneuve and Le Bourg. Seeking to outflank the German armour in action, aggressive manoeuvring by an unknown FGH tank commander would result in him damaging the Panther of *Hstuf.* Pfeiffer, killing its commander.

As the resurgent Royal Marines and FGH engaged the Germans, the *SS-Panzergrenadiere* were alerted that the Sherman tanks of No. 4 Troop had appeared to their rear, and they communicated this information to the tank of *Hstuf.* Pfeiffer, causing him to reverse slowly backward in the tight streets of Rots near the church. Reaching an open area when the turret could be traversed, Pfeiffer pointed the gun to the rear and continued to drive backwards, seeking to avoid a situation where the rear of the tank could be fired on.

Then, the worst possible thing happened to Pfeiffer and his crew: as the Panther retreated south along the main street in Rots from the church square, its turret traversed in the wrong direction, a Sherman appeared from the direction from which the Panther had retreated and began to aim at the German tank. The Panther's driver frantically gunned the engine, but to no avail, as he could not get out of the Sherman's field of fire.[36] Trapped by the tight confines of the street, the Panther was shot in the rear of the turret by the lone Sherman, killing Pfeiffer. The relentless Royal Marine counterattack and the Shermans firing into all buildings then drove back the *Begleitkompanie Züge*, and the survivors of the *1. Kp./SS-Pz.Gren.Rgt. 26* began to retreat as well, the *Kommandeur* of *IV. (Schwere) Zug* during this incident using a wheelbarrow to transport another wounded senior NCO out of the way of the FGH tank fire.

It would seem to the reader that the impact of the Panther tanks on the battle would have been expected to be much higher. While a sizeable number of FGH tanks and some other vehicles were destroyed, a large number of Royal Marines were not killed or wounded, the largest success being the 35 prisoners taken when the Germans counterattacked. It seemed the tight village streets, wooded areas and other obstacles gave the Royal Marines enough cover to avoid the worst of the tank and MG-42 fire. Had Pfeiffer lived and continued to fight, it is unclear what decision would have been made by the surviving *SS-Panzergrenadiere* officers on whether to continue to fight or pull back. Regardless of whether this was the critical event, after it occurred the *Waffen-SS* began to retreat along the main street of Rots and the surrounding fields.

In conclusion, both the Royal Marines and FGH tankers acted with the utmost determination to continue the battle in the face of the severe losses and destruction wreaked upon both A Squadron and the Royal Marines of B Troop, many of which had been forced to surrender in the tough urban fighting. Its renewed attack would clear the central area of Rots, though it must be made clear that this is all that they conquered during the course of the battle that went on into the hours of darkness. The battle had seen fierce combat and losses, and forces of the *Hitlerjugend* were driven back, albeit after successfully inflicting heavy armoured and infantry losses on Anglo-Canadian forces. Losses to the *1. Kp./SS-Pz.Gren.Rgt. 26* and the *4. Kp./SS-Pz. Rgt. 12* had been heavy and were not affordable for the division at this stage. One

4. Kompanie Panther tank was written off and a further three were badly damaged by tank and anti-tank gun fire during the defence of the village.[37]

The number of human losses on each side varies within historical accounts. The fighting in Rots is presented, especially in Canadian sources, as near apocalyptic, with both sides destroying one another, resulting in a sea of dead and wounded from both sides strewn through the square and side streets of Rots, the Royal Marines and FGH winning an almost pyrrhic victory over the *Waffen-SS* due to the scale of the losses. The regimental history of Regiment de La Chaudière supports this interpretation of the fighting as a bloodbath, and while the fighting was particularity heavy, the overall losses were not catastrophic for either side; the 46 RMC war diary for the date reports losses of only 22 dead. Despite the lack of access to the Fort Garry Horse war diary for June 1944 due to it being lost in Europe, Canadian Historian Mark Zuehlke lists seven killed from the FGH A Squadron and eight wounded.[38] Total German losses were 22 dead, 30 wounded and 15 missing from all units involved.[39]

Reassessment

In conclusion, the *Hitlerjugend* had performed reasonably well tactically in combat on 7 June, but during the period 8–10 June had suffered severe losses in return for non-existent territorial gains in its offensive operations. It could not mass its forces for a decisive thrust on a relatively small frontage, and like the other *Panzerdivisionen* to arrive as part of the *I. SS-Pz.Korps*, was simply overwhelmed by Anglo-Canadian forces that slowly but surely defeated their battalion-level attacks and then forced them into a defensive role simply because no other unit was there to hold the line.

Why were its battalions defeated in this time frame in battalion-on-battalion level combat operations? Poor coordination, lack of overwhelming combat power available for the job at hand, and a condition of complete 'shock' at an entirely new enemy and style of warfare all contributed to the failures. Poor coordination was a factor that seemed to plague all *Hitlerjugend* operations from 7 June onwards. Effective formation-to-formation radio communications, most importantly for tank and artillery support, simply did not occur due the threat of radio triangulation by enemy field artillery units and an arrogant, mistaken belief that what units were present would simply prevail over the Anglo-Canadian forces. All lessons learned from the North African and Italian campaigns against Commonwealth forces either had not been passed down or were simply ignored by the Eastern Front *Waffen-SS Kampfer* ('fighters') who waded into the fighting in small villages like Bretteville-l'Orgueilleuse in the same manner that they had attacked villages outside Kharkov in the winter of 1943.

Enemy air attacks, radio triangulation and a lack of proper planning due to real or imagined time pressures all combined to equal repeated defeats, robbing the *Hitlerjugend* of the battlefield initiative. The rough and ready tactics on the unbroken Ukrainian steppe that worked so well against groups of huddled Red Army soldiers with a few T-34s and one or two anti-tank guns now were completely ineffective due to constant pressure from Anglo-Canadian field artillery, naval gunfire and the never-ending strafing runs of the fighter-bombers, the hated Jabos that inhibited daytime supply runs, road marches and combat operations. Proper control at the *Armeekorps* and *Division* level was also a problem, as evidenced by the three *Panzerdivisionen Korps*-level attacks that simply could not get off the ground because of poor initial deployment too far from the beaches and their piecemeal commitment of forces that immediately became involved in combat or were forced to simply hold ground. The lack of infantry to support armoured attacks and vice versa was detrimental to *Hitlerjugend* attacks on villages and caused unduly heavy tank and infantry losses, the battles with the 7th Canadian Infantry Brigade being especially costly.[1] Aggression certainly was not lacking, nor was the desire to engage the enemy, yet this could not make up for poor *SS-Panzergrenadiere-Artillerie–Panzer* coordination.

This coordination problem hampered the proper mustering of the requisite force necessary for operations. Major force was needed to overcome the Allied fortress positions and their artillery-based doctrine. There were a total of four different *Waffen-SS* attacks on the twin village area of Bretteville-l'Orgueilleuse–Norrey-en-Bessin, none of which were successful. Despite many German units being in the area, including *SS-Panzer* and self-propelled *SS-Panzerartillerie* units, the proper coordination to mass the combat power of the sum of these forces did not occur. This was due to the Germans' overestimation of their capabilities and underestimation of Canadian RCA firepower and infantry resilience.

The Canadians were also prepared for German attacks and well trained by the British on the German doctrine. The severity of the Allied artillery fire shut down German operations totally and caused heavy *Waffen-SS* casualties. The coordination, speed and intensity of massed RCA and RA artillery fire was far superior to that of the of opposing SS gunners, despite their best efforts with what divisional ammunition assets were available.[2] Piecemeal *Blitzkrieg* tactics with light forces against this new enemy failed miserably, with Meyer, Wünsche and Mohnke all failing to make correct tactical battlefield decisions, despite their experience. The fact that the Canadians were not the Soviet Red Army was one of the main factors involved in the failures. Hasty attacks with inferior forces had very little chance of success in the west. Quoting British military historian Michael Reynolds in his work on the *I. SS-Pz. Korps* in Normandy, *Steel Inferno*: 'The shock tactics which had been so successful for the Germans in Russia, had failed miserably against the well-disciplined Canadian troops.'[3] Canadian Army official historian of the Second World War, C.P. Stacey, would go on to say: 'The German operations at this stage leave the impression of rather hasty and ineffective improvisations. The attacks were pressed with courage and determination but with no tactical skill.'[4]

Interestingly, the entire *Gen.d.Pz.Tr.* von Schweppenburg notion of allowing the enemy to land and attacking him with a massive, delayed panzer counterstrike was entirely discarded. The *Panzerdivisionen*, most notably the *Hitlerjugend*, were thrown piecemeal into the inferno and were occupied with defending a large frontage. Their *Kampfgruppen* battlegroups were not deployed en masse on a short frontage, where the possibility might exist that they could break through to the beaches and Allied rear areas.[5] They were forced to attempt the 'Rommel' battle but were far from properly deployed to do so, Allied aircraft slowing their transit times considerably. The entire destruction or severe depletion of almost all the affected formations of the Normandy *Atlantikwall* forced the arriving *Panzerdivisionen* into holding the line, not in any way in accordance with prescribed German *Panzerwaffe* doctrine. A concentrated and coordinated thrust, so stressed in German operational thinking, had been spurned in favour of small, hasty attacks that the British Second Army responded to with determination and superior defensive firepower.[6] Real or imagined time pressures to rapidly destroy the bridgehead, coupled with impossible travel demands due to a poorly planned deployment prior to the invasion, had led to failure.

Most of all, the Allied forces the *Hitlerjugend* were facing assumed at times a defensive, rather than offensive, posture that expected massed armoured counterattacks. The British tactical doctrine, proven in North Africa, had been developed to deal with the Germans, and the Canadian and British infantry divisions exercised it effectively. In doing so they maximised their strengths and advantages, while the opposite was true in the case of the Germans. The German attempt at the early war *Panzerwaffe* practice of mobile operations of a high-tempo nature, keeping the enemy on the run and rapidly penetrating his rear areas, was disrupted. Virtually all combat units within the *Hitlerjugend* had their noses bloodied, badly, and had not penetrated the beachhead perimeter nor retained the battlefield initiative.

Following this learning experience, the fighting style of the *Hitlerjugend* would change radically to a defensive posture, the reason for this being that forces needed to hold the front while the *Hitlerjugend* assembled for large assaults on a narrow frontage were not present. The Allied front above and to the west of Caen had stabilised and the initiative was now in their hands. The overall defensive might of the Anglo-Canadian forces was apparent, and would only grow stronger, as more ships unloaded their human and materiel cargo into the beachhead. The window to fight the swift, decisive 'Rommel' battle had come and gone. Even *G.F.M.* Rommel knew it was a time for pause, as the three *Panzerdivisionen* of *I. SS-Panzerkorps* were defensively pinned to the ground in front of Caen. He knew he had to replace them with *Infanterie-Divisionen* so that they could be used in their proper role, which certainly was not static defensive warfare.[7]

Total losses to the *Hitlerjugend* by nightfall on the evening of 11 June, taking the casualty figures from Hubert Meyer's divisional history at various points and adding them up, were 240 men killed, 586 wounded and 98 missing.[8] At total of 30 Panzers had been written off, and none of these were immediately replaced in the short term. The *SS-Panzergrenadiere* losses were almost solely concentrated in the combat arms *Kompanien* within the *Hitlerjugend*.[9] The fighting had at some stages been very intense, a factor made worse by the perpetration of war crimes against prisoners of war by a wide spectrum of *Hitlerjugend* officers, senior and junior NCOs and common *SS-Panzergrenadiere* post-battle.[10] For the majority of these incidents, there was no apparent reasoning behind the murders other than rage or the misguided belief that Anglo-Canadian troops had committed war crimes, and it speaks to the triumph of murderous criminality that characterised the Nazi regime over basic military professionalism, discipline and humanity.

Though these losses had occurred, the division was still very powerful, and in rather good shape if compared to other *Panzerdivisionen* on the Eastern Front in this time period. What was worrying for the Germans looking forward to further fighting in June and beyond was that while the division had taken losses and had its fighting capabilities slightly curtailed, its defensive responsibilities had not been reduced. In truth, following the landing of additional British forces in the days after the D-Day assault, it was facing a much more powerful enemy, one that would in mid-June pummel away at its left flank, and annihilate large portions of the division in a bitter battle of attrition, Operation *Epsom*.

Apart from establishing a firm front above Caen and limiting the size of the bridgehead, not much had been accomplished by the *Hitlerjugend* in accordance with German doctrine on mobile warfare. The *Hitlerjugend* was now caught in a deployment where it would be continuously worn down, this role being a total waste of its mobile offensive capabilities. It was now conducting warfare on Allied terms, and the campaign was progressing in the manner that Montgomery and other Allied generals had planned.

Mobile operations had come to naught, and all the formations and units of the *Hitlerjugend* had become engaged in fragmented actions rather than a unified push or divisional operation. *G.F.M.* Rommel, meeting with *Gen.d.Pz.Tr.* von Schweppenburg at *Pz.Gr.West Hauptquartier* at the Château La Caine on the evening of the 10 June, was greeted with a grim assessment from his subordinate. The offensive of *I. SS-Panzerkorps* would have to be postponed. The *21. Pz.Div.* was on the defensive, the *Panzer-Lehr* front had broken, and the *Hitlerjugend* was the only thing powerful enough to stop the Allies taking Caen. Ammunition and fuel were in short supply, and artillery and anti-aircraft corps-level units were on their way but were not near the front yet. Rommel had to agree that the planned three-division counter offensive could not begin.[11] As if to cap off the failure of the three *Panzerdivisionen* to make a concerted push, the *Hauptquartier* of *Panzergruppe West* was destroyed by an Allied air strike shortly after Rommel's departure. Schweppenburg survived, but his headquarters was effectively destroyed, and control of the *Panzerdivisionen* was given to *Ogruf.* Dietrich's *I. SS-Panzerkorps Hauptquartier* until it could be rebuilt.[12] This *SS-Panzerkorps*, with the *Hitlerjugend* being its most powerful component, would fight a desperate defensive battle from 12 June–12 July 1944, the period to be covered in the second volume of this series. In these battles, it would face some of the most devastating corps-level offensives ever launched by the British Army in the Second World War. It would be in these battles that its combat units would fight to near annihilation, these at times singlehandedly holding back attacking Commonwealth forces three and even four times their size.

Rank Equivalents

Comparative ranks: *Heer* – *Waffen-SS* – British Commonwealth Armies – US Army
(Officer aspirant tanks omitted)

Heer	Waffen-SS	Abbreviations used	Commonwealth Armies	US Army
Generalfeldmarschall	N/A	*G.F.M.*	Field Marshal	General of the Army
Generaloberst	*SS-Obergruppenführer und Generaloberst de Waffen-SS*	*Gen.O./ Obstgruf.*	General	General
General der Panzertruppen, Infanterie, Kavalerie, etc.	*SS-Obergruppenführer und General der Waffen-SS*	*Gen.d.Pz./ Ogruf.*	Lieutenant General	Lieutenant General
Generalleutnant	*SS-Gruppenführer und Generalleutnant der Waffen-SS*	*Gen.Lt./Gruf.*	Major General	Major General
Generalmajor	*SS-Brigadenführer und Generalmajor der Waffen-SS*	*Gen.Maj./ Brig.Fhr.*	Brigadier	Brigadier General
N/A	*SS-Oberführer*	*N/A/Obf.*	N/A	Senior Colonel
Oberst	*SS-Standartenführer*	*O./Staf.*	Colonel	Colonel
Oberstleutnant	*SS-Obersturmbannführer*	*Oberstlt./ Ostubaf.*	Lieutenant Colonel	Lieutenant Colonel

Heer	*Waffen-SS*	Abbreviations used	Commonwealth Armies	US Army
Major	*SS-Sturmbannführer*	*Maj./Stubaf.*	Major	Major
Hauptmann or Rittmeister	*SS-Hauptsturmführer*	*Hptm./Hstuf.*	Captain	Captain
Oberleutnant	*SS-Obersturmführer*	*Oberlt./Ostuf.*	Lieutenant	1st Lieutenant
Leutnant	*SS-Untersturmführer*	*Lt./Ustuf.*	2nd Lieutenant	2nd Lieutenant
Stabsfeldwebel	*SS-Sturmscharführer*	*Stabs Fw./N/A*	Regimental Sergeant Major (RSM)	Sergeant Major
Hauptfeldwebel	*SS-Stabsscharführer*	*H.Fw./Stab. Scha.*	Company Sergeant Major (CSM)	N/A
Oberfeldwebel	*SS-Hauptscharführer*	*Ofw./Hscha.*	Sergeant Major	Master Sergeant
Feldwebel	*SS-Oberscharführer*	*Fw./Oscha.*	Staff Sergeant	Technical Sergeant
Unterfeldwebel	*SS-Scharführer*	*Ufw./Scha.*	Sergeant	Staff Sergeant
Unteroffizer	*SS-Unterscharführer*	*Uffz./Uscha.*	Corporal	Sergeant
Obergrefreiter	*SS-Rottenführer*	*Ogrefr./Rttf.*	Lance Corporal	Corporal/ Specialist
Gregreiter	*SS-Sturmann*	N/A	Acting Corporal	Senior Private
Obergrenadier, Oberkannonier, etc.	*SS-Obergrenadier, Oberschütze,* etc.	N/A	Private 1st Class	Senior Private
Schutz, Kanonier, Grenadier	*SS-Schütze*	N/A	Private	Private

Glossary

Abteilung: Detachment. A German battalion-sized unit, usually used to designate armour, artillery or recce units, not *Pionier* or *Infanterie* units.

Armee: Army-sized formation within the German army and the *Waffen-SS*.

Bataillon: Battalion.

Befehlshaber: Army or army group commander with a rank of general or above.

Befehlspanzer: Command tank within a tank battalion or within the regimental headquarters of an armoured regiment.

Chef: Literally 'boss'. Used as a designation for a company commander.

Chef des Stabes: Chief of staff in a headquarters of *Korps* level or higher.

Ersatzheer: Replacement army organisation within Germany.

Feldgendarmerie: Military police within the German army and *Waffen-SS*.

Gefechtsstand: Headquarters of an *Abteilung*, regiment or division within the *Heer* or *Waffen-SS*.

Gepanzert: Armoured. Used to designate armoured infantry and armoured artillery.

Gruppe: Group. Used to designate a sub-unit within a wing in the *Luftwaffe*.

Hauptquartier: Headquarters of an *Armee*-level and above formation within the *Heer* and *Waffen-SS*.

Heer: German army.

Heeresgruppe (*H.Gr.*): Army group of several *Heer* armies.

Infanterie-Division: Infantry division within the *Heer*.

Infanterie-Geschütz: Small howitzer used within the *Grenadier* and *Panzergrenadier* regiments.

Jagdgeschwader: German Air Force wing of several groups or *Gruppen*.

Jagdpanzer: Hunting tank or tank destroyer; a turretless armoured vehicle designed to destroy other armoured vehicles in defensive operations.

Jäger: Designation for *Luftwaffe* ground troop infantry, similar to a *Grenadier* in the *Heer*.

Kampfgruppe: Battlegroup made up of several battalions or based on a regiment.

Kommandeur: Commanding officer of an *Abteilung* or battalion-level and above formation.

Kriegsmarine: German navy of the Second World War.

Landser: German army slang for an infantry soldier, similar to the US 'grunt'.

Luftflotte: Formation within the German air force, equivalent to an Allied air force such as the US Eighth Army Air Force.

Luftwaffe: German air force of the Second World War.

Nebelwerfer: 'Smoke thrower'. Name for rocket launcher artillery weapons.

Oberbefehlshaber: Higher commander, usually *Armee* or *Armeegruppe* commander.

Oberkommando der Wehrmacht (OKW): High command of the entire German armed forces, often misunderstood in Western military history works as the German army or high command of the army.

Panther: German medium tank.

Panzerabteilung: German tank unit of battalion strength.

Panzer: Shortened version of *Panzerkampfwagen*, or armoured combat vehicle.

Panzerabwehrkanone (Pak): German high-velocity anti-tank gun with trails that was towed by a vehicle when transported.

Panzergrenadiere: Armoured infantry carried in trucks or half-tracks.

Panzerkorps (*Pz.Korps*): An armoured *Korps* of two or more combat divisions.

Schützpanzerwagen (SPW): Armoured half-tracks, used to equip one battalion of a *Panzergrenadier* regiment.

Schwere Panzer Abteilung: Heavy tank detachment of battalion size. Usually equipped with Tiger I or II heavy tanks.

Staffel: Squadron-sized unit within a *Luftwaffe Geschwader* (wing). Smaller than an Allied fighter squadron but bigger than a flight.

Sturmgeschütz: Self-propelled gun on a tank chassis. The gun had limited traverse, and the fighting compartment was either open or enclosed.

Waffen-SS: Military wing of the NSDAP Party (Nazi Party) that ruled Germany during the Second World War, with its own rank structure and military units and formations.

Wehrmacht: Overall German armed forces, including the army.

Zug: Platoon-sized unit.

Zugführer: Leader of a platoon-sized unit, usually in an armoured or infantry unit.

12. SS-Panzerdivision Hitlerjugend
Order of Battle and command list,
1 June 1944

Note: '?' indicates 'unknown'.

Divisionsstab
Division Kdr.: *Brig.Fhr.* Witt
4. Ordonanzoffizer (04): *Ustuf.* Hausrath

Fuhrungsabteilung (Ia)
1. General St. Offz. (Ia): *Stubaf.* Meyer
1. Ord. Offz. (01): *Ostuf.* Meitzel
3. Gen.St.Offz. (Ic): *Ostuf.* Doldi
3. Ord. Offz. (03): *Ustuf.* Trommer
Div. Kartenstelle.: *Uscha.* Kriegge
Liter d. Nachrichtend. (LDN): *Ostuf.* von Brandis
Feldgendarmerie Kompanie: *Ostuf.* Buschausen

Hitlerjugend Begleitkompanie
Kompanie-Chef: *Ostuf.* Guntrum
1. Schutzen Zug. ?
2. S.M.G Zug. ?
3. Pak Zug. ?
4. Flak Zug. ?
5. s.I.G. Zug. ?

Quartiermeisterabt. (IB)
2. General St. Offz.: *Stubaf.* Buschein
2. Ord. Offz. (02): *Unstuf.* Lubbe
Waffenmuntion.: *Stubaf.* Schurer
Abt. IV-a. Div. Intendant.: *Stubaf.* Kos
Abt IV-b. Artz.: *Ostubaf.* Dr. R. Schutlz
Abt V, Div.Ing.: *Stubaf.* Manthey

SS-Panzerregiment 12
Rgt. Kdr.: *Ostubaf.* Wünsche

I. Abteilung
Abteilung Kdr.: *Stubaf.* Jürgensen
1. Kompanie: *Hstuf.* Berlin
2. Kompanie: *Ostuf.* Gaede
3. Kompanie: *Ostuf.* von Ribbentrop
4. Kompanie: *Hstuf.* Pfeiffer
Werkstatt Kompanie: *Ustuf.* R. Maier

II. Abteilung
Abteilung Kdr.: *Stubaf.* Prinz
5. Kompanie: *Ostuf.* Bando
6. Kompanie: *Hstuf.* Ruckdeschel
7. Kompanie: *Hstuf.* Brackner
8. Kompanie: *Ostuf.* Seigel
9. Kompanie: *Hstuf.* Buettner
Werkstattzug: *Ostuf.* D. Muller

Panzerjägerabteiling 12 (Note: Not deployed until later)
Abteilung Kdr.: *Stubaf.* Hanreich
1. Kompanie: *Ostuf.* Hurdelbrink
2. Kompanie: *Ostuf.* Wachter
3. Kompanie: *Hstuf.* Wost

SS-Panzergrenadierregiment 25
Rgt. Kdr.: *Staf.* Meyer
13. (s.I.G.) Kompanie: *Oblt.* Kaminski
14. (Flak) Kompanie: *Hstuf.* Brantl

15. (Aufklärung) Kompanie: *Hstuf.* von Büttner
16. (Pionier) Kompanie: *Ustuf.* Werner

I. Bataillon
Bataillon Kdr.: *Stubaf.* Waldmuller
1. Kompanie: ?
2. Kompanie: *Ostuf.* Knossel.
3. Kompanie: *Hstuf.* Peinemann
4. Kompanie: *Ostuf.* Wilke

II. Bataillon
Bataillon Kdr.: *Stubaf.* Scappini
5. Kompanie: *Hstuf.* Kreilen
6. Kompanie: *Hstuf.* Dr Thirey
7. Kompanie: *Hstuf.* Schrott
8. Kompanie: *Hstuf.* Breinlich

III. Bataillon
Bataillon Kdr.: *Ostubaf.* Milius
9. Kompanie: *Oblt.* Fritsch
10. Kompanie: *Oblt.* Dietrich
11. Kompanie: *Ostuf.* Stahl
12. Kompanie: *Oblt.*Worner

SS-Panzergrenadierregiment 26
Rgt. Kommandeur: *Ostubaf.* Mohnke
13. (s.I.G.) Kompanie: *Ostuf.* Polansk
14. (Flak) Kompanie: *Hstuf.* Stolze
15. (Aufklärung) Kompanie: *Oblt.* Bayer
16. (Pionier) Kompanie: *Ostuf.* Trompke

I. Bataillon
Bataillon. Kdr.: *Stubaf.* Krause
1. Kompanie: *Hstuf.* Eggert
2. Kompanie: *Ostuf.* Groschel
3. Kompanie: *Ostuf.* Duvel
4. Kompanie: *Ostuf.* Hartung

II. Bataillon
Bataillon Kdr.: *Stubaf.* Siebken
5. Kompanie: *Ostuf.* Gottard.
6. Kompanie: *Ostuf.* Schmolke
7. Kompanie: *Lt.* Henne
8. Kompanie: *Hstuf.* Fasching

III. Bataillon
Bataillon Kdr.: *Stubaf.* Olboeter
9. Kompanie: *Oblt.* Gobel
10. Kompanie: *Oblt.* Pallas
11. Kompanie: *Ostuf.* Hauser
12. Kompanie: *Ostuf.* Riede

SS-Panzer-Aufklärungsabteilung 12
Abteilung Kdr.: *Stubaf.* Bremer
1. Kompanie: *Ostuf.* Hansmann
2. Kompanie: *Ostuf.* Hauck
3. Kompanie: *Ostuf.* Keue
4. Kompanie: *Ostuf.* Beiersdorf
5. Kompanie: *Hstuf.* von Reitzenstein

SS-Panzerartillerieregiment 12
Rgt. Kdr.: *Ostubaf.* Schroder.

I. Abteilung
Abteilung Kdr.: *Stubaf.* Urbanitz
1. Batterie: *Hstuf.* Gille
2. Batterie: *Ostuf.* Timmerbeil
3. Batterie: *Ostuf.* Heller

II. Abteilung
Abteilung Kdr.: *Stubaf.* Schöps
4. Batterie: *Oblt.* Haller
5. Batterie: *Ostuf.* Kurzbein
6. Batterie: *Ostuf.* Kilchling

III. Abteilung
Abteilung Kdr.: *Stubaf.* Bartling
7. Batterie: *Ostuf.* Etterich
8. Batterie: *Ustuf.* Peschel
9. Batterie: *Ostuf.* Balschuweit
10. Batterie: *Hstuf.* Heydrich

SS-Werferabteilung 12 (Note: Not deployed until later)
Abteilung Kdr.: *Stubaf.* Muller
1. Batterie: *Hstuf.* Macke
2. Batterie: *Hstuf.* Zeisenitz
3. Batterie: *Ostuf.* Bay
4. Batterie: *Ostuf.* Dr Erhart

SS-Flakabteilung 12
Abteilung Kdr.: *Stubaf.* Fend
1. Batterie: *Ustuf.* Ritzel
2. Batterie: *Ostuf.* Reidel
3. Batterie: *Hstuf.* Dr Weygand
4. Batterie: *Ostuf.* Ritscher
5. Batterie: ?

SS-Panzerpionierbataillon 12
Bataillon Kdr.: *Stubaf.* Muller
1. Kompanie: *Oblt.* Toll
2. Kompanie: *Ostuf.* Kuret
3. Kompanie: *Hstuf.* Teidke
4. Kompanie: *Ostuf.* Bischof
Bruckendonne B Kompanie: *Ustuf.* Richter

SS-Panzernachrichtabteilung 12
Abteilung Kdr.: *Stubaf.* Pandel
1. Kompanie: *Ostuf.* Dinglinger
2. Kompanie: *Hstuf.* Kruger

SS-Panzerdivisionnachschubtruppen 12
Abteilung Kdr.: *Stubaf.* Kolitz
Krafft. Kompanien 1–6
Nachschub Kompanie

SS-Panzerinstandsetzungs-abteilung 12
Abteilung Kdr.: *Stubaf.* Manthei
Werkstatt Kompanien. 1–4

SS-Wirtschaftsbatallion 12
Abteilung Kdr.: *Stubaf.* Dr Kos

SS Sanitätsabteilung 12
Abteilung Kdr.: *Ostuf.* Dr R. Schulz

Feldersatzbattalion 12
Abteilung Kdr.: *Hstuf.* Urabl

Calculated Panzer losses and strengths within *SS-Pz.Rgt. 12*, 7–11 June 1944

Specific data on those on hand remaining operational, under short- or long-term repair, is *not listed*. No replacement tanks arrived to offset combat losses in this time period.

Date	Total Panzer IV tank losses on that date	Total Panzer IV tanks on hand at 2359 hrs	Total Panther tank losses on that date	Total Panther tanks on hand at 2359 hrs
7 June 1944	12	89	0	66
8 June 1944	0	89	3	63
9 June 1944	0	89	7	56
10 June 1944	1	88	0	56
11 June 1944	6	82	1	55
Totals: strengths, total losses	19	82	11	55

Endnotes

Acknowledgements

1   Keith Taylor, *The Waist-High Cornfield* (Hamburg: self-published, 2017), Keith Taylor, *Broken Bridges, Rivers to Cross* (Hamburg: self-published, 2021).

Introduction

1   Pim van Gelder, 'Operation Market Garden. Which time zone with which time?', retrieved 13 September 2023 from https://vriendenairbornemuseum.nl/public/docs/Operation_Market_Garden_Which_time_zone_with_which_time.pdf. Mr Van Gelder stresses in his analysis of Operation *Market Garden* time zones in place for both German and Allied forces that while there was a difference for September 1944, the times of both German and Allied armies in the summer months of 1944 were identical, changing only in September.

2   Hubert Meyer, *The History of the 12. SS-Panzerdivision Hitlerjugend* (Winnipeg: J. J. Fedorowicz Publishing, 1994). This English edition was based on a previous three-volume set, published earlier in Germany in 1982.

3   'Canada House of Commons Speaker Calls Ukrainian Nazi Vet a "Hero"', retrieved 10 October 2023 from https://www.youtube.com/watch?v=406huseHyJ4. Internet film clip of the incident.

4   Kurt Meyer, *Grenadiers. The Story of Waffen SS General Kurt "Panzer" Meyer* (Mechanicsburg: Stackpole Books, 2005), 249, 263, 298–99.

Chapter 1

1   Michael Reynolds, *Steel Inferno: I SS Panzer Corps in Normandy* (Barnsley: Pen & Sword Military, 2009), 40.

2   Friedrich Ruge, *Rommel in Normandy* (London: Presidio Press, 1979), 1–10.

3   Horst Boog, Gerhard Krebs, Detlef Vogel, *Germany and the Second World War Volume VII: the Strategic Air War in Europe and the War in the West and East Asia* (Oxford: Oxford University Press, 2006).

4   Walter Warlimont, *Inside Hitler's Headquarters 1939–1945* (Novato: Presidio Press, 1964), 414. Geoffrey P. Megargee, *Inside Hitler's High Command* (Lawrence: University of Press of Kansas, 2000), 210.

5   Frederich Ruge, *Rommel in Normandy*, 168–69.

6   Matthew Cooper, *The German Army 1939–1945* (London: Macdonald's and Jane's, 1978), 498. Discussion defence of the West and the Allied fighting potential between *G.F.M.* Rommel and *Gen. Maj.* Fritz Bayerlein, commander of the *Panzer-Lehr Panzerdivision*.

7   Heinz Guderian, *Panzer Leader. General Heinz Guderian* (New York: Da Capo Press, 1996), 263–65.

8   NARA, RG 338. MS-C024. Fritz Kraemer, *I SS Panzer Corps in the West* (Landsberg: US WWII Foreign Military Studies, 1954), 8.

9   Michael Reynolds, *Steel Inferno: I SS Panzer Corps in Normandy*, 41.

10   Michael Reynolds, *Steel Inferno: I SS Panzer Corps in Normandy*, 42.

11   John Ellis, *Brute Force* (New York: Viking, 1990), 146. The breaking of the communication codes of the German Enigma machines, beginning in 1941, gave the Allies a huge intelligence windfall that was crucial for developing a total intelligence picture of German deployments, beliefs and intentions. Each *Panzerdivision*, for example, had several Enigma machines.

12   Horst Boog, Gerhard Krebs, Detlef Vogel, *Germany and the Second World War, Volume VII*, 528–29.

13   Walter Gaul, 'The G.A.F. and the invasion of Normandy 1944', retrieved 2 January 2024 from https://www.ibiblio.org/hyperwar/Germany/LW/GAF-Normandy/index.html

14   Horst Boog, Gerhard Krebs, and Detlef Vogel, *Germany and the Second World War, Volume VII*, 531.

15   Horst Boog, Gerhard Krebs, and Detlef Vogel, *Germany and the Second World War, Volume VII*, 531.

16   Ian F. W. Beckett (ed.), *Rommel Reconsidered* (Mechanicsburg: Stackpole Books, 2013), 119.

17   NARA, RG 338. MS-C024. Fritz Kraemer, *I SS Panzer Corps in the West*, 5.

18   Ian F. W. Beckett (ed.), *Rommel Reconsidered*, 120.

19   NARA, RG 338. MS-C024. Fritz Kraemer, *I SS Panzer Corps in the West*, 7.

20   Horst Boog, Gerhard Krebs, Detlef Vogel, *Germany and the Second World War, Volume VII*, 511.

21   Ian F. W. Beckett, Editor, *Rommel Reconsidered*, 120.

22   R. J. Lahey, '"Hitler's Intuition", Luftwaffe Photoreconnaissance and the Reinforcement of Normandy', *The Journal of Military History*, 86 (January 2022): 77–109, 78.

23   Horst Boog, Gerhard Krebs, and Detlef Vogel, *Germany and the Second World War, Volume VII*, 565.

24   Horst Boog, Gerhard Krebs, and Detlef Vogel, *Germany and the Second World War, Volume VII*, 565.

25   Horst Boog, Gerhard Krebs, and Detlef Vogel, *Germany and the Second World War, Volume VII*, 565.

26   Horst Boog, Gerhard Krebs, and Detlef Vogel, *Germany and the Second World War, Volume VII*, 567.

Chapter 2

1   Bruce Condell (ed.), *Truppenführung: On the German Art of War* (London: Lynne Reinner, 2001). Originally published in 1933 under the leadership of *Generaloberst* Ludwig Beck, this book was the premier doctrine manual for the German *Heer*. However, it was woefully lacking in understanding or emphasising the importance of mobile armoured forces.

2   James S. Corum, 'The Development of Armour Doctrine', in *The Roots of Blitzkrieg: Hans Von Seeckt and German Military Reform* (Kansas City: University of Kansas Press, 1992), 122–43. Before Guderian, *Lt.* Ernst Volckheim had been the primary innovator in the field of armour as part of the *Reichswehr*'s Inspectorate of Motor Troops in the 1920s.

3   Matthew Cooper, *The German Army 1939–1945*, 137. The idea of outflanking and encircling the enemy was fundamental in German tactical and strategic doctrines. Joining the writings of the 19th-century Schlieffen with the new mobile warfare theories of British and German junior officers led to logical conclusions drawn up by Panzer leaders such as *Gen.O.* Heinz Guderian and strategic planners such as *G.F.M.* Erich Von Manstein.

4   J. B. A. Bailey, *Field Artillery and Firepower* (Annapolis: Naval Institute Press, 2004), 287. The low-cost armoured offensive *Blitzkrieg* warfare of the 1939–41 period stressed the reduced role of artillery and fire-intensive operations.

5   Matthew Cooper, *The German Army 1939–1945*, 470. An example of this was the counter-offensive of *XLVIII. Panzerkorps* to re-capture Zhitomir, November 1943.

6   Craig Luther, *Blood and Honor: The History of the 12th SS Panzer Division "Hitlerjugend Youth" 1943–1945* (Atglen: Schiffer Publishing, 2012), 244.

7   Michael Reynolds, *Steel Inferno: I SS Panzer Corps in Normandy*, 33. The attack was not a strictly controlled, over-planned affair with timed phases and objectives.

8   Bruce Condell (ed.), *Truppenführung: On the German Art of War*, 88–116. This chapter on the attack
    stresses a combined arms approach whenever possible in the attack. It must be noted that *Kampfgruppe*
    composition grew out of experience of the commander.

9   Roger Edwards, *Panzer: A Revolution in Warfare* (London: Arms and Armour Press,1989), 81–112.

10 Michael Reynolds, *Steel Inferno: I SS Panzer Corps in Normandy*, 146. One of which being the *Heer
    83. Nebelwerfer-Regiment*, a component of *Werfer Brigade 7*. It was used from time to time as support
    for the *Hitlerjugend*.

11 J. B. A. Bailey, *Field Artillery and Firepower*, 299. On the issue of counter-mobility, the best "stopper"
    to *Panzer* operations discovered in North Africa was the high-velocity anti-tank gun deployed in large
    numbers, matched with on-call heavy field artillery concentrations.

12 Roger Edwards, *Panzer: A Revolution in Warfare*, 210. In the initial period before and after the invasion,
    the RAF and USAAF attacked rail and road bridges, junctions, switching yards and crossroads, severely
    damaging the transport net.

13 Russell Hart, *Clash of Arms: How the Allies Won in Normandy* (Norman: University of Oklahoma Press,
    2001), 376. German counterattacks often developed within hours to regain the main line of resistance.

14 Roger Edwards, *Panzer: A Revolution in Warfare*, 81–112.

Chapter 3

1   Kamen Nevenkin, *Fire Brigades. The Panzer Divisions 1943–1945* (Winnipeg: J. J. Fedorowicz Publishing,
    2008), 904.

2   Kamen Nevenkin, *Fire Brigades*, 780–84.

3   See *Appendix 3*, *Hitlerjugend* Order of Battle.

4   See *Appendix 1* for *Waffen-SS* military rank equivalents.

5   Hubert Meyer, *The History of the 12. SS-Panzerdivision*, 3.

6   Omer Bartov, *The Eastern Front 1941–45, and the Barbarisation of Warfare* (New York: St. Martin's
    Press, 1986), 106–41. Using four German *Heer* divisions records and other sources, Bartov chronicles
    a descent into barbarism that sees a total disregard for the Geneva Convention in every possible way,
    and a pursuit of total, unrestrained war.

7   Craig Luther, *Blood and Honor*, 57.

8   Craig Luther, *Blood and Honor*, 60.

9   Hubert Meyer, *The History of the 12. SS-Panzerdivision*, 4–9.

10 Craig Luther, *Blood and Honor*, 71. This most certainly made the soldiers more committed to victory
    over the enemy. These were not draftee soldiers, but committed, ideologically brainwashed young men
    of high morale who received intensive infantry training. The Normandy fighting would not see Japanese
    Second World War 'Banzai' style infantry tactics, and *Hitlerjugend SS-Panzergrenadiere* did surrender if
    in hopeless situations. But if there was a chance to inflict harm on the enemy, it most certainly would
    be taken.

11 Michael Sullivan, 'Hitler's Teenaged Zealots: Fanatics, Combat Motivation, and the 12th SS Panzer
    Division *Hitlerjugend*', masters thesis, University of New Brunswick, Fredericton, 1999, 160. Sullivan
    believes that the motivation contained within the ranks of the *Hitlerjugend* was counterproductive, and
    quotes casualty figures in Hubert Meyer to support the argument. Comparing Sullivan's work to the
    findings of Niklas Zetterling's book *Normandy 1944* on the German land forces in Normandy, there
    is a list of estimated total casualty figures for all divisions involved. The *Hitlerjugend* suffered a total of
    8,000 casualties in the campaign. A division not caught in the Falaise pocket in 1944, the *21. Pz.Div.*,
    suffered 7,500. The *1. SS-Pz.Div. Leibstandarte*, which served from July on, suffered 5,000 casualties
    alone. Sullivan's argument that the *Hitlerjugend's* fighting style incurred far more casualties is somewhat
    baseless. The heavy casualties were due to *Hitlerjugend*, and other divisions like it, not being pulled out
    of the line for scheduled rest and refit purposes.

12 See *Appendix 3* Order of Battle for reference.

13 M. D. R. Foot and I. C. B. Dear (eds.), _The Oxford Companion to the Second World War_ (Oxford: Oxford University Press, 1995), 1103. Tank warfare in the Second World War. 'Regardless of improved anti-tank measures, the mobility, firepower, and protection of tanks, regardless of numbers, was as potent in 1945 as in 1939'.

14 Niklas Zetterling, _Normandy 1944. German Military Organization, Combat Power and Organizational Effectiveness_ (Winnipeg: J. J. Fedorowicz, 2000), 354. Each _Bataillon_ of _Heer Panzergrenadiere_ had 69 MG-42 belt-fed light machine guns.

15 Nicklas Zetterling, _Normandy 1944_, 354.

16 Niklas Zetterling, _Normandy 1944_, 354. The mechanised _III. Btl._ (_Gepanzert_)/_SS-Pz.Gren.Rgt. 26_ had one hundred and fifty-one MG-42 machine guns, six 8cm mortars, three 7.5cm Pak 40 anti-tank guns, four 3.7cm flak guns, two 7.5cm infantry howitzers, twelve SPW 251 half-tracks mounting the short L/24 7.5cm tank cannon and twelve SPW 251 half-tracks with twin flamethrowers.

17 Niklas Zetterling, _Normandy 1944_, 354.

18 This was the weapon known as the 'Moaning Minnie' to the Allies. Though rather inaccurate, it was particularly destructive and emitted a frightening howling noise as the rockets fired.

19 Niklas Zetterling, _Normandy 1944_, 142. The _Heer Werfer Brigade 7_, which supported the _Hitlerjugend_ in the Normandy battles, was equipped on 1 July 1944 with 110 _Nebelwerfers_ of all kinds.

20 Craig Luther, _Blood and Honor_, 86–87.

21 Craig Luther, _Blood and Honor_, 80.

22 Craig Luther, _Blood and Honor_, 81, 84. In total 86 Frenchmen were shot dead during and after the brief ambush by Marquis fighters. Most of these were innocent bystanders and shot as a matter of reprisal.

23 Craig Luther, _Blood and Honor_, 89. _Scenario A_ called for deployment between the mouth of the Somme and the Seine. _Scenario B_ called for deployment between the Seine and the Orne. Deployment _Scenario C_ called for action north and north-west of Caen.

24 Niklas Zetterling, _Normandy 1944_, 351.

25 Craig Luther, _Blood and Honor_, 58.

26 Hubert Meyer, _The History of the 12. SS-Panzerdivision_, 358. Appendix 7. Authorised combat strength per unit for a 1944 model _Waffen-SS Panzerdivision_.

27 Hubert Meyer, _The History of the 12. SS-Panzerdivision_, 8. All that was available to the division was a 3,000-litre fuel reserve.

28 Niklas Zetterling, _Normandy 1944_, 352–53. For example, if three Panther tanks were total write-offs because of a battle, they would not be replaced for months. In contrast, the Allies often replaced tanks in a matter of hours. The _Hitlerjugend_ received 13 replacement Panthers during the fighting in Normandy, which were sent off on 7 June and reached the division on 6–7 July 1944.

29 BA-MA RH 10/172. The _Heer Panzer-Lehr Panzerdivision_ was more lavishly equipped, especially with regard to tanks, tank destroyers and SPW 251 half-tracks.

30 Niklas Zetterling, _Normandy 1944_, 49. On 6 June 1944, only 7,172 tons of stockpiled artillery ammunition was present in Normandy.

31 Michael Reynolds, _Steel Inferno: I SS Panzer Corps in Normandy_, 16. After a November 1943 to April 1944 deployment to Ukraine, the _1. SS-Panzerdivision Leibstandarte SS Adolf Hitler_ fielded three panzers, four assault guns and roughly 1,200 men in its combat units. This was the core on which the division was re-built for service in Normandy in the summer of 1944.

32 M. D. R. Foot and I. C. B. Dear (eds.), _The Oxford Companion to the Second World War_, 298. The Anglo-Canadian amphibious operation was contained, and its troops withdrew or surrendered after several hours of fighting.

Chapter 4

1 Horst Boog, Gerhard Krebs, and Detlef Vogel, _Germany and the Second War, Volume VII_, 559. Map II. IV. 2 Deployment of Allied invasion forces, May 1944.

2   Marc Milner, *D-Day to Carpiquet, The North Shore Regiment and the Liberation of Europe* (Fredericton: Goose Lane Editions, 2007), 33.

3   Arthur Gullachsen, *An Army of Never-Ending Strength: Reinforcing the Canadians in Northwest Europe, 1944–45* (Vancouver: UBC Press, 2021).

4   Arthur Gullachsen, *An Army of Never-Ending Strength*, 93–100.

5   John English, *The Canadian Army and the Normandy Campaign* (Mechanicsburg: Stackpole Publishing, 2009), 159–75.

6   John English, *The Canadian Army*, 170. This reached what would become the First Canadian Army forces training in England by the way of the issued publication *Canadian Army Training Memorandum 28*.

7   John English, *The Canadian Army*, 172–73. It was discovered that most German casualties were inflicted during failed counterattacks.

8   Arthur Gullachsen, *An Army of Never-Ending Strength*, 13–22.

9   Mark Zuehlke, *Juno Beach: Canada's D-Day Victory, 6 June 1944* (Toronto: Douglas and McIntyre, 2004), 357. Appendix D.

10   David Greentree, *Hitlerjugend Soldier versus Canadian Soldier: Normandy 1944* (Oxford: Osprey Publishing, 2018), 15–16.

11   John English, *The Canadian Army*, 169. Diagram of four-echelon assault formation of a combined arms battlegroup.

12   George Blackburn, *The Guns of Normandy* (Toronto: McClelland & Stewart, 1995), 401. Though in the later stages of the Normandy campaign, rapid artillery moves by medium batteries were conducted to support operations of greater depth. The author in a map on page 401 shows seven different positions for 10–19 August 1944.

13   Russell Hart, *Clash of Arms*, 324. It must be noted that some of the most terrible Allied defeats occurred when dash and drive were displayed. The overcaution was representative of an army that realised it did not have the doctrine or the advanced technology to fight a rapid and fluid armoured battle.

14   Russell Hart, *Clash of Arms*, 148–49.

15   Russell Hart, *Clash of Arms*, 324–25.

16   Sean Summerfield, 'The 27th Canadian Armoured Regiment and the Battle of Authie: A Case Study into Manning, Training and Equipment Failures', *Journal of the Eastern Townships Studies*, No. 47, Fall, 117–26 (2016), 118.

17   Sean Summerfield, 'The 27th Canadian Armoured Regiment and the Battle of Authie: A Case Study into Manning, Training and Equipment Failures', *Journal of the Eastern Townships Studies*, No. 47, Fall, 117–26 (2016), 119.

18   Sean Summerfield, 'The 27th Canadian Armoured Regiment and the Battle of Authie: A Case Study into Manning, Training and Equipment Failures', *Journal of the Eastern Townships Studies*, No. 47, Fall, 117–26 (2016), 118.

19   Russell Hart, *Clash of Arms*, 304–6.

Chapter 5

1   R. J. Lahey, 'Hitler's "Intuition", Luftwaffe Photo Reconnaissance and the Reinforcement of Normandy', *Journal of Military History* 86, 77–109 (2022), 78.

2   Matthew Cooper, *The German Army 1939–1945*, 498.

3   Horst Boog, Gerhard Krebs, and Detlef Vogel, *Germany and the Second World War, Volume VII*, 561.

4   C.P. Stacey, *The Official History of the Second World War, Volume III: The Victory Campaign. The Operations in Northwest Europe 1944–1945* (Ottawa, ON: The Queen's Printer and Controller of Stationery, 1960), 6–7.

5   C.P. Stacey, *The Victory Campaign*, 17.

6   C.P. Stacey, *The Victory Campaign*, 76–80.

7   C.P. Stacey, *The Victory Campaign*, 77–79.

8   C.P. Stacey, *The Victory Campaign*, 102.

9   C.P. Stacey, *The Victory Campaign*, 81.

10 C.P. Stacey, *The Victory Campaign*, 81.

11 C.P. Stacey, *The Victory Campaign*, 80.

12 C.P. Stacey, *The Victory Campaign*, 76–77.

13 C.P. Stacey, *The Victory Campaign*, 77–79.

14 C.P. Stacey, *The Victory Campaign*, 69–70.

15 C.P. Stacey, *The Victory Campaign*, 50. Map of German defences.

16 Martin Middlebrook, Chris Everitt, *The Bomber Command War Diaries: An Operational Reference Book, 1939–1945* (London: Viking, 1985), 522–23.

17 C.P. Stacey, *The Victory Campaign*, 93.

18 Jack Goddard, *D-Day Juno Beach: Canada's 24 Hours of Destiny* (Toronto: The Dundurn Group, 2004), 87.

19 C.P. Stacey, *The Victory Campaign*, 99.

20 DND Military History and Heritage: Canadian Participation in the Operations in North-West Europe, 1944. Part 1: The assault and subsequent operations of 3 Canadian Inf Div and 2 Canadian Armed Bde 16–30 Jun 44. Appendix A to E Maps. 30 June 1952. Author: Reginald Roy. Retrieved 6 April 2024 from https://www.canada.ca/en/department-national-defence/services/military-history/history-heritage/official-military-history-lineages/reports/army-headquarters-1948-1959/nw-europe-1944-part-1.html

21 C.P. Stacey, *The Victory Campaign*, 74–75.

22 C.P. Stacey, *The Victory Campaign*, 104.

23 C.P. Stacey, *The Victory Campaign*, 108.

24 C.P. Stacey, *The Victory Campaign*, 109.

25 C.P. Stacey, *The Victory Campaign*, 108–9.

26 Norman Scarfe, *Assault Division. A History of the 3rd Division from the Invasion of Normandy to the Surrender of Germany* (Staplehurst: Spellmount, 2004), 110.

27 Daniel Braün, *Green Fields Beyond: The Story of the Sherbrooke Fusilier Regiment* (Research Triangle: Lulu Publishing Services, 2021), 183–84.

28 Daniel Braün, *Green Fields*, 183. Map of the advance to Villons-les-Buissons.

29 Daniel Braün, *Green Fields*, 184. Daniel Braün mentions these as 12.2cm gun-mortars, but these were most likely 8cm German mortars rather than 12.2cm captured Russian artillery pieces.

30 Daniel Braün, *Green Fields*, 111.

31 Daniel Braün, *Green Fields*, 187.

32 Niklas Zetterling, *Normandy 1944*, 277–80.

33 Werner Kortenhaus, *The Combat History of the 21. Panzerdivision* (Solihull: Helion and Company, 2014), 102.

34 Norman Scarfe, *Assault Division*, 78–79.

35 Norman Scarfe, *Assault Division*, 80.

36 Norman Scarfe, *Assault Division*, 81.

37 Norman Scarfe, *Assault Division*, 84–85.

38 Will Townend, Frank Baldwin, *Gunners in Normandy. The History of the Royal Artillery in Northwest Europe January 1942 to August 1944* (Cheltenham: The History Press, 2020), 161.

39 Norman Scarfe, *Assault Division*, 85.

40 C.P. Stacey, *The Victory Campaign*, 114.

41 Werner Kortenhaus, *The Combat History*, 109–10.

42 C.P. Stacey, *The Victory Campaign*, 118.

43 C.P. Stacey, *The Victory Campaign*, 115.

Chapter 6

1   Craig Luther, *Blood and Honor*, 101–2.
2   Craig Luther, *Blood and Honor*, 98.
3   Craig Luther, *Blood and Honor*, 100–1.
4   Walter Warlimont, *Inside Hitler's Headquarters 1939–1945*, 422.
5   NARA, RG 338. MS-C024. Fritz Kraemer, *I SS Panzer Corps in the West* (Landsberg: US WWII Foreign Military Studies, 1954), 8.
6   Hubert Meyer, *The History of the 12. SS-Panzerdivision*, 28, Craig Luther, *Blood and Honor*, 104.
7   Hubert Meyer, *The History of the 12. SS-Panzerdivision*, 28.
8   Craig Luther, *Blood and Honor*, 102.
9   Craig Luther, *Blood and Honor*, 108.
10 Hubert Meyer, *The History of the 12. SS-Panzerdivision*, 31.
11 Craig Luther, *Blood and Honor*, 108.
12 Craig Luther, *Blood and Honor*, 104. Niklas Zetterling, *Normandy 1944*, 370–77.
13 Craig Luther, *Blood and Honor*, 109.
14 Craig Luther, *Blood and Honor*, 110.
15 NARA T-312/1568/000950. *7. Armee* Telephone Log 6 June 1944.
16 Craig Luther, *Blood and Honor*, 114. Map of main routes leading to Caen.
17 NARA, RG 338. MS-C024. Fritz Kraemer, *I SS Panzer Corps in the West*, 9–12.
18 Vojenský ústřední archiv, *Kriegstagebuch Nr. 1 SS-Pz.Gren.Rgt. 25 1944*. 6 June 1944.
19 NARA, RG 338. MS-C024. Fritz Kraemer, *I SS Panzer Corps in the West*, 11.
20 NARA, RG 338. MS-C024. Fritz Kraemer, *I SS Panzer Corps in the West*, 12–13.
21 NARA, RG 338. MS-C024. Fritz Kraemer, *I SS Panzer Corps in the West*, 14.
22 Hubert Meyer, *The History of the 12. SS-Panzerdivision*, 28–29. Craig Luther, *Blood and Honor*, 105.
23 Hubert Meyer, *The History of the 12. SS-Panzerdivision*, 29–30. Craig Luther, *Blood and Honor*, 107.
24 Craig Luther, *Blood and Honor*, 107. Copy of Hansmann's radio report, originally presented in Huber Meyer's divisional history.
25 Vojenský ústřední archiv, *Kriegstagebuch Nr. 3 SS-Flak Abteilung 12 1944*. 6 June 1944 entry.
26 Vojenský ústřední archiv, *Kriegstagebuch Nr. 3 SS-Flak Abteilung 12 1944*. 6 June 1944 entry.
27 Vojenský ústřední archiv, *Kriegstagebuch Nr. 1 I. Btl./SS-Pz.Gren.Rgt. 25 1944*. 6 June 1944 entry. Hubert Meyer, *The History of the 12. SS-Panzerdivision*, 32.
28 Vojenský ústřední archiv, *Kriegstagebuch Nr. 3 II. Abt./SS-Pz.Rgt. 12 1944*. 6 June 1944 entry.
29 Vojenský ústřední archiv, *Kriegstagebuch Nr. 3 II. Abt./SS-Pz.Rgt. 12 1944*. 6 June 1944 entry.
30 Vojenský ústřední archiv, *Kriegstagebuch Nr. 2 III. Abt./SS-Pz.Art.Rgt. 25 1944*. 6 June entry.
31 Vojenský ústřední archiv, *Kriegstagebuch Nr. 3 II. Abt./SS-Pz.Rgt. 12*. 6 June 1944 entry.
32 Vojenský ústřední archiv, *Kriegstagebuch Nr. 1 SS-Pz.Gren.Rgt. 25 1944*. 6 June 1944 entry.
33 Vojenský ústřední archiv, *Kriegstagebuch Nr. 2 III. Abt./SS-Pz.Art.Rgt. 12 1944*. 6 June entry.
34 Stephan Cazenave, *SS-Panzer Regiment 12 in the Normandy Campaign 1944* (Winnipeg: J. J. Fedorowicz Publishing, 2020), 149.
35 Stephan Cazenave, *SS-Panzer Regiment 12*, 150.
36 Vojenský ústřední archiv, *Kriegstagebuch Nr. 1 I. Abt./SS-Panzer Regiment 12 1944*. 7 June 1944 entry.
37 Stephan Cazenave, *Sur le Front de Normandie. Panzerdivision Hitlerjugend 2: SS-Panzer Regiment 12 Normandie 1944* (Paris: Maranes Editions, 2014), 179.
38 Vojenský ústřední archiv, *Kriegstagebuch Nr. 1 I. Abt./SS-Panzer Regiment 12 1944*. 6–7 June 1944 entries.
39 Steven J. Zaloga, *Panther versus Sherman. Battle of the Bulge 1944* (Oxford: Osprey Publishing, 2008), 31. Looking at the late war employment of Panther units, American military historian Steven J. Zaloga argues that Panther units were transported by rail as far forward as possible to avoid breakdowns. This is true, but it was mainly to save fuel, which Germany was critically short of. The Panther was capable

of long road marches on good roads. In the Second World War, any tank unit forced to conduct long road marches would have some tanks fall out due to mechanical faults.

40 Two of most significant route marches involving Panther units were by *I.Abt./Pz.Rgt. 6* of the *Panzer-Lehr* and *I.Abt./SS-Pz.Rgt.12* of the *Hitlerjugend.*

41 Tank Museum Archives, Bovington, UK, No.2 Operational Research Section, Report No.18, Tank casualties during the exploitation phase after the crossing of the Seine, September 1944. During the period 28 August–7 September 1944, the 4th Canadian Armoured Division lost 57 tanks to mechanical causes and only 5 to enemy action.

42 Vojenský ústřední archiv, *Kriegstagebuch Nr. 1 I. Abt./SS-Panzer Regiment 12 1944.* 6–8 June 1944 entries.

43 Vojenský ústřední archiv, *Kriegstagebuch Nr. 3 II. Abt./SS-Pz.Art.Rgt. 12 1944.* 6 June entry.

44 Vojenský ústřední archiv, *Kriegstagebuch Nr. 3 SS-Pz.Art.Rgt. 12 1944.* 7 June entry.

45 Tim Saunders and Richard Hone, *12th Hitlerjugend SS Panzer Division in Normandy* (Barnsley: Pen and Sword Military, 2021), 50.

46 Craig Luther, *Blood and Honor*, 117.

47 Vojenský ústřední archiv, *Kriegstagebuch Nr. 3 SS-Pz.Art.Rgt. 12 1944.* 7 June entry.

48 Vojenský ústřední archiv, *Kriegstagebuch Nr. 1 SS-Pz.Gren.Rgt. 26.*

49 Craig Luther, *Blood and Honor*, 117.

50 Vojenský ústřední archiv, *Kriegstagebuch Nr. 3 SS-Pz.Art.Rgt. 12 1944.* 7 June entry. One artillery piece was a total loss and one was damaged in the bombing and strafing attacks of 6–7 June.

Chapter 7

1 Mark Zuehlke, *Holding Juno*, 28–32. LAC, RG 24, Volume 15,180. Le Régiment de la Chaudière War Diary. 7 June 1944 entry. Marc Milner, *Stopping the Panzers. The Untold Story of D-Day* (Lawrence: University Press of Kansas Press, 2014), 135. Map of German dispositions morning of 7 June 1944.

2 LAC, RG 24, Volume XV, 122. North Nova Scotia Highlanders War Diary. 7 June 1944 entry.

3 Marc Milner, *Stopping the Panzers*, 159.

4 Daniel Braün, *Green Fields*, 201. Marc Milner, *D-Day to Carpiquet*, 77.

5 Marc Zuehlke, *Holding Juno*, 86.

6 Marc Milner, *Stopping the Panzers*, 138.

7 Vojenský ústřední archiv, *Kriegstagebuch Nr. 1 SS-Pz.Gren.Rgt. 25 1944.* 7 June entry.

8 Vojenský ústřední archiv, *Kriegstagebuch Nr. 1 SS-Pz.Gren.Rgt. 25 1944.* 7 June entry.

9 Vojenský ústřední archiv, *Kriegstagebuch Nr. 3 SS-Flak Abteilung 12 1944.* 7 June entry.

10 Hubert Meyer, *The History of the 12. SS-Panzerdivision*, map section with German unit locations.

11 Vojenský ústřední archiv, *Kriegstagebuch SS-Pz.Art.Rgt. 12 1944 Anlagen.* 7 June 1944 divisional *Ia* operation order for the attack of *SS-Pz.Gren.Rgt. 25* north of Caen. Regimental copy held within the *SS-Pz.Art.Rgt. 12* records.

12 Craig Luther, *Blood and Honor*, 263–64. Appendix 11.

13 Craig Luther, *Blood and Honor*, 263–64. Appendix 11.

14 Vojenský ústřední archiv, *Kriegstagebuch Nr. 1 SS-Pz.Gren.Rgt. 25 1944.* 7 June entry. Vojenský ústřední archiv, *Kriegstagebuch SS-Pz.Art.Rgt. 12 1944 Anlagen.* 7 June 1944 divisional *Ia* operation order for the attack of *SS-Pz.Gren.Rgt. 25* north of Caen. Regimental copy held within the *SS-Pz.Art.Rgt. 12* records.

15 Vojenský ústřední archiv, *Kriegstagebuch Nr. 3 II. Abt./SS-Pz.Rgt. 12, 1944.* 7 June 1944 entry.

16 Stephan Cazenave, *SS-Panzer Regiment 12*, 156.

17 Marc Milner, *Stopping the Panzers*, 139.

18 Georges Bernage, Frederick Jeanne, *Three Days in Hell.* 7–9 June 1944 (Bayeaux: Editions Heimdal, 2016), 48–49. Tactical diagram showing order of march.

19 Marc Milner, *Stopping the Panzers*, 139–40.

20 Will Townend, Frank Baldwin, *Gunners in Normandy*, 178–79.
21 David Greentree, *Hitlerjugend Soldier*, 34.
22 Marc Milner, *Stopping the Panzers*, 146.
23 Mark Zuehlke, *Holding Juno*, 103.
24 Marc Milner, *Stopping the Panzers*, 166.
25 Vojenský ústřední archiv, *Kriegstagebuch Nr. 2 III. Abt./SS-Pz.Art.Rgt. 12 1944*. 7 June 1944 entry.
26 Vojenský ústřední archiv, *Kriegstagebuch Nr. 3 SS-Flak Abteilung 12 1944*. 7 June 1944 entry.
27 Georges Bernage, Frederic Jeanne, *Three Days in Hell*, 58.
28 Vojenský ústřední archiv, *Kriegstagebuch Nr. 1 SS-Pz.Gren.Rgt. 25 1944*. 7 June 1944 entry.
29 Stephan Cazenave, *SS-Panzer Regiment 12*, 162.
30 Stephan Cazenave, *SS-Panzer Regiment 12*, 167.
31 Marc Milner, *Stopping the Panzers*, 166.
32 Norbert Számvéber, *Waffen-SS Armour in Normandy. The Combat History of SS-Panzer Regiment 12 and SS-Panzerjäger Abteilung 12 Normandy 1944 based on their Original War Diaries* (Solihull: Helion and Company, 2012)., 217–18. Appendix II. German Cross in Gold submission for *Hstuf*. Ruckdeschel.
33 Stephan Cazenave, *SS-Panzer Regiment 12*, 166–67.
34 Stephan Cazenave, *SS-Panzer Regiment 12*, 166.
35 Marc Milner, *Stopping the Panzers*, 168.
36 Mark Zuehlke, *Holding Juno*, 104.
37 Mark Zuehlke, *Holding Juno*, 105.
38 Mark Zuehlke, *Holding Juno*, 105.
39 Mark Zuehlke, *Holding Juno*, 104.
40 Mark Zuehlke, *Holding Juno*, 106.
41 Hubert Meyer, *The History of the 12. SS-Panzerdivision*, 354. Appendix 6.
42 Howard Margolian, *Conduct Unbecoming: The Story of the Murder of Canadian Prisoners of War in Normandy 62 (Toronto: University of Toronto Press, 1998)*, 61.
43 Hubert Meyer, *The History of the 12. SS-Panzerdivision*, 42.
44 Vojenský ústřední archiv, *Kriegstagebuch Nr. 1. SS-Pz.Gren.Rgt. 25 1944*. 7 June 1944 entry.
45 Mark Zuehlke, *Holding Juno*, 118–19.
46 Hubert Meyer, *The History of the 12. SS-Panzerdivision*, 42.
47 Hubert Meyer, *The History of the 12. SS-Panzerdivision*, Map book. *The First Battle of Caen, 6–10 June 1944.*
48 Hubert Meyer, *The History of the 12. SS-Panzerdivision*, 43.
49 Hubert Meyer, *The History of the 12. SS-Panzerdivision*, 43.
50 Craig Luther, *Blood and Honor*, 141.
51 Craig Luther, *Blood and Honor*, 141.
52 Craig Luther, *Blood and Honor*, 142.
53 Craig Luther, *Blood and Honor*, 142.
54 Vojenský ústřední archiv, *Kriegstagebuch Nr. 1 SS-Pz.Gren.Rgt. 25 1944*. 7 June 1944 entry.
55 Howard Margolian, *Conduct Unbecoming*, 62. Hubert Meyer, *The History of the 12. SS-Panzerdivision*, 45. Vojenský ústřední archiv, *Kriegstagebuch Nr. 2 III. Abt./SS-Pz.Art.Rgt. 12 1944*. 7 June 1944 entry regarding heavy naval gunfire.
56 Vojenský ústřední archiv. *Kriegstagebuch Nr. 3 SS-Flak Abteilung 12 1944*. 7 June 1944 entry. Data is presented for each date in the *KTB* on ammunition use.
57 Georges Bernage, Frederick Jeanne, *Three Days in Hell*, 67.
58 Howard Margolian, *Conduct Unbecoming*, 61.
59 Howard Margolian, *Conduct Unbecoming*, 59.
60 Howard Margolian, *Conduct Unbecoming*, 61.
61 Howard Margolian, *Conduct Unbecoming*, 60.
62 Howard Margolian, *Conduct Unbecoming*, 58.

63 Georges Bernage, Frederick Jeanne, *Three Days in Hell*, 67.

64 Howard Margolian, *Conduct Unbecoming*, 61.

65 Howard Margolian, *Conduct Unbecoming*, 62–64.

66 Howard Margolian, *Conduct Unbecoming*, 63, 70.

67 Stephan Cazenave, *SS-Panzer Regiment 12*, 157.

68 Michaell Reynolds, *Eagles and Bulldogs in Normandy 1944: The American 29th Division from Omaha to St. Lo, The British 3rd Division from Sword to Caen* (Havertown: Casemate Publishers, 2020), 106–7. British military historian Michael Reynolds quotes the 2nd Battalion, Royal Ulster Rifles war diary as receiving 31 casualties, with 4 supporting tanks lost.

69 Hubert Meyer, *The History of the 12. SS-Panzerdivision*, 45. German *Hitlerjugend* forces on 7 June: Meyer suffered 99 dead, 250 wounded and 33 missing.

70 Vojenský ústřední archiv, *Kriegstagebuch Nr. 1 SS-Pz.Gren.Rgt. 25 1944*. 7 June 1944 entry.

Chapter 8

1 Vojenský ústřední archiv, *Kriegstagebuch SS-Pz.Art.Rgt. 12 1944 Anlagen*. 7 June 1944 divisional *Ia* operation order for the attack of *SS-Pz.Gren.Rgt. 25* north of Caen. Regimental copy held within the *SS-Pz.Art.Rgt. 12* records.

1 Hubert Meyer, *The History of the 12. SS-Panzerdivision*, 47–48.

2 British National Archives KEW, File 25/GS/Publications/1298. 'Current Reports from Overseas: No. 48. The War Office', 7. This report provides information on the effects of Allied air support. A sizeable percentage of German prisoners related tales of incessant air attack on major roads, severely hindering transport and movement. While *SS-Pz.Gren.Rgt. 26* was not destroyed from the air, its advance to the front was certainly severely delayed by Allied air activity combined with a lack of fuel and a terrible initial deployment.

3 Terry Copp, *Fields of Fire. The Canadians in Normandy* (Toronto: University of Toronto Press, 2003), 62.

4 Marc Milner, *Stopping the Panzers*, 205, 208.

5 Georges Bernages, Frederick Jeanne, *Three Days in Hell*, 77. Map of the 3rd Canadian Infantry Division–*Hitlerjugend* front lines during the bridgehead battles.

6 Mark Zuehlke, *Holding Juno*, 152.

7 Milner, *Stopping the Panzers*, 113.

8 Milner, *Stopping the Panzers*, 206.

9 David Greentree, *Hitlerjugend Soldier*, 44. The official designation of the 1st Hussars was the 6th Canadian Armoured Regiment.

10 Marc Milner, *Stopping the Panzers*, 260–61.

11 Marc Milner, *Stopping the Panzers*, 217–18.

12 'Infantry Training Part I: The Infantry Battalion: 1944 26/G.S. 1070 Publication', War Office. Ottawa: Controller, His Majesty's Stationery, 1944, 39. Retrieved 8 January 2019 from http://wartimecanada.ca/categories/training-manuals?tid=All&page=1

13 Marc Milner 'The Guns of Bretteville: 13th Field Regiment, RCA, and the defence of Bretteville-l'Orgueilleuse, 7–10 June 1944', *Canadian Military History Journal*, Vol. XVI: Iss. 4, Article 2 (2007), 2. Retrieved 25 March 2024 from https://scholars.wlu.ca/cmh/vol16/iss4/2, Marc Milner, *Stopping the Panzers*, 211, 235. Map showing RCA and RA field and anti-tank regiment dispositions.

14 Marc Milner, *Stopping the Panzers*, 235. Map showing RCA and RA field and anti-tank regiment dispositions.

15 Hubert Meyer, *The History of the 12. SS-Panzerdivision*, 49.

16 Terry Copp, *Fields of Fire*, 68. The fortress area was seized roughly 15 hours before the Germans reached it and the Canadians had entrenched themselves to good effect.

17 Georges Bernages, Frederick Jeanne, *Three Days in Hell*, 77. Map of events 7–8 June 1944.

18   Tim Saunders, *The Battle for the Bocage, Normandy 1944: Point 103, Tilley-sur-Seulles, Villers Bocage* (Barnsley: Pen and Sword, 2021), 43.

19   Tim Saunders, *Battle for the Bocage*, 46.

20   Tim Saunders, *Battle for the Bocage*, 57.

21   Jean-Claude Perrigault, *Album Historique: La Panzer-Lehr Division: Le Choc de Allies Brise L'Arme D'Elite de Hitler* (Bayeaux: Editions Hemidal, 1995), 158–59.

22   Jean-Claude Perrigault, *Album Historique: La Panzer-Lehr Division*, 160.

23   Jean-Claude Perrigault, *Album Historique: La Panzer-Lehr Division*, 159.

Chapter 9

1   Jean-Claude Perrigault, *Album Historique: La Panzer-Lehr Division*, 160.

2   Jean-Claude Perrigault, *Album Historique: La Panzer-Lehr Division*, 161.

3   Hubert Meyer, *The History of the 12. SS-Panzerdivision*, 47–48. The simple answer to why this could not be organised quickly was that the *Panzer-Lehr* was absent and the *Hitlerjugend* and *21. Pz.Div.* had involved themselves in heavy combat, making secluded assembly for massed attack somewhat difficult.

4   Vojenský ústřední archiv. *Kriegstagebuch III. Btl./SS-Pz.Gren.Rgt. 26 Anlagen 1944. Befehl 7.6.44.*

5   Vojenský ústřední archiv. *Kriegstagebuch III. Btl./SS-Pz.Gren.Rgt. 26 Anlagen 1944. Befehl 7.6.44.*

6   Vojenský ústřední archiv. *Kriegstagebuch III. Btl./SS-Pz.Gren.Rgt. 26 Anlagen 1944. Befehl 7.6.44.*

7   Stephan Cazenave, *Sur le Front de Normandie. Panzerdivision Hitlerjugend 1.2 Volume II: 6/6–7/7/44 Invasionsfront* (Paris: Maranes Editions, 2019), 116.

8   Vojenský ústřední archiv. *Kriegstagebuch SS-Pz.Gren.Rgt. 26 Anlagen 1944. Befehl 7.6.44.*

9   Hubert Meyer, *The History of the 12. SS-Panzerdivision*, 50.

10   Hubert Meyer, *The History of the 12. SS-Panzerdivision*, 49. Dr Frederick P. Steinhardt, Editor, *Panzer Lehr Division 1944–45. Helion WWII German Military Studies, Volume I* (Solihull: Helion and Company Ltd., 2008), 37–38. The divisional order is reprinted in full in this edited edition.

11   Vojenský ústřední archiv. *Kriegstagebuch Nr. 1 I. Abt./SS-Pz.Rgt. 12 1944.* 8 June 1944 entry. The Panther crews were not exhausted, and the drive of the last 16 kilometres was not enough to cause massive technical or engine failure in the tanks. The *2. Kompanie* did not depart due to a lack of fuel. The *3. Kompanie* went into the sector north of Caen and conducted securing tasks near the village of Gruchy.

12   Vojenský ústřední archiv, *Kriegstagebuch Nr 3 II. Abt./SS-Pz.Art.Rgt. 12 1944.* 7 June 1944 entry.

13   Vojenský ústřední archiv, *Kriegstagebuch Nr 3 II. Abt./SS-Pz.Art.Rgt. 12 1944.* 7 June 1944 entry.

14   Angelos N. Manolas, *The Reaper's Harvesting Summer. 12. SS-Panzerdivision: "Hitlerjugend" in Normandy* (Stroud: Fonthill, 2021), 67.

15   Stephan Cazenave, *Sur le Front de Normandie. Panzerdivision Hitlerjugend 1.2,* 116–17.

16   Stephan Cazenave, *Sur le Front de Normandie. Panzerdivision Hitlerjugend 1.2,* 117.

17   Hubert Meyer, *The History of the 12. SS-Panzerdivision*, Map Book 6–10 June 1944 operations.

18   Mark Zuehlke, *Holding Juno*, 197. The lack of artillery preparation and attempts at surprise attacks would continue as a favourite, if unsuccessful, tactic of the *Waffen-SS.*

19   Marc Milner, *Stopping the Panzers*, 237. Mohnke had been badly wounded in the Balkans in 1941 and had not seen front-line service since. *SS-Standartenführer* Meyer on the night of 6/7 June had also made his famous 'Little Fish' comment at the headquarters of the *716. Infanterie-Division.*

20   Brian A. Reid, *Named by the Enemy: A History of the Royal Winnipeg Rifles. The Story of Winnipeg's Famous Little Black Devils* (Montreal: Robin Brass Studio, 2010), 170–71.

21   Stéphane Jacquet, *Tilly-sur-Seulles 1944* (Bayeux: Editions Heimdal, 2019), 132. Map of routes taken by the division main groupings to the front, Brou to Villers-Bocage taken as a route distance example.

22   Tim Saunders, *The Battle for the Bocage*, 49–50.

23   Stéphane Jacquet, *Tilly-sur-Seulles 1944*, 43.

24   Jean-Claude Perrigault, *Album Historique: La Panzer-Lehr Division*, 162.

25 Dr Frederick P. Steinhardt, Editor, *Panzer Lehr Division 1944–45*, 41.

26 Helmut Ritgen, *The Western Front 1944: Memoirs of a Panzer-Lehr Officer* (Winnipeg: J. J. Fedorowicz Publishing 1995), 39.

27 Stéphane Jacquet, *Tilly-sur-Seulles 1944*, 143.

28 Stéphane Jacquet, *Tilly-sur-Seulles 1944*, 106, 168.

29 Hubert Meyer, *The History of the 12. SS-Panzerdivision*, 52.

30 Will Townend and Frank Baldwin, *Gunners in Normandy*, 202.

31 Tim Saunders, *Battle for the Bocage*, 67. Map of British 8th Armoured Brigade operations and *SS-Pz. Aüfkl.Abt. 12* dispositions.

32 Will Townend and Frank Baldwin, *Gunners in Normandy*, 202.

33 Jean-Claude Perrigault, *Album Historique: La Panzer-Lehr Division*, 160.

34 Vojenský ústřední archiv, *Kriegstagebuch Nr 3 II. Abt./SS-Pz.Art.Rgt. 12 1944*. 8 June 1944 entry.

35 Mark Zuehlke, *Holding Juno*, 167.

36 Mark Zuehlke, *Holding Juno*, 168.

37 Mark Zuehlke, *Holding Juno*, 168.

38 Mark Zuehlke, *Holding Juno*, 169.

39 Mark Zuehlke, *Holding Juno*, 171.

40 Jean-Claude Perrigault, *Album Historique: La Panzer-Lehr Division*, 162.

41 Tim Saunders, *Battle for the Bocage*, 53–54.

42 Helmut Ritgen, *The Western Front 1944*, 38.

43 Dr Frederic P. Steinhardt, Editor, *Panzer Lehr Division 1944–45*, 37–38.

44 Mark Zuehlke, *Holding Juno*, 170–71.

45 Mark Zuehlke, *Holding Juno*, 173–74.

46 Georges Bernage, Frederic Jeanne, *Three Days in Hell*, 95–99.

47 Hubert Meyer, *The History of the 12. SS-Panzerdivision*, 53–54.

48 Georges Bernage, Frederic Jeanne, *Three Days in Hell*, 100–3.

49 Mark Zuehlke, *Holding Juno*, 180.

50 LAC, RG 24, Volume XIV, 213. 6th Canadian Armoured Regiment War Diary. 8 June 1944 entry.

51 Mark Zuehlke, *Holding Juno*, 180.

52 Georges Bernage, Frederick Jeanne, *Three Days in Hell*, 107.

53 Hubert Meyer, *The History of the 12. SS-Panzerdivision*, 51–52. The total *Hitlerjugend* losses for the fighting on 8 June of June 1944 were 91 killed, 233 wounded and 45 missing. The Panther tanks of *I. Abt./SS-Pz.Rgt. 12* had not participated. While not losing any panzers on this day, the *Hitlerjugend* had suffered nearly 370 casualties of all kinds, the Canadians suffering slightly more due to the initial defeat and surrender of large numbers of the Royal Winnipeg Rifles, who were driven out of Putot-en-Bessin.

54 Hubert Meyer, *The History of the 12. SS-Panzerdivision*, 49–54.

55 Howard Margolian, *Conduct Unbecoming*, 80–81.

56 Marc Milner, *Stopping the Panzers*, 286.

57 Marc Milner, *Stopping the Panzers*, 287.

Chapter 10

1 Michael Reynolds, *Steel Inferno*, 106.

2 Marc Milner, *Stopping the Panzers*. Oliver Haller, 'The Defeat of the 12th SS: 7–10 June 1944', *Canadian Military History Journal*: Vol. III: Iss. 1, Article 2 (1994). Retrieved 10 December 2023 from https://scholars.wlu.ca/cmh/vol3/iss1/2, Mark Zuehlke, *Holding Juno*.

3 Vojenský ústřední archiv. *Kriegstagebuch Nr. 1 I. Abt./SS-Panzerregiment 12 1944*. Stephan Cazenave, *SS-Panzer Regiment 12*, Georges Bernage, Frederick Jeanne, *Three Days in Hell 7–9 June 1944*.

4 Terry Copp, *Fields of Fire*, 72–73.

5 Marc Milner, *Stopping the Panzers*, 264, 285.

6   Rudolf Lehmann, *The Leibstandarte III: 1. SS Panzer Division Leibstandarte Adolf Hitler* (Winnipeg: J. J. Fedorowicz Publishing, 1990), 105. Meyer and Wünsche conducted a surprise attack on village of Jefremowka, Ukraine, on 18 February 1943, with no artillery or air support preparation. In this attack, *SS-Panzer-Aufklärungabteiling 1*, commanded by Meyer, attacked the village frontally and the *Panzerabteilung* (tank battalion) of Wünsche made an enveloping attack. The attack was reported to be a complete success, with a reported 1,200 (inflated figure) enemy casualties inflicted and eight artillery pieces captured.

7   Rudolf Lehmann, *The Leibstandarte III*, 123.

8   Stephan Cazenave, *Sur le Front de Normandie. Panzerdivision Hitlerjugend 2*, 181.

9   John English, *The Canadian Army*, 51. Units of the 3rd Canadian Infantry Division had the better part of two and half years to prepare for the campaign in Normandy.

10   Kurt Meyer, *Grenadiers*, 227.

11   Kurt Meyer, *Grenadiers*, 228.

12   Terry Copp, *Fields of Fire*, 72.

13   Michael Reynolds, *Steel Inferno*, 95.

14   Hubert Meyer, *The History of the 12. SS-Panzerdivision*, 54. This screening force was made up of the *14. (Flak)*, *16. (Pionier)* and *15. (Aufklärung) Kompanien* of *SS-Pz.Gren.Rgt. 25*, and the divisional *Begleitkompanie* (Headquarters Escort Company).

15   Marc Milner, *Stopping the Panzers*, 259. As Canadian military historian Marc Milner notes: 'The Canadian Scottish Infantry Regiment and two squadrons of the 1st Hussars tank regiment had recently taken part in the 8 June counterattack on Putot. The artillery regiments behind the front were entirely unprotected.' 10 Centaur Tanks of the British 2nd Royal Marine Armoured Support Regiment were tasked to bolster the Canadian Field Artillery Regiment positions. Meyer could have been unaware of this gap in the Canadian positions, or simply too focused on Bretteville. Regardless, he let this opportunity pass by. The entirely unprotected left flank of the Royal Winnipeg Rifles remnants, recently defeated in Putot, could have been exploited in an attack on the axis Rots–Le Hamel–Bray straight north-west, bypassing Bretteville for the moment. The Royal Winnipeg Rifles were in no shape to resist, and the *Hitlerjugend* Panthers could have destroyed or attacked Canadian RCA field artillery and anti-tank units and reached dangerously close to the invasion beaches. D Company of the RRR battlegroup had recently abandoned its positions east of Bretteville near Rots and the way was clear. Hubert Meyer, *The History of the 12. SS-Panzerdivision*, 54. With Meyer and Witt being focused entirely on Bretteville, no mention is made in the *Hitlerjugend* divisional history of this possible opportunity.

16   Mark Zuehlke, *Holding Juno*, 195.

17   Stephan Cazenave, *Sur le Front de Normandie. Panzerdivision Hitlerjugend 2*, 181. Jürgensen was present. It is unclear if he was in his own command Panther, '155'.

18   Tim Sauders, *Battle for the Bocage*, 67. Map of German dispositions.

19   Wolfgang Schneider, *Panzer Tactics: German Small-unit Armour Tactics in World War II* (Mechanicsburg: Stackpole Books, 2005), 13.

20   Vojenský ústřední archiv. *Kriegstagebuch I. Abt./SS-Panzerregiment 12 Anlagen 1944. Kriegstagebuch* Appendix No.3. Stephan Cazenave, *Sur le Front de Normandie. Panzerdivision Hitlerjugend 2*, 181–90. As an example, *4. Kompanie* only had three *Züge*, or platoons, of a maximum of four Panthers each, maybe less, and possibly one *Kompanie* staff Panther for a total of eleven–fifteen Panthers versus the authorised strength of seventeen. Second World War tank units rarely if ever had 100 per cent of their vehicles operational at any one time, and some would have fallen out following the route march to the invasion front.

21   Niklas Zetterling, *Normandy 1944*, 351.

22   Stephan Cazenave, *SS-Panzer Regiment 12*, 188.

23   Hubert Meyer, *The History of the 12. SS-Panzerdivision*, 196. While the Wespe self-propelled guns were effective artillery assets, their value in the direct fire role in limited light conditions would be

restricted, and they had limited ammunition, carrying only 40 rounds per vehicle. A short but sustained bombardment would be all they could muster.

24 Vojenský ústřední archiv. *Kriegstagebuch Nr. 1 I. Abt./SS-Panzerregiment 12 1944.* 8 June 1944 entry.

25 Wolfgang Schneider, *Panzer Tactics*, 54.

26 Marc Milner, *Stopping the Panzers*, 262.

27 Milner, *Stopping the Panzers*, 235. On this page there is a map of the 7th Canadian Infantry Brigade's frontage map.

28 David Greentree, *Hitlerjugend Soldier*, 44.

29 Gordon Brown, Letter of Major Gordon Brown (ret.) dated 23 April 1994. The RRR B Company commander has often been listed as Lieutenant John Treleaven. Though the senior platoon commander who led the company to Rots on 7 June, he relinquished command of the company to Major Eric Syme on 8 June 1944.

30 David Greentree, *Hitlerjugend Soldier*, 44. Stewart A. Mein, *'Up the Johns': The Story of the Regina Rifles* (North Battleford: Senate of the Royal Regina Rifles, 1992), 113. It should be noted at this time two of the line companies in RRR were commanded by acting officers commanding (OCs), most of the majors becoming casualties in the previous two days.

31 'Infantry Training Part VI: The Anti-Tank Platoon 1943 26/G.S. 1023 Publication', War Office, Ottawa: Controller, His Majesty's Stationery, 1944, 11. Depth of all anti-tank assets in the infantry battalion defensive position was to be achieved in conjunction with deployed RCA anti-tank assets. Retrieved 8 January 2019 from http://wartimecanada.ca/categories/training-manuals?tid=All&page=1

32 Michael Reynolds, *Steel Inferno*, 98.

33 Marc Milner, *Stopping the Panzers*, 261.

34 G. W. L. Nicholson, *The Gunners of Canada: The History of the Royal Regiment of Canadian Artillery: Volume II: 1919–1967* (Toronto: McClelland and Stewart, 1972), 282.

35 Marc Milner, *Stopping the Panzers*, 262.

36 Georges Bernage, Frederick Jeanne, *Three Days in Hell*, 113. This page shows a map of RRR and 7th Canadian Infantry Brigade headquarters dispositions. The knowledge that he could have destroyed this headquarters as well and seized Bretteville seemingly would have ensured Meyer would requisition appropriate infantry forces to properly clear the objective. This proximity did have its advantages for the Canadians. Matheson would not have to travel far to communicate any urgency regarding his situation.

37 Marc Milner, *Stopping the Panzers*, 273. Footnote: Colonel Clifford interview, 2002.

38 Howard Margolian, *Conduct Unbecoming*, 104. Stephan Cazenave, *SS-Panzer Regiment 12*, 178.

39 Wolfgang Schneider, *Panzer Tactics*, 247.

40 Wolfgang Schneider, *Panzer Tactics*, 142, 247. It is stressed in German armoured doctrine to make use of indirect fire and to attach forward artillery observers.

41 C.P. Stacey, *The Victory Campaign*, 136.

42 'Infantry Training Part I: The Infantry Battalion: 1944. 26/G.S. 1070 Publication', War Office, Ottawa: Controller, His Majesty's Stationery, 1944, 43–44. Combat outposts could be supported by other assets, such as anti-tank guns and medium machine guns, to increase their strength. Retrieved 8 January 2019 from http://wartimecanada.ca/categories/training-manuals?tid=All&page=1

43 Ben Kite, *Stout Hearts: the British and Canadians in Normandy 1944* (Solihull, England: Helion and Company, 2014), 39. The carrier platoon of the RRR contained 13 vehicles, and it is unclear whether all of them drove off east of Bretteville.

44 Marc Milner, *Stopping the Panzers*, 266. Lee Windsor, Roger Sarty, Marc Milner, *Loyal Gunners: 3rd Field Artillery Regiment (The Loyal Company) and the History of New Brunswick Artillery, 1893 to 2012* (Waterloo: Wilfred Laurier Press, 2016), 344.

45 Terry Copp, *Fields of Fire*, 72.

46 Vojenský ústřední archiv. *Kriegstagebuch Nr. 1 I. Abt./SS-Panzerregiment 12 1944.* 8 June 1944 entry. Also, a total of six carriers are recorded as being destroyed in the war diary of *SS-Panzerregiment 12* for this date.

47 Marc Milner, *Stopping the Panzers*, 268. Vojenský ústřední archiv. *Kriegstagebuch Nr. 1 I. Abt./ SS-Panzerregiment 12 1944*. Panzer '427' was commanded by *SS-Unterscharführer* Hartmann. 8 June 1944 entry.

48 Marc Milner, *Stopping the Panzers*, 268.

49 LAC, RG 24, Volume *XIV*, 461. War Diary 12th Field Regiment, RCA. 8 June 1944 entry.

50 Eric Luxton, Editor, *1st Battalion the Regina Rifle Regiment: 1939–1946* (Regina: Regimental Association, 1946), 40. Howard Margolian, *Conduct Unbecoming*, 107. Mark Zuehlke, *Holding Juno*, 202. A total of eight members of the Cameron Highlanders of Ottawa and RRR were found shot at close range, indicating a possible battlefield execution by members of the *15. Kompanie, SS-Panzergrenadierregiment 25*. A total of six carriers were recorded as being destroyed in the war diary of *SS-Pz.Rgt. 12*.

51 Terry Copp, Gordon Brown, *Look to Your Front...Regina Rifles: A Regiment at War 1944–1945* (Waterloo: Laurier Centre for Military, Disarmament and Strategic Studies, 2001), 67–68.

52 Wolfgang Schneider, *Panzer Tactics*, 92.

53 Mark Zuehlke, *Holding Juno*, 202.

54 Mark Zuehlke, *Holding Juno*, 199

55 G. W. L. Nicholson, *The Gunners of Canada*, 282.

56 Georges Bernage and Frederick Jeanne, *Three Days in Hell*, 128–29. Stephan Cazenave, *SS-Panzer Regiment 12*, 180.

57 Kurt Meyer, *Grenadiers*, 228.

58 Mark Zuehlke, *Holding Juno*, 199.

59 G. W. L. Nicholson, *The Gunners of Canada*, 282. Bombardier Askin was killed in July 1944, but was mentioned in dispatches.

60 Marc Milner, *Stopping the Panzers*, 272.

61 Wolfgang Schneider, *Panzer Tactics*, 16.

62 Jean Bouchery, *From D-Day to VE-Day: The Canadian Soldier* (Paris: Histoire and Collections, 2003), 124.

63 Georges Bernage and Frederick Jeanne, *Three Days in Hell*, 110, 118–19.

64 Mark Zuehlke, *Holding Juno*, 203. PIAT stands for 'Projectile Infantry Anti-Tank.' RRR Able Company Rifleman Joe Lapointe, part of a PIAT crew, was instrumental in its destruction.

65 Eric Luxton (ed.), *1st Battalion the Regina Rifle Regiment*, 40.

66 Michael Reynolds, *Steel Inferno*, 99.

67 Stephan Cazenave, *SS-Panzer Regiment 12*, 182. The Panthers formed a firing line to south of Bretteville, with Wünsche to the rear in his command Panther, directing the fire.

68 Vojenský ústřední archiv. *Kriegstagebuch I. Abt./SS-Panzerregiment 12 Anlagen 1944*. Appendix No. 3.

69 Stephan Cazenave, *SS-Panzer Regiment 12*, 182.

70 Hubert Meyer, *The History of the 12. SS-Panzerdivision*, 55. Stephan Cazenave, *SS-Panzer Regiment 12*, 194. Cazenave in his account mentions Panther '116' was destroyed by PIAT fire.

71 David Greentree, *Hitlerjugend Soldier*, 56.

72 Hubert Meyer, *The History of the 12. SS-Panzerdivision*, 56.

73 Terry Copp, Gordon Brown, *Look to Your Front*, 80.

74 Luxton, Editor, *1st Battalion the Regina Rifle Regiment*, 40.

75 Luxton, Editor, *1st Battalion the Regina Rifle Regiment*, 41.

76 Wolfgang Schneider, *Panzer Tactics*, 248.

77 Michael Reynolds, *Steel Inferno*, 98.

78 Mark Zuehlke, *Holding Juno*, 207.

79 Michael Reynolds, *Steel Inferno*, 99.

80 Kurt Meyer, *Grenadiers*, 230.

81 Mark Zuehlke, *Holding Juno*, 207.

82 Vojenský ústřední archiv. *Kriegstagebuch Nr. 1 I.Abt./SS-Panzerregiment 12 1944*. Marc Milner, *Stopping the Panzers*, 273.

83   Stewart A. Mein, '*Up the Johns*', 115.

84   Mark Zuehlke, *Holding Juno*, 207–8.

85   Mark Zuehlke, *Holding Juno*, 210. The 13th Field Regiment, RCA, was led by Colonel F. P. T. Clifford and equipped with 24 M7 Priest 105mm self-propelled artillery pieces.

86   Mark Zuehlke, *Holding Juno*, 206.

87   Stephan Cazenave, *Sur le Front de Normandie. Panzerdivision Hitlerjugend 2*, 190. Multiple damaged Panthers were taken to the village of Venoix, the location of the *Pantherabteilung Werkstattkompanie* (Repair Company) for repairs.

88   Regina Rifles, 'Regina Rifles fatal casualties by date', for 8/9 June 1944. Retrieved 6 November 2018 from http://www.reginarifles.ca/bn_cas_list_d.htm

89   Georges Bernage, Frederick Jeanne, *Three Days in Hell*, 127. An unknown number of Canadian prisoners were killed by their captors in the early part of the battle, most coming from the outlying skirmish line positions east of Bretteville that were overrun. In keeping with the *Hitlerjugend* practice during the June 1944, many prisoners were shot arbitrarily after capture.

90   LAC, LAC, RG 24 *Volume XV*, 198. 1st Battalion, the Regina Rifle Regiment War Diary. 9 June 1944 entry. Tank support is recorded as arriving at 0515 hours.

91   National Archives, KEW WO 219/5326. File 461 (Volume II) SGS 'The Armoured Division in Battle'. 21st Army Group. Holland. December 1944. Doctrinal notes by Field Marshal Bernhard Law Montgomery. Nowhere in this pamphlet does it expressly forbid or warn against the use of tanks in night actions.

92   Wolfgang Schneider, *Panzer Tactics*, 247.

93   C.P. Stacey, *The Victory Campaign*, 137.

94   Hubert Meyer, *The History of the 12. SS-Panzerdivision*, 57.

Chapter 11

1   Stephan Cazenave, *Sur le Front de Normandie. Panzerdivision Hitlerjugend 1.2*, 172.

2   Stephen Cazenave, *SS-Panzer-Regiment 12 in the Normandy Campaign 1944*, 198.

3   Stephan Cazenave, *Sur le Front de Normandie. Panzerdivision Hitlerjugend 2*, 173.

4   Marc Milner, *Stopping the Panzers*, 290.

5   Vojenský ústřední archiv. *Kriegstagebuch Nr. 1 I. Abt./SS-Panzer Regiment 12 1944*. 9 June 1944 entry. Hubert Meyer, *The History of the 12. SS-Panzerdivision*, 58.

6   Hubert Meyer, *The History of the 12. SS-Panzerdivision*, D-4, D-5. Establishment strength report dated 1 June 1944.

7   Stephan Cazenave, *SS-Panzer Regiment 12*, 198.

8   Vojenský ústřední archiv, *Kriegstagebuch Nr. 3 II. Abt./SS-Pz.Art.Rgt. 12 1944*. 9 June 1944 entry.

9   Vojenský ústřední archiv, *Kriegstagebuch Nr. 3 II. Abt./SS-Pz.Art.Rgt. 12 1944*. 9 June 1944 entry.

10   Vojenský ústřední archiv, *Kriegstagebuch Nr. 1 I. Abt./SS-Panzer Regiment 12 1944*. 9 June 1944 entry.

11   Stephan Cazenave, *SS-Panzer Regiment 12*, 198.

12   Stephan Cazenave, *SS-Panzer Regiment 12*, 202.

13   Vojenský ústřední archiv. *Kriegstagebuch Nr. 1 I. Abt./SS-Panzer Regiment 12 1944*. 9 June 1944 entry.

14   Stephane Cazenave, *SS-Panzer-Regiment 12 in the Normandy Campaign*, 209.

15   Vojenský ústřední archiv. *Kriegstagebuch Nr. 1 I. Abt./SS-Panzer Regiment 12 1944*. 9 June 1944 entry.

16   Howard Margolian, *Conduct Unbecoming*, 108–9.

17   Hubert Meyer, *The History of the 12. SS-Panzerdivision*, 58–59.

18   Stephan Cazenave, *Sur le Front de Normandie. Panzerdivision Hitlerjugend 2*, 204–10.

19   Stepan Cazenave, *SS-Panzer Regiment 12*, 202. It is mentioned by Cazenave that the tanks took 10 days to repair, with some returning to *1. Kp./SS-Pz.Rgt. 12* by 19 June 1944.

20   Stephan Cazenave, *SS-Panzer Regiment 12*, 209.

21   Stephan Cazenave, *SS-Panzer Regiment 12*, 209.

22 Stephan Cazenave, *SS-Panzer Regiment 12*, 202.
23 Stephan Cazenave, *SS-Panzer Regiment 12*, 209.
24 Vojenský ústřední archiv, *Kriegstagebuch SS-Pz.Gren.Rgt. 26 Anlagen 1944*. 9 June 1944 list of casualties by *Bataillon*.
25 Vojenský ústřední archiv, *Kriegstagebuch Nr. 3 SS-Pz.Art.Rgt. 12 1944*. 9 June 1944 entry.
26 Vojenský ústřední archiv, *Kriegstagebuch Nr. 1. I. Abt./SS-Pz.Rgt. 12 1944*. 9 June 1944 entry.
27 Hubert Meyer, *The History of the 12. SS-Panzerdivision*, 61–62.
28 Will Townend and Frank Baldwin, *Gunners in Normandy*, 206.

Chapter 12

1 Hubert Meyer, *The History of the 12. SS-Panzerdivision*, 60.
2 Vojenský ústřední archiv, *Kriegstagebuch Nr. 3 II. Abt./SS-Pz.Art.Rgt. 12 1944*. 10 June 1944 entry.
3 Vojenský ústřední archiv, *Kriegstagebuch Nr. 3 SS-Pz.Art.Rgt. 12 1944*. 10 June 1944 entry.
4 Hubert Meyer, *The History of the 12. SS-Panzerdivision*, 60.
5 Stephan Cazenave, *Sur le Front de Normandie. Panzerdivision Hitlerjugend 1.2*, 187. Divisional order reproduced by Cazenave.
6 Vojenský ústřední archiv, *Kriegstagebuch Nr. 3 SS-Pz.Art.Rgt. 12 1944*. 10 June 1944 entry.
7 Vojensky Ustredni ArchivVojenský ústřední archiv, *Kriegstagebuch Nr. 3 I. Abt./SS-Pz.Rgt. 12 1944*. 10 June 1944 entry.
8 Stephan Cazenave, *SS-Panzer Regiment 12*, 212.
9 Vojenský ústřední archiv, *Kriegstagebuch Nr. 3, II. Abt./SS-Pz.Rgt. 12 1944*. 10 June 1944 entry.
10 Vojenský ústřední archiv, *Kriegstagebuch Nr. 3 II. Abt./SS-Pz.Art.Rgt. 12 1944*. 10 June 1944 entry.
11 Craig Luther, *Blood and Honor*, 177–78.
12 Stephan Cazenave, *SS-Panzer Regiment 12*, 220.
13 Will Townend and Frank Baldwin, *Gunners in Normandy*, 206. Hubert Meyer, *The History of the 12. SS-Panzerdivision*, 60.
14 Stephan Cazenave, *SS-Panzer Regiment 12*, 222.

Chapter 13

1 Jean-Claude Perrigault, *Album Historique: La Panzer-Lehr Division*, 161.
2 Vojenský ústřední archiv, *Kriegstagebuch Nr. 3 SS-Flak.Abt. 12 1944*. 8 June 1944 entry.
3 Vojenský ústřední archiv, *Kriegstagebuch Nr. 3 SS-Flak.Abt. 12 1944*. 8 June 1944 entry.
4 Hubert Meyer, *The History of the 12. SS-Panzerdivision*, 692.
5 Norman Scarfe, *Assault Division*, 98.
6 Hubert Meyer, *The History of the 12 SS-Panzerdivision*, 62.
7 Hubert Meyer, *The History of the 12 SS-Panzerdivision*, 62.
8 Hubert Meyer, *The History of the 12 SS-Panzerdivision*, 62.
9 Vojenský ústřední archiv, *Kriegstagebuch Nr. 1 SS-Pz.Gren.Rgt. 25 1944*. 8 June 1944 entry.
10 Will Townend and Frank Baldwin, *Gunners in Normandy*, 192. 2nd Battalion, The Royal Ulster Regiment War Diary. 8 June 1944. Retrieved 24 March 2024 from https://royal-ulster-rifles-ww2.blogspot.com/p/2rur-war-diary.html
11 Vojenský ústřední archiv, *Kriegstagebuch Nr. 1 SS-Pz.Gren.Rgt. 25 1944*. 8 June 1944 entry. Vojenský ústřední archiv, *Kriegstagebuch Nr. 2 III. Abt./SS-Pz.Art.Rgt. 12 1944*. 8 June 1944 entry. A group of eight–nine tanks are reported sighted at 1025 hours in the Les Buissons area.
12 Vojenský ústřední archiv, *Kriegstagebuch Nr. 1 SS-Pz.Gren.Rgt. 25 1944*. 8 June 1944 entry.
13 Vojenský ústřední archiv, *Kriegstagebuch II. Abt./SS-Pz.Rgt. 12. Anlagen 1944*. Table detailing *II. Abt./SS-Pz.Rgt. 12* Panzer IV tank strength and vehicles under repair.

14 Stephan Cazenave, *SS-Panzer Regiment 12*, 190–92.
15 Vojenský ústřední archiv, *Kriegstagebuch Nr. 3 II. Abt./SS-Pz.Rgt. 12 1944*. 9 June 1944 entry.
16 Werner Kortenhaus, *The Combat History*, 149.
17 Vojenský ústřední archiv, *Kriegstagebuch Nr. 3 SS-Flak.Abt. 12 1944*. 9 June 1944 entry.
18 Vojenský ústřední archiv, *Kriegstagebuch Nr. 3 SS-Flak.Abt. 12 1944*. 9 June 1944 entry.
19 Hubert Meyer, *The History of the 12. SS-Panzerdivision*, 63. Stephan Cazenave, *Sur le Front de Normandie. Panzerdivision Hitlerjugend 1.2*, 186. Vojenský ústřední archiv, *Kriegstagebuch Nr. 1 SS-Pz.Gren.Rgt. 25 1944*. 9 June 1944 entry. Four tanks were recorded destroyed at 1137 hours, and another two were destroyed at 1150 hours.
20 Vojenský ústřední archiv, *Kriegstagebuch Nr. 1 SS-Pz.Gren.Rgt. 25 1944*. 9 June 1944 entry.
21 Will Townend and Frank Baldwin, *Gunners in Normandy*, 192.
22 Will Townend and Frank Baldwin, *Gunners in Normandy*, 192. Norman Scarfe, *Assault Division*, 100.
23 Hubert Meyer, *The History of the 12. SS-Panzerdivision*, 62
24 Werner Kortenhaus, *The Combat History*, 150.
25 Hubert Meyer, *The History of the 12. SS-Panzerdivision*, 64.
26 Mark Zuehlke, *Holding Juno*, 261. Four Shermans were destroyed and the accompanying SDGH infantry suffered losses due to German artillery fire.
27 Tim Kilvert-Jones, *Sword Beach: 3rd British Infantry Division's Battle for the Normandy Beachhead* (London: Casemate Publications. 2002), 167. 9 June 1944 losses for the British assault on Cambes were 204 in total. Five AVRE tanks are mentioned as knocked out by German defensive fire.
28 Vojenský ústřední archiv, *Kriegstagebuch Nr. 3 II. Abt./SS-Pz.Rgt. 12 1944*. 9 June 1944 entry.
29 Vojenský ústřední archiv, *Kriegstagebuch Nr. 1 SS-Pz.Gren.Rgt. 25 1944*. 9 June 1944 entry.
30 Vojenský ústřední archiv, *Kriegstagebuch Nr. 1 SS-Pz.Gren.Rgt. 25 1944*. 10 June 1944 entry.
31 Stephan Cazenave, *Sur le Front de Normandie. Panzerdivision Hitlerjugend 1.2*, 186.
32 Vojenský ústřední archiv, *Kriegstagebuch Nr. 3 SS-Flak.Abt. 12 1944*. 10 June 1944 entry.
33 Vojenský ústřední archiv, *Kriegstagebuch Nr. 3 SS-Pz.Gren.Rgt. 25 1944*. 10 June 1944 entry.
34 Mark Zuehlke, *Holding Juno*, 294.
35 Mark Zuehlke, *Holding Juno*, 294–96.
36 Vojenský ústřední archiv, *Kriegstagebuch Nr. 3 SS-Flak.Abt. 12 1944*. 11 June 1944 entry.
37 Vojenský ústřední archiv, *Kriegstagebuch Nr. 3 SS-Pz.Art.Rgt. 12 1944*. 11 June 1944 entry. Niklas Zetterling, *Normandy 1944*, 120.

Chapter 14

1   Hubert Meyer, *The History of the 12. SS-Panzerdivision*, 66.
2   Hubert Meyer, *The History of the 12. SS-Panzerdivision*, 66.
3   Vojenský ústřední archiv, *Kriegstagebuch SS-Pz.Gren.Rgt. 26 Anlagen 1944*. 11 June 1944 entry. *SS-Pz. Aüfkl.Abt. 12* report on fighting near Hill 103 in June 1944.
4   Vojenský ústřední archiv, *Kriegstagebuch SS-Pz.Gren.Rgt. 26 Anlagen 1944*. 11 June 1944 entry. *SS-Pz. Aüfkl.Abt. 12* report on fighting near Hill 103 in June 1944.
5   Stéphane Jacquet, *Tilly-sur-Seulles 1944*, 247–49.
6   Vojenský ústřední archiv, *Kriegstagebuch SS-Pz.Gren.Rgt. 26 Anlagen 1944*. 11 June 1944 entry. *SS-Pz. Aüfkl.Abt. 12* report on fighting near Hill 103 in June 1944.
7   Stéphane Jacquet, *Tilly-sur-Seulles 1944*, 254–56 This information was taken from an account of the events on 11 June 1944 given by L/Cpl Weir, a veteran of the 4th/7th Royal Dragoon Guards.
8   Vojenský ústřední archiv, *Kriegstagebuch SS-Pz.Gren.Rgt. 26 Anlagen 1944*. 11 June 1944 entry. *SS-Pz. Aüfkl.Abt. 12* report on fighting near Hill 103 in June 1944.
9   Hubert Meyer, *The History of the 12. SS-Panzerdivision*, 67. Table on losses.
10 Hubert Meyer *The History of the 12. SS-Panzerdivision*, 67.
11 Tim Saunders, *Battle for the Bocage*, 129.

12 Tim Saunders, *Battle for the Bocage*, 123.
13 Hubert Meyer, *The History of the 12. SS-Panzerdivision*, 66.
14 LAC, RG 24, Volume *XIV*, 213. 6th Canadian Armoured Regiment War Diary, 11 June entry.
15 Frank Townend and Frank Baldwin, *Gunners in Normandy*, 196.
16 Terry Copp, Gordon Brown, *Look to Your Front*, 76. Account of Major Tubb on events of 11 June.
17 Tim Saunders and Richard Hone, *12th Hitlerjugend SS Panzer Division*, 90–91.
18 Vojenský ústřední archiv, *Kriegstagebuch Nr. 3 SS-Pz.Art.Rgt. 12 1944*. 11 June entry. *2. Batterie* provided defensive indirect fire support.
19 Terry Copp, Gordon Brown, *Look to Your Front*, 76. Account of Major Tubb on events of 11 June.
20 Terry Copp, Gordon Brown, *Look to Your Front*, 77. Account of Major Tubb on events of 11 June.
21 Mark Zuehlke, *Holding Juno*, 320.
22 Mark Zuehlke, *Holding Juno*, 324–26.
23 Vojenský ústřední archiv, *Kriegstagebuch Nr. 3 II. Abt./SS-Pz.Rgt. 12 1944*. 11 June 1944 entry.
24 Mark Zuehlke, *Holding Juno*, 327–28.
25 Vojenský ústřední archiv, *Kriegstagebuch Nr. 3 II. Abt./SS-Pz.Rgt. 12 1944*. 11 June 1944 entry.
26 Hubert Meyer, *The History of the 12. SS-Panzerdivision*, 68. Account of *Ustuf.* Jeran regarding the fighting on 11 June 1944 near Le Mesnil-Patry.
27 Mark Zuehlke, *Holding Juno*, 320.
28 Mark Zuehlke, *Holding Juno*, 323.
29 Mark Zuehlke, *Holding Juno*, 331–33.
30 Mark Zuehlke, *Holding Juno*, 331–33.
31 Mark Zuehlke, *Holding Juno*, 334.
32 Mark Zuehlke, *Holding Juno*, 336, 341.
33 Hubert Meyer, *The History of the 12. SS-Panzerdivision*, 69.
34 Hubert Meyer, *The History of the 12. SS-Panzerdivision*, 69.
35 Hubert Meyer, *The History of the 12. SS-Panzerdivision*, 69.
36 Norbert Számvéber, *Waffen-SS Armour in Normandy*, 200–2. Appendix II. Translated official award recommendation for *Stubaf.* Heinz Prinz.
37 John English, *The Canadian Army*, 164–65.

Chapter 15

1 Keith Taylor, *The Waist-High Cornfield*, 255.
2 Mark Zuehlke, *Holding Juno*, 302, Keith Taylor, *The Waist-High Cornfield*, 254.
3 Keith Taylor, *The Waist-High Cornfield*, 253.
4 Stephan Cazenave, *Sur le Front de Normandie. Panzerdivision Hitlerjugend 1.2*, 216.
5 Keith Taylor, *The Waist-High Cornfield*, 252.
6 Stephan Cazenave, *Sur le Front de Normandie. Panzerdivision Hitlerjugend 1.2*, 216.
7 Keith Taylor, *The Waist-High Cornfield*, 305. Statement of *Waffen-SS* veteran Otto Funk, a member of *15. Kp.(Aufklärung)/SS-Pz.Gren.Rgt. 25*, on the events of 11 June 1944 near noon in a field west of Rots close to the RN 13.
8 Hubert Meyer, *The History of the 12. SS-Panzerdivision*, 69.
9 Vojenský ústřední archiv, *Kriegstagebuch I. Abt./SS-Pz.Rgt. 12 Anlagen 1944. Anlage Nr. 5. 15.06.44*. Stephan Cazenave, *SS-Panzer Regiment 12*, 226.
10 Mark Zuehlke, *Holding Juno*, 302.
11 Vojenský ústřední archiv, *Kriegstagebuch I. Abt./SS-Pz.Rgt. 12 Anlagen 1944. Anlage Nr. 5. 15.06.44*.
12 Stephan Cazenave, *SS-Panzer Regiment 12*, 226.
13 Stephan Cazenave, *Sur le Front de Normandie. Panzerdivision Hitlerjugend 1.2*, 216.
14 Mark Zuehlke, *Holding Juno*, 300.
15 Will Townend and Frank Baldwin, *Gunners in Normandy*, 196–97.

16 Si Briggs, 'Royal Marines Armoured Support Group'. Royal Marines History. Retrieved 14 June 2023 from https://www.royalmarineshistory.com/post/royal-marines-armoured-support-group

17 Keith Taylor, *The Waist-High Cornfield*, 260.

18 British National Archives KEW, File ADM 202/105. 46 RMC War Diary. 11 June 1944 entry.

19 Keith Taylor, *The Waist-High Cornfield*, 257. LAC, RG24 Vol. XV, 180. Le Régiment de la Chaudière War Diary. 11 June entry.

20 Keith Taylor, *The Waist-High Cornfield*, 254.

21 Mark Zuehlke, *Holding Juno*, 300–1.

22 British National Archives KEW, File ADM 202/105. 46 RMC War Diary. 11 June 1944 entry.

23 Mark Zuehlke, *Holding Juno*, 302.

24 Keith Taylor, *The Waist-High Cornfield*, 261.

25 Mark Zuehlke, *Holding Juno*, 303.

26 Stephan Cazenave, *Sur le Front de Normandie. Panzerdivision Hitlerjugend 1.2*, 216.

27 Keith Taylor, *The Waist-High Cornfield*, 276. Map of the 46 RMC Y Troop advance over the Mue bridge into Rots.

28 Mark Zuehlke, *Holding Juno*, 303.

29 Keith Taylor, *The Waist-High Cornfield*, 292. Map of B Troop advance over the Mue bridge into Rots, showing the tank losses inflicted on the FGH A Squadron.

30 Stephan Cazenave, *Sur le Front de Normandie. Panzerdivision Hitlerjugend 1.2*, 217.

31 Stephan Cazenave, *Sur le Front de Normandie. Panzerdivision Hitlerjugend 1.2*, 218.

32 Hubert Meyer, *The History of the 12. SS-Panzerdivision*, 69–70.

33 Keith Taylor, *The Waist-High Cornfield*, 307.

34 British National Archives KEW, File ADM 202/105. 46 RMC War Diary. 11 June 1944 entry.

35 Mark Zuehlke, *Holding Juno*, 308–9.

36 Angelos N. Manolas, *The Reaper's Harvesting Summer*, 89.

37 John Buckley, *British Armour in Normandy* (London: Frank Cass, 2004), 93. The defensive effort by Anglo-Canadian forces of newly won objectives was particularly effective and used all combat arms.

38 Mark Zuehlke, *Holding Juno*, 310.

39 Hubert Meyer, *The History of the 12. SS-Panzerdivision*, 70.

Conclusion

1 British National Archives KEW, File PR25/GS publications/1316. 'Current Reports from Overseas. No.52. The War Office. Six Pounders versus Panthers'. 26 August 1944, 7. It was discovered during the fighting on the 8–10 June 1944 on the front of the 3rd Canadian Infantry Division that the 6-pounder anti-tank gun and other anti-tank weapons were quite effective, and poor German combined armoured tactics allowed multiple opportunities for their successful use.

2 British National Archives KEW, File PRO. 26/GS Publications/1329. 'Current Reports from Overseas, No.55'. The War Office. 16 September 1944, 2. Notes on the employment of artillery in Normandy. German artillery tactics are judged to be notably inferior shortly after 6 June 1944.

3 Michael Reynolds, *Steel Inferno*, 78.

4 C.P. Stacey, *The Victory Campaign*, 137.

5 Niklas Zetterling, *Normandy 1944*, 355. While a large regimental-sized force of the division went into battle on the 7 June, the mass of the *Hitlerjugend* was not in the line until the night of 9 June. Missing bits and pieces of the division, most notably *SS-Pz.Jg.Abt. 12*, did not show up until August 1944.

6 David C. Isby, Editor. *Fighting in Normandy: The German Army from D-Day to Villers-Bocage* (London: Greenhill Books. 2001), 47–48. *Gen.d.Pz.Tr. Geyr von Schweppenburg* statement of 8 June 1944 on *I. SS-Panzerkorps* operations. In this post-war statement, von Schweppenburg is insistent that even on the 8 June 1944, a decisive counter-stroke would have been successful.

7   Michael Reynolds, *Steel Inferno*, 82. *G.F.M.* Rommel's conclusions following the *Pz.Gr.West Hauptquartier* conference.

8   Hubert Meyer, *The History of the 12. SS-Panzerdivision*, 358. Appendix 7. These were mainly cosmetic losses. For example, the trench strength of a *SS-Panzergrenadier Regiment* was 3,316 officers and men.

9   Hubert Meyer, *The History of the 12. SS-Panzerdivision*. In the endnotes of his divisional history, Meyer gives the source for casualties as the Berlin *Wehrmacht* Information Office. This office was responsible for the notification of all family members of soldiers who became casualties. Data was compiled by date, unit, theatre, etc. Presumably its documentation survived the war. Meyer states only the war diary of the *I. Btl./SS-Pz.Gren.Rgt. 25* survived the fighting in Normandy, which is incorrect.

10   Howard Margolian, *Conducts Unbecoming*. Whether fired by rumours that Canadians did not take prisoners or rage at the losses incurred during this period of fighting, at least 156 Canadian prisoners of war were killed post-battle by the *Hitlerjugend*. Nearly all levels of ranks were involved, apart from the divisional headquarters. The shortage of officers and junior leaders who might have curtailed or halted the murders certainly could not have helped the situation.

11   David C. Isby, Editor. *Fighting in Normandy*, 114. *Gen.d.Pz.Tr.* von Schweppenburg post-war statement on the 10 June air strike. On this day, due to an Allied attack in the *Panzer Lehr Panzerdivision* sector the German lines were penetrated. Schweppenburg, with Rommel's agreement, cancelled the long-awaited *I. SS-Pz.Korps* counterattack, citing this breakthrough as the main reason.

12   Craig Luther, *Blood and Honor*, 180. In this raid, 61 RAF Medium B-25 bombers and 40 Typhoons and Spitfires hit the area, killing 32 of *Gen.d.Pz.Tr.* Geyr von Schweppenburg's staff.

Bibliography

Secondary sources

Bailey, J. B. A, *Field Artillery and Firepower*. Annapolis: Naval Institute Press. 2004.

Bartov, Omer, *The Eastern Front 1941–45, and the Barbarisation of Warfare* (New York: St. Martin's Press, 1986).

Beckett, Ian F. W. (ed.), *Rommel Reconsidered*. Mechanicsburg: Stackpole Books, 2013.

Bernage, Georges, and Jeanne, Fredrick, *Three Days in Hell. 7–9 June 1944* (Bayeaux: Editions Heimdal, 2016).

Blackburn, George, *The Guns of Normandy* (Toronto: McClelland & Stewart, 1995).

Boog, Horst, Gerhard Krebs, and Vogel, Detlef, *Germany and the Second World War, Volume VII: The Strategic Air War in Europe and the War in the West and East Asia, 1943–1944/45* (Oxford: Oxford University Press, 2006).

Bouchery, Jean, *From D-Day to VE-Day: The Canadian Soldier* (Paris: Histoire and Collections, 2003).

Braün, Daniel M., *Green Fields Beyond: The Story of the Sherbrooke Fusilier Regiment* (Research Triangle: Lulu Publishing Services, 2021).

Carell, Paul, *Invasion! They're coming!* tr. David Johnston (Algen: Schiffer Military History. 1995).

Cazenave, Stephan, *Sur le Front de Normandie. Panzerdivision Hitlerjugend 2: SS-Panzer Regiment 12 Normandie 1944* (Paris: Maranes Éditions, 2014).

Cazenave, Stephan, *Sur la Front de Normandie. Panzerdivision Hitlerjugend 1.2 Volume II : 6/6–7/7/44 Invasionfront* (Paris: Maranes Éditions, 2019).

Cazenave, Stephan, *SS-Panzer Regiment 12 in the Normandy Campaign 1944* (Winnipeg: J. J. Fedorowicz Publishing, 2020).

Condell, Bruce (ed.), *Truppenführung: On the German Art of War* (London: Lynne Reinner, 2001).

Cooper, Matthew, *The German Army 1933–1945* (London: Macdonald and Janes, 1978).

Copp, Terry, *Fields of Fire. The Canadians in Normandy* (Toronto: University of Toronto Press, 2003).

Copp, Terry, and Brown, Gordon, *Look to your Front…Regina Rifles: A Regiment at War 1944–1945* (Waterloo: Laurier Centre for Military, Disarmament and Strategic Studies, 2001).

Corum, James S., *Hans Von Seeckt and German Military Reform* (Kansas City: University of Kansas Press, 1992).

Edwards, Roger, *Panzer: A Revolution in Warfare: 1939–1945* (London: Arms and Armour Press, 1989).

Ellis, John, *Brute Force* (New York: Viking, 1990).

English, John, *The Canadian Army and the Normandy Campaign* (Mechanicsburg: Stackpole Books, 2009).

Foot, M. D. R., and Dear, I. C. B. (eds.), *The Oxford Companion to the Second World War* (Oxford: Oxford University Press, 1995).

Goddard, Jack, *D-Day Juno Beach: Canada's 24 Hours of Destiny* (Toronto: The Dundurn Group, 2004).

Greentree, David, *Hitlerjugend Soldier versus Canadian Soldier: Normandy 1944* (Oxford: Osprey Publishing, 2018).

Guderian, Heinz, *Panzer Leader. General Heinz Guderian* (New York: Da Capo Press, 1996).

Gullachsen, Arthur, *An Army of Never-Ending Strength: Reinforcing the Canadians in Northwest Europe, 1944–45* (Vancouver: UBC Press, 2021).

Hart, Russell, *Clash of Arms: How the Allies Won in Normandy* (Norman: University of Oklahoma Press, 2001).

Isby, David. C. (ed.), *Fighting in Normandy: The German Army from D-Day to Villers-Bocage* (London: Greenhill Books, 2001).

Jacquet, Stéphane, *Tilly-sur-Seulles 1944* (Bayeux: Editions Heimdal, 2019).

Kilvert-Jones, Tim, *Sword Beach: 3rd British Infantry Division's Battle for the Normandy Beachhead* (Oxford: Casemate Publishers, 2002).

Kite, Ben, *Stout Hearts: the British and Canadians in Normandy 1944* (Solihull: Helion and Company, 2014).

Kortenhaus, Werner, *The Combat History of the 21. Panzer Division* (Solihull: Helion and Company, 2014).

Lehmann, Rudolf, *The Leibstandarte III: 1 SS Panzer Division Leibstandarte Adolf Hitler* (Winnipeg: J. J. Fedorowicz Publishing, 1990).

Luther, Craig, *Blood and Honor: The History of the 12th SS Panzer Division* 'Hitlerjugend *Youth*' *1943–1945* (Atglen: Schiffer Publishing, 2012).

Luxton, Eric (ed.), *1st Battalion the Regina Rifle Regiment: 1939–1946* (Regina: Regimental Association, 1946).

Manolas, Angelos N., *The Reaper's Harvesting Summer. 12. SS-Panzerdivision: 'Hitlerjugend' in Normandy* (Stroud: Fonthill, 2021).

Margolian, Howard, *Conduct Unbecoming: The Story of the Murder of Canadian Prisoners of War in Normandy* (Toronto: University of Toronto Press, 1998).

Marteinson, John, and McNorgan, Michael, *The Royal Canadian Armoured Corps: An Illustrated History* (Toronto: Robin Brass Studio, 2000).

Megargee, Geoffery P., *Inside Hitler's High Command* (Lawrence: University of Press of Kansas, 2000).

Mein, Stewart A., *'Up the Johns': The Story of the Regina Rifles* (North Battleford: Senate of the Royal Regina Rifles, 1992).

Meyer, Hubert, *The History of the 12. SS-Panzerdivision Hitlerjugend* (Winnipeg: J. J. Fedorowicz Publishing, 1994).

Meyer, Kurt, *Grenadiers. The Story of Waffen SS General Kurt 'Panzer' Meyer* (Mechanicsburg: Stackpole Books, 2005).

Middlebrook, Martin, and Everitt, C., *The Bomber Command War Diaries: An Operational Reference Book, 1939–1940* (London: Viking, 1985).

Milner, Marc, *D-Day to Carpiquet, The North Shore Regiment and the Liberation of Europe* (Fredericton: Goose Lane Editions, 2007).

Milner, Marc, *Stopping the Panzers. The Untold Story of D-Day* (Lawrence: University Press of Kansas Press, 2014).

Mitcham, Samuel W., *Rommel's Last Battle: The Desert Fox and the Normandy Campaign* (New York: Stein & Day, 1983).

Nevenkin, Kamen, *Fire Brigades. The Panzer Divisions 1943–1945* (Winnipeg: J. J. Fedorowicz Publishing, 2008).

Nicholson, G. W. L., *The Gunners of Canada: The History of the Royal Regiment of Canadian Artillery: Volume II: 1919–1967* (Toronto: McClelland and Stewart, 1972).

Perrigault, Jean-Claude, *21. Panzer Division* (Bayeaux: Editions Hemidal, 2003).

Perrigault, Jean-Claude, *Album Historique: La Panzer-Lehr Division: Le Choc de Allies Brise L'Arme D'Elite de Hitler* (Bayeaux: Editions Heimdal, 1995).

Reid, Brian A., *Named by the Enemy: A History of the Royal Winnipeg Rifles. The Story of Winnipeg's Famous Little Black Devils* (Montreal: Robin Brass Studio, 2010).

Reynolds, Michael, *Steel Inferno: I SS Panzer Corps in Normandy* (Barnsley: Pen & Sword Military, 2009).

Reynolds, Michael, *Eagles and Bulldogs in Normandy 1944: The American 29th Division from Omaha to St. Lo, The British 3rd Division from Sword to Caen* (Havertown: Casemate Publishers, 2020).

Ritgen, Helmut, *The Western Front 1944: Memoirs of a Panzer-Lehr Officer* (Winnipeg: J. J. Fedorowicz Publishing, 1995).

Ruge, Friedrich, *Rommel in Normandy* (London: Presidio Press, 1979).

Saunders, Tim, *The Battle for the Bocage, Normandy 1944: Point 103, Tilley-sur-Seulles, Villers Bocage* (Barnsley: Pen and Sword, 2021).

Saunders, Tim, and Hone, Richard, *12th Hitlerjugend SS Panzer Division in Normandy* (Barnsley: Pen and Sword Military, 2021).

Scarfe, Norman, *Assault Division. A History of the 3rd Division from the Invasion of Normandy to the Surrender of Germany* (Staplehurst: Spellmount, 2004).

Schneider, Wolfgang, *Panzer Tactics: German Small-unit Armour Tactics in World War II.* (Mechanicsburg: Stackpole Books, 2005).

Stacey, C.P., *Official History of the Canadian Army in the Second World War. Volume III: The Victory Campaign* (Ottawa: The Queen's Printer and Controller of Stationery, 1960).

Steinhardt, Dr Frederick P. (ed.), *Panzer Lehr Division 1944–45. Helion WWII German Military Studies Volume I* (Solihull: Helion and Company Ltd., 2008).

Stirling, J. P. D., *The First and the Last: The Story of the 4th/7th Royal Dragoon Guards* (London: Art & Educational Publishers Ltd., 1946).

Számvéber, Norbert, *Waffen-SS Armour in Normandy. The Combat History of SS-Panzer Regiment 12 and SS-Panzerjäger Abteilung 12 Normandy 1944 based on their Original War Diaries* (Solihull: Helion and Company, 2012).

Taylor, Keith, *The Waist-High Cornfield* (Hamburg: self-published, 2017).

Taylor, Keith, *Broken Bridges, Rivers to Cross* (Hamburg: self-published, 2021).

Townend, Will, and Baldwin, Frank, *Gunners in Normandy. The History of the Royal Artillery in North West Europe January 1942 to August 1944* (Cheltenham: The History Press, 2020).

Warlimont, Walter, *Inside Hitler's Headquarters 1939–1945* (Novato: Presidio Press, 1964).

Windsor, Lee, Sarty, Roger, and Milner, Marc, *Loyal Gunners: 3rd Field Artillery Regiment (The Loyal Company) and the History of New Brunswick Artillery, 1893 to 2012* (Waterloo: Wilfred Laurier Press, 2016).

Zaloga, Steven J., *Panther versus Sherman. Battle of the Bulge 1944* (Oxford: Osprey Publishing, 2008).

Zetterling, Niklas, *Normandy 1944. German Military Organization, Combat Power and Organizational Effectiveness* (Winnipeg: J. J. Fedorowicz, 2000).

Zuehlke, Mark, *Juno Beach: Canada's D-Day Victory, 6 June 1944* (Toronto: Douglas and McIntyre, 2004).

Zuehlke, Mark, *Holding Juno. Canada's Heroic Defence of the D-Day Beaches, June 7–10, 1944* (Toronto: Douglas & McIntyre, 2005).

Journal articles

Oliver Haller, 'The Defeat of the 12th SS: 7–10 June 1944', *Canadian Military History Journal*, 3: Iss. 1, Article 2 (1994). Retrieved 12 June 2023 from https://scholars.wlu.ca/cmh/vol3/iss1/2

Lahey, R. J., 'Hitler's "Intuition", Luftwaffe Photo Reconnaissance and the Reinforcement of Normandy', *Journal of Military History*, 86 (2022), 77–109.

Summerfield, Sean, 'The 27th Canadian Armoured Regiment and the Battle of Authie: A Case Study into Manning, Training and Equipment Failures', *Journal of the Eastern Townships Studies*, No. 47, Autumn/Fall (2016), 117–26.

Primary archival sources

Bundesarchiv Militärarchiv, Freiberg, Germany

BA-MA RH 10/172.
BA-MA RH 10/321.

Canadian Armed Forces Directorate of History and Heritage, Ottawa, Canada

DHH 981.023 (D6) Summary of Sepp Dietrich Interrogation. Special Interrogation Reports on German Commanders. 1945–46.
DHH 20551.023 (D9) Exhibit No. 25. Kurt Meyer War Crimes Trial. Summary of Canadian 3rd Infantry Division Fighting. 6–11 June.
DHH 981.023 (D6) Special Interrogation Report *Brigadenführer* Kurt Meyer, Comd *12 SS Pz.Div.* 'Hitlerjugend'.
DHH 145.ZR11011(D7) Sept/1950 letter by C. S. T. Tubb summarising role of Regina Rifle infantry company on 8–11 June 1944 fighting.

Libraries and Archives Canada, Ottawa, Canada

LAC, RG 24 Vol. 14,213. 6th Canadian Armoured Regiment War Diary.
LAC, RG 24 Vol. 14,461. 12th Field Regiment, RCA War Diary.
LAC, RG 24 Vol. 15,036. Canadian Scottish Regiment War Diary.
LAC, RG 24 Vol. 15,076. Highland Light Infantry of Canada War Diary.
LAC, RG 24 Vol. 15,122. North Nova Scotia Highlanders War Diary.
LAC, RG 24 Vol. 15,127. North Shore Regiment War Diary.
LAC, RG 24 Vol. 15,168–15, 169. Queen's Own Rifles of Canada War Diary.
LAC, RG 24 Vol. 15,180. Le Régiment de la Chaudière War Diary.
LAC, RG 24 Vol. 15,198. 1st Battalion, the Regina Rifle Regiment War Diary.
LAC, RG 24 Vol. 15,223. Royal Winnipeg Rifles War Diary.
LAC, RG 24 Vol. 20,428. Sepp Dietrich Interview on Military Career.
LAC, RG 24 Vol. 20,512. 981.SOM(D54). Leo, Baron Geyr Von Schweppenburg Interview on activities of *Panzergruppe* West June–July 1944.
LAC, RG24 Vol. 10,517. 215A21-009(D167). 3rd Canadian Infantry Division Casualty Report. 6 June–16 August 1944.
LAC, RG24 Vol. 20,518. Heinz Guderian Interview on Normandy Fighting.
LAC, RG24 Vol. 20,519. 981 SOM. Fritz Bayerlein/Fritz Kraemer Report on Activities of I SS Panzer Corps 6 June–8 April 1948.
LAC, RG24. Vol. 10,685. 215C1.98. Canadian First Army Intelligence file on 12th SS Panzer Division.

Public Records Office of the United Kingdom, London, UK

British National Archives, KEW. File PRO. 25/GS publications/1316. Current Reports from Overseas. No.52. The War Office. 26 August 1944.
British National Archives, KEW. File PRO. 26/GS Publications/1329. Current Reports from Overseas, No.55. The War Office. 16 September 1944.

British National Archives, KEW. File ADM 202/105. 46 RMC War Diary
British National Archives, KEW. File 25/GS/Publications/1298. The War Office. 'Current Reports from Overseas: No.48'.
British National Archives, KEW. File WO 219/5326. File 461 (Vol 2) 'The Armoured Division in Battle'. 21st Army Group. Holland. December 1944.

Tank Museum Archives, Tank Museum Bovington, UK
Tank Museum Archives, Tank Museum Bovington, UK. 'No.2 Operational Research Section, Report No.18. Tank casualties during the exploitation phase after the crossing of the Seine, September 1944'.

Vojenský ústřední archiv, Prague, Czech Republic
Vojenský ústřední archiv. *Kriegstagebuch Nr. 1 I. Abt./SS-Pz.Rgt. 12 1944.*
Vojenský ústřední archiv. *Kriegstagebuch I. Abt./SS-Pz.Rgt. 12 Anlagen 1944.*
Vojenský ústřední archiv. *Kriegstagebuch Nr. 3 II. Abt./SS-Pz.Rgt. 12 1944.*
Vojenský ústřední archiv. *Kriegstagebuch II. Abt./SS-Pz.Rgt. 12 Anlagen 1944.*
Vojenský ústřední archiv. *Kriegstagebuch Nr. 1 SS-Pz.Gren.Rgt. 25 1944.*
Vojenský ústřední archiv. *Kriegstagebuch SS-Pz.Gren.Rgt. 25 Anlagen 1944.*
Vojenský ústřední archiv. *Kriegstagebuch Nr. 1 I. Btl./SS-Pz.Gren.Rgt. 25 1944.*
Vojenský ústřední archiv. *Kriegstagebuch SS-Pz.Gren.Rgt. 26 Anlagen 1944.*
Vojenský ústřední archiv. *Kriegstagebuch Nr. 3 SS-Pz.Art.Rgt. 12 1944.*
Vojenský ústřední archiv. *Kriegstagebuch SS-Pz.Art.Rgt. 12 Anlagen 1944.*
Vojenský ústřední archiv. *Kriegstagebuch Nr. 3 II. Abt./SS-Pz.Art.Rgt. 12 1944.*
Vojenský ústřední archiv. *Kriegstagebuch Nr. 2 III. Abt./SS-Pz.Art.Rgt. 12 1944.*
Vojenský ústřední archiv. *Kriegstagebuch Nr. 3 SS-Flak Abteilung 12 1944.*

United States National Archives and Records Administration, Alexandria, Virginia
NARA T-312/1568/000950. *7. Armee* Telephone Log, June 1944.
NARA, RG 338. MS-C024. Fritz Kraemer, *I SS Panzer Corps in the West*. Landsberg: US WWII Foreign Military Studies, 1954.

Dissertations and theses
Sullivan, Michael, 'Hitler's Teenaged Zealots: Fanatics, Combat Motivation, and the 12th SS Panzer Division *Hitlerjugend*', masters thesis, University of New Brunswick, Fredericton, 1999.

Miscellaneous
Laurier Centre for the Study of Canada Normandy Papers, 'Formation of the 8th Canadian Infantry Brigade assault craft and supporting warships, Operation *Neptune* 6 June 1944'.
Gordon Brown, Letter of Major Gordon Brown (Retd) dated 23 April 1994.

Websites
Biggs, Si, 'Royal Marines Armoured Support Group', Royal Marines History, retrieved 14 June 2023 from https://www.royalmarineshistory.com/post/royal-marines-armoured-support-group

'Canada House of Commons Speaker Calls Ukrainian Nazi Vet a "Hero"', retrieved 10 October 2023 from https://www.youtube.com/watch?v=406huseHyJ4

DND Military History and Heritage: Canadian Participation in the Operations in North-West Europe, 1944. Part 1: The assault and subsequent operations of 3 Canadian Inf Div and 2 Canadian Armed Bde 16-30 Jun 44. Appendix A to E Maps. 30 June 1952. Author: Reginald Roy. Retrieved 6 April 2024 from

https://www.canada.ca/en/department-national-defence/services/military-history/history-heritage/official-military-history-lineages/reports/army-headquarters-1948-1959/nw-europe-1944-part-1.html

Gaul, Walter, 'The G.A.F. and the invasion of Normandy 1944', retrieved 2 January 2024 from https://www.ibiblio.org/hyperwar/Germany/LW/GAF-Normandy/index.html

'Infantry Training Part I: The Infantry Battalion: 1944 26/G.S. 1070 Publication', War Office. Ottawa: Controller, His Majesty's Stationery, 1944, retrieved 8 January 2019 from http://wartimecanada.ca/categories/training-manuals?tid=All&page=1

'Infantry Training Part VI: The Anti-Tank Platoon 1943 26/G.S. 1023 Publication', War Office, Ottawa: Controller, His Majesty's Stationery, 1944, retrieved 8 January 2019 from http://wartimecanada.ca/categories/training-manuals?tid=All&page=1

Official History of the 2nd Battalion, Royal Ulster Regiment during World War II, '2nd Battalion, The Royal Ulster Regiment War Diary. June 1944', retrieved 25 February from https://royal-ulster-rifles-ww2.blogspot.com/p/2rur-war-diary.html

Regina Rifles, 'Regina Rifles fatal casualties by date', retrieved 6 November 2018 from http://www.reginarifles.ca/bn_cas_list_d.htm

Van Gelder, Pim, 'Operation Market Garden. Which time zone with which time?', 4. retrieved 13 September 2023 from https://vriendenairbornemuseum.nl/public/docs/Operation_Market_Garden_Which_time_zone_with_which_time.pdf

Index

Note: Italicised page numbers denote images or maps.